NAT

NATO and the Bomb
Canadian Defenders
Confront Critics

ERIKA SIMPSON

June 2002

Cris & Peter,
Thanks for your support and friendship over the years.
I have really appreciated you both!

All the best,
Erika

McGill-Queen's University Press
Montreal & Kingston · London · Ithaca

© McGill-Queen's University Press 2001
ISBN 0-7735-2088-0 (cloth)
ISBN 0-7735-2118-6 (paper)

Legal deposit first quarter 2001
Bibliothèque nationale du Québec

This book has been published with the help of
a grant from the J.B. Smallman Fund, Faculty
of Social Science, University of Western Ontario, and
with the support of the NATO Office of Information
and Press.

Printed in Canada on acid-free paper

McGill-Queen's University Press acknowledges the
financial support of the Government of Canada
through the Book Publishing Industry Development
Program (BPIDP) for its activities. It also acknowledges
the support of the Canada Council for the Arts for its
publishing program.

Canadian Cataloguing in Publication Data

Simpson, Erika, 1962–
  NATO and the bomb: Canadian defenders confront
  critics
  Includes bibliographical references and index.
  ISBN 0-7735-2088-0 (bound). –
  ISBN 0-7735-2118-6 (pbk.)
  1. North Atlantic Treaty Organization – Canada.
  2. Canada – Military policy. 3. Nuclear weapons –
  Government policy – Canada. I. Title.
  UA646.5.C35545 2001   355'.033571   C00-900517-X

Typeset in Palatino 10/12
by Caractéra inc., Quebec City

This book is dedicated to my parents

Contents

Acknowledgments

To help explain Canada's approach to the North Atlantic Treaty Organization (NATO) during the Cold War years, this book documents the underlying beliefs and assumptions of high-level policy-makers. Its central argument is that for over thirty years two belief systems – the "Defenders" and the "Critics" – significantly influenced Canadian defence policy regarding NATO. The beliefs and assumptions of these two groups affected decision-making between 1957 and 1963 – particularly regarding nuclear weapon acquisitions – and policy-making between 1963 and 1989 – especially regarding Canada's troop contributions to Europe. The release of previously classified materials and Cabinet documents from the Cold War years has made it possible to better appreciate some Canadian leaders' assumptions and approaches.

In the past, political scientists and historians who wrote about Canada and NATO were obliged to use secondary sources or rely on personal experiences. For this book, many heretofore-classified documents were obtained through the Access to Information Act (1982). A wide variety of newly released Cabinet minutes, memoranda, personal letters, diaries, original drafts of speeches, and departmental files were examined with a view to discerning the underlying beliefs of high-level decision-makers. The Historical Section of the Department of Foreign Affairs, the Directorate of History in the Department of National Defence, the Privy Council Office, the Public Archives of Canada, and the John G. Diefenbaker Centre provided material. Interviews were conducted in Ottawa and Toronto, as well as at NATO headquarters. I am particularly grateful to the Canadian Institute for International Peace and Security and the Department of Foreign Affairs and International Trade for grants enabling me to complete this book. These awards were a great encouragement to pursue research in Canadian security and defence policy. As well, scholarships awarded by the Department of National Defence Military and Strategic Studies Doctoral Fellowship program helped me pursue sources in Ottawa, Brussels, Toronto, and Saskatoon. The Department of National Defence and the Department of Foreign Affairs' interest in funding a long-term research project and providing travel funds was much appreciated. Special thanks also go to the Social Science and Humanities Research Council of Canada doctoral program for assistance. The opportunity in 1991–92 to work as a Research Fellow through the NATO Research Fellowship Programme, which aims to promote study on aspects relevant to NATO, was valuable too. At different times, the Centre for International Studies in Toronto and the Associates of the University of Toronto Travel Grant Fund helped finance travel to Ottawa and Toronto as well as research at NATO and SHAPE headquarters. The assistance of the Vice-President's (Research) Special Competition; the Agnes Cole Dark Fund, Faculty of Social Science; and the V.P. Smallman Fund of the University of Western Ontario is acknowledged as well. To all these organizations and a great number of individuals, I am truly thankful.

I am indebted as well to a number of persons who have offered advice and criticism. My particular thanks go to Professor Cranford Pratt, who read many different versions of each chapter, offered countless valuable suggestions, and was always a source of encouragement and sustenance. I would also like to thank Professor Janice Gross Stein for her support over the years, and Professor David Welch, who provided many astute suggestions. The book greatly benefited, too, from the insightful and constructive comments of Don Ward in Saskatoon.

I also wish to thank Wendy Dayton for her exceedingly helpful and meticulous assistance in editing this manuscript; Professor Bob Young for his pertinent advice; and Phil Cercone, Joan McGilvray, Joanne Pisano, and John Zucchi at McGill-Queen's University Press for their invaluable work in connection with the publication of this book.

The assistance of the following people was also very helpful during the research process: Isabelle Campbell and Owen Cooke in the Directorate of History at the Department of National Defence; Hector Mackenzie, John Hilliker, Greg Donaghy, Mary Halloran, and Ted Kelly in the Historical Section at the Department of Foreign Affairs; John Fletcher and Thelma Nicholson in the Privy Council Office; and Paul Marsden, Dick McClelland, Maureen Hoogenraad, and Loretta Barber at the National Archives of Canada. Geoffrey Pearson very kindly provided information about Canadian decision-making, as well as access to the Lester B. Pearson Collection. Roger Hill at the

Canadian Institute of International Peace and Security allowed me to cite from the CIIPS transcripts. Special thanks also go to Elizabeth Diamond, archivist at the John G. Diefenbaker Centre in Saskatoon, Saskatchewan for providing access to Diefenbaker's papers. In addition, Jane Barrett, Clayton Beattie, Gayle Fraser, Jack Granatstein, Knowlton Nash, and Basil Robinson provided invaluable information and inciteful comments.

In Ottawa and Brussels, I had the privilege of meeting many individuals who greatly contributed to my understanding of international affairs, alliances, and Canadian foreign and defence policy. Some of these are listed in the bibliography. The views and comments of delegates at NATO and the Supreme Headquarters Allied Power Europe (SHAPE) headquarters, many of whom have had considerable experience in NATO matters, provided an excellent cross-section of informed opinion.

Special thanks for their loving assistance go to my immediate family – Graham, Margarete, Janet, Michael, and Merran – and to my extended family – Howard, Marion, David, Susan, and Megan. My partner, Howard Peter Langille, offered many valuable suggestions and unfailing encouragement, proving that the best of friends can also be the best of partners.

Abbreviations and Definitions

ACE	Allied Command Europe
AEW	Airborne Early Warning
ALCM	Air-Launched Cruise Missile
ASW	Anti-Submarine Warfare
Bomarc	Surface-to-air anti-aircraft missile
CAST	Canadian Air-Sea Transportable brigade
CCF	Co-operative Commonwealth Federation
CFB	Canadian Forces Base
CFE	Canadian Forces Europe
CF-100	A.V. Roe Canuck jet fighter
CF-101	McDonnell Douglas Voodoo interceptor
CF-104	Lockheed Starfighter interceptor/ground attack aircraft
CF-105	A.V. Roe Avro Arrow interceptor
CF-5	Northrop Freedom Fighter interceptor
CINCNORAD	Commander-in-Chief, NORAD
CIIPS	Canadian Institute for International Peace and Security
DEA	Department of External Affairs
DEW	Distant Early Warning line

DFAIT   Department of Foreign Affairs and International
        Trade (formerly Department of External Affairs)

DND   Department of National Defence

DHist   Directorate of History, DND, Ottawa

F-101B US version of the CF-101, or Voodoo interceptor

F-104G US version of the CF-104, or Starfighter

GLCM   Ground-Launched Cruise Missile

GNP   Gross National Product

Hansard House of Commons Debates

H-bomb Hydrogen bomb

Honest John Short-range surface-to-surface dual-capable missile

ICBM   Intercontinental Ballistic Missile

JGD Centre Right Honourable John G. Diefenbaker Centre

Lacrosse Short-range dual-capable atomic missile

MBFR   Mutual and Balanced Force Reduction talks

MND   Minister of National Defence

MG   Manuscript Group

MP   Member of Parliament

NA   National Archives of Canada (formerly Public
        Archives of Canada)

NACC   North Atlantic Cooperation Council

NATO   North Atlantic Treaty Organization

NATO HQS NATO Headquarters, Brussels, Belgium

NDP   New Democratic Party

NORAD   North American Air Defence (now Aerospace)
        Command

OAS   Organization of American States

PAL   Permissive Action Link

PJBD   Permanent Joint Board on Defence

PCO   Privy Council Office

PMO	Prime Minister's Office
RCAF	Royal Canadian Air Force
SAC	Strategic Air Command
SACEUR	Supreme Allied Commander, Europe
SACLANT	Supreme Allied Commander, Atlantic
SAGE	Semi-Automatic Ground Environment radar detection system
SCEAND	Standing Committee on External Affairs and National Defence
SCOND	Standing Committee on National Defence
SHAPE	Supreme Headquarters Allied Powers Europe
SSBN	Ballistic missile-firing nuclear-powered submarine
SS-20	Soviet intermediate-range ballistic missile
STAFEUR	Special Task Force on Europe
Starfighter	CF-104 aircraft
TNF	Theatre Nuclear Forces
TNT	trinitrotuluene (high explosive)
UK	United Kingdom
UN	United Nations
US	United States
USAF	United States Air Force
USSR	Union of Soviet Socialist Republics
Voodoo	CF-101 interceptor

NATO AND THE BOMB

Leader's Belief Systems
and Canada's Defence Commitments

During the Cold War, Canada's stance toward the North Atlantic Treaty Organization (NATO) was one of shifting commitment. Canadian leaders often contemplated changes in the level of Canada's commitment to the military alliance, and at times made them, often abruptly. For example, John Diefenbaker's initial decision to acquire nuclear weapons systems for the Canadian Forces was followed by fervent debate within the Cabinet, especially during the Cuban missile crisis, and eventually both the prime minister and his minister of External Affairs came to oppose these nuclear commitments. Similarly, Lester Pearson, before becoming prime minister in 1963, reversed his opposition to acquiring nuclear weapons for Canadian Forces. But by the end of his prime ministership, Pearson was unsure as to whether Canada should retain its Alliance commitment of forces stationed in Europe. As well, Pearson's successor, Pierre Trudeau, initially intended to cut drastically, if not completely withdraw, Canadian Forces from Europe. The Cabinet eventually compromised, deciding to halve the forces instead. Under Trudeau, Canada eventually reverted to a unique, non-nuclear role within the Alliance. It was Trudeau's 1978 speech at the United Nations General Assembly, calling for the cessation of nuclear weapons testing and a "strategy of suffocation," which was followed by his government's controversial decision in 1979 to allow cruise missile testing on Canadian soil as part of the nation's commitment to NATO. In 1984, however, in an effort to encourage a more co-operative dialogue between NATO and the Warsaw Pact, the prime minister decided to undertake a last-ditch "peace initiative," travelling the world to advocate an end to the nuclear arms race.

With the fall of the Berlin Wall and the end of the Cold War in 1989, many Canadians assumed that the forty-year debate over

whether Canada should maintain its commitment to NATO or withdraw would come to an end. As the Soviet threat withered away, it
was thought that the demise of the Alliance was also inevitable. The
Mulroney government's decision to withdraw all Canadian Forces
from Germany thus fulfilled many nascent expectations (although
the announcement was met with disbelief among staunch NATO
defenders in both Canada and Europe). After withstanding some
criticism, the Canadian government reaffirmed its commitment to
European security through a renewed peacekeeping effort under UN
auspices in the former Yugoslavia. As well, the new Liberal government under Jean Chrétien decided to demonstrate its support for
NATO – and NATO expansion – through traditional military commitments. Under Chrétien, the federal government earmarked elements
of Canadian Forces stationed in Canada to NATO, and the federal
government supported NATO enlargement from sixteen to nineteen
members. Even during the debate over the war in Kosovo, the Chrétien
government was a strong backer of NATO. Although the Cold War
was over and the traditional threat from the Soviet Union had disappeared, it was apparent that the Liberal government had elected
to stay in NATO.

Today, despite the dissipation of the Soviet threat, the prohibitive
costs of NATO enlargement, and Canadian reservations about relying
upon NATO's strategy of nuclear deterrence, most indications are that
Canada will remain a NATO member. On the other hand, we can
expect that Canadian decision-making regarding the military alliance
will probably continue to be dominated by conflicting beliefs and
assumptions about the extent of Canada's obligations and commitment to the Alliance.

THE UNDERLYING BELIEFS AND ASSUMPTIONS OF CANADIAN LEADERS

Why has there been such variation in the support of Canadian leaders
for Canada's NATO commitments? What led some to defend and
others to criticize certain military commitments? During the Cold
War, these defence-related decisions were influenced by international
developments, domestic pressures, and individual concerns. International crises, NATO recommendations, bilateral pressures, electoral
concerns, and financial considerations – all affected the nature and
extent of Canada's NATO commitments. Nevertheless, the fact that
there were influential leaders who favoured, and others who simultaneously opposed, the various NATO commitments suggests the
presence of a variety of underlying beliefs and convictions.

This book's main contribution to the debate is its revelation that two competing belief systems – typified by the labels "Defenders" and "Critics" – significantly influenced defence decision-making between 1957 and 1989. The evidence demonstrates that the government's controversial stance toward NATO during the Cold War stemmed from new ways of thinking about everything from the nature of the threat to the suitability of a nuclear deterrence strategy. This new way of thinking first appeared around the time of the Cuban missile crisis, during Prime Minister Diefenbaker's tenure. It was not always logical or "rational," but it was embedded in a related set of assumptions that will be referred to here as typical of "Critics." It was, moreover, a *Weltanschaung* reflected later in the approach and policy direction of the Trudeau government. What was interesting and novel about the competing belief sytems of Defenders and Critics?

Behind the scenes, decision-makers who possessed beliefs typical of Defenders feared the consequences of Canada deserting its NATO allies and then finding itself abandoned in turn. Their fears grew out of a perception that the close ties among the allies were in danger of weakening, as well as a concern that the Canadian government was leaning toward neglecting its allies, which could lead to a wide array of unpleasant consequences. In contrast, other decision-makers, those with belief systems more typical of Critics, were preoccupied with the dangers of entrapment, including suspicions about the likelihood and possible consequences of the allies drawing Canada into an armed confrontation. They also had serious doubts about American undertakings. Whereas Defenders believed that Canada should maintain its support for NATO, by modernizing its military equipment, strengthening Canadian Forces overseas, and increasing defence spending, Critics sought to restructure and limit Canada's support for specific NATO commitments. Defenders perceived an opportunistic and aggressive threat to the Alliance from the Soviet Union; Critics argued that such fears were exaggerated and based on an inaccurate assessment of political realities. While Defenders assumed that Canada and the Alliance's weapons systems were necessary and non-threatening, Critics saw aspects of both NATO and the Warsaw Pact's arsenals as overly threatening. And while Defenders expressed their faith in different permutations of deterrence strategy, Critics often expressed concern about this doctrine and offered conditional support for it, at best. Indeed, some leaders shifted from one belief system to another as they learned more about the effects of nuclear weapons and the problems with deterrence strategy.

Thus, different belief systems led some influential decision-makers to press the government to maintain, if not strengthen, its NATO contributions, and others to seek a restructuring and de-emphasis of some of Canada's commitments to the Alliance. Due in large part to the presence of these opposing belief systems within the inner circles of high-level decision-making, Canada's approach to the Alliance and its NATO commitments often fluctuated and was frequently criticized. This study uncovers a new and original way of thinking about security that was typical of daring Critics such as Howard Green, John Diefenbaker, Norman Robertson, Pierre Trudeau, Donald Macdonald, Eric Kierans, Ivan Head, and Paul McRae – and that contributed greatly to the Canadian government's controversial stance toward NATO.

THE BELIEF SYSTEMS OF DEFENDERS AND CRITICS: GENERAL PATTERNS FROM 1963 TO 1989

Chapters 3 and 4 consider whether belief systems typical of Defenders and Critics influenced decision-making regarding a variety of NATO commitments between 1963 and 1989. In these chapters, I demonstrate that many high-level policy-makers interpreted events and developments differently because of contrasting core beliefs and assumptions related to the dangers of abandonment or entrapment, the source and salience of the threat, and the merits or demerits of the Alliance's weapons and strategy. Owing in large measure to the presence of these different beliefs among policy-makers, some leaders recommended maintaining or increasing particular NATO obligations, while others recommended decreasing or cutting selected commitments. Although a wide variety of other factors could have played a role in affecting defence decision-making, these chapters indicate that two distinct belief structures helped shape high-level discourse between 1963 and 1989. These chapters, in particular, show that competition between these beliefs significantly affected defence decision-making regarding Canada's overseas troop contributions to NATO.

A HISTORICAL CASE STUDY, 1957–1963

I have included a case study in order to show that, beginning in the late 1950s, certain influential decision-makers in the Diefenbaker administration espoused new beliefs and ways of thinking. The purpose of focusing on this period is to demonstrate the two belief systems that shaped and constrained the decision-making process as it related to fulfilling, or not fulfilling, Canada's nuclear commitments to the Alliance. The case study shows that, within the inner circle of defence decision-making, some policy-makers held belief systems typical of Defenders, which led them during their terms in office to advocate the acquisition of nuclear weapons to fulfill Canada's NATO commitments. But beliefs typical of Critics prompted other influential decision-makers between 1959 and 1963 to oppose that policy. As for Prime Minister Diefenbaker himself, his belief system gradually changed from that of a Defender to that of a Critic. This shift accounted for his initial advocacy of the nuclear commitment, his subsequent vacillation and search for options, and his eventual outright rejection of the nuclear systems. Thus, the evidence of this case study demonstrates that, owing to the onset of new ways of thinking critically, the defence policy-making process between 1957 and 1963 was significantly reshaped and constrained, thus contributing to Canada's shifting commitment to NATO.

THE ROOT CAUSES OF CONFRONTATION: REASONS FOR DEFENDERS' AND CRITICS' COMPETING BELIEF SYSTEMS

The final chapter explores possible explanations for the predominance of these belief systems during the Cold War. Since certain patterns of thought were repeatedly evident, this chapter analyses the roots of those beliefs – what might be called their antecedent causes. Like peeling layers from an onion, this chapter delves ever deeper into the question, exploring the roots of the two competing belief systems. It reveals that the principal elements of these two belief systems stemmed from various personal experiences and human characteristics, different historical lessons learned and absorbed, contrasting images about the source and salience of the threat, as well as alternative ways of approaching problems and participating in shared practices. By exploring some of the underlying reasons leaders advocated change, or consistency, with respect to Canada's past role in NATO, this section tries to deepen our understanding of the factors that have shaped past Canadian defence policy – and to broaden our appreciation of the various types of factors that could, in the future, shape Canadian policy in NATO.

LEADERS' BELIEF SYSTEMS AFFECT CANADIAN DEFENCE COMMITMENTS

By explaining some of the reasons Canadian leaders sought to increase, maintain, or decrease Canada's past commitments, we should be better able to understand some of the chief influences that have shaped Canadian defence policy-making. Although this country was a founding member of the Atlantic Alliance, controversy continued to focus on the exact nature and extent of Canada's military commitments to NATO. This book asks why such a variation in support for some of Canada's NATO commitments has persisted among influential Canadian decision-makers. What were the underlying beliefs of these decision-makers that led some to defend and others to criticize select NATO commitments? Perhaps by documenting, within a conceptual framework, many of the underlying ideas and convictions that influenced past high-level discussions about Canada's NATO involvement, we can enhance our understanding of defence decision-making and Canada's support, or lack thereof, for select NATO initiatives.

CHAPTER ONE

Canada's NATO Commitments during the Cold War

WITHDRAWAL FROM EUROPE AFTER THE COLD WAR

With the end of the Cold War, many Canadians assumed that the forty-year debate over whether Canada should maintain its commitment to the North Atlantic Treaty Organization (NATO) or withdraw would come to an end. They predicted the inevitable demise of the Alliance, as the Soviet threat waned. Some measure of a "peace dividend," derived from what Canada would have spent annually on NATO, seemed likely.[1]

The government's announcement in September 1991 of its intention to withdraw all but 1200 troops from the Central Front in Germany fulfilled many such expectations.[2] Estimates were that a gradual withdrawal, suitably cautious, would result in financial savings of some $1.2 billion over five years.[3] The government's promise that the remaining troops would be incorporated into some kind of "rapid reaction force" under NATO's multinational authority eased the fears of the "Atlanticists," who counselled that Canada not completely cut its military ties to Europe.[4]

Then in February 1992, Minister of Finance Michael Wilson announced plans to withdraw Canada's contingent from Europe completely. As Minister of National Defence Marcel Masse explained, "Canada's commitment to the Alliance is as strong as ever ... The pull-out decision is based on budgetary and fiscal reasons and we have absolutely no philosophical differences with NATO."[5] NATO defenders nevertheless reacted to the announcement with disbelief.[6] Members of the Canadian delegation, who had received only a few hours notice of the change in policy, found the decision difficult to justify initially, especially since Prime Minister Mulroney, only a few months before, had assured Chancellor Helmut Kohl of Germany that Canada intended to retain a visible military presence on European soil. The European allies and the American military representatives at Supreme Headquarters Allied Powers Europe (SHAPE) sharply criticized the timing of Canada's decision, particularly as it had been taken without consulting the other allies through proper channels.[7] But Canadian delegates to NATO and SHAPE in Brussels consoled themselves with thoughts of the significant role Canada's ambassador to NATO had played in establishing the North Atlantic Cooperation Council (NACC) and lauded Canada's commitment to European security through its peacekeeping efforts in the former Yugoslavia.[8] The idea of according former Warsaw Pact nations associate membership in NATO had been broached by Prime Minister Mulroney in 1991. When the possibility of associate status was rejected – mainly by Britain and France because of the security guarantee it entailed – the Canadian ambassador to NATO worked to institute some kind of NATO membership for the Eastern Europeans under NACC auspices.[9] The portrayal, by then Minister of National Defence and Minister of External Affairs Barbara McDougall, of Canada's contribution to the peacekeeping operation in Yugoslavia as a renewed contribution to European security was also a source of consolation to the Canadians in Brussels, whose diplomatic efforts were assisted by the high-media profile of the commander of the UN Forces, Canadian General Lewis Mackenzie.[10] Indeed, it was not long before Canadians at NATO headquarters were receiving requests from the other allies, including Americans, for more information on peacekeeping.[11] High-level representatives from allied countries such as Britain and Germany pointed to the maintenance on European soil of troops earmarked for NATO as Canada's most valuable contribution to European security. But in the early 1990s, it seemed as if the sudden shift of interest to peacekeeping might somehow brighten Canada's image at NATO headquarters.[12]

Indeed, although Canada's status at NATO headquarters diminished with the announcement of the troop withdrawal, the general attitude of the Canadian delegation was one of resignation; indications were that the Canadian announcement was a precursor to similar announcements of reductions and cutbacks among the other allies. It was clear that Canada would remain an active participant in the North Atlantic Council, in the hundreds of committees at NATO and SHAPE, and in the discussions surrounding the implementation of the new Strategic Concept.[13] Indeed, Canada's Associate Defence Minister Mary Collins maintained that the Strategic Concept's call for "lighter, more flexible forces," which could "more evenly focus" on all NATO's regions, was consistent with the principal themes of Canada's defence policy as announced in September 1991 and refined in February 1992. As Collins explained, after the troops were withdrawn from the two German bases by 1994, "we will continue to be an active member of the Alliance and our other Alliance commitments will remain unchanged."[14] In addition, NATO's secretary-general, Manfred Woerner, in February 1992, after the announcement of the troop withdrawal, assured the allies that Canada would meet its other commitments to NATO. As he saw it, these commitments "underline the intention of the Canadian government to continue to play a full role in the North Atlantic alliance and European security."[15]

CANADA'S CONTINUING ALLIANCE COMMITMENTS

Many of Canada's NATO commitments remained unchanged after the 1992 announcement. For instance, the nation could still dispatch an expeditionary brigade group, two squadrons of CF-18s, and an air defence battery to Europe. The government was still responsible for maintaining a Canadian Forces battalion prepared to deploy to Europe with either the Allied Command Europe (ACE) Mobile Force or the NATO Composite Force. Canadians continued to serve as part of the NATO Airborne Early Warning (AEW) system in Geilenkirchen, Germany, and as aircrew aboard NATO AEW aircraft. Canadian destroyers and frigates were still prepared to sail with the Standing Naval Force Atlantic, while eleven destroyers and frigates, one supply ship, three submarines, fourteen long-range patrol aircraft, and twenty-five helicopters retained their role in patrolling the North Atlantic as part of NATO's "augmentation" forces. Canada was still to do its part in defending NATO's Canada-U.S. region, as well as contribute to the North American Aerospace Defence Command (NORAD), the organization responsible for the defence of NATO's largest single land mass. Last but not least, Canada was to continue to offer the allied countries its facilities and territory for military training, such as those at CFB Goose Bay in Labrador and CFB Shilo in Manitoba, not to mention the underwater naval testing range at Nanoose Bay in British Columbia.[16]

The government continued to demonstrate its support for NATO through other means as well. The Canadian-paid portion of the infrastructure budget at NATO headquarters, although not widely known, was viewed as a significant contribution.[17] The government's intention to retain approximately 650 Canadian personnel at NATO and SHAPE as military planners, attachés, and representatives on the

Canadian delegation was seen too, as an important commitment. Finally, the announcement regarding the renewal of a ten-year contract to train approximately 6,000 German Armed Forces annually at CFB Shilo and CFB Goose Bay has been described as yet another example of Canada's intention to help strengthen the Alliance. As for CFB Goose Bay, although aboriginal residents complained about the environmental effects of low-flying jets and it was slated for closure because the United States deemed it too expensive for training purposes, it continued to serve as a training base for German and other NATO planes.[18]

Naturally, some politicians and defence analysts continued to discuss ways in which Canada could reinstate, if not strengthen, its symbolic NATO commitment of land forces to Europe. Some members of the Liberal party suggested that Canada retain the Lahr base in Germany as a forward-staging base for peacekeeping operations in Europe, Africa, and the Middle East, arguing that Lahr and CFB Cornwallis in Nova Scotia should become Canadian peacekeeping training centres for UN and NATO contingents. One high-level military commander at NATO suggested that Canada retain an "airhead" capability (i.e., a landing area for the Canadian air force) in Europe, and a former Canadian ambassador to NATO noted, tongue-in-cheek, that as long as Canada retained a piece of land in Europe with the flag flying overhead, and at least twenty-five people stationed there at Christmas, Canada's commitment to NATO could remain credible.[19]

Although the withdrawal of Canada's troops was seen by certain member states, not to mention some Canadians, as a weakening of the country's commitment to NATO, representatives of the government and members of the Canadian delegation to NATO continued to portray the decision as no lessening of Canada's support for NATO. As Canada's deputy permanent representative to NATO explained, the government remained committed to NATO, but would express that commitment in different ways.[20] Nevertheless, questions about how and whether Canada should maintain its commitment to NATO continued to surface. In effect, despite the near disappearance of the Soviet threat, a vocal minority in Canada seemed to favour a further strengthening of the country's NATO commitments. Proposals included re-equipping the augmentation forces based in Canada for their role in the Alliance's new Strategic Concept, acquiring new helicopters and submarines to support NATO's Anti-Submarine Warfare (ASW) strategy, enhancing Canada's diplomatic and consultative profile at NATO headquarters in Brussels, and training and equipping Canadian and multinational peacekeeping forces to participate in UN peacekeeping operations under NATO's direction.[21]

In November 1993, the new Liberal government of Jean Chrétien announced a comprehensive review of Canadian defence policy. By February 1994, a Special Joint Committee of the Senate and House of Commons was established to initiate consultations and report to the government. In testimony before the Special Joint Committee on Canada's Defence Policy, some policy-makers continued to argue that the Alliance should remain a priority for both defence and foreign policy reasons. They emphasized the wide array of new conflicts in the world, particularly in Europe; the instability of the Russian leadership; and the ongoing military threat. They advised the government to ensure that Canada had modern military equipment and sufficient tri-service personnel to fulfill the strategic requirements of both deterrence and NATO's new Strategic Concept. They suggested that the Canadian Forces be deployed and equipped in accordance with the Strategic Concept, which relied on rapid-reaction, main, and augmentation forces. Canada, they argued, must continue to structure and train its military for mid-to high-intensity combat operations. In testimony before the Special Joint Committee, it was frequently acknowledged that Canada should contribute to United Nations' peacekeeping and peacemaking operations, but that such contributions should remain a low priority for the Canadian Forces relative to their general combat capability for defending Canada and its allies. The alternatives, it was said, posed a risk to security and stability as well as to Alliance relations. Some policy-makers contended that NATO was adapting to this new environment of uncertainty, and that NATO alone retained the political coherence and military capability to ensure collective defence and security.[22]

Others argued that NATO was now less of a priority, given the dissipation of the Soviet military threat and the disappearance of both the Warsaw Pact and the Union of Soviet Socialist Republics (USSR). They noted the unlikelihood of an attack across Europe's Central Front and frequently cited the historic inability of military alliances to combat diffuse threats such as ethnic conflict, environmental degradation, and human rights violations. Some suggested that Canada should de-emphasize its military commitments to NATO, while retaining a diplomatic and consultative presence in the higher councils of the Alliance. Alternatively, many favoured increasing Canada's foreign aid and contributions to UN agencies and operations. Related proposals were advanced for new defence priorities, which would emphasize the monitoring and surveillance of Canadian territorial waters and airspace as well as expand the country's commitment to peacekeeping operations under UN auspices. Calls were heard for specialization rather than the maintenance of a general-purpose, combat-capable army, navy, and air force. The suggestion was to restructure and retrain the Canadian Forces to ensure a more productive contribution to peacekeeping and to the various initiatives outlined in the 1992 United Nations' Agenda for Peace. According to the critics, given this new environment, adherence to the prevailing assumptions, practices, and institutions of the past forty years could result in unnecessary risks and expenses.[23]

In the midst of this defence review, Prime Minister Jean Chrétien, Foreign Minister André Ouellet, and Defence Minister David Collenette announced the government's commitment to converting CFB Cornwallis into a multinational training centre for UN- and NATO-affiliated personnel, the Lester B. Pearson Canadian International Peacekeeping Training Centre. There, the government planned to sponsor training for military and civilian personnel from countries participating in NATO's Partnership for Peace (PFP), as well as from developing countries under Canada's Military Training Assistance Program.[24]

In December 1994 the Department of National Defence (DND) released the *Defence White Paper*, announcing that Canada would remain a full and active member of NATO. Its thrust was that, although the monolithic threat to Western Europe had disappeared and the principal responsibility for European defence lay with the Europeans, the government still valued the transatlantic link and recognized that the Alliance had made progress in adapting to a post-Cold War world. The White Paper noted, in particular, those aspects of NATO that reflected a co-operative approach to European security relations, including the creation of the North Atlantic Cooperation Council, PFP, and the development of the Combined Joint Task Force Concept.[25]

According to the White Paper, this perspective on NATO "underpinned" the future of Canada's Alliance commitments. In the event of a crisis or war in Europe, for example, the contingency forces Canada maintained for all multilateral operations would immediately be made available to NATO. Apart from this general commitment, the government announced changes to a number of specific peacetime NATO commitments. In the context of Canada's prior Alliance commitments, three important changes were envisaged. First, Canada would terminate its commitment to maintaining a battalion group to serve with Allied Command Europe's Mobile Force or the NATO Composite Force in the defence of northern Norway. The battalion group's equipment in Norway would be returned to Canada to help offset the needs of the regular forces and the militia. Instead, DND was willing to earmark an infantry battalion group to NATO's "Immediate Reaction Force." Second, in keeping with NATO's broader geographic focus, the government would supplement its one ship in NATO's Standing Naval Force Atlantic with the occasional assignment of a ship to NATO's Standing Naval Force Mediterranean. Third, Canada would scale back its contribution to NATO's infrastructure program and devote some of those funds to the expansion of its bilateral contract programs with Central and Eastern Europe under the Military Training Assistance Program.[26]

Some later additions were made to these changes to Canadian NATO commitments. The Defence department affirmed its commitment to providing, under UN auspices[27] or in defence of a NATO member state, the following: a naval task group; three separate battle groups or a brigade group; a wing of fighter aircraft; one squadron of tactical transport aircraft; and, within three weeks, the remaining elements of a "full contingency force." Canada's prior Alliance commitments were also largely maintained, although the number of personnel serving in NATO headquarters was to be reduced and the training of allied forces in Canada was put on a cost-recovery basis. Finally, the government indicated an interest in pursuing discussions with the United States, the NATO allies, and various other partners on the possible expansion beyond North America of the missile-warning function currently discharged by NORAD.[28]

Predictably, the release of this White Paper in 1994 did not terminate the debate over the extent of Canada's NATO commitments. Some high-level foreign and defence policy advisers gradually became concerned about the implications for Canada of NATO enlargement. Prime Minister Jean Chrétien had supported expanding NATO membership from sixteen to twenty member states (adding Poland, Hungary, the Czech Republic, and Slovenia). Estimates of the costs of enlargement had varied widely however, in part because of uncertainty about the number of new members that should be admitted. Nevertheless, in 1997, many high-level American officials agreed that NATO expansion would cost somewhere between US$27 billion and US$35 billion over the next thirteen years. For Canadian policy-makers, the concern was whether Canada's defence costs would jump with NATO expansion. Behind the scenes, some senior policy-makers began to worry about the looming costs of NATO expansion in the twenty-first century, as well as the extent to which Canada should or could support the rebuilding of the newer allies' defence systems. In the weeks prior to the ratification of the enlargement decision in the United States Congress, the US State Department had concurred with NATO's revised assessment, putting enlargement costs at only $1.5 billion. Yet these wide variations in estimates from such reputable analysts as the United States Congressional Budget

Office, the Pentagon, the State Department, and NATO headquarters raised still more questions about the extent of Canada's NATO commitments. Might these estimates prove to be too low? Even as the Alliance began to consider "opening the door" to a second round of expansion, various high-level Canadian policy-makers worried about the future cost of Canada's NATO obligations.[29]

Another debate in Canada revolved around whether the nuclear weapons states in NATO should demonstrate a stronger commitment to the elimination of their respective nuclear weapons (e.g., by fulfilling their obligations under Article VI of the Treaty on the Non-Proliferation of Nuclear Weapons). In 1996, Lloyd Axworthy, as the new minister of Foreign Affairs, asked the House of Commons Standing Committee and International Trade to review the nuclear issue. The minister asked the committee to focus on the various important developments and disarmament initiatives that had occurred in recent years, including the Project Ploughshares Report entitled *Canada and the Abolition of Nuclear Weapons*, the report of The Canberra Commission on the Elimination of Nuclear Weapons, and The International Court of Justice's advisory opinion on the threat or use of nuclear weapons – all of which had added new ideas and impetus to the nuclear weapons debate. The minister also requested that the committee's study reflect Canada's alliance commitments, including its membership in NATO, as well as future challenges to its security interests, including the security risks posed by the proliferation of other weapons of mass destruction and the practical challenges of effectively verifying complete nuclear disarmament.[30]

Accordingly, the standing committee issued a report in December 1998, *Canada and the Nuclear Challenge: Reducing the Political Value of Nuclear Weapons for the Twenty-First Century*, with fifteen recommendations concerning a wide range of nuclear issues. The committee recommended, for instance, that, during the next re-examination and update of the Alliance's Strategic Concept, the Government of Canada argue forcefully within NATO for a review of the nuclear component of its policy.[31] The Department of Foreign Affairs then coordinated *The Government Response* to these recommendations, which was tabled on 19 April 1999. *The Government Response* explained that "as an active member of NATO and a net contributor to overall Alliance security, as a friend and neighbour of the United States and its partner in NORAD and as a country that has a broad interest in (and ability to contribute to) building international peace and security, Canada balances its Alliance obligations with its disarmament and non-proliferation goals." Keeping these goals and constraints in mind, Canada proposed that the Alliance agree, at the upcoming Washington Summit in 1999 celebrating NATO's fiftieth anniversary, to review its nuclear policy and its relationship to proliferation, arms control, and disarmament. The government promised that Canada would "continue to urge NATO partners to consider the impact on potential nuclear proliferators when considering the characterization of the purpose of NATO nuclear forces." Moreover, the government promised to encourage the nuclear weapons states to demonstrate their unequivocal commitment to enter into and conclude negotiations leading to the elimination of nuclear weapons.[32]

In a development lost sight of in the media's focus on the Kosovo crisis, the NATO summit held 23–25 April 1999, in Washington, D.C., opened the door to a broad-ranging review of its nuclear weapons policy. At a news conference on 24 April, Minister Axworthy confirmed the willingness of NATO "to have a review initiated" of its nuclear weapons policies. Explaining that this was the thrust of the recommendations that came out of the report of Canada's Foreign Affairs Committeee, Axworthy added, "It's a message that the [Canadian] Prime Minister took [to] certain NATO leaders ... I think we have now gained an acknowledgement that such a review would be appropriate and that there would be directions to the NATO Council to start the mechanics of bringing that about."[33] While it is too early to say whether NATO's leadership will proceed to such a review willingly or grudgingly, the convoluted prose of the Washington Summit communiqué almost suggests to some that NATO policymakers wish the whole idea would go away.[34] Yet it is probably not too audacious to say that the approach of Foreign Affairs Minister Axworthy on behalf of the federal government indicates yet another important shift in Canada's policy and approach toward NATO and nuclear disarmament. It is too early to predict, however, whether Canada will withstand pressures from the NATO nuclear powers, especially the United States, and lobby hard to obtain changes in NATO's Strategic Concept.

Most recently, the federal government's unwavering support of NATO's actions in Serbia and Kosovo during the spring and summer of 1999 seemed, to many viewers, to be proof of Canada's loyalty to the Alliance. In effect, the fact that the Canadian government, along with most of the other allies, did not publicly raise doubts and reservations about the decision to bomb Serbia and Kosovo was taken as proof of Canada's allegiance to NATO.[35] However, many questions emerged about the extent to which Canada should be prepared to defend NATO's bombing of Kosovo, and about the measure of Canada's NATO obligations in case the war spilled over into the rest of the Balkans. For example, during the crisis in Kosovo, concerns were voiced about whether Canada should condone bombing a sovereign country that had not attacked any member of the Alliance and that was technically outside NATO's territory (i.e., out of area). The role of Canadian fighter planes (CF-18s) sent to assist with the aerial bombing of Serbia and Kosovo was also the subject of debate. Questions about whether Canada should contribute forces to a possible ground war provoked considerable discussion as well.[36] Although it is not yet known whether the federal cabinet was internally divided on these sorts of questions, certain comments by Lloyd Axworthy indicate that, as foreign minister, he harboured some serious reservations about unequivocally supporting NATO's actions in the Balkans. The war in Kosovo served to remind Canadians that NATO membership entailed obligations and commitments that could be difficult to sustain.[37]

In summary, recent debates in Canada about the foreseeable costs of NATO enlargement, the need for a review of NATO's Strategic Concept, and the extent of Canada's obligations vis-à-vis NATO's war in Kosovo are an indication of the debates to come about the extent of Canada's commitment to NATO. As the country moves into the next century, comparable questions about the measure of its alliance commitments will emerge. In effect, the debate has raged for the past fifty years, as efforts to maintain and enhance Canada's commitments to NATO have competed with attempts to restructure or de-emphasize those same commitments. In reality, the debate has been an ongoing feature of the country's involvement in the Alliance.

PAST DEFENCE DECISIONS REGARDING CANADA'S NATO COMMITMENTS

Historically, Canadian decisions about NATO have revealed a pattern of shifting, contrasting commitment. While nearly all high-level decision-makers, including most Cabinet ministers and senior advisers, have wanted to remain in the NATO "club," there has been little consensus as to the means by and extent to which Canada should contribute.

Under John Diefenbaker's administration between 1957 and 1963, for example, Cabinet ministers initially decided to deploy both nuclear-armed strike reconnaissance aircraft and nuclear missiles in Europe as part of Canada's NATO commitment. The prime minister agreed, as well, to sign the North American Air Defence (NORAD) agreement with the United States, further integrating Canadian and American air defence forces. Diefenbaker and many of his colleagues were convinced that NORAD should be a North American Command under NATO auspices. Additional announcements by the minister of National Defence regarding the planned acquisition of nuclear-tipped Bomarc missiles and nuclear-armed interceptor aircraft to be based on Canadian soil were then presented as part and parcel of Canada's expanding NATO commitments. Other Cabinet ministers and senior advisers, however, were increasingly reluctant to acquire nuclear warheads for the newly acquired weapons systems. In 1961, Howard Green, then minister of External Affairs, opposed the nation's nuclear commitments, while Douglas Harkness, then minister of National Defence, strongly favoured them. With the subsequent Cuban missile crisis, the public learned that the government had failed to fulfill its promises. A series of related events led to the fall of the government. In the general election that followed, Prime Minister Diefenbaker campaigned against the nuclear commitments his Cabinet had originally agreed to honour.[38]

In 1963, Lester Pearson, the leader of the Liberal party, exhibited a surprising *volte-face* as well. Whereas he had previously opposed nuclear warheads for the weapons systems the Diefenbaker government was acquiring, he suddenly announced his intention, if he were prime minister, to acquire the warheads, arguing that the commitments had to be fulfilled.[39] "I feel very strongly," he wrote in a letter dated 7 January 1963, a few days before announcing his decision, "that commitments made for Canada by a Canadian government should be honoured, until there is an opportunity to renegotiate and alter those commitments. This requires discussions with our allies in NATO and Washington."[40] Although Paul Hellyer strongly supported Pearson's decision, others felt that the Liberal leader's about-face was at least partly motivated by electoral ambitions.[41] Once he became prime minister, Pearson quickly replaced the ballast in the weapons systems with nuclear warheads.[42]

With the assistance of his minister of External Affairs, Paul Martin, and his minister of National Defence, Paul Hellyer, Pearson controlled the policy-making process sufficiently to ensure that the government was not swayed from fulfilling Canada's nuclear commitments.[43] By the end of his mandate in office, however, he was privately debating whether Canada should maintain a different NATO commitment – the contribution of 10,000 men stationed in Western Europe. In his last few months as prime minister, Pearson requested a secret review of the Canadian overseas commitment to NATO. Norman Robertson, formerly under-secretary of the Department of External Affairs, along with two active diplomats, Geoffrey Murray and Geoffrey Pearson, helped write the review that recommended retaining the status quo.[44] After stepping down in April 1968, Lester Pearson said, in an appearance on an American television program, that he supported the idea of withdrawing Canadian Forces from Europe.[45] However, Pearson was hardly consulted during the campaign for the Liberal leadership and the general election that followed.[46] In 1968, Pierre Elliott Trudeau assumed the prime ministership on a platform that promised a re-examination of Canada's foreign and defence policy, including all its NATO commitments.

During his campaign for the Liberal leadership, Trudeau had supported the withdrawal of Canadian Forces from Europe, while retaining a NATO role for the defence of North America.[47] After he was elected leader, he declared: "We will take a hard look in consultation with our allies at our military role in NATO and determine whether our present military commitment is still appropriate to the present situation in Europe. We will look at our role in NORAD in the light of our technological advances of modern weaponry and of our fundamental opposition to the proliferation of nuclear weapons."[48] Thus, in July 1968, the Trudeau government undertook a comprehensive examination of foreign and defence policy, beginning with the question of Canada's continued participation in NATO. Prime Minister Trudeau, President of the Privy Council Donald Macdonald, Postmaster-General Eric Kierans, Secretary of State Gerard Pelletier, and Trudeau's chief advisers Ivan Head and Gordon Robertson were all initially inclined to cut back, or possibly withdraw, Canadian Forces from Europe. They were opposed in Cabinet by Minister of National Defence Leo Cadieux; Minister of External Affairs Mitchell Sharp; Minister of Transport Paul Hellyer; and Paul Martin, leader of the government in the Senate.[49] In April 1969, after much heated discussion in Cabinet and among various advisory groups set up to discuss the issue, Prime Minister Trudeau and his foreign policy adviser Ivan Head decided to reduce the forces in Europe by two-thirds.[50] When this decision was announced to the NATO allies and members of Parliament, however, it was forcefully opposed.[51] So the prime minister and the Cabinet changed tactics once again. This time it was announced that the troops would be reduced by fifty percent. For ministers who were utterly opposed to Canada's NATO involvement, such as Eric Kierans, it was a disappointing turn of events.[52]

Once Canada's NATO policy seemed settled, Trudeau turned his attention elsewhere. Although the country's other Alliance commitments received little media attention during the 1970s, Canada was pressured during this time to increase defence spending to levels commensurate with that of the other NATO allies.[53] In the late 1970s, the government also agreed to provide a Canadian Air-Sea Transportable (CAST) brigade for the defence of Norway on NATO's northern flank.[54] The issue that finally came to preoccupy the prime minister and Cabinet, however, had little to do with Canada's financial contribution to NATO or the extent of the country's overseas troop commitments. Rather, it had to do with the nature of Canada's obligations to test weapons systems for NATO and the United States. Once again, a different NATO commitment (apart from nuclear weapons, stationed forces, or defence spending) came to the fore in domestic debates about what should be the measure of Canada's commitment to the Alliance.

Questioning the extent of Canada's NATO obligations had its roots in Pierre Trudeau's 1978 speech to the United Nations Conference on Disarmament. There, the prime minister had propounded a "strategy of suffocation," based partly on a proposal to desist from, or suffocate, the testing of nuclear weapons carriers – planes, missiles, and so on.[55] In 1979, however, it became apparent that the United States was going to ask Canada to test the air-launched cruise missile (ALCM), a system designed to carry nuclear warheads.[56] The contradictions were apparent, and by the time the government was formally asked to test the cruise, a significant portion of the Canadian public was vociferously opposed to the notion. Many worried about President Ronald Reagan's provocative comments about the "evil empire" of the then USSR and the increasingly tense relations between the superpowers. Questions arose as to whether Canada was testing ALCMS for the second phase of NATO's two-track strategy in Europe or for an American first-strike strategy.[57] Within Cabinet, some ministers opposed the testing while others favoured it.[58] As the prime minister privately told visiting Vice-President George Bush, several ministers were expressing their constituents' concerns that the cruise missile was a technological development that created exceptionally difficult problems with regard to arms control verification. They feared it was a new leap forward in the arms race, with enormous risks for instability in a situation where parity had existed.[59] Trudeau attempted to quell debate by writing a general letter to the public that defended cruise testing as part of Canada's fair share of the burden shouldered by NATO allies.[60] In the end, the tests went ahead. But the issue clearly divided the government, the Liberal party, and the public.[61]

In 1983–84, in an effort to mitigate his and the public's concerns about the likelihood of nuclear war between the United States and the Soviet Union, and as part of what some have referred to as his "last hurrah," Prime Minister Trudeau undertook a peace initiative.[62] He visited fifteen NATO and Warsaw Pact capitals to encourage a more co-operative dialogue, while emphasizing the security of NATO and the Warsaw Pact.[63] As he explained: "We want to change the trend-line. We want to make it clear not only that the Alliance is strong; that it will defend itself; that it will not be intimidated; but that it is also pursuing peace."[64] Once Trudeau stepped down, though, his government's record of commitment to NATO between 1968–71 and 1978–84 seemed contradictory.

Those who thought Canada had failed to honour its commitments welcomed the Conservative election victory of September 1984.[65] The government's subsequent *Defence White Paper* (1987) promised to increase spending and strengthen Canada's NATO commitments. The general direction of the White Paper was toward expansion in all areas of the armed forces, including growth in capital expenditures, re-equipment of both the army and air force, revitalization of a three-ocean navy, and the buildup of military capabilities appropriate for meeting the continued Soviet threat. Specifically, the government announced its intention of acquiring a fleet of nuclear-powered submarines, as well as consolidating Canada's forces and modernizing its equipment on the Central Front.[66] The government had committed itself to spending $183 billion on defence over fifteen years, with approximately $58 billion earmarked for new equipment. As then minister of National Defence, Perrin Beatty, explained, this "modernization" program would "present unparalleled opportunities and challenges for Canadian industry."[67]

However, the cancellations and cutbacks announced by the Conservatives in April 1989 marked a conspicuous change in direction. Policy direction now moved toward a freeze on defence spending, cancellations or cutbacks on all major capital expenditures, and a reduction in the number of troops. Plans for submarines were cancelled and the number of battle tanks to be acquired was halved. As well, plans were annulled for the deployment of up to a division of troops in Europe.[68]

After the fall of the Berlin Wall in November 1989 and the Persian Gulf War in the winter of 1991, public debate continued as to whether there was any good reason to maintain Canada's expensive troop commitment in Europe.[69] The government's announcement in September 1991 of a reduction to 1,200 troops, followed by notice in February 1992 of its intention to withdraw completely from Germany by 1994, was opposed by a few but accepted with equanimity by many others.[70] The government's intention to withdraw all Canadian troops from the Central Front, although surprising in light of Mulroney's recent statements in Germany that the government would continue to honour its European commitments,[71] should not have been entirely unexpected, however, given the sea change in East-West relations, the inclination among the allies to reduce military spending and reap a peace dividend, as well as the erratic record of different Canadian governments regarding the nation's commitment to NATO. As Geoffrey Pearson, former ambassador to Moscow, has pointed out: "There has been, over time, a fairly constant Canadian withdrawal and return, and withdrawal and return, to NATO, as a centre for our foreign policy. If you looked at the history of our NATO policies, you would be struck by the way that the graph goes up and down."[72]

It is apparent that the Canadian government has expended a significant amount of money, training, military equipment, and diplomatic energy on NATO since 1949. It is estimated that Canada spent anywhere between $1 to 1.2 billion a year to maintain troops in Europe. Added to that should have been the purchase of submarines, the construction of frigates, and the maintenance of anti-submarine aircraft in order to carry out Canada's NATO role in the North Atlantic, according to Admiral Robert Falls (ret.), the former Chief of the Defence Staff and chairman of NATO's Military Committee in 1983.[73] But this was not all. The total costs attributed to the Canadian Forces Europe (CFE) would have been much higher, according to Major-General Leonard V. Johnson (ret.), if transportation, training, national logistics support, administration, and other items charged to other commands had been included. Moreover, these costs did not include the land and air forces assigned to the defence of Norway, the training and exercising of those forces, any maritime forces assigned to NATO in wartime, or the augmentation needed to transport Canadian Forces' units to war establishments, all of which were included in other Defence Department allocations.[74]

Of course, some Canadians now assume that the forty-year debate about whether Canada should continue its commitment to the Alliance or withdraw ended with the withdrawal of the CFE from the Central Front in Europe. But many of Canada's other NATO commitments are still in place; the federal government remains committed to NATO membership; and efforts are under way to strengthen Canada's commitments to the Alliance in different ways. For example, 1,000 personnel of the Canadian Forces continue to be deployed in the former Yugoslavia under NATO's direction, although they were originally moved there from Germany as part of a United Nations' peacekeeping operation. Questions remain, too, as to whether the government should continue to channel significant amounts of money, capital, training, and equipment toward the cost of NATO expansion. Estimates are that the cost of inviting new members such as Hungary, the Czech Republic, and Poland into the club could cost non-US NATO members hundreds of millions of dollars in additional assessments. Moreover, the Liberal government under Jean Chrétien is committed to rebuilding war-torn Kosovo, in part by deploying hundreds of Canadian Forces personnel there as part of a NATO peacekeeping force.

Although the Cold War is over, many elements of the old belief systems about the nature of the threat, the relevance of deterrence, and the need for a strong collective defence organization such as NATO persist. During the Cold War, many decision-makers had conflicting reasons for contemplating – and, at times, changing – Canada's NATO commitments. An appreciation of Defenders' belief systems can help explain prevailing thought patterns. On the other hand, a few Canadian leaders rejected prevailing American defence strategy and weapons systems to pursue alternative approaches to managing Canada's complex bilateral and multilateral defence relationships. New ways of thinking among Canadian leaders competed with traditional attitudes and approaches.

CHAPTER TWO

Canadian Belief Systems in Context

In seeking to broaden our understanding of defence decision-making and Canada's support – or lack thereof – for selected NATO commitments, this study outlines the belief systems of influential policy-makers within a conceptual framework. Such an approach necessarily raises theoretical questions and methodological issues that need prior clarification.

WHY IS IT NECESSARY TO EXPLORE THE FACTORS AFFECTING CANADIAN DEFENCE POLICY-MAKING?

Assuming that the study of defence policy-making will deepen our understanding of Canada's approach to its NATO commitments, why is it necessary to explore the factors affecting defence policy-making? Perhaps Canada's record of commitment might be more satisfactorily explained by studying other factors, such as developments arising out of the international system or the domestic environment?

Let us look at a variety of other "systemic-level," "state-level," and "individual-level" variables in light of their effect on Canada's approach to NATO. At the "systemic-level" of analysis, for instance, international crises, historical developments, and systemic-level power configurations might be analysed for their effect on the country. It could be posited that, as a result of the Cuban missile crisis, the Pearson government decided to acquire nuclear weapons for the Canadian Forces. Alternatively, one could say that, owing to the relaxation of tensions between NATO and Warsaw Pact countries, the Mulroney government withdrew Canadian Forces from Europe and closed its bases. Historical developments, such as advances in technology, might also help explain Canada's record of commitment. One could hypothesize, for example, that the emergence of Soviet bombers capable of reaching Canadian territory contributed to the country's decision to acquire nuclear-armed Bomarc missiles as part of its commitment to preserving NATO's deterrent capabilities or, similarly, that Soviet development and deployment of the ss-20 missile led to Canada's decision to test the cruise missile as part of NATO's "two-track" strategy.

One might also group bilateral pressures under the general rubric of international variables affecting Canada's NATO commitments. It could be hypothesized, for instance, that it was the United States' request that Canada acquire nuclear-armed missiles and interceptors that prompted the government to acquire Bomarc missiles and Voodoo interceptors, or that it was American pressure to equip the Bomarcs and Voodoos with nuclear warheads that contributed to the Canadian government's disinclination to acquire these systems. Alternatively, it might be postulated that it was American pressure that compelled Canada in the early 1980s to test the cruise missile or, conversely, that a surfeit of American pressure pushed Canada, a few years later, into taking an intermediary role between opposing alliances.

One could also examine the influence of international organizations such as the NATO Council and the United Nations. Perhaps the NATO Military Committee's recommendation in 1952 that military authorities make plans based on the assumption that nuclear weapons would be used in NATO's defence from the outset prompted the Canadian government to acquire nuclear weapons systems? Negative allied reaction to Canada's 1969 announcement of a two-thirds cut to Canadian Forces in Europe may have contributed to the government's subsequent decision to cut the Forces by only one-half. The effect of UN directives could be considered another possible stimulant, for Canada has frequently supported various arms control and disarmament resolutions at the United Nations. For instance, did the "Irish resolution," with its recommendation for restraints on the spread of nuclear weapons, prompt Canada to reconsider acquiring nuclear weapons for the Canadian Forces?

In fact, many systemic-level variables probably affected Canada's record of commitment. For example, systemic changes in power configurations might well account for Canada's contrasting approaches to the Alliance. Paradoxically, allied requests that Canada contribute to the defence and rebuilding of post-war Western Europe may have led to the strengthening of Canada's NATO commitments, whereas the gradual recovery and growing ability of Western Europe to defend itself may have contributed to a weakening of Canada's overall commitments. Clearly, further exploration of systemic developments and pressures might well broaden our understanding of Canada's support, or lack thereof, for various NATO commitments.

As for other possible factors operating at the state level, perhaps economic pressures affected Canada's NATO record. It could be argued, for example, that the Bomarcs or cruise missiles were a relatively less expensive alternative to the mounting cost of fielding trained military personnel in Europe, or that financial imperatives contributed to the Trudeau government's interest in withdrawing some of the Forces stationed overseas. Also, the Washington Summit's recommendation that each NATO ally increase its percentage of GNP devoted to defence spending may well have affected Canada's NATO spending. On the other hand, the prospect of a "peace dividend" could have enticed Canada into reassessing its commitments.

Also at the state level, domestic pressures may have influenced Canada's approach to NATO. Growing domestic criticism, for example, could have contributed to Canada's decision under Diefenbaker not to fulfill its nuclear commitments, whereas later, under Trudeau, domestic interest groups representing defence and industrial interests appeared to pressure the government to strengthen its NATO commitments. It seems evident that different state-level variables, including financial imperatives, domestic pressures, and domestic interest groups, may well have influenced the resources Canada earmarked for NATO.

These sorts of systemic- and state-level variables all suggest promising areas for further analysis. Why, then, does this study focus on factors affecting defence policy-making at the level of the individual? Although it makes sense to argue that it was the interplay of many different factors which contributed to Canada's overall record of commitment to NATO, this position does not help in developing a conceptual framework that is sufficiently parsimonious, explanatory, and illuminating. In any conceptual model, complex reality needs to be partitioned with boundaries; humans cannot deal with too much information at once. In a project of this nature, boundaries of inquiry need to be drawn. Therefore, this book does not purport to explain all the reasons for Canada's support, or lack thereof, for select NATO commitments. It merely suggests that studying the factors affecting defence decision-making can significantly deepen and broaden our understanding of Canada's overall approach to the Alliance. Let us begin with the premise that factors affecting individual-level decision-making need to be explored.

One problem to date with much of the analysis of NATO and Canadian defence policy has been the attribution of individual human assumptions and inclinations to actor units, such as the state or government, when, in effect, it is only individuals who are subject to these kinds of beliefs. Phrases such as "Canada decided" or "the federal government committed" beg the question of who decided for Canada, and who committed. To speak of actors, governments, and systems obscures the fact that it is leaders who usually make decisions on behalf of the collectivity called Canada. The individual level of analysis – with its focus on discerning the psychological factors that affect policy-making – presumes that there is merit in focusing on the field of individuals who participate in the decision-making process. The idea is that people are subject to experiences, images, and fears, while institutional abstractions such as "Canada" or "the government" are not, except in a metaphorical sense. In other words, this book is premised on the assumption that understanding the factors affecting individual defence policy-makers can significantly contribute to our understanding of Canada's overall approach to, and role within, the NATO Alliance.

WHY IS IT NECESSARY TO EXPLORE WHETHER BELIEFS AFFECTED CANADIAN DEFENCE POLICY-MAKING?

This book does not purport to explain all the factors affecting Canada's overall approach to NATO. It does, however, suggest that individual-level factors in the form of beliefs and assumptions have played a significant role in defence policy-making with regard to Canada's NATO commitments. Of course, a variety of other influences may have had an equal, if not greater, effect on decision-making, including international crises, technological developments, bilateral pressures, and historical trends. It could be posited, for instance, that Prime Minister Diefenbaker's perception of a relaxation of superpower tensions in the wake of the Cuban missile crisis led him to delay fulfilling his government's commitment to acquire nuclear weapons, or that the 1968 Soviet invasion of Czechoslovakia prompted some Cabinet ministers to advocate that Canada strengthen its forces in Europe. Alternatively, it could be suggested that technological developments, not international crises, had the greater impact on policy-making. The perception of some policy-makers that Canada should have the best weapons available may have inclined some politicians to favour the acquisition of tactical nuclear weapons for the Canadian Forces. By the same token, confusion over whether the cruise missile could be used in a first-strike role may have contributed to some Cabinet ministers' inclination to oppose cruise testing.

Bilateral pressures may also have affected defence decision-making. For example, the US State Department's press release taking the Diefenbaker government to task for not fulfilling its nuclear commitments was a form of bilateral pressure that had a contrary influence on the prime minister's inclinations. As well, decision-makers could have been particularly influenced by UN and NATO directives during select time periods. For instance, NATO's Harmel report of 1967 (stressing the need for allied consultation and the reduction of East-West tensions) or the Reykjavik Declaration of 1968 (in which the allies pledged to seek mutual and balanced force reductions) may have contributed to the perception among decision-makers that Canada could ease tensions by withdrawing its forces from Europe. On the other hand, a decade later, UN initiatives reflecting increased worldwide interest in arms control and disarmament may have incited Prime Minister Trudeau to propose his "strategy of suffocation" and, later, to undertake a peace initiative.

Clearly, while a wide range of international factors may well have affected policy-makers, other state-level variables, such as domestic pressures and financial concerns, may have affected them equally. For example, shifts in the public's support for NATO, both for and against, could conceivably have led some decision-makers to recommend either increases or cutbacks in defence expenditures. On the other hand, changes in the overall defence budget may have prompted others to advocate either new equipment or cuts in spending. As well, representations from domestic interest groups and interested academics may have influenced some Canadian leaders to either support or criticize Canada's NATO commitments. It seems self-evident that a wide variety of subjective factors arising from the international and domestic environment, including changes in perceptions of the threat, changes in allied attitudes toward Canada, fluctuations in public opinion, and ebbs and flows in defence spending, impinged on the attitudes of influential decision-makers toward Canada's NATO commitments.

But again, if it is so evident that the interaction of international and national factors affected decision-making, why does this book nonetheless focus on individual leader's beliefs and assumptions? First, that there were some influential decision-makers who favoured, while others simultaneously opposed, select NATO commitments suggests contrasting attitudes on the part of the various high-level defence policy-makers. After all, they were all influenced by the same international developments, bilateral pressures, domestic concerns, and political imperatives. And yet many emerged still diametrically opposed in their attitudes toward NATO. Second, a preliminary survey indicated that the various leaders' underlying ideas and convictions frequently influenced high-level decision-making. Indeed, many heretofore classified documents – including confidential correspondence, secret memoranda, and restricted Cabinet meetings – referred to decision-makers' own beliefs, fears, and assumptions. Third, this particular line of inquiry is, to date, relatively unexplored as an area of analysis. Thus, given the availability of many formerly classified documents pertaining to Cabinet discussions, I feel now is the time to ask whether certain beliefs and assumptions have consistently affected defence policy-making. In the end, outlining some of these commonly held beliefs within a conceptual framework can only enhance our understanding of defence decision-making and Canada's support, or lack thereof, for select NATO initiatives.

WHAT IS A BELIEF OR AN ASSUMPTION?

For the purposes of my research, a belief is conceived of as "the mental concept at the basis of an argument or action," while an assumption is "the taking of anything for granted as the basis of an argument or action." For example, the very lack of war between NATO and the countries of the Warsaw Pact for over fifty years might be used to support a belief in the strategy of deterrence. Implicit in this kind of reasoning is the assumption that the possession of nuclear weapons deters war.[1]

A great deal of the literature about NATO has ignored the beliefs and assumptions of leaders and NATO decision-makers. Although beliefs and assumptions are important for increasing our understanding of those who hold them, they are often difficult to discern. Since they are the initial links in a chain of reasoning, they may seem obvious, not at all contentious, or at times even unworthy of notice. They can also often be hidden from view in the guise of images, analogies, and metaphors. Decision-makers, for example, may justify Canada's membership in NATO as a kind of "insurance policy." Just as the payment of an insurance premium entails no risk for the policy-holder, Canada's membership in NATO is then deemed risk-free and responsible. But the presence of an important belief or assumption is also sometimes indicated by an omission. If, for example, decision-makers rarely mention the Soviet threat to the Alliance, this would suggest either that they assume it to be of little consequence, or that the threat is accepted as axiomatic of international affairs, thereby providing the context for decision-making.[2]

WHO WERE THE DECISION-MAKERS?

In general, *decision-makers* are defined as those individuals who have the greatest opportunity to act on their preferences and fears; those individuals whose attitudes, concerns, fears, and belief systems most affect the outcome of decision-making processes regarding national defence and NATO issues; and those individuals who possess the power both to commit the government and to prevent other decision-makers from reversing that commitment.[3]

"Influential" decision-makers have been categorized still further, according to their relative distance from the centre of decision-making. Paul Pross first suggested that a "policy community" could be represented by means of a diagram of concentric circles illustrating the position of various institutions and pressure groups, with the "Cabinet," the "Central Policy Structures," and the "Lead Agency" at the centre of the diagram.[4] This study builds on that idea, suggesting that influential decision-makers can be subdivided into concentric circles consisting of individuals (not roles) positioned in the "centre," the "inner" and "outer" core, the "periphery" or "margins," and outside the policy community (the "marginalized"). In this study, I focus on those individuals at the centre of decision-making, those who wield the most influence. However, I also pay attention to decision-makers within the inner and outer cores of decision-making. Excluded are those on the periphery of defence and alliance policy-making, as well as the marginalized.

DO LEADERS POSSESS CLUSTERS OF INTERCONNECTED BELIEFS?

This study suggests that certain beliefs and assumptions have played an important role in influencing policy-making. Like ideologies, which act as guides to action, certain beliefs – related to the dangers of abandonment or entrapment, the nature of the threat, and the utility of NATO's strategies and weapons to deter war – shaped and constrained decision-making. Over time, these belief systems exerted a major impact and contributed to Canada's support, or lack thereof, for select NATO commitments.

Initially, it was thought that one type of belief would dominate at a particular time, within a certain context, or even within a particular group of decision-makers. During the course of my research, however, it became apparent that different leaders possessed different clusters of assumptions and beliefs. These interconnected ideas related to the dangers of abandonment, the perils of entrapment, the threat to the Alliance, the utility of nuclear and conventional weapons, and the merits or demerits of deterrence doctrine. For some leaders, these clusters of beliefs and assumptions seemed more akin to ideologies or world views at the opposite ends of a pole. Some leaders possessed coherent, all-encompassing world views, of which certain beliefs – such as their fears about possible abandonment or entrapment – were important elements. Others had less coherent schema through which they filtered and organized information. All leaders, however, did have mindsets that revolved around several core assumptions, although some mindsets were highly interrelated while others seemed less coherently connected. Finally, I settled on the term *belief system* as the most appropriate to describe these sets of core beliefs and assumptions.[5]

WHICH BELIEF SYSTEMS ARE DELINEATED?

Two sets of beliefs and assumptions typical of Defenders and Critics, respectively, were developed inductively and deductively. The choice of just two belief systems was based on the frequency with which the components of these belief structures were encountered in my research. Indeed, there seemed to be a good deal of agreement (or disagreement) among high-level decision-makers on either one set of pivotal assumptions or the other. Chapter 3 explains the beliefs and assumptions of Defenders by referring to pertinent historical examples drawn from the classified records of Canadian decision-making. Chapter 4 describes the beliefs and assumptions of Critics using new information pertaining to high-level decision-making processes. In effect, the typical profiles of Defenders and Critics are painted with broad brushstrokes in chapters 3 and 4. The obvious question then becomes whether profiles of merely two belief systems will result in a vast over-simplification or, conversely, an amplification of our understanding.

In this book, the Defender and Critic profiles, as outlined in chapters 3 and 4, may seem to portray these decision-makers as more single-minded and intolerant than they actually were. The real world, as decision-makers perceived it, was infinitely complex; indeed, the actors were driven by a multiplicity of beliefs, assumptions, and motives. Nevertheless, categorizing leaders' beliefs and assumptions about a variety of important concepts – ranging from the nature of the threat, to the intentions of the allies, to the utility of nuclear and conventional weapons – into two broad categories can help simplify the issues and increase one's understanding. Indeed, by deriving the profiles from historical evidence arising out of an extended time span (chapters 3 and 4) and an in-depth case study (chapters 5, 6, and 7), I tried to avoid imposing dangerously simplistic psychological distinctions on any one category. In the end, the classification of influential decision-makers' beliefs and assumptions into two broad categories – Defenders or Critics – provides a useful conceptual framework with which to help explain Canada's approach to NATO over selected time periods.

CAN TWO DIFFERENT BELIEF SYSTEMS PROVIDE A SATISFACTORY EXPLANATION?

Throughout my research, I recognized that most decision-makers' beliefs and assumptions were more complicated than two, three, or more profiles would suggest, especially in the abnormal and stressful situations in which the decision-makers frequently found themselves. I presumed, too, that the leaders involved were intelligent people who had thought deeply about Canada's NATO commitments. In other words, my intention is not to suggest that Canadian leaders did not think through the issues carefully. Rather, the research suggests that their beliefs and assumptions owed a great deal to the past – to the lessons learned from events and history, to views conditioned by war, and to perceptions of nuclear reality.

Although this book will demonstrate that the presence of two different types of belief systems or mindsets can help explain Canada's support, or lack thereof, for various NATO commitments, one might still ask whether three, four, or even five categories might not have provided a better explanation. Certainly, the proclivity of scholars to situate policy-makers in two or more neat categories can be seen in a wide variety of scholarly analyses regarding defence policy-making.[6] Indeed, while this study suggests that the descriptive labels of Defender and Critic are more illuminating than others – such as dove versus hawk, realist versus idealist, isolationist versus internationalist – it does recognize that typecasting decision-makers into two categories can oversimplify and underestimate the complexity of some leaders' beliefs. Moreover, whereas it was important to broaden understanding by categorizing the main elements of two different mindsets, not all leaders could be categorized once and for all as either Critics or Defenders. At times, some espoused important elements of both belief systems, others were undecided or ambivalent, or the categories themselves proved to be too rigid. I have tried throughout, then, to explain any apparent confusion of the leaders, as well as their conversion from one set of beliefs to another. Chapter 9, the conclusion, considers whether this book would have been improved, for instance, by positing a third or fourth belief system.

METHODOLOGICAL ISSUES

Chapters 3 and 4 show that many high-level Canadian decision-makers possessed entire belief systems, or elements of belief structures, that were typical of Defenders or Critics. The case study in chapters 5, 6, and 7 illuminates the extent to which these sorts of beliefs influenced high-level decision-making processes. The following three approaches were used to assess whether these belief systems affected the decision-making process pertaining to Canada's NATO commitments.

First Approach: Assessing evidence arising out of the psychological milieu

This study focuses on discerning different leaders' beliefs and assumptions in order to understand their impact on defence decision-making. Thus the evidence collected required a focus on the psychological milieu (the world as leaders saw it) rather than the operational milieu (the world in which defence policy was carried out). As a result, it was critical to examine evidence arising out of defence policy-making processes in which the leaders themselves were involved in discussing what should be the measure of Canada's NATO commitments. It was not important to study time periods in which there was little or no high-level debate. Whereas in the real world, where defence policy was carried out, many Canadian commitments to NATO remained unchanged, in the world as various leaders saw it, different kinds of NATO commitments came to the fore. For example, the issue of whether Canada should fulfill its nuclear commitments dominated defence decision-making in the period between 1959 and 1963 under Diefenbaker, while questions about how many military personnel Canada should deploy in Europe took precedence in secret discussions beginning in 1968. During different time periods and under different governments, the type of commitment making up the topic of high-level discussion and debate shifted. For that reason, this book does not explore defence decision-making as regards one kind of NATO commitment over time (for example, the Canadian Forces in Europe between 1957–92). Nor does it attempt to fully explain the factors affecting decision-making apropos all of Canada's NATO commitments during one select time period (for example, the Diefenbaker government's commitments to nuclear and conventional equipment as well as military and diplomatic personnel, and its related commitments to NORAD). Instead, I have focused my analysis on defence policy-making with regard to the particular NATO commitment that preoccupied decision-makers during the time period in question.

The instrumental model: assessing evidence with a view to its context   The "instrumental," as opposed to the "representational," model of analysis works on the assumption that the speeches and public documents of a politician and bureaucrat may be designed to influence the general public and may, therefore, be a less than accurate reflection of the speaker's or writer's true beliefs. I have therefore given more weight to handwritten notes, diaries, personal memoranda, letters, and secret Cabinet documents than to departmentally prepared speeches, policy papers, *ex post-facto* interviews, and memoirs.[7]

Based on an instrumental model of analysis, I assessed the material for this study with attention to its particular context. Highly-classified documents (e.g., top secret, secret, for Canadian eyes only, confidential, and personal) were accorded more credibility than papers written for wide distribution by the Department of External Affairs (DEA) or the Canadian delegation at NATO headquarters.[8] Similarly, handwritten drafts of speeches and scrawled amendments to notes and memos were studied with greater care than were final drafts, while personal letters to friends and colleagues were considered more reflective of a decision-maker's beliefs than were standard departmental replies. The original version of a carefully prepared speech to a specialist audience, for example, received greater attention than newspaper articles reporting the speech. And a contemporary diary was accorded more validity than an autobiography or recollection of events written years later. Finally, verbatim responses to journalists and transcripts recorded in *Hansard* were considered more representative of a decision-maker's underlying beliefs and concerns than were interviews conducted months or years later.

Second Approach: Using research questions to draw out
the main elements of each belief system

To mitigate against the possibility of biased evidence selection and researcher subjectivity, as well as to clarify the research agenda, I derived two sets of questions inductively and deductively. The context is the following. Many documents describing high-level discussions indicated, for example, that some important decision-makers believed that the Soviet Union posed an opportunistic and aggressive threat, while others assumed the threat was exaggerated and misunderstood. Some leaders feared that if Canada did not fulfill its NATO commitments the country would abandon its allies, while other policy-makers feared entrapment in a nuclear war much more than they feared abandonment. Beliefs about the reliability or unsuitability of nuclear deterrence doctrine also conflicted. Accordingly, questions pertaining to these contrasting core beliefs were posed, and the evidence was examined to answer these research questions. For example, the tendency to fear abandonment rather than entrapment was caught in the form of two questions: "Did decision-makers fear abandonment?" and "Did decision-makers fear entrapment?" Similarly, to discover whether belief in deterrence strategy was a salient consideration for decision-makers, the evidence was evaluated according to two questions: "Did decision-makers believe deterrence doctrine was suitable and reliable?" and, alternatively, "Did decision-makers believe deterrence doctrine was unsuitable and unreliable?" Once it was found that many decision-makers held substantive interrelated beliefs, two sets of five questions each were posed. The two sets of questions, again derived inductively and deductively, are summarized below.[9] The book was written, then, to answer these questions. In doing so, it profiles the Defenders and Critics, using evidence from different decision-making processes over the periods 1957–63 and 1963–89. Much of this evidence is documented so that others can review and confirm the findings.[10]

Research Questions: Mapping Canadian Thinking about NATO

NATO Defenders

- Did decision-makers fear abandonment?
- Did decision-makers believe Canada should pursue closer ties to its allies through established kinds of military commitments?
- Did decision-makers believe that the external threat to the Alliance was opportunistic and aggressive?
- Did decision-makers assume both Canada's and the Alliance's weapons were necessary and non-threatening?
- Did decision-makers believe that deterrence doctrine was suitable and reliable?

NATO Critics

- Did decision-makers fear entrapment?
- Did decision-makers believe Canada's established military ties to the allies should be restructured and de-emphasized?

- Did decision-makers believe the external threat was exaggerated and misunderstood?
- Did decision-makers believe that both sides' weapons were unnecessarily threatening?
- Did decision-makers believe deterrence doctrine was unsuitable and unreliable?

These two sets of questions effectively guided the research process and can be conceived of as maps to Canadian thinking about NATO. Of course, no one decision-maker can be held up as a perfect example of the Defender or the Critic (just as none can be described as perfectly rational). The evidence, however, shows that many influential decision-makers possessed beliefs and assumptions typical of Defenders or Critics, and that these belief structures significantly affected Canadian defence decision-making regarding the country's NATO commitments.

Third Approach: A historical case study

For the third approach, I conducted a historical case study – an in-depth analysis of the Diefenbaker period in office, 1957–63 (chapters 5, 6, and 7). The premise was that such an approach could help in assessing the influence of various kinds of intervening variables. As well, it would aid in refining deductively derived abstractions by linking them to inductively deduced conclusions. Moreover, the results would allow for the incorporation of additional, initially unconsidered factors into the discussion of the evidence, thus producing a stronger explanation.[11] In effect, chapter 5 reviews the defence decision-making process during the Diefenbaker period, while chapters 6 and 7 provide historical examples from the period to demonstrate that contrasting belief systems not only influenced decision-making but also contributed to the Cabinet's shifting nuclear commitment.

SELECTION OF THE HISTORICAL CASE STUDY

The selection of the case study fulfilled several requirements. First, the research had to focus on defence policy changes apropos one type of Canadian commitment to NATO. The concept of commitment could be used broadly, in the sense that Canada is committed to the Alliance. Or it could be used narrowly to describe a particular commitment to NATO, such as the government's undertaking to provide equipment such as the Honest John missiles for the Canadian Forces in Europe.[12] To enable a rigourous comparison, it was decided to focus the case study on narrowly defined commitments to NATO.

Second, the case study had to focus on a single Canadian government's decision – to either strengthen or weaken its commitment to NATO – that was subsequently reversed. It was deemed important that the case study focus on a decision-making process that involved the same influential decision-makers and contrasting decisions over time. In the end, it proved impossible to satisfy these requirements entirely. Some of the key players resigned, died, or lost interest in the decision, while others suddenly came on the scene and proceeded to wield considerable influence. Nevertheless, as long as it was essentially the same sample group of influential decision-makers at the centre of defence policy-making who stayed in power, the requirements of a controlled comparison were considered to have been reasonably satisfied.

Third, the case study had to cover a time period that generated considerable empirical evidence so that underlying beliefs and assumptions could be discerned using an instrumental model of analysis. Many primary documents, personal letters, memoranda, diaries, off-the-record commentary, minutes of in camera meetings, as well as handwritten drafts of speeches were necessary; this in turn created a number of problems, mainly because of access restrictions to NATO-related documents, especially information associated with high-level decision-makers' beliefs about nuclear weapons, the nuclear threat, and the other countries in the Alliance.[13] Another problem was the size of the information pool, which shrank through the 1970s, '80s, and '90s. Alternative information sources in the form of *ex post-facto* interviews were not a good source of evidence because of the nature of the research.[14]

In the final analysis, two historical periods proved adequate for the case study.[15] One, encompassing the defence decision-making process under Prime Minister Pierre Trudeau between 1968 and 1971, provided much of the evidence for the broadly delineated categories of Defenders and Critics depicted in chapters 3 and 4. Another encompassed an earlier decision-making process that transpired under Prime Minister Diefenbaker between 1957 and 1963.

THE CASE STUDY: NEW SOURCES OF PRIMARY AND SECONDARY EVIDENCE

Today, a wealth of primary and secondary material related to defence policy-making between 1957 and 1963 is available for research purposes. Indeed, despite restrictions on access to NATO-related documents, particularly information on nuclear weapons, a few collections have recently been opened. As a result, journalists, retired government officials, and academics have returned to explore the period.[16] Despite such valuable resources, however, obtaining access to relevant documents and archival sources is still a problem. For example, even after repeated requests, many of Howard Green's papers at the National Archives (NA) remain inaccessible, and the Privy Council Office (PCO) continues to excise large sections of the Cabinet minutes or "Cabinet Conclusions." At times, therefore, a very few references have had to serve as representative of a decision-maker's particular beliefs, while other instances saw a plethora of comments which then had to be assessed for their sincerity and representativeness.

SUMMARY

In summary, chapters 3 and 4, with their overviews of the substantive beliefs and assumptions of each belief system, demonstrate that many influential decision-makers held beliefs typical of Defenders or Critics and that these, in turn, affected decision-making between 1963 and 1987. The two distinct belief structures helped to shape high-level discourse and, in particular, show that competition between the two significantly affected defence decision-making regarding Canada's overseas troop contributions to NATO.

Chapters 5, 6, and 7 reveal that some of the most influential decision-makers in place between 1957 and 1963 possessed belief systems typical of one or the other profile, and that these mindsets, in turn, affected decision-making regarding Canada's nuclear commitments. As well, the case study explores the onset of Critics' belief systems and the commencement of new ways of thinking about Canada's nuclear weapons. By documenting within a conceptual framework many of the underlying ideas and convictions that led the government to acquire nuclear weapons – and then to disarm – the book attempts to broaden our understanding of some of the reasons for nuclear acquisition and the subsequent disarmament. After all, Canada was the only country during the Cold War that sought to acquire its own stockpile of nuclear weapons and then to disarm them.

Chapter 8 considers deeper questions: What were some of the underlying reasons for such opposing world views? What led some policy-makers to defend and others to criticize Canada's NATO commitments? This chapter delves still further into the issue, asking what particular events, crises, and dilemmas impelled Canadian leaders to take a stand in favour of (or against) the acquisition of nuclear weapons, the deployment of more Canadian troops overseas, the testing of cruise missiles for the United States, and the withdrawal from Europe. By considering key antecedent factors that contributed to the prevalence of these two belief systems, we can better appreciate the reasons for their predominance. Indeed, although the Cold War has ended, the kinds of reasoning and arguments put forward by NATO policy-makers and Canadian decision-makers – for example, during the bombing of Kosovo – would indicate that many of the same events, incidents, and lessons of the twentieth century, including the lessons of Munich and Vietnam, continue to affect the belief systems of Canada's leaders today.

By explaining why Canadian leaders sought to increase, maintain, or decrease Canada's past commitments, we may be better able to understand some of the important influences that have shaped defence policy-making in this country. Over the years, Canada, although a founding member of the Atlantic Alliance, has faced continual controversy about the measure of its military commitments to NATO. The final chapter, which briefly examines the forty-year dilemma of Alliance membership for Canada, concludes with an analysis of the theoretical and policy-relevant implications of this research for international relations theory and Canadian foreign and defence policy.

CHAPTER THREE

The Belief Systems of Defenders: General Patterns between 1963 and 1989

Since 1957, efforts to maintain and strengthen Canada's commitments to NATO have competed with contrary efforts to restructure or de-emphasize select NATO commitments. This competition among policy-makers has been a distinguishing feature of Canada's involvement in NATO for the past forty years. Many policy-makers based their defence of Canada's NATO commitments on an interlocking set of beliefs and assumptions typical of Defenders.[1] These beliefs led them to support maintaining, even strengthening, Canada's NATO commitments.

SUBSTANTIVE BELIEFS AND ASSUMPTIONS OF DEFENDERS

Defenders feared abandonment

The most important belief held by many Defenders was that the close ties among the allies would be threatened unless Canada maintained or strengthened its NATO defence commitments. If these commitments were weakened or abandoned and Canada deserted its closest allies, they feared that Canada would be in danger of being itself abandoned. These persistent concerns about the neglect of friends and allies that could result in an array of negative consequences can be grouped together as evidence of the Defenders' widespread tendency to fear abandonment.

Many Canadians harboured fears about the consequences of abandoning the NATO allies. Between 1963 and 1987, stark scenarios were frequently advanced concerning what could happen if Canada failed to nurture its military relationship with its allies. High-level discussions and correspondence throughout the period dwelt on the possibility that equivocation by the government regarding its defence ties could threaten the Alliance's solidarity, along with Canada's interests in Europe. One high-level policy-maker wrote to the minister of External Affairs in 1969 as follows: "Unpalatable though it may be, we must recognize that the public debate on collective security and specifically on NATO that has been going on in Canada has been most unsettling to the Alliance and damaging to Canadian interests in Europe. There is need to redress the balance decisively and I fear that this will not be accomplished unless we draw a line under our national period of hesitation and resume our place in the Alliance without qualification."[2]

Predictions about unsettling the Alliance and damaging Canadian interests in Europe were common, as was the fear that any measure of Canadian withdrawal from Europe might lead to other threatening scenarios, such as German domestic pressures leading to "an expansion of German military strength and the development of an independent nuclear weapons capability." Indeed, senior defence officials predicted in 1968 that any weakening, or withdrawal, of Canadian support from NATO could "affect the solidarity of the Alliance out of all proportion to Canada's relative force contribution at present."[3]

Many Defenders also assumed that if the government withdrew Canadian Forces from Europe or shifted defence expenditures away from NATO, Canada's allies would react sharply. The Ad Hoc Committee on Defence Policy, which in 1963 reported directly to the minister of National Defence, emphasized that the consequences of withdrawing from NATO "would be a sharp reduction in Canada's stature in Europe and in Washington."[4] According to a high-level, secret document written five years later, Canada's image in Europe would be "damaged" if the government was to withdraw its forces from Europe: "Rightly or wrongly, the Europeans have chosen to consider our forces in Europe as an earnest of our desire for close association with them and as a symbol of our internationalist spirit. Any unilateral action to withdraw them for reasons which our Allies did not find convincing would damage that image and modify the regard in which we are held by Europeans."[5]

When questions arose about reducing the forces' defence expenditures in Europe, Cabinet ministers often warned that the allies would disapprove of any shift of emphasis from Europe to Canada. Mitchell Sharp, minister of External Affairs in 1969, cautioned his colleagues that our allies "would not want to do the dirty work while we do the nice things."[6] Some influential decision-makers emphasized that, unless Canada strengthened or maintained its NATO commitments, the country could become isolationist or neutralist or that a wave of pacifism would overtake governmental decision-making, leading to a detachment from all allied affairs. As the Ad Hoc Defence Committee warned in 1963: "A policy of isolationism would permit Canadian defence policy to be disentangled from alliance commitments. However, the price would be that Canada's foreign policy as well as Canadian defence policy would cease to be relevant to Canadian national interests or to the contemporary world. Moreover, no feasible operation of Canadian foreign policy or Canadian defence policy can disentangle Canada from the Twentieth Century or the American continent."[7] Some Defenders also viewed Prime Minister Trudeau's effort in 1968–69 to withdraw, or at least reduce, Canadian Forces in Europe as indicative of a dangerous trend toward neutralism. According to Ross Campbell, Canada's ambassador to NATO at the time: "And believe me, Pierre Trudeau did not get the outcome that he had at that time wanted. He wanted the outcome to be that we would become a neutral nation. You may remember ... he envisaged that as one option, and that's where I think he wanted it to come out. And it didn't come out that way because that's not the instinct of most Canadians."[8]

The concern among Defenders about negative consequences if the government were to abandon NATO was not limited to the possible results of abandoning Canada's Western European allies. Many Defenders also predicted dire consequences if the country's commitments to the United States, under NATO auspices, were weakened. As Paul Hellyer, minister of National Defence during the Pearson era, told his Cabinet colleagues in 1963, "The consequences of a failure to honour Canada's nuclear commitments would be far-reaching; it might, for example, jeopardize extensive sales to the United States of the Caribou II aircraft or lead to the withdrawal of u.s. concessions on the importation of Canadian oil."[9] According to the minutes of another Cabinet meeting six years later, "consideration would have to be given to the possibility of an adverse reaction in the United States to any reduction in military expenditures." As the president of the Treasury Board saw it, "United States authorities, while granting that we had freedom to choose military roles, were always concerned as to the relative size of the burden that Canada was assuming." Another minister pointed out that the Cabinet was drawing conclusions based on the possibility of fearful consequences, the reality of which Postmaster-General Eric Kierans seriously questioned. Other Cabinet ministers, including Minister of External Affairs Mitchell Sharp and Minister of National Defence Leo Cadieux, nevertheless continued to insist that there would be grave consequences if the government chose to de-emphasize its NATO defence commitments to the United States.[10]

Dire consequences were also predicted whenever the question of neutrality or non-alignment arose. If Canada decided to pursue neutrality, the argument went, "the USA could find that the penalty to its security interests was intolerable."[11] According to a secret intradepartmental report presented to Cabinet in 1969, the Americans

could not tolerate the military use of Canadian territory by any power deemed hostile to US interests, and they would, therefore, undoubtedly meet with armed force – perhaps even without invitation – any attempt at the invasion, occupation or subjection of Canada ... [Non-alignment could] increase Canada's exposure to the indirect threat of foreign subversion ...[and] tend to introduce an element of instability into the strategic nuclear balance, i) because it would impose a penalty on the USA by denying access to Canadian territory and air space needed for the defence of US territory and the protection of the US strategic retaliatory forces, and ii) because a non-aligned Canada would interpose between the USA and the USSR a large geographical area of defence concern to both, but which would be an unknown political quantity in times of international tension.[12]

Many Defenders also cautioned that Canada might face difficult problems with the United States if the government did not agree to American requests to store or test nuclear weapons systems in Canada. In 1966, for example, Minister of External Affairs Paul Martin warned that the government had to agree to store nuclear weapons at the us-leased Argentia base in Newfoundland because "a nuclear capability at Argentia is considered by the US to be a highly desirable increment of deterrence to missile attack on North America ... Should we reject this request we would be likely to face some difficult problems. A rejection would be taken very seriously by the US ... It would also add an important new item to the list of current Canadian positions about which Washington is unhappy, whereas a favourable decision could help to offset adverse US reaction on such matters as the Soviet air agreement."[13]

Over the past four decades, many Defenders have warned as well that the government had to maintain, if not strengthen, its commitments to the North American defence system in order to avoid encroachment and excessive control by the United States. As a senior adviser argued in 1964, "our sovereign control" and "the durability of the French-English partnership" could depend on strengthened military commitments to North America: "In terms of our continuing relations with the US, there is an urgent political need to maintain Canada's contribution to North American defence at the highest possible level, especially when our sovereign control over other elements of our society and economy are under heavy US pressure. The durability of the French-English partnership in Confederation may well be dependent in part on our ability to resist US encroachment in all fields, including military."[14] Another high-level memorandum in 1968 advised that any reduction in Canada's military commitments could provoke the United States into making arbitrary decisions about Canadian defence policy:

Certainly substantial reductions in air defence and maritime defence could have grave repercussions on our bilateral relations with the US. It would be strongly resisted by the US because it would affect their own security. To compensate for the loss of US security, Canada would be pressed to agree to free access to Canadian air space and facilities for US air defence forces and accept US assumption of operational control of the ocean approaches to Canada. In both cases, but especially in the case of air defence, such a situation would involve stationing substantial numbers of US military personnel in Canada. At the same time, the USA would be making vital decisions affecting Canada's security and in a context which would have removed the incentive for close and easy consultation and exchange of information which Canadian participation in North American defence creates.[15]

In addition to worrying about the need to resist American encroachment and American control over Canadian decision-making, many Defenders projected the fear that if Canada were to weaken or withdraw its military commitments to NATO, the United States could slide into isolationism. Some Cabinet ministers argued in 1969 that if Canada withdrew from NATO, "this would be a plus for isolationism in the US" and would affect Canada's interest "in the preservation of western civilization."[16] In that same year, other Defenders expressed concern that many facets of Canada's political, economic, and defence relationship with the United States could dissipate if Ottawa were to weaken its NATO commitments. According to Marcel Cadieux, under-secretary of state for External Affairs in 1969, "even if Canada were prepared to ignore its own security, it could not ignore the U.S.A.'s security interests; otherwise the U.S. would be pressed to take unilateral steps which would deny us the advantages we derived from co-operation and would at the same time threaten our autonomy."[17] Similarly, another high-level restricted memorandum written in 1984 stated: "Should our support of NORAD (and NATO) decline, Canada could lose lucrative business to our 'more committed' Allies. Any reduction in our contribution might spill over to other segments of the bilateral relationship. USA trade policy, protectionism, environmental and broad political issues could be influenced by our attitudes towards defence relations."[18]

A related theme put forward by Defenders was that of the danger of Canada no longer being treated as a full partner, and the government not being consulted by the allies. According to the intradepartmental "Defence Policy Review" prepared for Cabinet in 1969: "The termination of Canadian defence co-operation with the USA and Western Europe would mean that Canada would no longer be participating in the formulation of Western policies on such matters as European security and disarmament, and that Western governments would regard Canada as essentially an outsider which no longer saw political interests in common with them. The result would be a decline in the hearing which Canada was able to obtain for its views in Western capitals, even if those views, in Canadian eyes, continued to have intrinsic merit."[19] Another senior policy-maker in External Affairs wrote his minister in 1969 that Canada's voice would be respected only if it fully cooperated with, and remained a reliable member of, NATO: "For Canada, this means in simple terms that it is only through continued participation in NATO that we can be sure of being part of a future process which is certainly going to alter profoundly the world scene over the next decade. But it also means that our voice in that process will be a respected one only if we are a fully cooperating and reliable member of the sole organization which is to be an integral part of the United States' far-reaching experiment in direct negotiation with the USSR."[20]

Defenders assumed that Canada needed to participate fully in NATO military activities in order to be regarded by the allies as a full partner. They also pointed out that the government, by weakening its military commitments to NATO, would lose its "seat at the table" in NATO discussions and have little say on decisions of great importance. In 1968, defence experts advised the Special Task Force on Europe that the government's ability to participate in the formulation of the nuclear policies of the Alliance would be threatened if Canadian forces in NATO should no longer be equipped with nuclear weapons: "Nuclear matters lie at the core of NATO strategy and there is no logic to the claim that Canada would somehow be better off if it dissociated itself from the decisions that must in any case be taken. Any decision to withdraw from the nuclear role in Europe simply on moral grounds would be difficult to justify."[21] More than two decades later, other high-level policy-makers continued to assume that "it's really by having had forces in Europe that we are a player in this business."[22] According to Paul Dick, associate minister of National

Defence in 1988 and a strong advocate of increasing Canada's commitments to the Alliance: "It is the leader of the NATO group who squares off with the leader of the Warsaw Pact group. If we did not have that seat at the NATO table, then we would have no more voice than many other countries in this world who do not even participate in discussions about disarmament and arms control."[23]

The fear that the allies would abandon Canada was also expressed in the notion that the Europeans might cut trade links if the government decided to withdraw from Europe, or that the United States might cease to grant Canada preferential trading status if Canada chose to reduce its military commitments. According to a secret memorandum circulated in 1968 in the Department of External Affairs:

Our refusal to cooperate in continental defence would cause serious concern to the USA authorities and USA public opinion, and would adversely affect the USA's attitude towards economic cooperation with us. We would incur heavy direct costs through the termination of the USA-Canada defence production sharing agreements; as indirect costs, our present exports of oil and natural gas and potential exports of uranium to the US might be affected, as well as our trade in such commodities as copper scrap, potash, lead, zinc, etc. The US authorities might be considerably less inclined to make mutually beneficial special arrangements with us in the financial field (eg. the interest equalization tax) or to enter into new areas of cooperation similar to the Auto Parts agreement. In summary, there could in the long term be extremely serious adverse consequences for our economy.[24]

Still other decision-makers were wary of the dangers of abandonment because they had witnessed previous allied reaction to reductions in Canada's defence spending. As one high-level official recalled in 1982, "Canada's decision to reduce our contingent in Europe in the early 1970s was criticized on the grounds that we were weakening NATO's strength in Europe. Subsequently, we continued to draw criticism because of the low percentage of our GNP spent on defence, compared to most other members of the Alliance." [25] In particular, the allies' criticism of Canada's failure to meet the pledge to devote three percent of GNP to real growth in the defence budget alerted some decision-makers to the possibility that there could be future negative consequences if Canada did not meet its NATO commitments.[26] As a senior adviser wrote Michael Pitfield in the PCO in 1980:

Canada's defence effort has been severely criticized recently, particularly by the US, in the annual multilateral examination in NATO's Defence Review

Committee. I think we may expect Mr. Vance to raise the subject in critical terms when he visits Ottawa later this month ... I thought I should draw this criticism to your attention because of my concern at the adverse effect in foreign policy terms that a failure by Canada to make every effort to achieve the 3% real growth in defence expenditures will have, particularly in Washington, but also among our major NATO allies.[27]

Aside from the idea that the allies might punish Canada for reducing its military commitments, some Defenders emphasized the possibility that a Canada estranged from NATO would be left alone with its great neighbour to the south. The domination of Canadian defence and foreign policy by the United States would inevitably result. Another ambassador to NATO, Arthur Menzies, argued that "there was an advantage to Canada being in a larger organization with a number of others rather than in a position which would have been as unequal as a Canada/United States type of organization."[28] According to another Defender, Ross Campbell, one of the "absolutely deadly" consequences of the growth of "the European centre within NATO" was that Canada would be "left on the shelf with the Americans."[29] One way to avoid this outcome, he later argued, was for Canada to commit to NATO, not reduce or withdraw its overseas military commitments.

Along with their fears of abandonment, some Defenders occasionally worried that the United States, in a fit of pique over any Canadian decision to withdraw from NATO, might abruptly cease consulting with Canada on other defence issues and renegotiate its defence agreements with Canada. As Marcel Cadieux, the deputy minister of External Affairs, pointed out in 1969 in a secret memorandum to his minister, if Canada chose to become non-aligned, the United States would have to abrogate various defence agreements with Canada, and the process of disengagement would "be extremely acrimonious and also expensive in terms of trade in defence-related items and in terms of possible US compensation claims against Canada."[30] In the opinion of another high-level policy-maker in 1966, the capacity and willingness of the United States to share in the burden of providing "global security" could be "circumscribed" by Canada's unwillingness to share the defence burden. As he saw it, there would be "new strains" in Canada's relations with the US if Canada "faltered" in any significant way.[31]

The important message underlying all these warnings about the consequences of not fulfilling the government's NATO commitments was that, unless the government strengthened, or at least maintained, its NATO commitments, Canada risked abandoning its allies and being itself abandoned. Many high-level decision-makers who pressed the government to strengthen or maintain its NATO commitments had a strong tendency, both publicly and behind the scenes, to project fearsome images and threatening scenarios related to the dire consequences of abandonment.

Defenders believed that Canada should pursue closer ties to the allies through established kinds of military commitments

Although Canadian decision-makers have suggested a variety of ways to pursue closer ties in the NATO Alliance, the tendency among Defenders was to consider only traditional, established ways of fostering such ties. Established means of pursuing closer ties included commitments to maintain or increase the number of Canadian Forces personnel earmarked for NATO purposes, particularly those deployed in Europe, as well as promises to modernize or designate more weapons systems and equipment to Canadian Forces in NATO, particularly in Europe. Traditional ways of signalling Canada's allegiance to the allies also included commitments to maintain or increase the percentage of the federal government's defence budget or the percentage of GNP directed toward the defence of the Alliance.

To a great extent, those who believed that Canada should contribute to NATO by such traditional means held long-established opinions as to how the nation should participate in the Alliance. During World War II and the Korean War, the United States and Canada were the only allied countries capable of providing Western Europe with military forces, equipment, and money. These traditionalists seemed to assume that maintaining Canada's overseas commitments was the most appropriate method of signalling its intention to support friends and allies.[32] As John Holmes later explained, the perception that Canada had performed as a great military power during World War II persisted, contributing to the view that Canada should continue to make commitments to NATO concomitant with being a great power.[33] This conviction was reinforced by the fact that Soviet and Warsaw Pact troops continued to be stationed along the Central Front. Although written references to this threat were infrequent, the general assumption among Defenders continued to be that Canadian troops were in Europe to help deter a Soviet attack from behind the Iron Curtain and, if war broke out, to assist in keeping it below the nuclear threshold. As explained in a paper written in 1969 by DND officials for the Special Task Force on Europe:

Canadian participation in collective defence arrangements with European allies essentially serves the purpose of helping to minimize the risk of U.S./ USSR conflict or, if it breaks out, helping to contain it below the level of an all-out nuclear exchange. Since the formation of the NATO Alliance in 1949 the risk of a deliberate all-out assault by the USSR on the West has greatly receded. But as long as settlement of European political problems is lacking, particularly over Germany, and as long as formidable armed forces continue to be massed in Eastern Europe, there is a major risk of great-power conflict by accident or miscalculation.[34]

Established ideas about how Canada could help deter the threat dominated, too, because Canadians kept in touch with other NATO decision-makers who continued to assume that the defence of Western Europe was of utmost importance.[35] That the allies still considered Canada's forces and equipment stationed overseas as the most appropriate type of commitment Canada could make to NATO was sometimes a source of frustration, but for the most part Defenders accepted it. As Mitchell Sharp explained to the Cabinet Committee on External Policy and Defence in 1969:

The majority of observers agree that the Soviet Union would use its nuclear force only as a last resort. It would not be employed in a premeditated sense. Rather the real possibility [exists] that a miscalculation or accident would change the balance of power in Europe and thereby a local conflict, once it began, could escalate into a nuclear confrontation. The military role of western powers [is] to contain that local conflict and to manage any possible crisis that might exist. The contribution of conventional forces [is] most significant in this context. The presence of our military force in Europe also [serves] as a warning to the Soviet empire that Canada [is] committed to the struggle for the peaceful resolution of European problems. Our men must be stationed there as evidence of our intentions and our commitment.[36]

It is noteworthy that the defence of Canada was not widely regarded as a NATO priority. According to another high-level confidential source in 1984:

[Our European allies] simply do not accept the idea that, in the nuclear age, North America is as vulnerable as Europe, or that Canada, lying between the superpowers, risks becoming [a] no-man's-land in a nuclear war. These are notions that stir Canadian imaginations powerfully. Europeans, however, are convinced that it is they who are in the front line, and that it is still Europe which is far the more vulnerable. To them, North America is a sanctuary, even in the nuclear age, and Canada one of the safest places in the world.

When we commit forces in places our allies see as specially vulnerable – in Germany or northern Norway – we make a commitment that is immediately understood. A commitment in North America – even justified as part of a larger and arguably more rational contribution to the general defence of the North Atlantic region – would carry nothing like the same weight ...[37]

Defenders generally conceded, without any detailed argument, that the military alternatives to stationing the forces overseas would be less effective than the current arrangements, and that objections could be raised to other alternatives. For example, according to the "Defence Policy Review" of 1969:

Since it is generally conceded that the likelihood of being able to redeploy the force from Canada in time to be of military use in Europe is small ... objections could be raised at the time that the deployment of the force would serve to add to international tensions ... this alternative would not be cheaper and could well be considerably more expensive than the current cost of the mechanized brigade ... [and] it has already been argued that for the present without some form of military contribution stationed in Europe Canada would not be regarded by its allies as making an appropriate contribution to NATO.[38]

Similarly in 1984 the Defence Evaluation Group assumed that Canada had no option but to maintain its CAST commitment to Norway, because the CAST Brigade had always been a purely Canadian commitment:

Reaction of our Alliance partners to any unilateral redeployment of Canadian forces from the CAST commitment to Northern Europe must be viewed in light of the question – who would be willing to take over Canada's commitment? The answer lies in why Canada is involved with CAST to begin with. The CAST Brigade is a purely Canadian commitment for a number of reasons. The USA would not be accepted because of their high profile; the West Germans would not be tolerated because of historical circumstance, while the Belgians, Dutch and Danes all have political and economic problems of their own. Thus, should Canada withdraw the CAST commitment, a gap could occur in Northern European defence strategy.[39]

A number of important advisory groups (such as the Cabinet Committee on External Policy and Defence; the Ad Hoc Committee on Defence Policy, 1963; the intragovernmental Defence Policy Review, 1969; the Special Task Force on Europe, STAFEUR study, 1969; the Defence Studies Review Steering Group, 1972; and the Defence Evaluation Group, 1984) were tasked to consider alternatives to stationing

Canadian Forces in Europe. The general tendency, however, was to reaffirm conventional wisdom and make the case for maintaining the status quo. As noted by the Ad Hoc Committee on Defence Policy:

Withdrawal of Canada's participation in the defence of Europe would lead logically to the withdrawal of Canadian forces from Europe and their disbandment. The principal attraction in this course of action is the potential saving in costs. The principal disadvantage is in the reduction in Canada's stature and influence within NATO. In this respect there can be no possible room for illusion. There is no alternative role for Canada, military or non-military, which could serve as a comparable support of Canadian diplomacy.[40]

In keeping with the tendency to argue that Canada should maintain if not strengthen its traditional commitments to European defence, Defenders also assumed that Canada should strive to meet NATO's goal of three-percent annual real growth in defence spending. Although this was a general assumption, behind the scenes there was ongoing controversy about how to measure, fairly, the percentage of a country's GNP devoted to NATO.[41] A major consideration was that the allies, particularly the United States, could criticize a Canadian shortfall in defence spending. According to one secret memorandum written in 1968, the American attitude toward Canada "would be influenced by their conviction that with the US spending 10% of its National Income on defence, Canada should certainly be able to continue to spend at least 3% of its GNP."[42] As another influential Defender saw it in 1974:

By the traditional criteria used by NATO, Canada is already making one of the most modest contributions to collective defence of an Alliance country (e.g. we are amongst the lowest in terms of GNP devoted to defence and the proportion of the overall budget devoted to defence). This situation and the fact that our own inflationary problems are not as severe as in some other countries would lead our allies to look with considerable concern at any decision by the Canadian government to reduce the level of the Canadian defence program particularly if it would affect adversely our military capacity.[43]

Similarly in 1980, a high-level official warned the under-secretary of External Affairs that the "failure of Canada to achieve the minimal NATO goal of a 3% annual real growth would undoubtedly have negative effects in foreign policy terms, particularly in our relations with the US and our major European allies".[44] Also, according to a Canadian ambassador in 1980: "If we do not meet these obligations (i.e. 3% increase in real terms of defence spending), of course, the

Government could count on it that it will be under persistent institutionalized pressure to do so within the framework of NATO, as well as bilaterally. We can expect also, as in the past, that our principal allies – who are also our principal economic partners – will not fail to relate our performance as a military ally to other aspects of our relations with them."[45] In other words, an important concern of many Defenders was that the allies could severely criticize the government if it failed to meet the three-percent goal.[46]

A review of these documents and statements reveals that three streams of thought on Canada's traditional commitments to NATO developed among Defenders in the higher echelons of defence policy-making.[47] The *first stream* assumed that Canada's traditional contribution of forces, equipment, and money to defend Western Europe was of key importance to the continuing function of the Alliance. A memorandum written for the minister of External Affairs to use in Cabinet in 1969 instructed him to emphasize that "the Canadian contribution is certainly not insignificant and our air component ranks fourth in size and striking power after the U.S., U.K. and Germany. To believe that our departure would cause barely a ripple would be to underestimate seriously the weakening of NATO defences which would result from our withdrawal."[48] This first-stream assumption could be likened to the propensity among humans to see our own behaviour as central to the behaviour of others.[49]

In a somewhat different fashion, the *second stream* of thought assumed that the Alliance's overall conventional balance in Western Europe would help prevent war and potentially affect the outcome of war. A high-level correspondent in 1969 emphasized that if Canada were to shift its conventional defence effort to North America, its role in preventing war would be almost entirely removed. That would also

remove us entirely from any active role in preventing war where it is most likely to ignite and expand into global war (Europe) ... [T]he defence of North America is impossible and therefore defence activities in that theatre are by their nature either only damage-limiting in character or a marginal contribution to protection of deterrent forces in the USA. It should be brought out [in the STAFEUR report] that our contribution to North American defence is largely an exercise in sovereign protection against USA encroachment rather than a major contribution to deterring the Soviet Union.[50]

Such a second-stream assumption – that the overall balance of conventional forces in Europe would both prevent and affect the outcome of war – seems similar to the military thinking that predated the nuclear era.[51]

On the other hand, a *third stream* of thought among Defenders took
for granted that, given the strategic nuclear balance, Canada's military commitments to NATO made no great difference, being important only insofar as they signalled a unified resolve and Alliance
solidarity. In 1963, the Ad Hoc Committee on Defence Policy pointed
out that if Canada were to undertake only those programs "which
were demonstrably essential to Western security or to the maintenance of distinctively Canadian interests," the Canadian Forces in
Europe could be disbanded, the Royal Canadian Navy could be
reduced to a coastguard, and the present defence budget could be
reduced by at least fifty percent. However, according to this committee, "the adverse consequence would be to diminish Canada's international stature and to place severe strains upon Canada's relations
with the USA."[52] As well, a restricted memo written in 1984 by senior
defence officials pointed out that, although Canada's military contribution to NATO made no real difference, it was important in terms
of signalling unified Alliance resolve. As high-level defence officials
put it, "While the Canadian strategic contribution to the Eastern flank
of NATO is small, the Warsaw Pact could use the issue [of redeployment to Canada] to their own political ends, namely that the Alliance
was losing its political will to defend itself."[53] The conviction that
Canada's contribution to NATO was symbolically important albeit
insignificant, was most succinctly expressed by Ross Campbell: "Sure
we can't save NATO with our contribution, or change the balance with
the Soviet bloc with our little contribution to the Armed Forces, but
make no mistake, they are of vital consequence to the coherence of
this thing, to the solidarity of NATO."[54]

These three streams of thinking tended to assume that Canada
should maintain or strengthen its ties to the allies by committing itself
to acquiring additional forces, modernizing or strengthening weapons systems, and increasing its financial resources for NATO defence
purposes. In addition, some Defenders promoted traditional commitments that appeared to strengthen Alliance ties without assessing the
strategic rationale or implications of these commitments. There is
evidence, for example, that some ministers in Pearson's Cabinet were
initially prepared to negotiate a further agreement – to acquire "anti-
submarine weapons" (the "fifth commitment") – into the general
agreement concerning nuclear warheads. When it was pointed out
that it was unclear if an original commitment had been made to
obtain these weapons and if there was a strategic requirement for air-
dropped anti-submarine nuclear weapons in the near future, Prime
Minister Pearson suggested instead that the "Annex" stipulating the
scope of the proposed agreement and the naming of the weapons be
dropped, in favour of a paragraph referring merely to weapons and

weapons systems "as specified by agreement between the two countries from time to time." The Cabinet agreed.[55]

Other evidence that decision-makers sometimes did not assess the purported strategic purpose of different weapons systems is found in the Trudeau Cabinet's discussions. Faced with the Soviet invasion of Czechoslovakia, the ministers considered whether the strength of the Air Division should be decreased to 88 aircraft, as previously announced, or maintained at 108. They discussed, at length, the allies' possible reaction to a reduction as opposed to the political consequences of a reaffirmation of this commitment. Only near the end of their discussion did Paul Hellyer, then minister of Transport, draw attention to the strategic purpose of the aircraft. In the larger context of the Cabinet's debate, however, Hellyer's assessment was inconsequential. Indeed, most ministers were concerned with whether the contemplated reduction would damage Canada's relationship with the allies or whether maintaining the CF-104s at their present level would increase tensions.[56]

At times, then, decision-makers espoused some types of weapons systems and force structures as appropriate commitments to NATO with no real appreciation of their strategic purpose. Although these types of endorsements could be attributed to ignorance or even disingenuity, they also reveal that the beliefs of some Defenders about the need to maintain and strengthen Alliance ties were sometimes so thoroughly entrenched that no strategic rationale was needed to support a particular commitment.[57]

Defenders believed the external threat to the Alliance was opportunistic and aggressive

A decision-maker's *perception of threat* is defined here as the anticipation of impending harm to the state, usually of a military, economic, or political kind. Any event, series of incidents, or statement that is (or is not) deliberately communicated can spark a leader's anticipation of future harm to the state. Although the perceived threat may be neither real nor credible, a decision-maker's interpretation can be highly influential.[58]

From 1949 to 1960, many Defenders perceived the external threat to the Alliance as an aggressive, monolithic bloc.[59] As Arthur Menzies, a former ambassador to NATO and head of the Defence Liaison Division in External Affairs later explained:

I think at that time it was the natural approach for people like Mr. St. Laurent and Mr. Pearson to talk about global Communism as a movement across Eurasia. And certainly when the Communists took power in China, just before the outbreak of war in Korea, it looked as if there was a certain monolithic unity and that unity did remain for the first ten years or so until the Soviets probably overreached themselves or the Chinese got more conscious of their own particular national interests which they decided they wanted to defend.[60]

During this period, Defenders tended to believe that the threat was to the Alliance's very stability. As Air Marshall Hugh Campbell cautioned the RCAF Staff College in 1960, there was "little hope of the Communists departing from their avowed aim of world domination and of keeping the international pot boiling." He called it "the practice for the past generation," saying there is "little hope of change."[61]

Over the 1960s, the idea of a monolithic threat to the Alliance took on a mythic stature that most Defenders recognized as not entirely based on reality. Despite a growing recognition that the Communist threat was divided and diffuse, the Defenders tended to continue to project an image of the Communist world as a unified, aggressive bloc. Among individual Defenders, the external threat was referred to variously as "Soviet Russia,"[62] "the Soviet Empire,"[63] "Soviet Imperialism,"[64] "Communism,"[65] and "the Communist camp"[66] or "East European national forces."[67] The threat, moreover, appeared in various guises and phrasings. The labelling included: "Marxist-Leninism as a rationale and blueprint for revolution,"[68] "the danger of Europe being overturned by Communists,"[69] "the power of the Soviet armed forces,"[70] "Soviet expansionist aims,"[71] "the possibility of a spillover of internal unrest in Warsaw Pact countries,"[72] and "the self-appointed leader of an international revolutionary movement."[73] The common tendency, however, was to perceive an aggressive challenge to the Alliance, one relentlessly bent on expansion.[74]

At times it was difficult to discern whether policy-makers viewed this threat as opportunistic and aggressive or whether they were merely projecting its continued existence. According to Paul Martin, minister of External Affairs in 1967, the Russians were continuing to develop their already formidable military power, despite improved relations with the West: "We cannot be sure that their earlier appetite for expansion would not revive if NATO were to lower its defences.[75] And as Marcel Cadieux, under-secretary of state for External Affairs, stated in 1969: "The prospect for long-term improvement in relations with the USSR [is] promising. But it [has] not yet happened. While the communist countries [are] taking steps to make themselves more acceptable, they [have] not abandoned their basic objective of supplanting Western influence around the world."[76] During the 1980s, many high-level decision-makers continued to decry the aggressive and opportunistic threat posed by the Soviet Union. According to Perrin Beatty, minister of National Defence in 1987, it was imperative that countries work collectively to face the common peril: "In two world wars and in Korea we built an honourable reputation for pulling more than our weight when called upon to defend our way of life, our national institutions and our democratic values. It is perhaps difficult for some to accept that these values remain under threat today. But they are, and these threats are not uniquely ours. We cannot defend this vast country against possible enemies on our own. We must seek our security through collective measures with other nations who face the common threat."[77] And the 1987 Defence White Paper *Challenge and Commitment: A Defence Policy for Canada* contained the following warning:

Since the end of the Second World War, the Soviet Union has persistently expanded its military power. At the expense of the civilian economy, it has devoted vast resources to its armed forces. The result is a military establishment that has reached rough parity with the United States in strategic weapons while maintaining numerical superiority over Allied conventional forces in Europe. During the same period, it has transformed its fleet from a defensive coastal force to a powerful navy with global reach. The Soviet Union has further increased its military potential through its sponsorship and dominance of the Warsaw Pact.[78]

The tendency toward repeated confirmation of the existence of an aggressive threat led some decision-makers to reject any evidence that challenged their fundamental assumptions about the Soviet Union. The 1963 Ad Hoc Defence Committee, for example, condemned "the recent tendency" in Canada "to err in the direction of underestimating the threat of Soviet imperialism" and to mistakenly believe that "Soviet policy aims to avoid general war." In the committee's view, to underestimate the existence of this threat was a "profound error" because "the aims of Soviet policy are imperialistic ... [as] has been true of nearly every great empire since the world began."[79] Similarly, Robert Ford, long-time Canadian ambassador to Moscow, explained privately in 1969 that although "few observers would claim that the Soviet Union by design would unleash a nuclear attack," there were "few restraints on the use of Soviet military power for political ends." As he saw it, "dialogue with Soviet Government officials on issues affecting the supremacy of their authority" was "in essence a dialogue with the deaf."[80]

Indeed, the tendency of some Defenders to reject evidence that contradicted their convictions about the nature of the threat continued into the 1980s and 1990s. According to a confidential dispatch from a high-level Canadian policy-maker in 1984, "prudent Western planning" had to assume that "whatever rulers came to power in the Soviet Union" would "probably look on their foreign policy interest in Europe in a traditional way." As the dispatch explained, "In the immediate future, there is no prospect of progress in East-West relations, certainly not of a kind that would radically alter the political context in Europe ..."[81] Even as late as 1988, the associate minister of National Defence indicated a similar tendency to reject evidence that contradicted his strong convictions:

In the last two years we have had *glasnost* and a seeming willingness by the Soviet Union to change. We welcome it and hope it is sincere, continuing and long-lasting. We all want to work towards achieving peace in the world. They have also made other comments here and there which look good on the surface. One of them of course concerns the zone of peace in the Arctic. They made much comment about northern Scandinavia, the North Atlantic and other areas, but did not make reference to their own areas. Of course they have a great mass of military might in their Arctic. It seems they wanted to have us lay down our arms but keep their Arctic areas fully armed.[82]

Although by this time other decision-makers were rethinking their imagery of the external threat to the Alliance, Perrin Beatty, Paul Dick, and other senior defence policy-makers continued to conceive of the Soviet threat as aggressive and opportunistic.[83]

Defenders assumed both Canada's and the Alliance's weapons
were necessary and non-threatening

Defenders tended to downplay Canada's capabilities and to regard NATO's weapons systems and intentions as defensive, not offensive. Although others criticized some NATO weapons as being potential first-strike systems, Defenders usually portrayed Canada and the Alliance's weapons systems as part of a second-strike deterrent.

As this study focuses on the psychological rather than the operational milieu, questions about whether Canada and the other allied countries actually possessed offensive or defensive weapons are unimportant. What is important is whether the leaders, themselves, regarded Canada and the Alliance's weapons as non-threatening and defensive.

Most public debate during the Cold War focused on just one dimension of the opposition between nuclear (offensive) and conventional (defensive) arms. But weapons can be distinguished as offensive or defensive with reference to both the perceived capabilities of the systems and the subjective motivations that may be attached to them. In other words, the best judge of whether a system is offensive or defensive is the possible target of the system, the adversary, just as we, in self-defence, would be the best judge of the adversary's offensive or defensive weapons systems. However, the distinguishing of offensive versus defensive weapons can also be done based on geographical terms. Thus, if a weapon can be effectively used abroad, on the adversary's territory, it is labelled "offensive"; if it can be used at home once an attack has taken place, it is labelled "defensive." The offensive/defensive distinction can also be based on the weapon's range variables (e.g., immobile, local, limited versus extensive, long, highly mobile) or impact variables (e.g., high explosive, weapon of mass destruction, chemical, toxic, biological, nuclear), or whether it is strategic or tactical. For example, a weapon capable of reaching the enemy's homeland or attacking deep behind its echelons might be classified as strategic and offensive, whereas a weapon that operates on or close to the battlefield might be conceived of as tactical and defensive.[84] From a perusal of the records of Cabinet meetings and high-level debates, however, it would appear that most Canadian leaders made no subtle distinctions between offensive and defensive weapons, whether on objective grounds or in terms of commonly accepted technical definitions. Rather the tendency of Defenders was simply to assume that Canada and the Alliance's weapons systems were defensive.

For many years the Canadian CF-104 strike reconnaissance aircraft deployed in Europe were represented as non-threatening components of a defensive strategy. In 1959, when the minister of National Defence directed that Canada acquire nuclear-armed strike reconnaissance aircraft to help "penetrate the area between the combat zone and the Russian border for reconnaissance and for strikes on targets of opportunity such as advancing columns of troops," Defence Minister Pearkes maintained that "such action would only be taken after hostile ground forces had commenced operations in western Europe." As Pearkes explained, "To prevent the overrunning of NATO Europe it would be essential to defeat enemy forces launching such an attack."[85] From Pearkes's perspective, these weapons were defensive and non-threatening.

During the 1960s, questions arose in Canada about whether the Starfighters could be perceived by the Soviets as first-strike weapons, inasmuch as they were capable of departing before hostilities had begun so as to locate and attack targets on the ground. Pierre Trudeau incited a furor within the Departments of National Defence and External Affairs in 1968 when he asked whether the government should rethink the role of Canada's Air Division in Europe precisely because it could be perceived by the Soviet Union as instrumental in a first-strike scenario. Indeed, Trudeau asked an audience of Liberals in 1969:

And has the scenario ever been explained to you, to the Canadian people, as to under what conditions our aircraft would fly nuclear weapons and unleash them on Europe? Will it only be as a second strike, will it only be as a deterrent? Are these 104s, are they soft targets? In the eyes of the Soviets, in the eyes of the Warsaw Pact countries, are they not entitled to ask themselves: "Well, what are these 104s flown by Canadians going to serve? Are they going to be first strike or second strike? ... They are soft targets, they are on the ground, we know where the airfields are. Isn't it likely that they might be used to attack us first?" These are the questions that our enemies, the Soviets, are asking themselves.[86]

Despite such questions, high-level officials continued to conceptualize the CF-104s as second-strike, defensive weapons. According to a secret 1968 memo advising Prime Minister Trudeau to phase out these aircraft, "public questioning of our forces in Europe has focused particularly on the strike aircraft. This aircraft which has a nuclear attack capability might be expected to be an early target of pre-emptive attack in a war and is, therefore, not likely to be a particularly effective weapon."[87] Thus, even as Trudeau was considering phasing out the strike aircraft, his advisers were not acknowledging the prime minister's argument that the CF-104s could be perceived as an offensive weapons system.[88] Until Trudeau succeeded in phasing out the nuclear components of these aircraft in 1971, most defence advisers continued to present the nuclear-armed CF-104s as entirely defensive.

The extent to which some Canadian decision-makers downplayed the Alliance's nuclear capabilities is also noteworthy. In the 1950s and 1960s, many Defenders "conventionalized" the Alliance's own nuclear weapons by presenting them as usable weapons capable of defending allied soil. As Lieutenant General Charles Belzile (ret.) recollects: "We tended to look at nuclear weapons with a certain amount of awe, but we considered that training and planning for their use, and defending against them, on the tactical side, in the case of the army particularly, was a very logical and a very necessary extension of our training ... We didn't have an all-pervasive fear of nuclear weapons, in my memory, in those days."[89] Such portrayals of the allies' nuclear weapons systems as capable of protecting and safeguarding allied territory, rather than as instruments of war that threatened to destroy both sides' terrain, occasionally led to undue faith in the Alliance's nuclear capabilities. According to a 1965 secret memorandum for the proposed "NATO Working Group on Nuclear Planning," the allied forces under NATO command "would be entirely incapable of protecting the countries of Western Europe against a Soviet attack" if not for the fact that they were backed by the "strategic power of the US" along with the "national strategic capability of small British and French elements."[90] The underlying assumption was that, in the event of a Soviet attack, American strategic nuclear forces and British and French nuclear weapons would protect Western European countries.

In 1983, in a similarly unconvincing fashion, former Minister of External Affairs Flora MacDonald told the House of Commons that the Europeans had requested the deployment of cruise and Pershing missiles because they wanted to have "some defensive mechanism" to protect themselves. "As long as the people of the countries of western Europe feel that way," said MacDonald, "I feel that we as a member of NATO supporting them must agree to that kind of defensive system which, in this case, means the Cruise missile and the Pershing II." In effect, MacDonald incorrectly portrayed these weapons as systems capable of defending allied territory rather than as instruments of mass destruction that contributed to NATO's deterrent posture.[91]

The widespread inclination to regard the Alliance's nuclear and conventional weapons as fundamentally non-threatening led to the use of reassuring analogies to describe them. Charles Nixon, a former deputy minister of National Defence, likened Pershing and cruise missiles to a "comfort blanket,"[92] while the conventionally armed CF-104 aircraft was disparaged by the minister of National Defence, Leo Cadieux, and Cabinet colleague Bud Drury as "a pea shooter" and a "second-hand Cadillac."[93]

The assumption that Canada's own weapons were necessary and defensive prompted some Defenders to reason that the Alliance's nuclear and conventional deployments were a "measured response" to the enemy's initially threatening provocations. Thus, cruise missiles were presented as the Alliance's reluctant response to the Warsaw Pact's SS-20 intermediate range ballistic missiles.[94] Canada's contribution of frigates and submarines to the Alliance's Anti-Submarine Warfare (ASW) strategy was deemed necessary on the grounds that the Soviet Union had already developed a significant submarine capability.[95] In hindsight, it was rationalized that a decision by Canada to develop its own stockpile of nuclear weapons would have been an appropriate response.[96]

There was a worrisome tendency among many Defenders, particularly in the 1950s and '60s, to rely on the Alliance's nuclear weapons to the point that their use was contemplated almost with equanimity.

In 1963, the Ad Hoc Defence Committee recommended that air defence weapons be armed with nuclear weapons for "policing" and "coastguard" duties because of their "improved cost-effectiveness."[97] And in 1968, a working group from the Departments of National Defence and External Affairs reasoned that, "in the field of air defence, Canada is likely to have a long-term requirement for nuclear weapons simply because they would provide the most effective defence in the event of attack."[98] Especially during the 1950s and '60s, decision-makers contemplated the use of nuclear weapons with little concern as to their possible effects. A prevailing assumption at that time, according to Lieutenant-General Charles Belzile, was that:

Nuclear weapons were still controllable. And they were, by and large, those that were being considered by the Canadian forces for arming some of their aircraft or arming the tips of some of the missiles or indeed some artillery shells which could be fractional yield nuclear weapons. We studied those things and we saw them as just another extension, if you want, of the available spectrum of weapons systems, to allow you to fight a war if you ever had to fight it. And we did not look at nuclear weapons with the same global unease that I think we all do today.[99]

By the 1970s and 1980s, not all Defenders regarded nuclear weapons as non-threatening. Many recognized that, to be credible, the weapons had to be seen as both threatening and usable; they realized that what mattered in signalling a deterrent message was not how the Alliance saw it, but how others would understand it. As J. Gilles Lamontagne, the minister of National Defence in 1983, pointed out: "The entire purpose of nuclear weapons is to deter aggression, to deter their use by others ... But there is a paradox in the strategy of deterrence which must be recognized. If nuclear weapons are to be useful to deter aggression, they must be credible. To be credible, there must be confidence, especially on the part of the opposition, that is the other side, that they will work."[100] Yet, despite recognizing that NATO's strategic and tactical nuclear weapons had to be seen as threatening to be credible, Defenders, by and large, tended to present Canada's own weapons systems as defensive. They assumed that Canadian weapons systems would only be used as part of a second-strike strategy. When questions were raised in the 1980s about whether the cruise missiles being tested in Canada could be used as offensive battlefield weapons in a limited nuclear war, high-level officials emphasized that "neither the air-launched nor the ground-launched cruise [missile] systems have the high speed capability required for a 'first-strike' weapon and are therefore exclusively retaliatory in character."[101] The cruise missile was portrayed solely as a second-strike weapon. Later, critics charged that the so-called advanced cruise missile could be used as part of an offensive strategy, even though this missile was categorized in high-level discussions as an improved version of the slower, second-strike model. In fact, a high-level briefing note written in February 1983 entirely overlooked the stealth missile's potential as a first-strike weapon. According to this adviser, "future models of the cruise missile (e.g. 'the stealth cruise missile') are expected to incorporate technical improvements designed to make them less vulnerable to radar detection and therefore less likely to be shot down. These improvements form part of a continuing effort to improve the deterrent capability of US and NATO forces and will therefore enhance Canadian security."[102] Although questions were raised about the offensive capabilities of the stealth missile, many high-level decision-makers maintained that they would not be used unless deterrence failed or the enemy decided to strike first.

Finally, in keeping with the assumption that Canada's weapons were necessary and non-threatening, Defenders often assumed that technological advances in the nation's own weapons systems were acceptable. Thus, the new tactical nuclear weapons were widely conceived of as "a usable kind of weapon which limited damage."[103] The Alliance's cruise missile was initially conceptualized as relatively harmless and innocuous,[104] while Canada's maritime contribution to NATO's ASW strategy was conceived of as appropriate because it would solve the kinds of problems experienced during World War II and the Cuban missile crisis – specifically, problems relating to the protection of supply convoys travelling to Europe from North America.[105] In many such instances, Defenders were inclined to see reassuring similarities between different kinds of military equipment, and to place various sorts of weapons in the same non-threatening category. From their perspective, technological advances in our defence systems were both appropriate and warranted.

Defenders believed deterrence doctrine was suitable and reliable

Many influential decision-makers premised their support for maintaining or strengthening Canada's NATO commitments on the changing requirements of deterrence doctrine. Most Defenders expressed considerable faith in deterrence, a faith they retained as nuclear strategy evolved and technology advanced. Before 1957, most Defenders believed that credible deterrence should rely mainly on the United States' monopoly of ballistic nuclear missiles.[106] By the late 1950s, however, many Defenders assumed that deterrence doctrine had to be based on the threat of massive retaliation.[107] In the 1960s, deterrence doctrine had evolved such that a credible deterrent at all levels was deemed necessary so as to ensure a "flexible response."[108] By the late 1970s and early 1980s, many Defenders equated credible deterrence with the deployment of tactical nuclear weapons in Western Europe, together with each side's surfeit of nuclear and conventional weapons.[109] Finally, by the early 1990s, those acquainted with NATO's Strategic Concept believed that a balance of fewer nuclear weapons, a core of rapid-reaction forces, and a backup of main and augmentation forces was now required to achieve "minimal deterrence."[110] Despite these changes, the stability of deterrence doctrine was grounded in the assumption that, to deter the threat, the allies had to ensure that the cost of attacking would be perceived to be greater than the benefits. According to DND's Defence Planning Guidance in 1970, stable mutual deterrence "is a situation in which neither of the nuclear adversaries can perceive any advantage to be gained from a massive strategic attack on the other due to the other's ability to respond, after absorbing the attack, with a counter-attack which would cause unacceptable damage to the initial attacker."[111] Similarly, according to DND's Directorate of Strategic Analysis in 1983: "deterrence is relatively stable insofar as both sides feel they and their opponent possess an adequate capability for retaliation even after absorbing a first strike. It is felt that if both sides maintain such a capability, neither will attack first, out of the realization that such an action would trigger an almost certain devastating response."[112]

   Although this assumption appeared relatively straightforward, the commitments that were deemed necessary to ensure stable and credible deterrence varied from one decade to the next, and from one decision-maker to another. To cite one example, in 1963, then Minister of National Defence Douglas Harkness argued in favour of the deployment of nuclear-armed Bomarc missiles in Canada at North Bay and La Macaza. He thought this "would allow potential air engagements to take place away from the densely populated areas of Canada and move the air defence line closer to the periphery of the ground radar system."[113] But by 1971, Minister of External Affairs Mitchell Sharp informed the Cabinet Committee on Defence that these missiles would be retired from service, "since their immobility makes them highly vulnerable to missile attack and they would be certain targets before the follow-on bombers were within range." By this time, it was thought that stable nuclear deterrence no longer relied on a credible anti-bomber defence but on the assured second-strike capability of a range of strategic weapons from intercontinental ballistic missiles to submarines. According to Sharp, "while the Bomarc missiles had been a valid contribution in the day when a full anti-bomber defence was required to protect the deterrent, and before the USSR had deployed a substantial missile force, this was no longer the case."[114] By 1983, however, many influential Canadian decision-makers assumed that, were it not for the Alliance's entire array of strategic, tactical, and conventional weapons systems, the stability of deterrence could be severely threatened. The Minister of National Defence explained in 1983: "We have no doubt that in doing what we do now, for example, flexible response, inter-continental missiles, short and long range nuclear force, what we used to call TNF, and also through our conventional forces we can create a credible deterrence. The minute, however, that our deterrent is no longer credible, we lose completely the effect of it. That could mean that you have to go to the horror of nuclear war or to submit to whatever the aggressor decides to do with you."[115]

Thus, in each decade, different kinds of commitments by Canada to NATO were deemed necessary to help ensure a credible deterrence posture. Indeed, some Canadian decision-makers at times supported one approach to deterrence strategy while NATO headquarters espoused another. For example, the Alliance's doctrine of "mutual assured destruction" was still widely accepted among Canadian decision-makers after it had been informally jettisoned by NATO's higher echelons in favour of a strategy of "flexible response." As the Ad Hoc Committee on Defence reported in 1963, many Canadians continued, mistakenly, to support the doctrine of massive retaliation and to support acquiring military capabilities that would contribute to the deterrence of all-out thermonuclear war: "[A common misconception widely held by many Canadians, including many alleged experts on defence] is that military capabilities which do not contribute to the deterrence of all-out thermonuclear war are essentially useless. This view, in fact, implies an extreme version of the Dulles-Radford doctrine of massive retaliation. It is a curious fact that this horrendous doctrine has secured an intellectual acceptance in Canada which it never secured in the United States."[116] Such different approaches to the problem of credible deterrence were the result of evolving ideas among NATO strategists about how to signal credibility and deal with advances in nuclear technology.[117] But the thinking of influential Canadian policy-makers was divergent as well. As Admiral Robert Falls (ret.), Chief of the Defence Staff from 1977 to 1980, later explained, ideas about how to ensure a credible deterrent posture in Europe changed even as tactical nuclear missiles were deployed in Germany:

Most of the weapons of mass destruction would have fallen, it seems to me, on German soil, and I think what they were trying to generate there, in retrospect, was to get a little less emphasis on nuclear warfare and on the trip wire concept. In other words, it was a genuine desire to have a more deterrent posture I think ... And so, I think, probably, it was in trying to respond to Germany's concern that the Americans, and I think quite rightly, decided it was time to put more emphasis on conventional forces and therefore less reliance, no less numbers or anything else like that, heaven forbid, but less reliance on the nuclear trip wire aspects.[118]

While some Defenders changed their minds about what was necessary to signal a credible deterrent posture, others remained beholden to NATO's declared strategy until it eventually came to their attention that another permutation of the doctrine needed to be defended.[119] As Ross Campbell explains, each permutation of deterrence strategy seemed sensible at the time:

We've watched it [NATO strategy] evolve from trip wire and massive retaliation, in the days when we had total superiority over the Soviet Union, to other pragmatic adjustments that took place when they finally got the nuclear capability. All of a sudden we decided on graduated response, flexible response, which meant that there's no point in committing suicide. Let's develop a doctrine that is a little more realistic and that says we'll respond with the degree of force needed to restore the *status quo*. We won't attract a holocaust if we can help it. Well, you know you can laugh about this, in retrospect, but when you're at the peak of a Cold War, it is another matter and these policies look sensible. They look ridiculous in retrospect. At the time they looked very sensible because we didn't really know what was going to happen in the future.[120]

Over time, some Defenders came to believe nuclear deterrence was an appropriate and suitable strategy precisely because the Alliance never had to use its nuclear weapons. As Gilles Lamontagne, then minister of National Defence, explained in 1983: "Deterrence is not an attractive way of ensuring peace, but it has worked."[121] Certainly, for some Defenders, it was unthinkable to suggest that nuclear deterrence could fail, or that deterrence might not ensure peace in Europe. Charles Nixon, a former deputy minister of National Defence and a strong NATO Defender, recalled: "Trudeau would ask repeatedly: 'Is this going to be a short war or long war?' Immediately you respond to that question, you are lost because you accept war as being inevitable. As soon as I perceived this, when I was in the PCO, I advised the Prime Minister: 'You're asking the wrong question. If we get into any war, we have failed in the important thing, and that's to deter it.' So your question should be: 'What posture should we have to deter war?'"[122] To Nixon, and other Defenders, it was unthinkable that nuclear deterrence might fail to keep peace in Europe.

Defenders partly based their support for Canada's NATO commitments on the requirements of nuclear deterrence doctrine. Many also believed that, in order to ensure its reliability – that is, to prevent deterrence from failing – the Alliance had to ensure its conventional defences were credible and that NATO could prevail in a limited war. For these decision-makers, a credible defence system and possible victory in a limited war were conceivable and attainable objectives. It was widely accepted, for instance, that the Canadian Forces should prepare for war across the spectrum of conceivable scenarios, with particular attention to high-intensity warfare in Europe.[123] It was also assumed that NATO's conventional defences should be strengthened "to the point where the net deterrent, the combined deterrent effect, is credible again." As John Halstead, a former ambassador to NATO explained, it was thought that NATO's conventional arms buildup had to be sufficient to halt a Soviet attack and put the onus for the first-use of nuclear weapons on the Soviet Union.[124]

Besides focusing on a credible conventional defence, many Defenders also believed that, to prevent deterrence failure, an equivalent or superior military balance was required. Although not many Defenders steadfastly believed that superior forces were necessary to deter attack, it was generally assumed that "a military balance is essential in today's world to our own security and that of our allies."[125] In the words of James Taylor, former under-secretary of state for External Affairs and ambassador to NATO, a balanced combination of nuclear and conventional forces was necessary to ensure a credible deterrent:

The key words are, I think, stability and balance. You can maintain a balance at different levels, and we must try to maintain it at the lowest level we can arrange, but if it has to be maintained at a relatively high level, for reasons not of our seeking, then really you have to find the resources to do that. It does not mean that you have to maintain forces on a one for one basis. No one in NATO has ever argued that and NATO never has maintained forces on that basis. It simply means that you have to maintain some adequate combination of nuclear and conventional forces to constitute a credible deterrent.[126]

Placing their faith in nuclear and conventional postures based on deterrence doctrine often meant that Defenders tended to ignore or dismiss threatening scenarios that could not be averted by issuing a deterrent threat. The possibility of uncontrollable escalation in Europe leading to general nuclear war, for example, was only cursorily examined.[127] The chance of a minor conflict or border skirmish escalating into a nuclear confrontation was also downplayed.[128] The possibility of accidental nuclear war was only briefly scrutinized.[129] The idea that there could be an armed conflict, even a war between members of the Alliance, was for the most part unthinkable,[130] just as undeterrable threats involving harm to the environment, human rights violations in Eastern Europe, nuclear proliferation in the Third World, terrorism, or nuclear waste dumping were seldom considered.[131] Based on both classified and declassified evidence, it seems that many defence decision-makers either ignored or dismissed scenarios that could not be averted by the threat of nuclear and conventional retaliation. In effect, little, if any, attention was accorded to alternative scenarios that could not be controlled by relying on deterrence. Instead, based on their faith in deterrence, Defenders pressed the government to contribute to NATO's various nuclear and conventional force postures.

CONCLUSION

While there is no question that nearly all influential Canadian decision-makers believed that the USSR was a significant and salient threat, in many situations the concerns of high-level decision-makers about abandoning the allies or being abandoned by them took precedence over customary and traditional preoccupations with the Soviet Union. For this reason, I examined the assumptions of Defenders about abandonment first, before dealing in detail with their particular beliefs regarding the threat, the utility of nuclear and conventional weapons, and the merits of deterrence.

Defenders tended to believe that the consequences of neglecting the allies, or being themselves abandoned, were best averted by maintaining, if not strengthening, Canada's established contributions of forces, equipment, and money to NATO. Defenders simultaneously projected a belief that the threat to the Alliance from the Soviet Union, the Communist camp, or the Warsaw Pact was aggressive and opportunistic. As they saw it, Canada and the Alliance's defence capabilities were necessary and non-threatening. And, as another important element of their worldview, Defenders tended to advocate maintaining, if not modernizing, Canada's military commitments to NATO's deterrent posture, based on the belief that this doctrine continued to be suitable and reliable.

The main elements of this belief system impelled many influential decision-makers to support maintaining, if not strengthening, Canada's NATO commitments. During secret high-level debates, decision-makers were influenced by a variety of factors stemming from the international system and their domestic environment. However, it was adherence to a distinctive belief system typical of Defenders that appeared to contribute significantly to the support for Canada's NATO commitments. As well, although many of the comments cited in this chapter were attributed to confidential sources between 1963 and 1987, it is clear that most influential defence decision-makers espoused many of the main elements of one belief system. They included Paul Martin, Sr., Paul Hellyer, Mitchell Sharp, Leo Cadieux, Marcel Cadieux, Ross Campbell, Robert Cameron, Robert Ford, John Halstead, Gordon Smith, James Francis, Jim Nutt, Alan Gotlieb, Arthur Menzies, James Taylor, General Jean Allard, General Charles Belzile, Charles Nixon, J. Gilles Lamontagne, Perrin Beatty, and Paul Dick. Paul Martin was minister of External Affairs between 1963 and 1968 under Prime Minister Lester Pearson, and the leader of the Government in the Senate and acting secretary of state for External Affairs under Prime Minister Trudeau. Martin, a taciturn yet strong NATO Defender, argued consistently in both Pearson's and Trudeau's Cabinets in favour of maintaining, if not strengthening, Canada's NATO commitments. Mitchell Sharp, as minister of Finance under Lester Pearson from 1965 to 1968 and minister of External Affairs under Prime Minister Trudeau from 1968 to 1974, proved to be an articulate and well-briefed NATO Defender. He consistently pressed other Cabinet ministers and senior advisers in his department to favour retaining or strengthening Canada's overseas stationed forces. Paul Hellyer, serving as Pearson's minister of National Defence between 1963 and 1967 and Trudeau's minister of Transport between 1968 and 1969, quickly became an astute and well-informed critic of the structure of the Canadian Forces. Hellyer favoured unification and a shift toward mobile, light-armed forces capable of being deployed in Canada and Europe. Yet in the final analysis, he generally sided with other Defenders in support of fulfilling Canada's nuclear and conventional commitments to NATO.

Between 1967 and 1970, Minister of National Defence Leo Cadieux worked with Canada's ambassador to NATO, Ross Campbell, to oppose cutbacks and the contemplated withdrawal of Canadian Forces from Europe. Although Cadieux and Campbell opposed the Trudeau government's announcement of a two-thirds cutback in April 1969, they were forced to defend the announcement to other NATO representatives. In letters, telegrams, and personal appeals (Cadieux even threatened resignation), they argued against the reduction and, in September 1969, Cadieux was able to announce that the reductions would constitute only half of the previous force, rather than the two-thirds decrease originally contemplated. Both parties based their arguments on fundamentally the same underlying assumptions as other Defenders.

Among the senior advisers to Cabinet during this period, there were also a number of less influential, but stalwart, Defenders. Marcel Cadieux, under-secretary of state for External Affairs between 1964 and 1970, consistently perceived a salient threat from the Soviet Union, and was more concerned about the dangers of abandonment than the possible consequences of entrapment. (Cadieux wrote many of the internal memoranda and briefing notes for Mitchell Sharp in defence of Canada's overseas forces and its nuclear commitments.) Another influential decision-maker, Robert Cameron, rose through the ranks of the civil service in the 1960s to become head of NATO and the North American Division in Ottawa between 1969 and 1970, director general of the Bureau of Defence and Arms Control in 1970, and eventually assistant under-secretary of state for External Affairs in 1981. For nearly twenty years, Cameron exerted an influence on Canadian defence decision-making, and his early views generally reflected many of the commonly held beliefs of Defenders. John Halstead was also a vigorous defender of Canada's Alliance commitments. As the principal writer of the STAFEUR report in 1969, assistant and then deputy under-secretary of state for External Affairs during the 1970s, and ambassador to NATO between 1980 and 1982, Halstead worked diligently to defend Canada's link to Europe through established NATO commitments. Other influential civil servants in the Department of External Affairs such as Robert Ford, James Ross (J.S.) Francis, Alan Gotlieb, Jim Nutt, and Gordan Smith shared many of the typical assumptions of Defenders as well. They prepared many of the memoranda and briefing notes informing Cabinet ministers of the grounds for arguing in favour of Canada's NATO commitments. Briefly, Ford served as Canada's ambassador to Moscow between 1964 and 1980. Francis, who had joined the Department of External Affairs in 1954, rose to become director of the Defence Relations Division in 1983. Gotlieb, who joined the Department of External Affairs a few years later in 1957, served as an assistant undersecretary between 1967 and 1968, before moving to the new Department of Communications as deputy minister from 1968 to 1973. Between 1977 and 1981, he returned to External Affairs as under-secretary with a final stint as ambassador to Washington under both Liberal and Conservative prime ministers. Nutt, who joined the department in 1949, was named a counsellor in Washington in 1960, deputy under-secretary of state in 1977, and a consul general in New York in 1979. Smith, who wrote the original drafts of the 1971 White Paper on Defence, served as Canada's ambassador to NATO during the 1980s and eventually served as deputy minister of Foreign Affairs.

Because of access restrictions, it is difficult to discern the extent to which Defenders retained their influence during the 1978–89 period. The CIIPS transcripts indicate that policy-makers who espoused the convictions of typical Defenders during the mid- and late-1970s included Ambassadors James Taylor and Arthur Menzies, Generals Belzile and Allard, and Deputy Defence Minister Charles Nixon. The House of Commons transcripts seem to indicate that two Trudeau Cabinet ministers – Minister of National Defence Gilles Lamontagne and Minister of External Affairs Alan MacEachen – as well as two Mulroney ministers – Minister of National Defence Perrin Beatty and Associate Defence Minister Paul Dick – based their arguments on reasoning typical of Defenders. But as we move forward in time – specifically after 1978 – it becomes increasingly difficult to ascertain, first, who the most influential defence decision-makers were and, second, their respective underlying beliefs and assumptions during their time in power. It is premature, then, to say whether the belief systems of Defenders had a significant effect on defence policy-making after 1978.

Much of the available evidence nevertheless indicates that, between 1963 and 1978, the presence of a number of Defenders in the inner circles of defence decision-making contributed to the Pearson and Trudeau governments' support for select NATO commitments. This is not to say that it was only their presence that accounted for the Pearson Cabinet's decision to fulfill its nuclear commitments while maintaining its other NATO commitments virtually unchanged between 1963 and 1968. Nor does it entirely explain the Trudeau government's eventual decision to remain in NATO and to reduce the Canadian Forces in Europe by half. A host of other factors contributed to these outcomes. There can be little question, however, that between 1963 and 1978 many of the beliefs typical of Defenders significantly influenced defence decision-making apropos Canada's NATO commitments.

This chapter shows, broadly speaking, that certain beliefs and assumptions played an important role at various times in Canada's defence decision-making with regard to its NATO commitments. Within the inner circles of decision-making, certain policy-makers advocated that Canada strengthen or maintain these commitments because of their own beliefs about the foreseeable consequences of abandonment, the nature and salience of the threat to the Alliance, and the utility of NATO's defence systems, not to mention the requirement that Canada help buttress deterrence strategy. The following chapter delineates some of the contrasting ideas and convictions that influenced high-level decision-making between 1963 and 1989.

CHAPTER FOUR

The Belief Systems of Critics:
General Patterns between 1963 and 1989

Some decision-makers opposed to Canada's Alliance commitments were united by similar underlying beliefs and assumptions. This chapter identifies elements of a belief system shared by many of these individuals, referred to here as "Critics."[1]

SUBSTANTIVE BELIEFS AND ASSUMPTIONS
OF CRITICS

Critics feared entrapment

In contrast to Defenders, Critics were preoccupied with the dangers of entrapment. They were suspicious about the likelihood and possible consequences of the allies drawing Canada into an armed confrontation and had doubts about NATO undertakings, particularly American strategic objectives.

Fears of entrapment were expressed in different circumstances and with varying degrees of intensity. Some Critics feared that Canada was in danger of once again becoming entangled in European affairs. According to Eric Kierans, a member of the Cabinet Committee on External Policy and Defence in 1969, "people like [my] Mother had left Europe to get away from it and not bring it with her."[2] It was Kierans' opinion that: "Cabinet Ministers should not be so acutely conscious of our allies' pleas as to the desperate need for Canada's continued military contribution abroad ... In the context of European problems it [is] important that the Soviet empire be put on notice that any of its adventures in Western Europe would be contained and met with resistance but European countries should look after that basic problem at this point in time and we should be devoting our resources to other priorities."[3] Other decision-makers suspected that Canada was so entangled in NATO that the Alliance, not the Canadian government, dictated Canada's foreign and defence policies. Shortly after assuming power in 1968, Prime Minister Pierre Trudeau assessed the situation in the following terms: "And I am afraid, in the situation which we had reached, NATO had in reality determined all of our defence policy. We had no defence policy, so to speak, except that of NATO. And our defence policy had determined all of our foreign policy. And we had no foreign policy of any importance except that which flowed from NATO. And this is a false perspective for any country."[4]

Critics also tended to suspect that the government was trapped into fulfilling military commitments to NATO that the other allies, not Canada, deemed necessary. Certain sectors within the government were criticized for shaping the armed forces not in view of "prior Canadian needs" but "for fear of the approbation of our allies."[5] As was declared in one secret Cabinet meeting in March 1969, "External Affairs should not explain to Cabinet what the Dutch, Italians and Germans think our [NATO] policy should be. They should explain to other countries what our situation is and what our policies are."[6]

Aside from concerns about the extent of the Alliance's impact on Canadian defence policy, Critics also expressed doubts about NATO strategies and undertakings. A few senior advisers to Prime Minister Trudeau, including his foreign policy adviser Ivan Head, considered it irresponsible "for Canada to continue in NATO without attempting to make rational many of the inconsistencies in NATO policy which weaken the organization's credibility." According to Head's secret report for Cabinet, Canada should not continue to participate in NATO simply "because of the exhilaration of 'consultation' or the entreaties of the Europeans."[7]

Critics also worried that the United States might unwillingly draw Canada and the other allies into an armed conflict. As Lester Pearson wrote in a personal letter in 1961 (when he opposed acquiring nuclear weapons), there was a danger that the United States could entrap NATO in a global holocaust: "The Liberal party also believes that NATO should reduce its dependence on nuclear weapons in US hands which might only serve the purpose – in the absence of adequate conventional strength – of converting a limited military incursion into a global nuclear holocaust."[8]

As well, a number of decision-makers were alarmed by shifts in emphasis in American policy; they were leery, too, about the emotionalism, partisanship, and interservice rivalries that affected American defence policy-making. Once again, as Pearson's comments indicate, certain American viewpoints left him discomforted and uneasy. As he told the Institute for Strategic Studies during an *in camera* lecture in 1965:

I was in Washington a few months ago. I spent an evening talking about a lot of things to some people who are pretty important in the present administration. I was surprised and somewhat disturbed to learn that there is a view in Washington that there is no use trying to do much about this, that it is inevitable, and that while we have to go through the motions and make all the usual declarations about the desirability of putting an end to nuclear weapons and especially to stop the proliferation of them, there is not only very little that we can do about it but, perhaps, in the long run it would not be a bad thing to have neighbours, who are on bad terms with each other having nuclear weapons as a deterrent on both sides to aggression … Well, that may be, but I must say that I do not get very much comfort from a world organized on that basis.[9]

The idea that American defence policy-making was dominated by unsound military thinking or by excessive fear and antipathy was often posited. During the 1980s, Prime Minister Trudeau expressed concern about the influence of President Reagan's views on American defence policy-making. During a private meeting with West German Foreign Minister Hans-Dietrich Genscher, Trudeau expressed the opinion that Reagan held unrealistic views about the possibility of bringing the USSR to its knees and withering away the Soviet empire. According to Trudeau, President Reagan and his Californian advisers were "the problem" while US Secretary of State George Shultz "might be more open to flexibility."[10] Similarly, a close adviser to Trudeau, MP Paul McRae, wrote Trudeau that Reagan was dangerously aggressive, and that members of the American military were intent on inciting war.[11] Whereas some Critics apparently feared that individual Americans, such as the president, posed a problem, others believed that the United States' superpower status ensured expansionist policies; they warned that segments of American opinion were dangerously aggressive, and that important members of the élite and the American military were bent on inciting war. For many, the chance that the Alliance leader might drag Canada into an armed confrontation not of its own choosing was in itself a salient threat.

If there was an underlying theme to these diverse comments and concerns, it was that involvement in the Alliance brought with it dangers of entrapment. Indeed, the imperative became that Canada should avoid, or avert, any action that might risk the country becoming embroiled in a deadly superpower conflict.

Critics believed Canada's established military ties to the allies should be restructured and de-emphasized

Critics sought to de-emphasize, if not restructure, Canada's traditional military ties to the allies. In general, these decision-makers opposed maintaining or increasing the number of Canadian Forces personnel earmarked for NATO, including the number of Canadians deployed in Europe. They were generally critical of the government's promises to modernize and commit more weapons systems and equipment to NATO, and they were generally intent on decreasing the percentage of the federal defence budget and the GNP directed toward Alliance purposes.

Several Critics thought the government should sever its military ties to the Alliance in order to encourage other countries within NATO and the Warsaw Pact to de-escalate. Some recommended Canada withdraw entirely from military alliances such as NATO and NORAD in order to hasten the process of disarmament on both sides. As Eric Kierans argued in an important speech in January 1969, "Canada's withdrawal from its military commitments would hasten this day of reckoning – the realization by people on both sides of the Berlin wall that these billions are being spent each year, not as a deterrent against the other side but to impose order on themselves."[12]

While some sought to sever Canada's traditional ties to NATO, others recognized that, even if Canada withdrew from the Alliance, its territory would remain a target in a nuclear war. They nevertheless pressed the government to begin symbolically disentangling itself from NATO as an example for other nations. As James Richardson, minister without portfolio, told his Cabinet colleagues in 1969, by reducing its military power in NATO, Canada could set an example for the Warsaw Pact and other non-aligned nations to follow. In Richardson's view, a symbolic reduction of Canada's military commitments would challenge the other side to de-escalate as well as foster a climate of international understanding.[13] Prime Minister Trudeau argued similarly in 1968, saying that by restructuring, if not withdrawing, its military commitments from Europe, Canada could set a precedent and thus contribute to world peace. As the newly elected prime minister, he pressed Ottawa bureaucrats, "When are we going to start trying to de-escalate? When are we going to arrive at a plan to achieve peace by not getting stronger militarily?"[14] In Trudeau's view, the government could promote world peace by reducing its traditional military commitments to NATO and rechannelling resources into other avenues. Prime Minister Trudeau commented to the British prime minister at a closed meeting in 1969:

The question which the Canadian government was asking itself was whether Canada could do something else which might be more effective in promoting the common objectives of the West. The escalation of military power between the USA and the Soviet Union was reaching frightening proportions. How much further could it go without by its very weight destroying our system of

values? Could we not do something to augment the chances in favour of peace
rather than the chances against war? ... For example, the provision of aid on
a more massive scale, the construction of more "exemplary societies" in the
West, the development of the standards of social justice ... Was it not possible
that if NATO were not so strong militarily, the Soviet Union might not be so
afraid of liberalizing tendencies in Eastern Europe? The Canadian government
was asking itself whether the time had not come to de-escalate NATO, whether
guidelines could not be developed for negotiations with the Soviet Union to
that end, whether the Soviet Union might not be prepared in particular for a
quid pro quo for a Canadian military withdrawal from NATO.[15]

Whereas Trudeau initially assumed that reducing the number of
Canada's overseas stationed forces would de-escalate the arms race
and promote world peace, other high-level Critics thought that
reducing Canada's military ties to Western Europe might contribute
to détente and peaceful co-operation with the Soviet Union. Donald
Macdonald argued in 1969 that Canada now had a "particularly
unique opportunity" to promote détente with Eastern Europe. As
president of the Privy Council, he told the Cabinet that, by withdrawing from Europe, "Canada would be in a far better position to play
a more active diplomatic role and exercise all of the options on
détente with Eastern Europe." Moreover, withdrawal of Canadian
Forces from Europe "could contribute to a lifting of the military siege
against the Soviet Union ... influence the siege mentality of the Soviet
Union's leaders ... penetrate the Warsaw bloc countries to encourage
liberalism and western contracts ... [and accentuate] internal problems
within the Soviet empire to force a more rapid accommodation ..."[16]
Clearly, Critics at times assumed that by withdrawing or de-emphasizing
Canada's traditional military commitments to NATO, the country
could help foster world peace, détente, or disarmament.

While many Critics believed the government should sever or
reduce its established ties to the Alliance, some argued that Canada
could divert its resources into less traditional commitments. Instead
of withdrawal, they suggested a restructuring.[17] A few months after
assuming power, Pierre Trudeau, Ivan Head, and others pressed for
and obtained a reordering of Canadian defence priorities. The protection of Canadian sovereignty was now in first place, while the
fulfillment of NATO commitments was in third place, after "the
defence of North America in cooperation with US forces."[18] Trudeau
characterized these efforts to increase defence and surveillance over
Canadian territory as another way of contributing to NATO's overall
security.[19] In fact, he personally wrote NATO's secretary-general in
1969, saying, "It is my view that Canada's forces deployed in North

America and the adjacent oceans for the protection of the United States deterrent contribute to the security of the European members of NATO just as the defensive efforts of NATO members in Europe contribute to the security of Canada."[20] Trudeau also made it clear to Cabinet, however, that "in the allocation of resources to the defence of North America, when the choice was between the first and second priority, the Canadian government would spend money on the first priority and only spend money on the second priority, primarily, if it assisted the first and, secondly, if it was necessary for political reasons."[21] Fulfilling Canada's NATO commitments was now the government's third-ranking priority.

Some Critics proposed that, as an alternative to established military ties, Canada should attempt to foster greater economic interdependence among the allies. This was one of the major themes explored by Lester Pearson as part of his work on NATO's "Committee of Three."[22] While NATO's role in fostering economic interdependence was never very important to the other allies, John Holmes wrote later that "Pearson and [Escott] Reid and company did not simply want to pretend that NATO was more than a military alliance in order to fool the public. They really believed it, they really wanted it to be something more."[23]

Critics also argued that Canada might contribute in a different way to Alliance solidarity by helping open up channels of communication among the allies, pressing for increased allied consultation, and seeking to give the smaller allies greater influence over Alliance decision-making. Pearson believed that NATO could be strengthened, for instance, by according greater power and influence to "the European side of the coalition," although "nobody did anything about it."[24] Later in his tenure, Trudeau also pressed for a more open exchange of views and what he called a "deepening of consensus" among the allies. As he told reporters in 1971, during his first trip to meet with Soviet leaders:

Canada is a great friend and neighbour of the USA and its ally in NORAD. But it is important for Canada to diversify its channels of communication because of the overwhelming proximity of the USA. Economically, culturally and even militarily it threatens our national identity. We are good allies but we need to diversify our communications with all the significant powers of the world. Hence we remained in NATO. This is even more true with the USSR – another superpower. If they can take time to discuss with us we are glad to do so.[25]

In keeping with his emphasis on opening channels of communication "with all the significant powers of the world in NATO," Prime Minister

Trudeau also criticized the practice of inviting heads of state to NATO meetings in order to "rubber-stamp" documents which were already, in his words, "cooked" and "pre-cooked." As Trudeau remarked to the press at the NATO Summit meeting in 1982, it was a pity that allied representatives could not communicate with one another more openly:

People come in with a speech which has been drafted by their officials in Brussels who have been working for years together, and then they each make speeches which are nothing more than paraphrases of the Communiqué which has been drafted in Brussels by people who have been working for years together. And so we all make speeches repeating what we are all saying in the Communiqué, and nobody has a chance to say: "Well, why did you say that? And where did you get this idea? And what makes you think that? The people across the river here have not got another point of view." So that is a bit of a pity.[26]

Some influential decision-makers proposed that Canada contribute to international peace and security by diverting more resources to other multilateral organizations such as the United Nations. For example, devoting more human and diplomatic resources to the role of "helpful fixer" at the UN was proposed as an alternative, less costly way in which Canada could promote international – and thereby the Alliance's – security. Thus, according to one drafter of the Department of External Affairs' 1980 foreign policy review:

The main argument for Canadian membership in NATO and NORAD and the expenditure by Canada of about four billion dollars a year on defence is that Canada is contributing to a deterrent which makes it less likely that the Soviet Union will follow policies involving serious risks of precipitating a world war. There are other and less expensive ways by which Canada can promote its security. Lester Pearson by his activities during the Suez crisis in 1956 substantially reduced the chances that the crisis might lead to a world war. He did the same by his contribution to the achievement of an armistice in Korea in 1953. It is impossible to put a price tag on this. One could hazard the guess that the value of Pearson's contributions to Canadian security by helping to prevent a world war arising out of Korea in 1953 or the Suez in 1956 was greater than all the Canadian defence expenditures since the second world war. Helpful fixing costs the Canadian taxpayer almost nothing.[27]

Other Critics suggested that, as an alternative contribution to the Alliance, Canada should promote multilateral arms control and disarmament discussions. According to an important speech by Pierre Elliott Trudeau in 1969, " it so happened that NATO after 20 years in our opinion had developed too much into a military alliance and not enough into a political alliance, not enough into an alliance which is interested not only in keeping the balance of deterrence of tactical power in Europe but into an alliance which is interested in arms control and de-escalation."[28]

Despite these suggestions about how Canada's established military ties to the Alliance might be de-emphasized or restructured, Critics usually did not see themselves as deliberately trying to undermine the Alliance. Most simply saw NATO from a different perspective, viewing it as an institution based on irrelevant and outmoded patterns of military thought and interaction. Lester Pearson admitted in his autobiography that, "by 1956, in fact, I was losing hope that NATO would evolve beyond an alliance for defence; and even there I was beginning to have doubts about its future."[29] During his first couple of years in office, Pierre Trudeau also believed that the Alliance had lost its relevance and it was time to consider other ways to reorient Canadian defence and foreign policy. He explained to reporters in 1969: "That is why we have embarked on a defence and foreign policy review, to say that NATO is good, it has played a role, but perhaps there is something else. Perhaps there are other ways to forward the cause of peace and, perhaps other ways of influencing the strategic decisions."[30] In a fashion typical of Critics, Trudeau did not deliberately seek to undermine NATO. During the defence and foreign policy review period between 1968 and 1971, Trudeau shifted from favouring the withdrawal of Canadian Forces from Europe to being critical of NATO. He began to support continued Canadian membership as long as the government first pursued defence alternatives of a higher priority (i.e., sovereignty, North American defence). It may have been, as Admiral Robert Falls, former Chief of the Defence Staff suggested, that Trudeau felt "there were certain things he could do politically and certain things he couldn't, both domestically and internationally."[31] Once Trudeau and his colleagues agreed in 1969 to reject the option of non-alignment and remain in NATO, Trudeau adhered to what he referred to as the Canadian public's position.[32]

Over the years, however, Trudeau continued to criticize NATO decision-making processes, to question the extent of Canada's different commitments, and to express dissatisfaction with select NATO commitments and strategic initiatives.[33] He saw fit in 1969, for example, to express his scepticism to US Secretary of State Henry Kissinger and Defence Secretary Robert McNamara about the value of a small Canadian mechanized unit in the West German plains. Rather than agreeing to maintain or increase the size of the Canadian brigade,

Trudeau inquired whether it would not be more appropriate for Canada to be assigned the job of watching Soviet nuclear submarines in Hudson Bay. He asked if a case should not be made for a substantial maritime role in the Atlantic for Canada, and he pointed out that Canada's military presence in Europe was intended not so much to scare "our potential enemies" as "to impress our friends."[34] While this line of questioning reflected Trudeau's scepticism about maintaining Canadian land forces in Western Europe and an ASW role in the Atlantic, others saw it as an indication of the prime minister's fundamental opposition to NATO.[35] Probably the most concise synopsis of Trudeau's viewpoint as it evolved between 1968 and 1979 is found in a transcript of a 1974 press conference. In reply to questions about NATO, Trudeau commented:

It's not that we want to become good members of NATO, I think we are good members of NATO ... we are part of the Alliance, we want to remain part of the Alliance. We are not pacifists, though we are pacific. We believe that in our position neutralism is not the best solution, that being members of these two alliances – NATO and NORAD – is Canadian policy. We have discussed it publicly in Parliament and with the Canadian public and it was and remains our position ... In other words, don't be afraid as some of them appear to be that Canada is dissatisfied with the idea or the reality of the Alliance, but do realize that criticism within Canada is not on the existence of it but on certain insufficiencies or incapacities that it has demonstrated ...[36]

Trudeau felt, then, that it was appropriate to criticize "certain insufficiencies or incapacities" of NATO, but did not see himself as deliberately trying to undermine the Alliance. It merely seemed that, from his perspective, NATO was an irrelevant and outmoded institution. It was not until 1991, when he was out of office, that Trudeau told Chief of the Defence Staff John de Chastelain that he could not understand why it had taken Canada so long – twenty more years – to get out of NATO.[37]

Generally speaking, three streams of thought developed among Critics with respect to the consequences and implications of restructuring and de-emphasizing Canada's established military commitments to NATO. The *first stream* assumed that reducing or withdrawing Canada's contribution of forces, equipment, and money from Western Europe would be of little importance to the continuing function of the Alliance or to Canada's influence on the allies. As some Cabinet Ministers pointed out in 1969, "In pure numerical terms there was minimal military significance to our contribution [and] the Canadian contribution added little to the overall balance of conventional forces in the Warsaw and NATO Pact countries."[38] According to Critics such as Donald Macdonald, Ivan Head, and Eric Kierans, Canada's contribution to European security could be withdrawn because past experience showed it was neither needed nor appreciated by the other allies; moreover, it certainly played no role in influencing Canada's other ties with Europe, such as trade. As Macdonald told the Cabinet in 1969:

Western Europeans are now mature enough to defend themselves without the intervention of Canadian support. Additionally, there is no evidence that Canadian presence or absence will be a major determinant in the United States' decision to continue to play the great power role in Europe. The Europeans will continue to defend themselves because it is in their interest to do so and the United States will continue to participate in European defence as long as it considers it to be in its interest to do so. A negative decision by Canada will not affect those choices ... in purely military terms, there cannot surely be any serious claim that we have very great influence ... that we have a diplomatic position which we exercise out of all proportion to our military addition ... I would regard the argument as basically not proven...[39]

In his report to Cabinet, Ivan Head echoed Macdonald's concerns: "It must be remembered that the European members of NATO have a combined population of 300 millions and a combined GNP of U.S. $500 billion. Measured in these terms, any possible Canadian contribution of military forces would be of marginal military influence."[40]

Similarly, the first stream of thought among Critics believed that Canada's contributions to Europe's defence made no difference to the way in which the allies treated Canada in other issue areas. According to notes taken during one Cabinet meeting of a debate between Kierans and Mitchell Sharp, Kierans argued:

The fact that we had been in Europe in two world wars and were a member of NATO did not influence in the slightest the position of European negotiators in the trade area. France was now telling us that if we spent $20 million on the European Launcher Development Organization that they would finally be convinced of our interest in Europe. Next year we would be asked to demonstrate our interest in Europe in some other way. Mr. Sharp had not proved ... that a single economic decision was favourably influenced by our NATO membership.[41]

In reply to the argument that Canada would encounter a hostile reaction from its allies if the government was to sever or de-emphasize its established military ties, Critics often asserted that cutting

Canada's traditional military contributions would likely have little impact. As Donald Macdonald argued, "I do not believe that we would be subject to increasing hostility in GATT, in the OECD, or in functional multilateral dealings with European countries merely because we were not participating in the security arrangements."[42]

Whereas this first stream assumed that Canada's nuclear and conventional commitments to Western Europe were of little significance, the *second stream* believed that the acquisition of nuclear or conventional weapons could increase the likelihood of war either by accident or miscalculation; and reducing Canada's NATO commitments might therefore decrease levels of international tension. Prime Minister Trudeau was himself initially inclined to cut back, perhaps withdraw, Canadian Forces from Europe, because he thought their withdrawal might contribute to a lessening of tensions and a reduction of the possibility of unintentional conventional war. As he explained to the minister of National Defence and the minister of External Affairs, "If NATO should engage in a conventional war with the Warsaw Pact, NATO would eventually lose because of the Warsaw Pact's superior conventional forces. If NATO resorted to nuclear weapons everything would be lost. In these circumstances, what is the point of NATO maintaining substantial military forces?"[43]

The *third stream* of thought did not presume that Canada's commitments to NATO made a large difference in military terms, nor were these commitments important as evidence of Alliance resolve and solidarity, given the overall balance of strategic nuclear forces. As Gordon Robertson, clerk of the PCO and secretary to Cabinet, wrote the prime minister in 1969, owing to the bilateral nuclear balance of terror, Canada's conventional commitments to Europe were no longer meaningful.[44] Similarly, Ivan Head counselled that Canada's traditional commitment to defend Western Europe and North America was relatively inconsequential in military terms as well as in terms of signalling Canada's resolve to retaliate against the Soviet Union; rather, he argued, what was important was whether Canada's military forces impressed "our friends." Head's top secret report for the prime minister and the Cabinet in 1969 asked: "What size, and directed to what ends, should be our military force in order to ensure the continued goodwill and co-operation of our United States neighbour and, to a much lesser extent, our other friends and allies? (Briefly, the role of the Canadian Armed Forces is not, initially, to impress our enemies, but rather our friends. This is a political, not a military, role.)"[45] For those in this third stream of thought, contributing to the balance of strategic, tactical, and conventional forces was no longer a critical pursuit. In the nuclear age, whatever the balance of both sides' forces prior to an armed conflict, the final outcome would be equally and totally devastating.

The first stream, then, assumed Canada's military contribution to the Alliance was relatively insignificant and might therefore be reduced. The second stream was primarily concerned that strengthening Canada's military commitments would exacerbate a dangerous situation and increase the likelihood of escalation. The third stream presumed that, because of the nuclear balance, Canada's contribution of conventional forces to NATO was largely unnecessary. In addition to these three streams of thinking, Critics sometimes recommended that Canada de-emphasize or sever particular military commitments to the Alliance without assessing their strategic rationale and implications. It was sometimes recommended, too, that certain weapons systems be cancelled, reduced, or not acquired because Critics wanted, above all, to depart from a prescribed course of action or policy direction. Cabinet ministers Donald Macdonald and Eric Kierans, for example, recommended cutting back the number of CF-104 aircraft Canada deployed in Europe from 108 to 88. After the invasion of Czechoslovakia, "other delegations at Brussels made clear their concern about Canadian plans to reduce the number of aircraft in its air division in Europe ..." During the subsequent Cabinet debate, Macdonald, Kierans, and to a lesser extent Trudeau, dwelled on the continued importance of signalling Canada's intention to promote general de-escalation by reducing the number of aircraft, rather than on the strategic purpose for deploying these aircraft and their military implications.[46] Although such recommendations were sometimes attributed to naiveté about strategic matters, they indicated that Critics at times sought, above all, to depart from a previous policy direction.

Critics believed the external threat to the Alliance
was exaggerated and misunderstood

Whereas Defenders portrayed the external threat to the Alliance as aggressive and opportunistic, their counterparts tended to argue that the nature of the communist threat was exaggerated, that the malign intentions of the Soviet Union had been misinterpreted, or that the Russians could be trusted. Trudeau's frustration with the orthodox opinions advanced in the STAFEUR report prompted him to secretly appoint Ivan Head as coordinator of a study of Canadian defence policy, which was unexpectedly presented to Cabinet in March 1969. Head was unconvinced that there existed "a probable, direct and credible threat to Canadian territorial integrity": "This leaves the

Canadian government, unlike the governments of its NATO allies, free to make the major decisions concerning Canadian defence policy solely upon political considerations – what size, and directed to what ends, should be our military force in order to accord with the very real desire of a large element of the Canadian public that we maintain some form of armed forces ..."[47] As one who worked in a different milieu in the PCO and with Treasury Board, Head seemed relatively uninhibited about rethinking the nature of the threat and Canada's options in that regard. Another mandarin from the PCO, Gordon Robertson, viewed the threat with less attention to the military's established perspective and more attention to "political" considerations. He argued in 1969:

Once it is clearly recognized that broad political considerations are more important than military factors in determining Canadian defence policy, the next step is obvious. It is simply to shape defence policy to accord primarily with the most important political factors involved. This guideline suggests that the size, roles and structure of our forces should be developed in the future primarily as a function of our relations with the United States and Canadian internal security ... [a military presence in Europe] may represent to a significant extent a by-product of our relations with the United States.[48]

While some Critics assumed the external threat to the Alliance was exaggerated, others noted that this threat was misunderstood. As Paul McRae wrote the prime minister, his impression of the Soviet Union was "of a nation very insecure, internally and externally, and with a government that is extremely conservative, and with a neurotic passion for secrecy ... The internal problems ... would seem to me to make any idea of invading the NATO powers rather ridiculous. Their inability to manage their satellites, the failure in Afghanistan, and the string of failures in other parts of the world, would lead me to believe that the shrill statements of Mr. Reagan, and his associates appear much overdone."[49]

Many Critics assumed, too, that NATO's chief adversary was motivated by many of the same concerns. "Is the Soviet Union not as afraid of us as we are of it?" Trudeau asked Ottawa bureaucrats in 1968.[50] Similarly, James Richardson told the Cabinet Committee on External Policy and Defence in 1969 that the Soviet government faced "the same type of domestic demands and difficulties" as Canada. In Richardson's view, "an alternative should be sought whereby Canada could signal to members of the Soviet empire that we realized and understood that their basic concerns were similar to ours."[51]

As a consequence of their refusal to accept conventional threat assessments, Critics were often labelled as "naive," "simplistic idealists," or "doves." Their beliefs about the measure of the threat to the Alliance were usually based, however, on plausible evidence and logical reasoning. For instance, whereas some argued that the Pentagon and the CIA were exaggerating both Warsaw Pact military spending and the Soviet lead in arms technology and weaponry,[52] others contended that the Russians had established an Eastern European buffer-zone and were acting aggressively in client states such as Czechoslovakia or Afghanistan because of insecurity, not malign motives fuelled by expansionist tendencies.[53] Others maintained that self-interest, the threat of nuclear destruction, or modern verification techniques now ensured that the Soviet leadership could be trusted to disarm;[54] a few, however, argued that the prevailing view of the threat was based not so much on historical fact as on American ideological conviction or the attendant demands of American domestic politics.[55]

Owing in part to their conviction that the threat to NATO from the Soviet Union was exaggerated, Critics were often concerned about the spiraling arms race and the increased likelihood of accidental or miscalculated nuclear war. It was frequently argued that adversaries could justify arms buildups and bellicose defence postures based solely upon each other's threatening demeanour. As Eric Kierans explained in 1969: "NATO may or may not have been the appropriate answer to a particular threat in 1948. As a continuing institution, it is something else again. Instead of a genuine deterrent against a genuine threat, it has become a self-justifying deterrent against a non-existent military threat. NATO's existence guarantees that of the Warsaw Pact, each needs the existence of the other to justify its own existence. Two military bureaucracies leaping upon each other for reassurance."[56] In a similar fashion, Prime Minister Trudeau emphasized that the real problem now was how to halt the spiral. In a speech to the UN General Assembly in 1982, Trudeau said: "We arm out of fear for our security and we will disarm only if we are convinced that the threat to our security has abated ... Security, unfortunately, is an elusive concept. It is not only a matter of weaponry. It is also a matter of perception. When each side acts in ways which the other perceives to be threatening, the gulf of suspicion widens between East and West."[57]

For many Critics, the main threat to Canada's security was no longer the Soviet Union but the threat of nuclear war arising out of both sides' surfeit of weapons. The greatest threat to Canada was not an armed attack, but the danger of a miscalculated or accidental conflict escalating uncontrollably to full-scale nuclear warfare. As Cabinet Minister Walter Gordon wrote to Prime Minister Pearson in 1964: "In the opinion of many people, including myself, the prospect of all-out war with the Soviet Union was less than it had been some years before. If there should be a war it would almost certainly be a thermonuclear war in which Canada's contribution would be insignificant ... I, for one, have thought for some time that the Europeans should assume a greater responsibility for the defence of Western Europe and that Canada's commitments there should be very substantially reduced."[58] According to a draft statement issued by Trudeau in 1969, " to say that there is no present threat to Canada's territorial integrity is not to say that there is no present threat from without to Canada's physical security. Should a major world conflict break out, it will not involve territorial aggrandizement at Canada's expense, but it could easily involve mass destruction within Canada."[59] Writing twenty years later, Paul McRae also referred to the danger of accidental war escalating to thermonuclear war: "There is no doubt that the Pershing II missile, the Stealth Cruise, a host of anti-satellite and satellite weaponry, all escalate the danger of an accidental war and lessen the chances of meaningful survival."[60] For many Critics, the threat of nuclear war was much more dangerous and salient than any threat from the Soviet Union or the Warsaw Pact. As Trudeau remarked in 1983: "Today we have long since lost the ability to comprehend the force of a nuclear blast in terms of any comparison with traditional explosives ... The choice we face is clear and present. We can without effort abandon our fate to the mindless drift toward nuclear war. Or we can gather our strength, working in good company to turn aside the forces bearing down on us, on our children, on this Earth."[61]

Some Critics viewed the Soviet threat in the context of a structural problem arising out of the competition between two heavily armed superpowers. Fearing that Canada was in danger of being entrapped, and subjected to great power ambitions, conflicting ideologies, and ominous military capabilities, they saw the Soviet menace as part of a larger threat system dominated by opposing military alliances and an ongoing arms race. As a result, Critics were sometimes not averse to suggesting that the United States was also provocative and dangerous. For some, the prospect of America undertaking independent military initiatives was fearsome, along with the prospect of the Soviet threat being manipulated to justify such initiatives. These worries were often exacerbated by American behaviour in a variety of domestic, continental, and international incidents, from McCarthyism to North

American defence policy to Cuba. The demonstrated penchant of Americans to indulge in sabre-rattling, their willingness to resort to aggressive military tactics, their propensity to escalate the arms race without sufficient allied consultation – a number of Critics focused on these concerns in their dealings with Canada's closest neighbour.[62]

Critics believed both sides' weapons were unnecessarily threatening

While Defenders focused on the adversary's intentions and capabilities, Critics tended to portray both sides' weapons systems and strategies as unnecessarily offensive. They feared that both opposing blocs would perceive each other's military equipment and forces as overly threatening, leading, in turn, to a spiraling arms race and the dangers of unintentional escalation. Many Critics pointed out, therefore, that Canada's own weapons and strategies were not necessarily required, and might, indeed, be perceived by the enemy as dangerously offensive.

In his top-secret 1969 study, Ivan Head pointed out that Canada's capabilities in anti-submarine warfare "broke the rules" that ensured the stability of the deterrent system precisely because they were intended to undermine the Soviet Union's second-strike capability. As he warned the prime minister and Cabinet, "The purpose of our ASW program is to harass and destroy the Soviet missile-carrying submarine which is designed to perform a second-strike role." Head went on to criticize the government's commitment to supply nuclear-tipped CF-104 aircraft to Europe for their first-strike capability: "Our air division in Europe is based a few minutes flying time from East Germany, is a soft target, and is armed with air to surface nuclear weapons ... In the eyes of the Soviets it is credible *only* as a first-strike system."[63]

Another highly influential policy-maker under Trudeau, Gordon Robertson, warned that Canadian weapons systems might be perceived by the Soviet Union as designed for attack. In a memorandum to the prime minister, Robertson explained: "The Canadian nuclear strike aircraft are almost certainly already targeted by the other side. The logical deduction is either that these aircraft might never get off the ground if shooting started or, as viewed from the east, that they are deployed for a surprise attack, i.e. for aggression not defence. The heavy mechanized brigade is not designed to contain local conflicts which may erupt somewhere along the boundaries which now divide the opposing blocs in Europe."[64]

As well, several Critics felt compelled to point out to the other NATO allies, behind closed doors, that their weapons systems and strategies might be interpreted by the enemy as overly threatening. In 1969, Trudeau voiced his own doubts to Henry Kissinger about American intentions to defend the United States' second-strike capability (in the form of Intercontinental Ballistic Missiles [ICBMs], bombers, and submarines). According to the secret report of Trudeau and Kissinger's discussion:

The Prime Minister voiced his reservations about the United States' determination to take additional measures to protect not only Minutemen sites but also SAC bases and Polaris-carrying submarines. I saw Kissinger and Reston raise eyebrows and exchange surprised glances as if they had been warned that the Prime Minister might hold such views ... My impression is that ... the [US] authorities had not been prepared to believe that our Prime Minister would question in such a basic and thorough fashion present defence policies.[65]

The idea that allied weapons were overtly threatening led some Critics to warn, too, that, by storing or testing US nuclear weapons in Canada, the country would contribute to international tensions, new combat capabilities, and possibly provoke a Soviet first-strike or an accidental nuclear war. If the Canadian government agreed to test the air-launched cruise missile for the United States, Paul McRae warned the prime minister, Canada would possibly contribute to the development of an American first-strike capability. If Canada consented to deploy Pershing and cruise missiles, there was a danger that the Soviet Union would not back down but continue to deploy weapons to more troublesome areas: "Thus the deployment of the Pershing II missile with a 6 to 8 minute run from Europe to a Soviet silo, evoking a launch-on-warning situation, could result in the deployment of a [Soviet] missile off the U.S. shore, with a comparable flight period. A computer error, due to the short time for verification left under such a situation, would, or could, bring about World War III ..."[66]

Sometimes the belief that both sides' weapons were unnecessarily offensive produced arguments that were new and disturbing to others. Mitchell Sharp, Leo Cadieux, and Paul Hellyer, for example, were perturbed by the strange new hypotheses the prime minister suggested should undergird future Canadian defence policy. In a secret memorandum to Cabinet ministers in 1969, Trudeau proposed that the government establish a new defence policy which would exclude first-strike capabilities, confine nuclear weapons to a second-strike or defensive posture, and permit Canadian territory to be used for only solely defensive purposes. As Trudeau explained, "It would be of great assistance to make public that it was Canadian foreign policy that our military arrangements were purely defensive in character, that Canadian territory was to be used for defensive purposes."[67] The prime minister hoped his proposals would receive Cabinet's concurrence and "be the hypotheses upon which military planners could develop practical policies." Sharp, Cadieux, and Hellyer initially rejected them on the grounds that it would be too conceptually difficult to categorize weapons as "offensive" or "defensive,"[68] although the changes were finally mentioned in the 1971 Defence White Paper.[69] It may have been Trudeau's emphasis on psychological factors – the need to empathize with the adversary's perceptions – that disturbed his Cabinet colleagues. Evidently, Trudeau believed that the "preservation of peace" rested principally on psychological variables. As he explained in his proposal: "It can, of course, correctly be pointed out that the enforcement of the proposal could not prevent the initiation of a nuclear exchange from the array of weapons systems which are completely outside Canadian jurisdiction. While this is so, it is also true that preservation of peace, and progress towards arms control depend above all on psychological factors."[70]

In addition to the disturbing idea that elements of both sides' weapons systems were unnecessarily threatening, some Critics pointed out that certain Canadian commitments seemed unnecessary. During one Cabinet briefing, Trudeau rejected the Canadian military's reasons for contributing to NATO's submarine surveillance program. Instead, he asked a series of logical questions undermining the military's traditional assumptions for supporting Canada's role in NATO's anti-submarine warfare strategy. The prime minister's reasoning is reflected in the Cabinet Conclusions:

If it were assumed that Canadian destroyers could closely identify and track Soviet submarines and if it were assumed that no offensive action would be taken by those Canadian destroyers, then what value would there be in acquiring knowledge of the submarine's location and what comfort could there be in knowing that you tracked successfully, if the submarine attacked ... Destroyers only become totally effective if they can strike and destroy. If Canadian destroyers attacked in the first instance without warning then the allies would have instigated a nuclear attack. That possibility must be ruled out. If destroyers were attacking submarines, then it must be assumed that a nuclear exchange through ICBMs or bombers had already taken place. At that point it would be difficult to maintain that there was any deterrent value in the destroyer program ... In other words, are destroyers really needed for this type of activity and in particular, is there a need for 24 destroyers as shown in the model for forces 1972/73.[71]

Admiral Robert Falls, former Chief of the Defence Staff, remarked years later that, during his tenure, Trudeau had capably used "a kind of Jesuit logic" to try to destroy the military's traditional arguments in favour of contributing to NATO's ASW capability: "There was one time when he [Trudeau] talked of submarines to me, and that allowed me to believe that he knew a hell of a lot more about the ASW aspects of the Navy than I certainly expected him to, and that he differentiated very clearly between an attack submarine and a "boomer," an SSBN. He was in fact using this kind of Jesuit logic, I suppose, to try and destroy what he thought was my position ... He was very clear that, you know, it was destabilizing to be trying to develop an ASW capability against SSBNs."[72]

Rather than directly attack or undermine the military's grounds for different types of commitments, many Critics also put forward original metaphors and new strategic rationales for opposing certain types of commitments. For instance, those Defenders who seemed preoccupied with counting and comparing nuclear stockpiles were labelled "nuclear accountants" or workers in the "spagetti factory."[73] The enemy's threatening posture, they argued, was no more than a "measured response" to NATO's initial provocations. Moreover, the Soviet Union's nuclear missiles could be justified as modernized versions of previously acceptable missile systems.[74] Indeed, before the UN General Assembly in 1978, Prime Minister Trudeau argued for a new "strategy of suffocation," maintaining that continued flight-testing of new strategic delivery vehicles would justifiably force the Soviet Union to respond in kind, thus contributing to the dynamics of the arms race and to both sides' arsenals of threatening weapons.[75]

Critics believed deterrence doctrine was unsuitable and unreliable

Many Critics lacked faith in certain aspects of deterrence doctrine and disparaged its underlying assumptions. To rely on the Alliance's nuclear and conventional forces to deter war, they argued, would exacerbate, not reduce, the chance of war. To believe, furthermore, that the Alliance could credibly defend itself with nuclear or conventional forces was, to their way of thinking, misguided. Instead of relying solely on deterrence, Critics drew attention to alternative scenarios and options.

In an analysis of "the present super-power deterrent system," for example, Ivan Head concluded: "The balance is an unhealthy one, because of the danger of accident, because of the danger which would follow the entry of new participants, because of the danger it may not be maintained." Although Head advised in 1969 that "the balance appears to be a necessary evil," he recommended that Canada restructure its defence posture so as not to further undermine the security of both side's second-strike capacity. He suggested

Canada restructure its defence structure in order to: "(a) do whatever it can to protect the United States second-strike capability; (b) avoid doing anything which would have the effect of intimidating the Soviet second-strike capability; [and] (c) avoid adopting any posture or role which is credible in the eyes of the Soviets only as a first-strike role." Nevertheless, as Head concluded in his secret document for Cabinet, "in our present defence role, we break all three of these rules."[76] Head considered it important that the basic assumptions underlying the Alliance's doctrine of flexible response be challenged. As he warned the prime minister, "Any assumption that the use of 'tactical' nuclear weapons will not escalate immediately to a full intercontinental strategical nuclear weapon holocaust must be challenged because there is no provable criteria for its premise. With the continued existence of mankind at stake, some extraordinary degree of certainty should be required."[77]

As well, other influential policy-makers criticized Canada's reliance on deterrence doctrine to prevent escalation. Trudeau informed the Cabinet in 1969 that Canada's contemplated contribution to NATO of CF-5 squadrons and its current contribution of 108 CF-104 aircraft to Europe (which, as had already been announced, would be reduced to eighty-eight aircraft) should be reassessed. "In the event of hostilities in Europe, the French would retaliate with an atomic bomb and it was illusory to think otherwise," he stated.[78] At the Second United Nations Special Session on Disarmament in 1982, Trudeau also criticized the counterintuitive logic of nuclear deterrence: "The nuclear debate is difficult and seems to pursue an inverse logic. It deals with power that, by common consent, is unusable. It argues for more nuclear weapons in order that, in the end, there may be fewer. It perceives the vulnerability of cities and of human beings as an element of stability in the nuclear balance. And worst of all, the debate goes on without much evidence of any light at the end of the tunnel."[79] Trudeau became increasingly concerned about the possibility that new intercontinental strategic weapons could be so mobile as to be virtually invisible. To his mind, this buttressed the stability of the doctrine of mutual assured nuclear deterrence, while calling into question the ability of both sides, or any international body, to verify arms control agreements:

You see the paradox. These questions are so intellectually difficult that, too often, the public and their leaders are tempted to leave these problems to experts, to nuclear accountants, to people who understand the technology, but do not consider the political dimension of the issue. If missiles stay in one place, the enemy knows where they are, and could destroy them by launching a first strike, so that the side under attack could not respond with an attack of its own. One side would win the war simply by destroying the other's nuclear missiles. That is why these weapons are destabilizing. You must use them or lose them. For that reason, making these missiles mobile also makes them more stabilizing weapons, in the sense that a first strike by the enemy would not destroy exactly where they are, and so he will not start a war, because the other side will still be able to send missiles back at him. That would assure the destruction of both sides, which is not in the interest of the side which might otherwise be tempted to launch a first strike. But there is a further paradox in the fact that, if these missiles are too mobile, you could not count them, even by using satellites. And if you cannot count them, neither side could verify that the other was respecting the treaties, such as SALT I, and other agreements that might be reached.[80]

For the prime minister, like other Critics, many aspects of nuclear deterrence were troubling, especially given the rapid development of new technologies.

Many Critics also believed that threatening to use nuclear or conventional weapons of mass destruction to prevent attack fundamentally undermined national and global security. Trudeau remarked in 1984:

The experts would have us believe that the issues of nuclear war have become too complex for all but themselves. We are asked to entrust our fate to a handful of high priests of nuclear strategy. And to the scientists who have taken us from atom bombs to thermonuclear warheads, from missiles with one warhead to missiles with ten or more, from weapons that deter to weapons that threaten the existence of us all. Canadians, and people everywhere, believe their security has been diminished, not enhanced, by a generation of work spent on perfecting the theories and instruments of human annihilation.[81]

Paul McRae concluded, similarly, that new developments in weapons technology had increased the likelihood of any conflict escalating into a major war. As he put it: "There is no doubt that the Pershing II missile, the Stealth Cruise, a host of anti-satellite and satellite weaponry, all escalate the danger of an accidental war and lessen the chances of meaningful survival. The fate of civilization is rapidly passing from the control of humans to control by a computer."[82] For Trudeau and McRae, like other Critics, deterrence imperilled rather than ensured Canadian security and the future of human civilization.

As a result of these sorts of concerns, some Critics were willing only to provide conditional support for deterrence. Several argued that, in future, Canada should try to safeguard the Alliance's second-strike capabilities, not help enhance an American first-strike capacity. Ivan Head wrestled with the problem of whether Canada should contribute to the doctrine of flexible response or the doctrine of preserving a balance of deterrents in the form of an assured second-strike capability (i.e., mutual assured destruction). He concluded that "the balance appears to be a necessary evil," and that Canada should therefore concentrate its defence efforts on protecting the United States' second-strike capability and, secondarily, assume a defence posture that related to NATO's flexible response posture.[83] Similarly, in 1969 Prime Minister Trudeau questioned whether Canada's naval force should be prepared to destroy the Soviets' second-strike capability. As Trudeau asked a group of Liberals in land-locked Alberta: "Our contribution in the naval area to our anti-submarine warfare – is this the right contribution? Should we be having the kind of naval force which is prepared to destroy the Soviet nuclear-armed submarines, which are a deterrent for them as the Polaris is a deterrent for the United States? ... [Soviet] submarines are by nature, I suppose, in this capacity – they are second strike, they are deterrent. Is our policy right to be armed essentially against them?"[84]

Some Critics were troubled, too, by the argument that nuclear deterrence was a successful strategy simply because there had been no war in Europe.[85] Some maintained that, in the nuclear era, wars would be neither deterred nor conducted according to historical principles or precedents. As Paul McRae wrote Trudeau, "What I am surprised to find, and what worries me, are those who apply pre-World War I – and II – thinking, including the Munich syndrome, and who don't seem to have any concept of what is in store for civilization if the two superpowers ever go beyond the brink."[86] Still others found it difficult to believe that a war in the European theatre would not immediately become a global conflict. The assumption that a nuclear exchange could be limited and tactical, or that there could be a winner in any nuclear war, was summarily rejected;[87] meanwhile the old "win-lose" mentality was criticized as outdated, and the notion of a balance, superiority, or sufficiency of nuclear forces was seriously challenged.[88]

A number of Critics also questioned the need to strengthen the Alliance's conventional forces, fearing such a move would exacerbate, not reduce, tensions and the arms race. Essentially, they assumed that "the moment one side was unsuccessful in matching the conventional forces of the other in a military confrontation then there would be reliance upon nuclear weapons."[89] Critics often questioned the point of maintaining substantial conventional forces, given that it would be difficult for both sides to refrain from escalating any conflict to all-out nuclear war. As Trudeau's adviser in the Privy Council Office Gordon Robertson wrote, it was difficult to justify the presence of Canadian Forces in Europe:

First, if the European members of the Alliance are not capable of containing a local conflict in Europe, then it is neither reasonable nor credible to expect Canadian troops to perform this function ... Second, the presence of Canadian troops in Europe, unlike U.S. forces, does not directly guarantee the credibility of the nuclear deterrent ... it is very doubtful whether NATO has the capacity to effectively carry out a strategy of flexible conventional response in the first place ... the Canadian contribution [i.e. of conventional forces to Europe] is not sufficient to make the doctrine of flexible response workable; nor, if it were workable, would the absence of the Canadian contribution make it unworkable ...[90]

Like Head and Robertson, many Critics considered it unnecessary to commit additional conventional forces and military equipment to NATO in order to signal the Alliance's resolve to retaliate against limited aggression. Their preferred solution was to raise the nuclear threshold, establish a lower balance of conventional forces, and promote nuclear disarmament and arms control, including mutual and balanced conventional force reductions. As Trudeau reasoned in 1983, the "sensible approach" would be for both sides to reduce their conventional forces to mutually agreed levels:

As long as this imbalance of conventional forces persists, so does the risk that nuclear weapons would be brought into action at an early stage of any conflict. That is why we say that the nuclear threshold in Europe is too low. And of course we can never be certain that the use of nuclear weapons in the European theatre would not escalate rapidly to ever more massive nuclear retaliation on an international scale. The conclusion we draw is that the best way to raise the nuclear threshold is to establish a more reasonable balance of the conventional forces on each side. How then do we achieve this balance? ... The simple, though expensive answer is for the West to increase its conventional forces until they match those of the Warsaw Pact. I see this as a last resort. The far more sensible approach would be for both sides to reduce their conventional forces to mutually agreed levels, a task to which we have devoted the past ten years at the Mutual and Balanced Force Reduction (MBFR) talks in Vienna.[91]

Finally, Critics drew attention to alternative scenarios that could not be resolved or averted by issuing a traditional deterrent threat.

Such scenarios included nuclear arms races in the Third World;[92] armed revolution and insurrection in trouble spots outside Europe;[93] as well as civil uprisings, famine, and poverty in the Third World.[94] For Critics, these threats to international peace and security could not be offset by a doctrine they deemed both unsuitable and unreliable in the nuclear era.

CONCLUSION

Some Canadian decision-makers harboured fears about entrapment and doubts about NATO initiatives. Their worries about being trapped in an American-led incursion were voiced more fervently than were their fears about the possible threat from the Soviet Union and the Warsaw Pact. Moreover, in many situations, when issues of maintaining, de-emphasizing, or strengthening Canada's NATO commitments arose, these influential decision-makers tended to dwell on the probable reaction of the NATO allies rather than on the Soviet Union.

Critics believed the dangers of entrapment could best be averted by restructuring and de-emphasizing Canada's traditional contributions of forces, equipment, and money to NATO. They worried that these commitments otherwise increased tensions and the likelihood of a nuclear holocaust. They were united by a concern that Canadians avoid entrapment in potentially provocative and expensive NATO undertakings. Critics also viewed both blocs' weapons as posing unacceptable risks. Many aspects of both sides' weapons and strategies, being unnecessarily offensive, could, they felt, contribute to dangerous arms races and escalating tensions. Yet another essential element in their belief system was the conviction that the external threat to the Alliance was often exaggerated and misunderstood. Rather than rely solely on deterrence as a strategy for war prevention, Critics tended to challenge conventional thinking and draw attention to alternative courses of action.

A number of examples in this chapter were attributed to confidential sources. Yet it is possible to affirm that, at different times between 1963 and 1987, Walter Gordon, Lester Pearson, Pierre Trudeau, Ivan Head, Gordon Robertson, Donald Macdonald, James Richardson, Gerard Pelletier, Eric Kierans, and Paul McRae held beliefs typical of Critics. As the minister of Finance under Lester Pearson between 1963 and 1965, Walter Gordon questioned many aspects of government policy. That the Soviet threat might be exaggerated, that overseas forces might not be necessary, and that the government needed to re-examine the extent and measure of its NATO commitments – these were all issues that Gordon personally raised with the prime minister in 1964, before his resignation after the general election of 1965. Under Pearson's tenure, however, the control over foreign and defence policy-making exerted by himself, External Affairs Minister Paul Martin, and Defence Minister Paul Hellyer resulted in few Cabinet debates and little questioning of Canada's NATO commitments between 1963 and 1967. Indeed, the Cabinet quickly agreed on 9 May 1963 to fulfill Canada's nuclear commitments. And Pearson, Martin, and Hellyer steered Cabinet policy toward consistent support of Canada's other Alliance commitments. Thus between 1963 and 1967, the government's NATO policy did not undergo any important shifts in emphasis and commitment.

In fact, it was not until 1967–68 that Lester Pearson began to question the need for Canada's deployment of a large contingent of Forces in Europe. Indeed, by the late 1960s, Pearson was beginning to espouse beliefs more typical of Critics than Defenders. Although Pearson was a defender of Canada's membership in NATO for most of his life, questions about the extent and measure of those commitments began to vex him in the late 1960s. Whereas Pearson had helped found the Alliance in 1949, he gradually became disappointed with its military character and the nonemphasis on Article II of the Treaty, which had called for greater economic, social, and cultural ties within the Atlantic Community. That Pearson cannot be unequivocally categorized as either a Defender or a Critic seems evident by his differing attitudes toward the issue of acquiring nuclear weapons for the Canadian Forces. In the months prior to the 1963 election, for instance, there was some confusion about the implications of the Liberal party's non-nuclear stance and Pearson was on record as being opposed to the weapons systems. Owing in part to Paul Hellyer's advice, though, Pearson changed his mind and promised that, if elected, he would renegotiate these agreements. Once elected, he proceeded to replace the sand ballast in all the weapons with nuclear warheads. It seems that, in his later years, Pearson walked a fine line between the roles of Defender and Critic; if he had doubts or criticisms, they were expressed in the form of "quiet diplomacy." Although his doubts about whether Canada should retain a 10,000-strong military force surfaced more openly in 1967, it was not until he stepped down from office that he publicly criticized the practice of stationing Canadian Forces in Europe.[95]

Pierre Trudeau assumed power in 1968 on a platform that was openly critical of NATO and the extent to which membership in the Alliance dominated Canadian foreign and defence policy. By 1971, he seemed convinced that while Canada should remain a member of NATO, the kinds of commitments the country made to defend NATO's territory should be North American-based. His initial inclination to withdraw Canadian Forces from Europe was tempered by the process of Cabinet debate and extra-Parliamentary discussion, such that he and Ivan Head eventually settled for a two-thirds reduction in the number of overseas forces. When this reduction was heavily criticized by the NATO allies and Cabinet ministers alike, and was also attacked in Parliament, the prime minister compromised again, settling for a fifty-percent cut. Thus, although Trudeau espoused many of the beliefs typical of Critics between 1968 and 1971, as prime minister he was obliged to make compromises. In the mid-1970s, his approach became more publicly supportive, and less openly critical, of NATO. Like Pearson before him, Trudeau's views defy easy categorization. He was at once a supporter of Canada's continued membership and involvement in NATO and a critic of select NATO initiatives and directions. By the time he undertook his peace initiative in 1983–84, however, many of his statements and off-the-cuff remarks reflected the reasoning frequently espoused by Critics.

Other influential decision-makers between 1968 and 1971 – Ivan Head and Gordon Robertson, for example – are more easily classifiable as Critics. As Trudeau's chief adviser on foreign policy, Head wrote, at Trudeau's request, a brief for Cabinet that outlined many of the reasons for reducing the number of overseas stationed forces, de-emphasizing Canada's NATO commitments, and restructuring the shape of the Canadian Forces based in Canada.

Within the Cabinet itself, President of the Privy Council Donald Macdonald, backed by Minister-without-Portfolio James Richardson and, to a lesser extent, Secretary of State for External Affairs Gerard Pelletier, often put forward arguments and reasoning that were typical of Critics. As we have seen, Donald Macdonald was a well-informed, outspoken Critic who took a keen interest in these issues, even preparing his own detailed briefs for discussion in Cabinet. Although he supported some form of co-operative arrangement with the United States for the defence of North America, he questioned Canadian military contributions to NATO. Richardson focused more on the implications for world peace if Canada was to withdraw, or at least weaken, its military commitments to NATO. Among other considerations, Richardson believed Canada would have a unique opportunity to contribute to a lessening of East-West tensions. Pelletier also favoured non-military approaches to the lessening of world tensions, and quietly sided with Macdonald – and presumably, Trudeau.[96]

Postmaster-General Eric Kierans was another vigorous NATO Critic. He frequently argued against Canada's continued membership

in NATO, and was one of the few high-level decision-makers who
recommended that Canada withdraw entirely from the Alliance.
(Trudeau encouraged him to make this argument so as to incite a
national debate.)[97] In fact, nearly all Canadian decision-makers
believed that Canada should remain a NATO member – the recurring
debate centred on what should be the measure and extent of Canada's
military and non-military NATO commitments. In the end, Kierans's
influence over the long term was marginal, as he resigned in April
1971 in opposition to the general direction being taken by the
Trudeau government. As one who was seen to "meddle too much"
in departmental matters that were not his affair,[98] Kierans had less
apparent influence on defence policy than other Cabinet ministers
such as Mitchell Sharp, Leo Cadieux, and Donald Macdonald.

Although Pierre Trudeau, Ivan Head, Donald Macdonald, Gordon
Robertson, James Richardson, Gerard Pelletier, and Eric Kierans were
vigorously opposed by Defenders such as Mitchell Sharp, Leo
Cadieux, Marcel Cadieux, and Ross Campbell, they were able, particularly between 1968 and 1971, to moderately reshape Canada's
NATO commitments in a direction consonant with their underlying
beliefs and assumptions. Nuclear weapons were phased out, Canadian Forces in Europe were at least symbolically cut back, and the
emphasis of the 1971 Defence White Paper was on defensive forces
based in Canada as a contribution primarily to sovereignty and North
American defence.

Access restrictions limit the extent to which one can draw a similar
profile of decision-makers in the period between 1978 and 1989.
Confidential briefing notes written by MP Paul McRae for Prime
Minister Trudeau indicate that McRae's viewpoint was largely shared
by the prime minister. But in the late 1970s and 1980s, it is difficult
to determine whether beliefs typical of Critics had a significant
impact on defence decision-making. Many of Trudeau's public comments during the peace initiative indicate that the prime minister
held the beliefs of Critics to be self-evident. Yet his convictions are
not in themselves a sufficient explanation for the shifts in Canada's
approach toward NATO between 1978 and 1989. Many other factors
– such as the United States' request that Canada test the cruise
missile, the tone of President Reagan's anti-Soviet remarks, and the
emergence of a vociferous peace movement in Canada – could have
contributed to this prime minister's shift in approach toward Canada's
NATO commitments. Until the relevant Cabinet documents are
released (1998–2009), researchers will be unable to discern whether
beliefs typical of Defenders or Critics had a critical effect on defence
decision-making in the last decade of the Cold War.

We can conclude, however, that between 1968 and 1978 the presence of several Critics in the inner circles of decision-making had a significant impact on the Trudeau government's lack of support for some NATO initiatives. This is not to say that it was solely the presence of Trudeau, Head, Robertson, Macdonald, Richardson, Pelletier, and Kierans that accounted for the government's intention to disarm the nuclear weapons and reduce or withdraw Canadian Forces from Europe. Naturally, other systemic- and domestic-level factors contributed to these shifts in policy as well. There seems no doubt, though, that many of the substantive beliefs of Critics significantly affected the high-level debate regarding Canada's NATO commitments between 1968 and 1978. Despite DND's established policy in favour of nuclear weapons for the Canadian Forces, despite the Soviet invasion of Czechoslovakia, and contrary to the recommendations and recriminations of other allies, the convictions of a few politicians brought about significant changes in the government's defence policy.

CHAPTER FIVE

A Case Study:
The Diefenbaker Government's
Shifting NATO Commitments,
1957–1963

This case study considers the Diefenbaker government's legacy with respect to Canadian defence policy and the onset of "new thinking" about nuclear weapons; it also asks why Prime Minister Diefenbaker and some of his advisers began to question whether Canada should take on a nuclear role. Two questions take centre stage: What beliefs about nuclear weapons and the nature of the threat led some high-level policy-makers to argue against acquiring nuclear warheads? What assumptions about the dangers of abandonment, entrapment, and nuclear deterrence incited some to oppose the nuclear commitments? Apparently, a new way of thinking – typical of Critics – significantly influenced decision-making and led to the Diefenbaker government's shifting approach to nuclear weapons. Diefenbaker's legacy was that he was the first Canadian prime minister, but certainly not the last, to take an anti-nuclear stand.

My purpose here is to explain when and to what extent the belief systems of Critics began to influence the defence decision-making process. This chapter retells the story of the Diefenbaker government's controversial defence policy. The new findings are based largely on the recently declassified records of Cabinet; the newly opened personal papers of Prime Minister Diefenbaker; and the declassified documents now available from DND's Directorate of History, such as the recently opened "Raymont Series."

THE EARLY YEARS: FIRM COMMITMENTS
(JUNE 1957 TO JUNE 1959)

John Diefenbaker's predecessor, Louis St. Laurent, had delayed making defence-related decisions for fear of inciting public furor. Thus, it was left to Diefenbaker to decide whether Canada should join NORAD, cancel the production of the Avro Arrow, and acquire nuclear weapons for the Canadian Forces.

The decision to integrate operational control of the Royal Canadian Air Force (RCAF) with the United States Air Force (USAF) had been under discussion since December 1956. The chairman of the Canadian Chiefs of Staff, General Charles Foulkes, advised the newly appointed minister of National Defence, General George Pearkes, that this urgent matter be taken up by the Cabinet Defence Committee. However, Pearkes suspected that the prime minister would be disinclined to set up a Cabinet Defence Committee before the entire Cabinet was itself organized. On 24 July 1957, barely two weeks into the government's mandate, Pearkes proceeded to discuss the matter privately with the prime minister, his long-time friend, returning shortly with the latter's written endorsement. A press release announcing the establishment of the North American Air Defence (NORAD) agreement was quickly prepared. A Canadian deputy commander was appointed, and the matter was later briefly discussed in Cabinet. That appeared to be the end of the matter.[1]

The decision to cancel the production of the Avro Arrow was taken with more circumspection, if only because of its domestic implications. The costs of producing a state-of-the-art interceptor almost entirely in Canada, combined with factors such as managerial inefficiency, limited demand, a short production line, and news of the successful *Sputnik* launch and ICBM tests, impelled Diefenbaker to announce, on 23 September 1958, the government's decision to delay Arrow production pending further review. A sustained attempt to find foreign buyers yielded no takers. At that time, the other allies were concerned about the new ICBM threat, not about a Canadian-made interceptor to counter the bomber threat. The government was finally forced to shut down the A.V. Roe industry, putting tens of thousands of highly skilled employees out of work. For some, this signalled the end of Canada's economic independence in more than just defence production.[2]

The decision to acquire nuclear warheads for the Canadian Forces as part of Canada's commitment to NATO was initially accorded little importance. Indeed, in 1957, politicians were largely unconcerned about the extent of Canada's non-nuclear commitments to NATO, and the question as to whether Canada should maintain a standby battalion overseas under NATO auspices was not even an issue. Not long after the Diefenbaker government assumed power, however, questions about whether to acquire nuclear warheads for the Canadian Forces committed to NATO began to assume a great deal of importance.

THE DECISION TO ACQUIRE NUCLEAR WEAPONS
FOR THE CANADIAN FORCES

Diefenbaker attended his first meeting of the NATO heads of government in December 1957. At this meeting, the leaders of the Alliance finally endorsed NATO document MC 14/2, which called for development of the Alliance's ability to defend its territories and seas as far forward as possible to maintain the integrity of the NATO area. The MC 14/2 counted on the use of nuclear weapons from the outset. The leaders also agreed to a complementary NATO document, the MC 48/2, authorizing the NATO Council to plan and make preparations on the assumption that nuclear weapons would be used from the outset. It was agreed that NATO would establish stocks of nuclear warheads for the defence of the Alliance.[3]

Although Diefenbaker agreed to MC 14/2 and MC 48/2, he was very much preoccupied at the NATO meeting with the NORAD issue. The recent well-informed criticism of Lester Pearson, leader of the Opposition and former minister of External Affairs, was forcing Diefenbaker to tread carefully on the issue of NORAD's relationship to NATO.[4] His chief concern was to present the concept of a bilateral arrangement with integrated air forces in North America as an integral part of NATO's multilateral military structure. Indeed, with General Pearkes's and Foulkes's support, he would have liked to declare NORAD a NATO command. But Diefenbaker, Pearkes, and Foulkes knew this would fly in the face of the American military's reluctance to establish a multinational command in North America, with its attendant implications for American disclosure policy.[5] Consequently, the prime minister had to choose his words carefully when speaking to the Heads of Government at the December 1957 NATO meeting. If his political sense had already warned him to question American proposals to stockpile nuclear weapons in Europe, these doubts were not aired. His comments on NORAD's relationship to NATO were designed to avoid consternation, as was his endorsement of the concept of acquiring nuclear weapons. He reasoned, simply, that "the proposal to form a NATO stockpile of atomic warheads ... follows logically from the decision taken in 1954 to organize our forces in Europe on the understanding that they would be able to use such weapons to repel attacks."[6]

It is difficult to determine whether Diefenbaker fully understood that these words implied his agreement to the concept of nuclear weapons for Canadian air and land forces in Europe. On the one hand, as prime minister he was supposed to be informed about NATO's total force requirements for planning purposes. On the other, it is unlikely that he took any interest at this time in the implications of MC 14/2 and MC 48/2 for the structure of his own country's forces. Preoccupied, and perhaps unprepared for his first NATO meeting, he seems to have had little understanding of what he was committing Canada to.

In terms of exact commitments, the "planning guidance" issued by SHAPE headquarters for 1958 recommended that Canada obtain the Honest John and Little John nuclear missile units, as well as nuclear-tipped fighter-bombers. The government eventually acquired an interlocking network of five expensive nuclear weapons systems. Ministers shortly began to discuss these different systems in secret Cabinet meetings. Before the public, however, they were careful to make it seem as if the burgeoning nuclear weapons issue primarily revolved around the question of obtaining nuclear warheads for the Bomarc missiles and the interceptors to be deployed on Canadian soil.

AN EXTENSIVE NETWORK OF NUCLEAR-CAPABLE WEAPONS SYSTEMS

The commitment to acquire Bomarc missiles

On 23 September 1958, at the same time as his announcement concerning the Avro Arrow, Diefenbaker announced that the government would acquire two squadrons of Bomarc missiles. The decision to acquire the Bomarcs appeared tainted from the beginning, however, for Diefenbaker misrepresented the grounds for their deployment. Indeed, he conveyed the impression that the Bomarc missiles would be acquired as a substitute for the obsolete Arrow interceptors. Although he may have been confused about the strategic purpose of the Bomarc and primarily concerned about alleviating the political impact of the Arrow cancellation, in hindsight he seemed deliberately disingenuous. Moreover, his speech mystified the public, contributing to the impression that the Bomarc was necessary because it was strategically superior to the Arrow.

The new Bomarc missile to which Diefenbaker had committed the country was designed as an anti-bomber projectile that could intercept Soviet bombers carrying conventional or nuclear warheads. Whereas the original version, the Bomarc A, carried a conventional warhead, the USAF-preferred newer model was armed with a nuclear warhead. The USAF maintained that the Bomarc A's disadvantage was its conventional charge, which would need to be exploded in close proximity to an attacking aircraft. The Bomarc B's nuclear explosion, on the other hand, could destroy enemy aircraft without needing the same precision of interception. A second argument in support of the Bomarc B was that its warhead could destroy all the warheads on the Soviet carrier vehicle. Since the fear was that Soviet bombers would carry "dead man fuses" preset for certain altitudes, at which point they would detonate regardless of whether the bomber's crew was dead or alive, the USAF favoured the nuclear-tipped model. To counter arguments that the explosion from the Bomarc B would cause nuclear fallout over Canada, American experts pointed out that fallout levels would be insignificant compared to the nuclear fallout showered down on Canada by the release of a conventional bomb.[7]

Whether Diefenbaker understood from the outset that the Bomarc would carry a nuclear, not a conventional, warhead remains unclear. Years later, he professed not to have understood the distinction between the two models, and only to have consented to the acquisition of the Bomarc A missile because it carried a conventional warhead.[8] However, the Parliamentary record shows that, on 20 February 1959, the Prime Minister told the House of Commons:

The full potential of these defensive weapons is achieved only when they are armed with nuclear warheads ... Problems connected with the arming of the Canadian Brigade in Europe with short range nuclear weapons for NATO defence tasks are also being studied. We are confident that we shall be able to reach formal agreement with the United States ... It will be of course some time before these weapons will be available for use by Canadian forces ... It is our intention to provide Canadian forces with modern and efficient weapons to enable them to fulfill their respective roles.[9]

These words clearly seem to mean that Diefenbaker accepted that the Canadian Forces would have nuclear weapons. From his perspective in 1959, however, the chief advantage of the Bomarc stemmed not from its warhead but from its relative inexpensiveness. The Bomarc was cheaper to build and maintain than most aircraft. Instead of a pilot, it relied on a ground-based system of radars referred to as the SAGE system. State-of-the-art technology, it was nevertheless vulnerable to jamming and deceptive tactics. American strategists concluded that, for the sake of credible deterrence, the Bomarc should complement, not replace, manned interceptors. In 1959, Diefenbaker may not have fully understood this.[10] Cabinet documents indicate, however, that by May 1960 ministers recognized that Canada was bound by agreement with the United States to construct two bases for nuclear-armed Bomarc missiles, although the threat of the manned bomber had rapidly decreased and the ministers were advised that the threat would be negligible by 1965. The Cabinet's quandary about whether to acquire the Bomarcs was exacerbated by news that US tests of Bomarc B missiles were unpromising and the cost of buying more interceptors prohibitive. Nevertheless, the consensus in Cabinet was that the Canadian commitment "could not be cancelled in present circumstances without precipitating a crisis in Canada's relations with the U.S."[11]

This fear prompted the Cabinet to continue to advocate construction of the Bomarc missile sites, at a cost of $15 million. Ironically, the American Congress held a heated debate several weeks later about whether or not to drop the entire Bomarc program owing to its cost and unpromising trials. It was a measure of the Canadian government's commitment to the missiles that Diefenbaker decided to visit President Eisenhower.[12] In telegrams, the Canadian ambassador to Washington Arnold Heeney sought, too, to reassure officials that he was seeking the preservation of the Bomarc program: "We understand that USA officials are fully aware that approval by Congress of a curtailed Bomarc program aimed solely at providing for the installation of Bomarc 'B' in Canada would create difficulties for the Canadian government. It might be useful, however, if I were to reiterate this point at a suitable level in the State Department before the House-Senate conference convenes."[13] Evidently, high-level representatives of the Canadian government pressed the United States to continue the project.[14] The extent of the government's lobbying activities is portrayed by one American senator's comment that, "what with Boeing lobbyists and the Canadian Cabinet Ministers twisting our arms, we might have to spend more money on a thoroughly bad weapon."[15] Although the United States Congress finally reinstated some money for the Bomarc program, it reduced the missile strength originally contemplated for the two Canadian bases by seventy-five percent.[16] However, the decision as to whether or not to supply nuclear warheads for the missiles was still being debated in Cabinet two years later, during the Cuban missile crisis. In Peter Newman's words, "The fifty-six Bomarc missiles, guarding Canada's industrial heartland, pointed at the sky, supposedly alerted but in reality unarmed and totally useless."[17]

The Commitment to acquire CF-101 air defence interceptors

In the years between 1958 and 1961, the government also considered whether to replace 162 CF-100 air defence interceptors with 66 CF-101 Voodoo interceptors. Although the Voodoos carried bomber-destroying missiles armed with atomic warheads, they were also capable of carrying conventional weapons.[18] The USAF gave the nuclear-fitted Voodoos to the RCAF in July 1961 in exchange for a Canadian commitment to operate eleven Pinetree Radar stations. Although the ICBM was expected to become the principal intercontinental weapon by 1963, the military warned that the enemy would also use bombers to "augment the weight of attack for some time to come." Therefore, high-level military representatives thought that a "family" of complementary weapons would be required, consisting of interceptor aircraft and surface-to-air missiles for area defence. In such a configuration, they wanted the Voodoos to provide "positive armed identification" and "fire-power back-up."[19]

It was reported that the Americans tried, unsuccessfully, to write into the Voodoo transferral agreement a clause that they would be armed, like the American interceptors, with Genie nuclear warheads.[20] The Cabinet vacillated on this issue for months; then in June 1961, the prime minister announced the decision to arm the 66 F-101B aircraft with conventional weapons only.[21] Although the commitment was seldom mentioned again publicly,[22] the Cabinet confronted the dilemma again in August 1961. The minister of National Defence advised that nuclear warheads were necessary for the interceptors so that they could destroy the nuclear weapons on attacking bombers. Furthermore, special storage sites would be needed at each interceptor base in Canada for the nuclear MB1 missiles.[23] According to George Ignatieff, Diefenbaker's adviser on defence and nuclear issues and assistant deputy minister of External Affairs beginning in November 1960, this belated request for nuclear warheads for the Voodoos enraged the prime minister. At one point he accused Chief of the Air Staff Hugh Campbell of "time and time again" deliberately misleading him about the bomber threat, and then the interceptor threat, so that he felt faced with a *fait accompli*.[24]

The Cabinet's decision about whether to acquire nuclear or conventional warheads for the CF-101s was further complicated by an American request to stockpile MB1 nuclear missiles for their interceptors at Goose Bay, Labrador, and Harmon Field, Newfoundland.[25] The minister of National Defence suggested, and Cabinet agreed, that this matter be dealt with when questions relating to the nuclear weapons for Canadian Forces were settled. Diefenbaker, however, secretly decided to defer his consent to the American request as a lever to persuade the United States to grant joint control of use. When Diefenbaker explained his plan to Arnold Heeney, Canada's ambassador to the United States, Heeney was unable to conceal his dismay, allowing that "this was an exceedingly difficult matter altogether." Diefenbaker was undeterred. He agreed with Heeney that early conclusion of an agreement with the United States would be desirable, but reminded him that there was a great deal of sentiment in Canada against nuclear weapons. As he explained in a rare moment of disclosure, ultimately Canadian Forces would need arming with nuclear weapons. Nevertheless, he preferred to defer his approval on the American MB1 storage issue until there were satisfactory arrangements for joint control over the use of Canadian nuclear weapons systems.[26] In the end, the issue of nuclear warheads for the Canadian and American interceptors was left undecided until the last few months of the government's tenure.

The commitment to acquire nuclear depth charges and torpedoes

Another rarely mentioned commitment was the government's decision to acquire nuclear depth charges and torpedoes for Canadian and American maritime forces in the North Atlantic.[27] The intention was to drop them from aircraft or launch them in anti-submarine missiles from surface vessels. The anti-submarine missiles were also meant to destroy nuclear-missile-carrying submarines and to prevent the offshore bombing of Canada and the United States. Indeed, their small size and short range rendered them useful only for an anti-submarine role. The issue of supplying these warheads to Canadian maritime forces raised parallel questions. Of concern to the Cabinet was the plan to store them for American use at the American-leased naval base at Argentia, Newfoundland. Rarely, though, did the public hear about this arrangement.

The commitment to obtain CF-104s

Once the allies agreed to develop NATO's ability to defend its territories and seas as far forward as possible, counting on the use of nuclear weapons, the Supreme Allied Commander Europe (SACEUR), General Lauris Norstad, recommended that Canada convert four of its squadrons to one "strike" and three "attack fighter" bomber squadrons. At that time, both strike and attack fighter-bomber squadrons were capable of delivering nuclear weapons. It was then up to the Canadian government to decide whether to fulfill the request. In its highly-classified reply, the government stated that the recommendation was not entirely acceptable to Canada, but that discussions with SHAPE on the future of the RCAF No. 1 Canadian Air Division would take place once the present equipment became obsolete. General Norstad had to accept this reply. Again in 1958, SHAPE's planning guidance recommended that Canada provide, by

1961, one nuclear-capable strike and one nuclear-capable attack fighter-bomber squadron of twenty-five aircraft each, to be increased to one strike and three attack fighter-bomber squadrons by 1962. The government replied that the decision was under study. Finally, in May 1959, Norstad proposed that Canada replace its F-86 Sabre squadrons with not one but eight strike-reconnaissance squadrons consisting of eighteen aircraft per squadron. The Canadian government accepted this recommendation and decided to prepare for the recommended strike-reconnaissance role by replacing the F-86 squadrons with the Lockheed F-104G aircraft. The F-104s were low-level jet bombers that could carry a one-megaton nuclear bomb and had a radius of action of some 500 miles. The RCAF calculated that Canada would then be able to contribute about twenty percent of NATO's tactical nuclear force in Europe.

General Pearkes publicly announced the decision to acquire the F-104s (renamed the CF-104s or "Starfighters") in July 1959, although the aircraft were not expected to come into service for two years. In his speech, Pearkes explained that the NATO military authorities had asked Canada to fulfill a nuclear strike-reconnaissance role, and that the views of General Norstad about the roles and equipment needed by the Canadian Air Division were important considerations. In Pearkes's view, "The decision now taken is in accordance with the recommendations of the supreme allied commander and re-emphasizes the fact that Canada, as a member of the NATO alliance, intends to continue to meet its agreed commitments as we have in the past, despite the heavy costs involved."[28] In a personal letter to General Norstad, Diefenbaker indicated that the general's briefing to Cabinet had been "most helpful and of distinct benefit in making the decision."[29]

NATO welcomed the Canadian government's decision to acquire the CF-104s. Norstad replied to Diefenbaker shortly afterward, describing the "stimulating effect" in NATO circles that had followed the decision to re-equip:

Militarily, of course, the effect is very significant for it means that the Air Division, which enjoys a record second to none, will continue to play a leading part in deterring aggression and in defending the nations of the Alliance. More important, perhaps, the decision is a reaffirmation of solid support and backing of the principles of the NATO Treaty. Traditionally, Canada has demonstrated such support in several distinct ways; by the high calibre of her personnel, by the quality of her equipment, by the generosity of her aid to other nations, and by the leadership displayed in higher Councils. I feel that once again by the way in which this decision was communicated to the Canadian Parliament and the NATO Council, accompanied as it was by a re-statement of Canadian policy, the cause of NATO has been tangibly strengthened and, by the same token, the prestige of Canada has been greatly enhanced. Coming as it did at a rather critical time, this fillip was all the more gratifying. It has had a noticeable effect on Council members and, I am certain, on the nations which they represent.[30]

In the end, however, this "fillip" did not have as stimulating an effect on Council members as Norstad had hoped. Although at the time Norstad wrote the letter no indication had emerged as to a lack of Canadian interest in obtaining nuclear warheads for the CF-104s, when the CF-104s came into operational service two years later they were deemed ineffective. Moreover, the decision as to whether to supply the Air Division with nuclear weapons had still not been made.

The commitment to acquire Lacrosse and Honest John missiles

The decision-making process surrounding the acquisition of nuclear-tipped surface-to-surface missiles for the Canadian Forces in Europe was similar to the process for the CF-104s. Cabinet simply had to approve two costly types of missile systems instead of one. In 1957, SACEUR recommended that Canada acquire the Honest John rocket in order to support the infantry brigade group in Europe. The Honest John surface-to-surface missile was a land-force atomic support requirement, with a range of approximately twenty miles and a nuclear warhead with a comparatively low yield. The government did not accept SACEUR's recommendation, claiming it was considering providing a ground-to-ground missile suitable for the support of the land forces when such a missile became available. Norstad could only concur with this course. A year later, SHAPE recommended that, by 1958, Canada include an Honest John unit of two launchers in support of the Infantry Brigade Group and, by 1961, a Little John unit of two launchers. The government again rejected the recommendation, claiming that it was considering a ground-to-ground missile suitable for the support of the land forces. On 1 October 1958, on the recommendation of the minister of National Defence, Cabinet authorized the procurement of one battery of Lacrosse II missiles.

By 1960, however, it was apparent that the complexity of the Lacrosse system prevented its use in forward areas.[31] The Cabinet Defence Committee therefore decided to approve, at an estimated cost of $2.8 million, the procurement of six Honest John launchers instead of the Lacrosse missile system.[32] They chose the Honest John system because it was already in service – or about to be introduced

– with other NATO forces at the brigade and divisional level. Most importantly, Canada's reply to NATO's 1960 Annual Review stated that the new Honest John launchers were capable of carrying either a conventional or nuclear warhead.[32]

The government intended to deploy the Honest John missiles early in 1962. Unit training on the Honest John battery took place, and, in Canada's reply to NATO's 1961 Annual Review, reference was made to the planned deployment of the missiles to Europe. As had happened with the CF-104s, however, the missiles did not come into operational service because of the debate in Cabinet about whether or not to acquire nuclear warheads for the launchers.

Firm commitments to acquire nuclear weapons

By 1960 it appeared that the government was firmly committed to acquiring nuclear weapons in order to fulfill its NATO commitments. The presence of the prime minister and his top military advisers at the NATO summit in December 1957, authorizing the establishment of nuclear stockpiles for the use of NATO forces in Europe; the prime minister's announcements of 23 September 1958 and 20 February 1959, referring to the acquisition of Bomarc missiles; the announcements regarding the CF-101 and CF-104 interceptors for Canada and Europe; and the statements about the intended acquisition of the Lacrosse and Honest John nuclear missiles all indicated that the Diefenbaker government was firmly committed to the acquisition of nuclear weapons for Canadian Forces in both Europe and Canada.[34] General Pearkes's comments to the House of Commons in July 1959 reflected this decision:

Of course it is Government policy that Canadian troops should be armed as efficiently and as effectively as the troops with which they are cooperating ... On February 20 of this year ... the Prime Minister announced that as far as our troops in Europe were concerned and as far as our Air Force and troops in Canada were concerned we were entering into a series of negotiations with the United States in order to arrange the details of the storing of and equipping [of] our forces with nuclear weapons as and when they would be available and as and when we would have the weapons to launch them. By the time we get the Bomarc and by the time we get the Lacrosse over to the Brigade and by the time we get the new aircraft for the Air Division I am confident that these programs will be completed.[35]

It is apparent that the Diefenbaker government announced several defence commitments in this period that it did not fulfill. It is evident, too, that several decision-makers in the Department of External Affairs exerted considerable influence in order to reverse avowed government policy.

THE MIDDLE YEARS: WANING COMMITMENT (JUNE 1959 TO DECEMBER 1962)

Diefenbaker appointed his good friend Howard Green as secretary of state for External Affairs in June 1959.[36] Within a few weeks, Green had begun a disarmament campaign in External Affairs, focusing on the need to rid Canada and the world of nuclear weapons. Once it became clear that the minister was "attracted by the anti-nuclear viewpoint," Norman Robertson, under-secretary of state for External Affairs, gave him his support. Although Robertson already harboured doubts about the government's direction, under Green's predecessor he had felt he should be careful about voicing his concerns so as not to put disconcerting pressure on his minister. He also believed that it was sometimes necessary to be pragmatic and wait for the current of opinion to run its course. Once Green assumed control of the department, however, External's most senior mandarin was reassured that his dissenting beliefs could be more openly expressed.[37] For other high-level decision-makers in the inner and outer core of decision-making, such as the ambassador to the United States Arnold Heeney and the principal secretary to the Cabinet Robert Bryce, the strength of the Green/Robertson coalition was alarming. As Heeney wrote in his diary: "H.G. [Howard Green] himself, though he continues to have the loyalty, even affection, of those who work with him, and who supports the dept. stoutly, is sadly miscast in his office. Nevertheless, his own attitudes and prejudices, in a curious way, combine with NAR's [Norman Robertson's] cosmic anxieties, particularly w.[with] our defence relationships external and domestic to produce a negative force of great importance."[38] Despite Heeney's assessment, Green inspired keen admiration among civil servants such as Robinson and Ignatieff, who held great affection for "the old guy" and for his guts and determination.[39] Howard Green and Norman Robertson were largely responsible, then, for heading External Affairs in the direction of disarmament, toward more support for the United Nations, and, ultimately, onto a collision course with General Pearkes, Douglas Harkness, and the Department of National Defence.

Joint control

The first public sign of waning support for nuclear weapons among Cabinet ministers emerged in 1960. On 4 July the prime minister stated that there must be "Canadian control" over the nuclear weapons. Ten days later he amended this to "joint control" by Canada and the United States.[40] By November 1960, Diefenbaker was referring to

Canada's sovereign right to exert joint control over the nuclear weapons "when and if" such weapons were required:

We have taken the stand that no decision will be required while progress towards disarmament continues. To do otherwise would be inconsistent. When and if such weapons are required we will have to take the responsibility ... We have made it equally clear that we shall not in any event consider nuclear weapons until as a sovereign nation, we have quality of control – a joint control. In other words, this problem is not one requiring immediate decision. The course to be taken will be determined in light of what happens in connection with disarmament and in the light of events as they transpire and develop in the months ahead.[41]

Although "when and if" frequently appeared in public statements by Diefenbaker and others after July 1960, behind the scenes Diefenbaker still seemed to accept the necessity of ultimately arming the Canadian Forces with nuclear weapons. As he disclosed to Heeney at a meeting in November 1960, the problem was that there was a great deal of sentiment in Canada against nuclear weapons; in addition, the Liberal party was opposed, as was the CCF [Co-operative Commonwealth Federation]. Diefenbaker himself thought this a "totally unrealistic attitude," and believed the Canadian Forces would "ultimately" have to be armed with nuclear weapons once satisfactory arrangements for joint control of use were in place. It was at this November meeting that Diefenbaker told Heeney of his plan to use Canadian consent to the storage of American MB1 nuclear weapons as leverage in persuading the United States to grant joint control of use. Overall, Heeney gained the impression that Diefenbaker recognized the necessity of acquiring nuclear warheads, but that he planned to strike a hard bargain to obtain the desired joint control.[42] However, Green, after talking with Heeney and Robertson immediately after this meeting, came to a different conclusion. He surmised that Diefenbaker's reference to joint control and the use of the MB1 "as a sanction for insistence thereon" was based on the prime minister's underlying assumption that "the US would never meet our requirement for participation in the decision to use the weapon." In Green's opinion, Diefenbaker knew the United States would "never give us satisfaction on joint control."[43]

The Irish resolution

A few weeks after these discussions, Cabinet met to discuss the implications of "the Irish resolution." The declassified records of this meeting in December 1960 reveal that the ministers had already recognized the quandary concerning their NATO commitments. Briefly, the government's stand on the disarmament resolutions it had sponsored at the UN, particularly the Irish resolution, greatly concerned the Cabinet. The Irish resolution was calling for temporary and voluntary restraints on the spread of nuclear weapons. Howard Green explained to Cabinet that no country would vote against the Irish resolution; all would either vote in favour or abstain. To date, he noted, the United States had persuaded the United Kingdom and some other NATO countries to abstain. Although the United States was not pressing Canada to abstain, Green believed that a Canadian vote in favour of the Irish resolution would split the country from its NATO partners. Green was in an impossible position. As a co-sponsor of the resolution on disarmament, he thought Canada should not abstain. On the other hand, the secretary-general of NATO was attacking the resolution in the NATO Council because NATO was proposing that a unified deterrent be put in place under NATO's control. In effect, Green worried that he might have to speak out against the secretary-general in the NATO Council.[44]

In their discussion, "some ministers" pointed out that to vote in favour of the Irish resolution would make it impossible to hold discussions with the United States on the acquisition of nuclear weapons for all of Canada's proposed systems.[45] Furthermore, after supporting NATO's position in 1957 on the stockpiling of nuclear weapons in Europe and the placing of intermediate-range ballistic missiles at SACEUR's disposal, the government "could hardly turn around now" and vote for the Irish resolution. The concern was that the public would feel that the government had washed its hands of nuclear weapons, and the next step would be strong criticism of the government for spending so much money on carriers for these weapons. Indeed, some ministers feared "the government would be acutely embarrassed by having very expensive but virtually useless equipment on its hands."[46]

During the discussion, Diefenbaker argued that the government was bound by the agreement reached at the meeting of the NATO Heads of Government. He declared that the Canadian delegation to the upcoming NATO meeting should recognize that the government was "morally bound" by the 1957 decision, and discussions should continue with the United States on acquiring the weapons and warheads. As for disarmament, Diefenbaker stated that he personally did not have much hope for success in this field. While disarmament was a laudable purpose, he said, he was afraid the Conservative party would be dubbed "the disarmament party."[47] Diefenbaker planned to

reconcile Green's disarmament stance at the UN with his own stand
on nuclear weapons by, first, insisting that Cabinet members refrain
from publicly airing their conflicting opinions. In future, he declared,
only he would make statements on policy regarding nuclear weapons, and these statements would be made as far as possible in Parliament. If other ministers had to refer to Canadian policy, he added,
they should quote the prime minister or use his wording. As for the
Irish resolution, Diefenbaker asked that it be modified to clarify that,
if there was no progress in the immediate future on preventing the
spread of nuclear weapons, Canada would review its position. He
noted, however, that this did not mean that Canada would slow down
the procurement of carriers for nuclear weapons; nor did it rule out
discussions, when the time was ripe, on the acquisition of warheads.
Finally, he warned his colleagues, without explaining exactly what he
meant, that the government would only acquire nuclear weapons if
the United States accepted the principle of "joint control."[48]

In accordance with the prime minister's wishes, the Cabinet
instructed Green to vote in favour of the Irish resolution but with a
caveat. Green was to add the following clause to the resolution: "If,
however, there is no significant progress in this field in the immediate
future we will reconsider our position on the temporary measures
which are proposed in this resolution."[49] In effect, Diefenbaker had
reconciled the Cabinet's conflicting points of view by suggesting
policies based on delay and prevarication.

First meeting with Kennedy and growing confusion about joint control

John Kennedy's political victory in the United States initially dis-
mayed the prime minister for he greatly valued his friendship with
Dwight Eisenhower and had doubts about his brash successor. Nevertheless, Diefenbaker's first meeting with Kennedy in February 1961
was singularly successful. The prime minister proudly reported to
Cabinet that he had insisted negotiations continue regarding "joint
custody and control and joint authority over use" of the nuclear
weapons to be stored at Harmon Field and Goose Bay. As for the
American submarine base at Argentia, he claimed he had told
Kennedy that Canada would require joint custody but that NATO
would determine the actual use of the nuclear weapons. Diefenbaker
also reported that he had indicated to Kennedy that, as long as
serious disarmament negotiations continued, Canada did not propose to determine whether to accept nuclear weapons for the Bomarc
bases or the Canadian interceptors. In the event that such weapons
were accepted by Canada, however, "joint custody and joint control"
would be required. According to Diefenbaker, the president had

raised no objections, and only asked whether the same sort of "two-key" arrangement as the United Kingdom had would be satisfactory. Diefenbaker said it would, and both leaders concluded that negotiations for the necessary agreements could now continue based on a "package deal."[50]

Satisfied with Diefenbaker's report of the arrangements, Cabinet let the matter lie for more than six months. By October 1961, however, Diefenbaker had again made several contradictory statements regarding the spread of nuclear weapons and the issue of joint control. He told journalists and petitioners against nuclear weapons that his government had accepted the "Kennedy declaration" that there should be no extension of the "nuclear club." In terms of the declaration's implications, however, he stated that "the Bomarc is in the position it has always been in – also the F-104 – that they are equipped so that if nuclear warheads become necessary to be used in the event of war they would have the launch capacity."[51] In response to questions about how Canada would obtain nuclear warheads for these systems in the event of an attack, Diefenbaker seemed either not to know or to be deliberately disingenuous. As he put it, "I am not telling you something that is a matter of security. I am simply telling you that if there is no extension of the nuclear club then all other answers are available."[52]

Was Diefenbaker opposed to the acquisition of nuclear weapons in 1961? His comments at the time indicate that he was undecided and confused. He seemed to believe that Canada could abide by the principle of not spreading nuclear weapons if it acquired defensive, rather than offensive, weapons and if the warheads were neither manufactured nor tested in Canada. He was also confused about whether Canada's acquisition of nuclear weapons would extend the nuclear club, inasmuch as Canada was a member of NATO, which already had nuclear weapons.[53] Nevertheless, during the tense weeks of the Berlin crisis in August 1961, the prime minister seemed to decide in favour of nuclear warheads:

There are some in Canada who advocate we should withdraw from NATO in the event that nuclear weapons are made available for the possession and control of NATO. I believe that to follow that course would be dangerous to the survival of the forces of NATO that are there now, should war begin. And it would be dangerous for the survival of freedom itself ... Would you in 1961, faced by the overwhelming power of Soviet might in East Germany close to West Berlin with large divisions fully armed, would you place in the hands of those who guard the portals of freedom nothing but bows and arrows? They would stand against overwhelming power – it is as simple as that.[54]

Diefenbaker was not alone during this time, either in his insistence on joint control or in his confusion about what was meant by the spread of nuclear weapons and the expansion of the nuclear club. Confusion was also apparent in Cabinet. At a Cabinet meeting in August 1961, some ministers expressed concern that "there was no move underway in NATO" to work out "a system of joint control" over nuclear weapons. At the time, control over the American nuclear weapons deployed in the United States, Turkey, Greece, and Italy was solely in the hands of the United States. And the United Kingdom controlled its own, much smaller arsenal. As the allies preferred this system, some ministers in Ottawa feared that Canada's insistence on some form of joint control would fly in the face of the arrangements made for the nuclear weapons stored in Turkey, Greece, and Italy. They wondered, furthermore, whether the question of German acquisition of nuclear weapons would be brought to the forefront if Canada acquired nuclear weapons under joint control. In these ministers' opinion, the United States did not want Germany to have nuclear weapons because the Soviet Union, which "had legitimate reason to fear Germany, might then strike the first blow." Consequently, they were concerned that Canada would break "more than new ground" if the principle of joint control were negotiated.[55]

During Cabinet debates, ministers seemed to split into three different sets of opinion concerning nuclear commitments. Some argued that Canada was obliged to contribute to the defence of the American deterrent, not only because of Canada's location but because of Canada's involvement in NORAD and in the other collective defence arrangements of the Western Alliance. In their view, "the defence of Canada and the United States was inseparable and it was not acceptable that the United States' forces under CINCNORAD [the Commander-in-Chief NORAD] were armed with nuclear weapons and the Canadian forces were not."[58] Other ministers referred to the crisis over Berlin and similar tense international situations that could only be exacerbated if Canada acquired nuclear weapons. In the middle, either unwilling or unable to come to a decision, was the prime minister. If Canada acquired nuclear weapons, he argued, it was essential that it be only on the basis of "joint control," amounting to a power of veto over their use. According to Diefenbaker, even the nuclear weapons to be stored by the United States on American-leased bases in Canada would have to be under joint control, or this would "be an abandonment of responsibility on the part of Canada."[57]

Although Diefenbaker and others often referred to the principle of joint control, no one seemed to understand what it really meant. Ministers fretted over NATO's lack of movement in working out "a new system of joint control" and the implications of Canadian joint control for a possible German acquisition of nuclear weapons. Dave McIntosh, a newspaper reporter who followed the defence debate and had a firm grasp of defence concepts, put forward the most plausible explanation: "What it boils down to is this: the United States president could authorize use of nuclear weapons in Canada but Canada would determine whether these weapons would be fired. Canada by itself could not order the firing of a nuclear warhead but it could veto any such firing approved by the US. This is known as the 'two-key' system and has applied for years to American nuclear warheads stored in Britain."[58]

At the behest of Green and Robertson, the Cabinet inquired in 1961 and 1962 into the possibility of storing nuclear warheads in the United States, which would then be flown to Canada and installed in launching systems in the event of an emergency. The chairman of the Canadian Chiefs of Staff, Air Marshal Frank Miller, noted the suggestion "with some concern." "This is not regarded as an acceptable military solution," he warned.[59] However, the idea was not abandoned. Cabinet members such as Diefenbaker and Green continued to refer to the possibility of storing "missing parts" for the nuclear weapons in the United States. It was not until after the Cuban missile crisis in December 1962 that Howard Green and Douglas Harkness were informed by Dean Rusk and Robert McNamara that the missing part proposal was considered impracticable by the United States government.[60]

Throughout this confusing period – October 1961 to October 1962 – ministers were aware that the issue could have serious repercussions in Parliament. Nevertheless, the expected admonitions and questions failed to materialize. When Minister of National Defence George Pearkes retired, Diefenbaker replaced him in November 1961 with Douglas Harkness. Harkness's chief of staff warned that an article by Professor Peyton Lyon criticizing Diefenbaker for clouding the nuclear issue could have serious repercussions for him in Parliament, but nothing ever materialized.[61] Indeed, nuclear weapons were not a major issue during the June 1962 election campaign, although by that time Diefenbaker seemed to support their acquisition. He also seemed to oppose expansion of the family of nuclear powers, and to advocate a distinctly different version of joint control. In truth, by baffling everyone, he was able to avoid the issue.

It was around the spring of 1962 that Diefenbaker's closest advisers began to worry about the prime minister's preoccupation with burgeoning anti-American sentiment in Canada and his own growing antipathy toward President Kennedy. Before Eisenhower stepped down, Diefenbaker had already begun to refer to the "avalanche of anti-Americanism" in Canada. According to Heeney's diary in March 1962:

The first major evidence of this change was his expression of concern to me late last summer [1961] ... as to the alarming [rise] in anti-US sentiment among Canadians. At that time he dissociated himself from this sentiment and referred to it as a grave problem with which he had to deal. On a number of occasions since – in person and over the telephone – he has given me the impression increasingly that he has little confidence in the USA Admin., that he resents their failure to take effective account of Canadian interest – and that his feeling for the President has changed to one of, yes, resentment, as well as lack of confidence ...[62]

The development that concerned Diefenbaker's advisers most, however, was the prime minister's reference to a paper Kennedy inadvertently left behind after their April 1962 meeting. The memo, entitled "What We Want from Ottawa Trip," contained "instructions" from Walt Rostow to the president about American objectives regarding the Organization of American States (OAS) and foreign aid.[65] Although the objectives it recommended were relatively innocuous, the memo was punctuated by references to "pushing" Canada. Its language incensed the prime minister, and he decided to hold onto it. But it was Diefenbaker's demeanour concerning this incident that so alarmed Arnold Heeney and Basil Robinson. The prime minister was no longer concerned about the rising anti-American sentiment in Canada – he embodied it.

The Cuban missile crisis

On 22 October 1962, the former American ambassador to Canada, Livingston Merchant, arrived with an important message for the prime minister. At a meeting with Diefenbaker, Green, and Harkness, unaccompanied by attending officials, Merchant spoke about the intelligence situation in Cuba and the action contemplated by the American government. A couple of hours later, Kennedy addressed the American people about the gravity of the threat from Cuban missile installations. He spoke of a peril which "menaced most of the major cities in the Western Hemisphere, ranging as far north as Hudson's Bay, Canada and as far south as Lima, Peru."[64] Emphasizing that Soviet Foreign Minister Andrei Gromyko had lied to him about Soviet assistance to Cuba, he announced a strict quarantine of all offensive military equipment under shipment to Cuba. There was no doubt that the American armed forces were preparing for any eventuality.

An hour after the television address, the chairman of the Chiefs of Staff asked the minister of National Defence for permission to put the Canadian Forces on a state of alert equivalent to that of the American forces. Harkness agreed to the Air Chief Marshal's request, but said he needed to consult with the prime minister first. Diefenbaker, who balked at alerting the Canadian Forces, suggested that such a move required the entire Cabinet's approval. That evening, in an address to a jittery Parliament, Diefenbaker appealed for calm. He cast doubt on the deductions arrived at from American aerial photographs of the missile sites in Cuba, and recommended that a group of non-aligned nations from the UN Disarmament Committee make an on-site inspection in Cuba to ascertain the facts. His public demeanour throughly downplayed the sense of crisis.[65]

At the emergency Cabinet meeting the following day, Harkness reiterated President Kennedy's request that the Canadian Forces go on alert. Diefenbaker and Green urged that Canada reject the request. Unable to come to any decision after much divisive argument, the Cabinet met again, on 24 October. After yet another inconclusive meeting, Diefenbaker finally consented to Harkness's request to alert the forces. Unbeknownst to the prime minister, however, Harkness had secretly alerted the Canadian Forces forty hours previously. Within an hour of President Kennedy's television speech, the defence minister had gone ahead and put the Canadian Forces on alert without Diefenbaker's approval.[66] Whether Harkness was right to take matters into his own hands remains a matter of debate, but journalists criticized the government severely for purchasing $700 million worth of nuclear weapons that turned out to be utterly ineffective as a deterrent because they lacked the necessary warheads.[67]

Like many crises, the Cuban missile crisis delineated opinion, erased ambiguity, and hardened soft-liners. Some sections of the Cabinet Conclusions continue to be excised, and the secretary to the Cabinet did not keep a record of all the discussions. But Harkness wrote a detailed diary describing the Cabinet debate shortly afterward.[68] Both the existing Cabinet records and Harkness's account corroborate that there were at least two opposing opinions in Cabinet.

One group of ministers, led by Harkness and supported by Associate Defence Minister Pierre Sevigny and Minister of Veterans Affairs George Hees, argued that, as partners in defence, Canada should put the Canadian component of NORAD in readiness. They regarded the situation as "perilous," believed that "Canadians would not panic" and thought "Russia would, in any case, not expect Canada to do anything else." Furthermore, they said, "not to move in pace with the American forces would embarrass Canadian troops."[69]

Another coalition, led by Diefenbaker and supported by Green, argued that Canada should not appear to be "stampeded," as this would only intensify the excitement and increase the pressures. In their view, "Canada was not automatically embroiled any time the United States was. Practically, however, Canada was." They argued that there were great dangers in rushing in at this time. "Quick action brought quick judgement," they warned, and "it would be dangerous to have the present moves interpreted as offensive rather than defensive action." Furthermore, in their view, there were "domestic political overtones in the US decision," and Canada should appear to be behaving normally and deliberately.[70]

The only issue the entire Cabinet could agree on was the need to consult with the other NATO allies. Yet apparently the British, French, and West German governments had pledged their full support to the United States when consulted by Dean Acheson, and the issue was discussed at the NATO Council meeting.[71] It was only after the news that the US Strategic Air Command and some American naval forces had gone to the Defcon 2 alert level, which meant "immediate enemy attack expected," that Diefenbaker ruefully told Harkness, "Oh, well, all right, go ahead … go ahead."[72]

As Diefenbaker admitted, "The Cuban crisis brought a new urgency to the defence debate in Cabinet, in Parliament, and in the country as a whole."[73] Military personnel were angry that, when alert status was ordered, the newly acquired nuclear weapon systems lacked warheads. "No one wants a nuclear war," wrote one brigadier-general to Diefenbaker, "but the best way to ensure peace under present conditions is to be strong. If proof is necessary the Cuban situation is an example."[74] Others were frightened that the world had narrowly avoided nuclear war, yet the Canadian government was still intent on acquiring nuclear warheads for its weapons systems. And some interpreted the Cuban crisis as evidence that, in an emergency, nuclear warheads could not be acquired quickly, if only because a hasty call by Canada for nuclear arms could rapidly unhinge a tense world situation.[75] In the wake of the Cuban missile crisis, the entire issue of nuclear warheads for the Canadian Forces in Canada and Europe suddenly assumed a very high profile.[76]

Diefenbaker reacted to the complaints and the uproar by deciding to proceed with secret negotiations for "joint control" over the nuclear warheads. He insisted, however, that he was only willing to continue the discussions on the understanding that if there were any leak concerning the negotiations, they would stop forthwith. As for joint control, the prime minister still believed it was possible; indeed, only if it were proven that joint control with the United States was impossible would he be willing to consider other alternatives. Also during this Cabinet meeting, ministers began to reconsider whether or not to hold warheads for the Bomarcs and the CF-101s in the United States, to be brought into Canada on request by the Canadian government if an emergency occurred or NORAD was alerted.[77] Over the next few weeks, Diefenbaker began to refer to this alternative as "the missing part approach." To his mind, the missing part approach called for an agreement with the United States whereby nuclear warheads would not be physically located on Canadian soil in peacetime, but could be rapidly acquired from the United States should war break out. According to Diefenbaker, the missing part approach would be rec-oncilable with all the stated policies of his government, and prove a satisfactory solution to the problem of North American defence.[78]

Another option the Cabinet considered in the wake of the Cuban crisis was to negotiate the storage of weapons for the Canadian Forces in Europe on bases under NATO command.[79] On 30 October the Cabinet agreed to pursue negotiations with the United States, under which nuclear warheads would be held in storage for, and made available to, Canadian Forces in Europe under NATO command for use in CF-104 aircraft and Honest John rockets. Harkness and Green agreed to the prime minister's request that they discuss with the American *chargé d'affaires* the possible implementation of this alternative as well as the missing parts approach.[80]

American reaction was strongly disapproving. According to one high-level source, the frustration of American authorities with Canada became acute in December 1962, once US Secretary of Defence Robert McNamara and Secretary of State Dean Rusk met Harkness and Green. McNamara and Rusk decided there would be no further satisfactory progress toward Canadian acceptance of nuclear weapons.[81] Whereas the American authorities were entirely dissatisfied with Canada's delays in fulfilling its NATO and NORAD commitments, Green's report to Parliament about the NATO meeting was reassuring: "We were very pleased to have it pointed out, not by ourselves but by the military authorities and the United States, that Canada had lived up to her commitments and, for example, that our brigade was the only combat-ready unit in the NATO forces other than those of the United States. In spite of rumours which I have seen in the press at home since my return, there was not a word of criticism of Canada's military efforts in NATO."[82] Apparently, the European allies refrained from criticizing Canada's overall military effort because Canada was the only member of the Alliance, besides the United States, which had met all its conventional military com-mitments to Europe. With little media attention, the government had strengthened its conventional forces in Europe the year before at the time of the Berlin crisis.[83] Although American defence officials were acutely frustrated by the endless delays in negotiations to obtain nuclear warheads, the European allies were satisfied with Canada's conventional contribution. Green felt justified in asserting that "accusations that we are the bad boys of NATO or have let the side down are completely false ... I have seldom encountered as much friendliness toward Canada as at this meeting."[84]

THE FINAL YEAR: LACK OF COMMITMENT (JANUARY 1963 TO APRIL 1963)

A succession of events in January 1963 led to the fall of the government. The entire issue of nuclear commitments came to the fore again when about-to-retire SACEUR General Norstad visited Ottawa on 3 January. Speaking frankly, he told journalists that until the Canadian government acquired nuclear warheads for the Canadian air division and army brigade group in Germany, it would not fulfill its NATO commitments. Based on arrangements made at the NATO meeting in 1957, he explained, a stockpile of atomic weapons had been developed in Europe to meet the requirements of NATO forces. Under the atomic energy law of the United States, however, the president retained authority, custody, and control over these warheads and could only make them available to a NATO ally that had signed a bilateral agreement. Such agreements had been reached between the United States and essentially all NATO countries, and did not imply any expansion of "the nuclear club." Until a bilateral agreement with the United States was signed, Norstad stated, Canadian soldiers and airforce crews could not be given information enabling them to train for up to six months in the use of the nuclear weapons. Norstad concluded his remarks by pointing out that Canada was one of two, perhaps three, countries that had done its best in meeting its commitments, but "it's an obligation on every country in the alliance to contribute what they can contribute, and I think this is an obligation which the Canadians have accepted."[85]

Lester Pearson took the opportunity to deplore again a situation whereby, having accepted the NATO commitments, the government was neither fulfilling nor changing them. Government representatives continued to defend the "joint control" and "missing part" approaches, and Green continued to maintain that Canada was living up to its NATO commitments. Then on 9 January, Pearson announced a *volte-face* in Liberal nuclear policy. The government, he stated, had an obligation to fulfill its commitments to acquire nuclear warheads for all the weapons systems it had acquired at great expense. Moreover, he promised that, as prime minister, he would first fulfill those commitments and afterward negotiate for disarmament of the weapons systems.[86]

Pearson's new resolve to support the acquisition of nuclear warheads profoundly disturbed Diefenbaker, and he elected to make a keynote policy address to the House of Commons on 25 January 1963. In his speech, Diefenbaker claimed he had realized at a recent meeting in Nassau with President Kennedy and Prime Minister Macmillan that new concepts were planned for the NATO forces: "I was in Nassau. I formed certain ideas. I read the communiqué that was issued there and I came to certain conclusions based on that communiqué ... that nuclear war is indivisible, that there should be no further development of new nuclear power anywhere in the world, that nuclear weapons as a universal deterrent are a dangerous solution." Diefenbaker also declared that the current state of disarmament negotiations meant that the world was entering a new era in which NATO would rely on a multilateral nuclear force. Consequently, "all our planning to date, or most of it, will be of little or no consequence." Specifically referring to the Bomarc missile, he hinted that it would be scrapped. "Every now and then some new white hope of rocketry goes into the scrap pile ... [W]ho would have guessed three years ago that today the fear would be an attack with intercontinental missiles?" As for the nuclear weapons systems in Europe, he pointed out that, "all the nations made mistakes, $3 billions worth of mistakes and more, up to 1960, but the fact that a mistake may have been made, or may not have been made, should not be a basis for the continuation of a policy just because to admit it would be wrong."[87]

To everyone's surprise, Harkness issued a press release shortly after the speech to clarify Diefenbaker's remarks. He explained that, although the speech contained "nearly all the varying theories and ideas which have been put forward on nuclear arms," the prime minister's remarks indicated that he did intend to equip certain weapon systems with nuclear arms. After vigorous argument in Cabinet, however, Harkness realized that Diefenbaker would not support his stand and submitted his resignation.[88]

The resignation of the minister of National Defence was accompanied by yet another embarrassing incident. The US State Department issued a press release on 30 January 1963 directly contradicting Diefenbaker's speech. The release stated that the agreement at Nassau raised "no question of the appropriateness of nuclear weapons for Canadian Forces in fulfilling their NATO or NORAD obligations." It also contradicted Diefenbaker's assertion that Canada could secure nuclear weapons if circumstances made such a course necessary: "The Canadian government has not yet proposed any arrangement sufficiently practical to contribute effectively to North American defense." Finally, the release affirmed that the bomber threat would remain a significant element in the Soviet strike force for the rest of the decade. Canada needed, therefore, to fulfill its obligations to acquire nuclear weapons for North American defence.[89]

The press release made glaringly apparent the displeasure of American authorities over Canada's defence policy. Although it was rumoured that Kennedy's national security adviser, McGeorge Bundy, had released it against the president's better judgement, Diefenbaker later attributed the release to Kennedy's machinations to remove him from power. According to the prime minister, "President Kennedy concluded that he could fix things so that he would no longer be obliged to deal with me or my government."[90] Preoccupied with fears about American intentions, Diefenbaker refused to acknowledge the mounting frustration of the media and the population with his equivocating stand on Canada's nuclear commitments. There followed a debate in Parliament in which the Liberals and the CCF both attacked the government for failing to issue a clear statement respecting Canada's defence policy. Finally, on 5 February 1963, a motion of non-confidence in the government was carried, Parliament was dissolved, and an election was called for 8 April 1963.

The election campaign

During the election campaign, Diefenbaker crusaded against the acquisition of nuclear warheads. In speeches across the country, he referred continuously to the Liberal party's intention to make Canada a "nuclear dump,"[91] and to an old press release concerning the conventional warhead on the Bomarc A as proof that his government had definitely not committed Canada to a nuclear role.[92] Once he received Robert McNamara's testimony to the United States House of Representatives regarding the Bomarc sites, Diefenbaker's resolve to oppose nuclear weapons was even more apparent. In his testimony, McNamara admitted the Bomarc sites were "soft" and offered practically no protection from Soviet bomber attack. He acknowledged that, at the very least, they would "cause the Soviets to target missiles against them and thereby increase their missile requirement or draw missiles onto these Bomarc targets that would otherwise be available for other targets."[93] Diefenbaker reacted to McNamara's testimony with: "Happy days are here again. McNamara's really put the skids under Pearson. This is a knockout blow." He continued: "The Liberal party would have us put nuclear warheads on something that's hardly worth scrapping. What's it for? To attract the fire of intercontinental missiles. Never, never, never,

never has there been a revelation equal to this. The whole bottom fell out of the Liberal program today. The Liberal policy is to make Canada a decoy for intercontinental missiles."[94] But his efforts had little effect on Canadian voting preferences. The Liberal party took enough seats to form a minority government under Lester Pearson. A few months later, after reaching a quick agreement with the United States, Pearson replaced the sand ballast in the missile systems with nuclear warheads.[95]

WHO WERE THE INFLUENTIAL DECISION-MAKERS?

The centre

A close reading of the primary and secondary documents relating to the Diefenbaker government's period in office indicates that between 1957 and 1963 only a few individuals exerted a strong influence on the defence policy-making process. Between June 1957 and April 1963, Prime Minister John Diefenbaker, Minister of National Defence George Pearkes and his successor Douglas Harkness, and Minister of External Affairs Howard Green dominated the decision-making process. Indeed, these four were effectively at the centre of policy-making. They had the greatest opportunity to act on their preferences and fears. It was their attitudes, concerns, and beliefs that most affected the outcomes of decision-making processes regarding Canadian policy toward the Alliance. They were the ones who wielded the most power to commit the government, along with the ability to prevent other decision-makers from reversing that commitment. As prime minister, Diefenbaker was very influential throughout the period from June 1957 to April 1963. As minister of National Defence from June 1957 to October 1961, General George Pearkes also wielded a great deal of influence. Of the two ministers of National Defence, however, his successor Douglas Harkness had a greater opportunity to dominate the decision-making process. Harkness influenced defence policy-making from November 1961 until his resignation in January 1963. Finally, as minister of External Affairs from June 1959 to April 1963, Howard Green had a considerable impact on defence decision-making. The study of their beliefs and assumptions is therefore key to illuminating the reasons for the government's contrasting commitments to NATO.[98]

The inner and outer core

At different times, an inner core and an outer core of decision-makers also wielded considerable influence. The inner core seems to have consisted of Under-Secretary of External Affairs Norman Robertson, Ambassador to Washington Arnold Heeney, and Chairman of the Chiefs of Staff General Charles Foulkes. In the outer core, exercising less influence, were Minister of External Affairs Sidney Smith; Associate Defence Minister Pierre Sevigny; Chief of the Air Staff Hugh Campbell; Air Chief Marshal Frank Miller; as well as Assistant Deputy Minister of External Affairs and Diefenbaker's special adviser on defence, George Ignatieff.

The leader of the Opposition, Lester Pearson; the ambassador to the UN, General E.L.M. Burns; Heeney's successor to the post of ambassador in 1962, Charles Ritchie; Minister of Trade and Commerce George Hees; Minister of Veterans' Affairs Gordon Churchill; the first under-secretary of External Affairs Jules Leger; and Diefenbaker's External affairs liaison Basil Robinson were at the periphery. On the margins were those who occasionally influenced the course of events, people such as Pearson's external affairs critic Paul Hellyer; the Canadian ambassador to West Germany, Escott Reid; and Senator William Brunt. Finally, the marginalized, who were largely excluded from directly taking part in the decision-making process, included representatives of anti-nuclear organizations such as the Voice of Women and the leader of the CCF, Tommy Douglas.

Primary documents and most of the secondary literature confirm that certain figures – Diefenbaker, Harkness, Green, and, to a slightly lesser extent, Pearkes – dominated the defence decision-making process during this time period and that, at different times, an inner and outer core also wielded considerable influence.[99] The following chapters analyse these decision-makers' underlying beliefs and assumptions. They also establish the dynamic generated by the presence of two competing belief systems – that of the Defenders and the Critics – as an important reason for the variation in the government's nuclear commitments.

CHAPTER SIX

The Traditional Beliefs and Assumptions of Defenders, 1957–1963

In 1957, the Diefenbaker government made firm commitments to acquire five different nuclear weapons systems. Between 1960 and 1961, however, the government wavered on these decisions. And by 1962, high-level decision-makers, including the prime minister, were expressing outright opposition to them. As we have seen, between 1957 and 1960 many different factors seemed to impel the prime minister and his Cabinet, as well as senior military and civilian advisers, toward acquiring nuclear systems as part of Canada's NATO commitment. Technological developments such as the development of the Russian *Sputnik* in 1957 and the successful testing of the Bomarc B in 1959 initially prompted Diefenbaker to support the Bomarc acquisition. At the same time, bilateral pressures spurred military advisers such as General Pearkes and Foulkes to favour acquiring these nuclear-capable weapons systems. NATO directives – including MC 14/2 and MC/48/2, premised on using nuclear weapons from the outset – appeared to sway Diefenbaker and his Defence minister. Financial imperatives, such as the cancellation of the Avro Arrow and its substitution with the relatively inexpensive Bomarc missile, affected Diefenbaker's attitude as well. Military recommendations, such as General Norstad's briefing to Cabinet and SHAPE's recommendations, exerted considerable influence, too, on members of Cabinet and the Chiefs of Staff. Influential defence policy-makers had to consider all these international and domestic variables when deciding to acquire nuclear weapons systems.

Between 1961 and 1963, it was apparent that other systemic- and state-level factors were interacting to dissuade Canadian leaders from fulfilling their commitments. Momentous international events such as the Cuban missile crisis and the subsequent easing of tensions led decision-makers such as Green to question the necessity of acquiring nuclear weapons at all. UN recommendations pertaining to the Irish resolution, for instance, or to Canada's high-profile position in the UN's Eighteen-Nation Disarmament Committee also influenced the Cabinet's debate. American behaviour (Kennedy's failure to consult during the Cuban missile crisis and the publication of the US State Department's press release), electoral considerations (the influence of increasingly divided public opinion and Pearson's unexpected *volte-face* regarding the nuclear issue), as well as domestic criticism (e.g., the outpouring of letters and complaints from groups such as the Voice of Women) – all contributed in some measure to different decision-makers' lack of support for nuclear weapons.

Yet neither international pressures nor domestic concerns provide sufficient explanation for the changes in Canadian defence policy. One key reason for the government's waffling support appears to have been rooted in individual attitudes: the fact that some decision-makers in the inner circle of decision-making favoured, and others opposed, fulfilling Canada's nuclear commitments. In other words, one unexplored explanation for the government's fluid attitude regarding nuclear weapons may be the significant influence of individual policy-makers' underlying beliefs on defence policy-making.

This chapter examines whether beliefs typical of Defenders affected high-level decision-making between 1957 and 1963. Although no one decision-maker is singled out as the archetypal exemplar of a Defender, the evidence shows that many important decision-makers held belief systems typical of Defenders. These beliefs, in turn, skewed defence decision-making toward acquiring nuclear weapons as part of Canada's NATO commitment.

SUBSTANTIVE BELIEFS AND ASSUMPTIONS OF DEFENDERS

Defenders feared abandonment

Minister of National Defence Douglas Harkness was profoundly influenced by fears of abandonment. Harkness feared that the government could, in the near future, "disassociate" from NATO if "pacifists" and "neutralists" overtook governmental decision-making processes. He claimed that he himself had "squarely faced the fact" that "we lie between the world's two greatest protagonists, and if war comes, we will be in the middle of it whether we are neutralists, isolationists or active supporters of the West; and whether we are unarmed or are armed with conventional or nuclear weapons." Accordingly, he was frustrated that "neutralists," like "ostriches with their heads in the sand," wanted to disassociate Canada from its allies.[1] As he told a closed audience of supporters from the Royal Canadian Military Institute, "These people, by some weird intellectual gymnastics, come to the conclusion that if we disassociate ourselves from our allies no one will drop any bombs on us."[2]

Throughout his tenure as Defence minister (1961–1963), Harkness worried that Canada's "full partnership" in the Alliance would be jeopardized. He feared the allies would be frustrated with Canada because of the government's delays in fulfilling its nuclear commitments, and he worried about the implications of Howard Green's disarmament stand at the United Nations. His fears prompted him to write his Cabinet colleagues: "On the one hand there is our national desire to pursue disarmament unfettered by the commitments we have made to NATO ... On the other hand, this places in doubt our position as a full partner in NATO which provides the collective defence alliance vital to our national security in the absence of effective disarmament." Instead of following Green's course of "unilateral disarmament," Harkness proposed that Canada pursue a "collective approach" to disarmament and defence: "Canada should press within NATO for a more vigorous collective approach to disarmament in order to avoid the erosion of the strength of the alliance by unilateral national disarmament activities ... Effective disarmament negotiations should be conducted from a position of strength ... [and] in the absence of substantive progress in the field of disarmament, Canada should pursue collective defence through NATO."[3] Harkness's blanket assertions that Canada's pursuit of "unilateral disarmament" would erode the Alliance's strength and that all disarmament negotiations should be conducted from a position of superiority were based on two assumptions. First, Harkness assumed that not acquiring nuclear weapons and advocating disarmament at the UN meant that Canada would be responsible for initiating a process of disarmament that would undermine and threaten the Alliance. Second, he believed that disarmament negotiations were unlikely to succeed, but should nonetheless be conducted from a "position of strength." He assumed that disarmament negotiations would have a better prospect of succeeding if Canada contributed in some measure to the Alliance's nuclear superiority.[4]

As we have seen in chapter 3, decision-makers' fears of abandonment were frequently expressed via dire predictions and negative expectations about what could happen if Canada's allied ties to Europe or the United States were weakened. Harkness, for example, focused almost entirely on the grave consequences for Canada's heretofore smooth working relationship with the United States. He privately warned the prime minister about the dangerous consequences if the government decided not to acquire the nuclear-capable F-104 interceptors from the United States: "I should think there would be some danger that the Americans would want to have a complete revision of the NORAD arrangement set up, with quite unforeseeable implications for us."[5] Harkness also considered warning Green that, "if we should now limit the armament of these aircraft to the non-nuclear weapons, the result would be a significant reduction in NORAD's defence capability – a result patently distasteful to the United States."[6]

In keeping with this tendency to invoke the fear of American retaliation, Harkness warned, too, about the implications of Green's disarmament stance at the United Nations. In a confidential letter, he advised the prime minister not to encourage Green's support of the "neutral" resolution at the UN, calling for the suspension of nuclear tests, because of possible adverse American reaction. It was not in Canada's interests, he said, to "place pressure upon the Americans to accept an agreement which would be contrary to the essential requirements of American security and therefore of Canadian security." Moreover, it would also be inadvisable "to place a major strain upon Canada's diplomatic credit in Washington by voting in favour of a moratorium on testing."[7]

Compared to Harkness's almost constant preoccupation with the consequences of Canada abandoning its allies, the prime minister expressed relatively little concern about the possibility. Diefenbaker assumed that if "the aggressor" attacked any of the allies, there would be no alternative but for Canada to go to war. As he wrote, "These are the very facts of survival that face us as a nation ... [and] the facts on which our defence policy decisions have to be made."[8] It also appears that Diefenbaker held strong convictions about the imperatives of Alliance solidarity; in the margins of one speech, he saw fit to scrawl: "The imperative need of Western Solidarity transcends all other conditions."[9] And in a draft of another speech, he inserted: "The alliance between Britain, the United States and Canada and the other Nations of NATO in an unbreakable chain of responsible co-operation is a major element for the survival of the free world."[10] During the 1961 Berlin crisis, the prime minister rejected any notion that Canada not support its allies. Although he admitted that some of those who had served and sacrificed in two world wars against Germany might understandably possess an ambivalent attitude toward Berliners, Diefenbaker believed that Western eviction from Berlin would have repercussions throughout Germany and Europe. Canada could not abandon this Western European outpost because of what it represented, he argued; to retreat now "would mean that the pledged word of the West would be called in question everywhere in the world with consequences impossible to calculate for the future of freedom."[11]

During the first few years of his tenure, Diefenbaker was relatively unconcerned that Canada's close relations with the Alliance leader were possibly threatened or dissipating. He acknowledged that there were "difficulties" for Canada arising from the fact that the United States had worldwide commitments and responsibilities, many of which were not shared by Canada. Nevertheless, he showed no hesitation in welcoming American leadership of the free world "so long as the American leaders did not take Canadian support for granted."[12] He liked to point out that the close relationship between Canada and the United States was geographically, socially, and ideologically natural, since it was based on a common heritage and a common aspiration. In reply to questions about stronger military ties with the United States, he asserted that "cooperative arrangements which are designed to ensure survival in the military sense" were acceptable, so long as Canada's national, political, and economic identity was not jeopardized.[13] In fact, Diefenbaker confided to the British prime minister in 1960 that although Canada's close relationship with the United States was sometimes interpreted as subservient, he felt the United States had done nothing that could be interpreted as "condescension" or "putting Canada in a subservient position."[14]

As prime minister, Diefenbaker initially believed there was no possibility that his government could desert the allies. Nor did he fear that the allies might disassociate from Canada. Like other Defenders, however, he expressed some concern about the effects of "neutralism" and "pacifism" on Canada's "responsibilities under NATO." And in 1959 he acknowledged that "neutralist sympathies" were beginning to surface in "certain quarters." Nevertheless, he was determined to make clear to the public that there was no neutralism in Canada's thinking or conduct, and no weakening of support for NATO:

What is our position in Canada? Some seem to have the view that we could be neutral in any war that may take place, neutral in the event that the United States was involved – or Britain, or France, or West Germany. There is no neutrality of that kind today. Our responsibilities under NATO, under the agreement entered into with the full cognizance and support of all Members of Parliament will not allow any choice to be made in the future. There can be no academic debates in Parliament or of Parliament on the question of whether or not we are automatically at war in the event that any of the nations in NATO are at war.[15]

Between 1957 and 1960, Diefenbaker assumed that allied relations were strong and only to a limited extent threatened by neutralists. A few other high-ranking decision-makers, however, including Harkness and Ambassador to Washington Arnold Heeney, worried a great deal about the negative message they thought the government was sending the allies by not forthrightly fulfilling its nuclear commitments. Heeney, in particular, feared that the "attitudes and prejudices" of Minister of External Affairs Howard Green and his under-secretary of state Norman Robertson threatened Canada's defence relationship with the United States. As Heeney confided to his diary in 1962, he was concerned that Green's attitudes and prejudices combined with Robertson's "cosmic anxieties" were producing "a negative force of great importance."[16]

Underlying Heeney's apprehension about the effect Green and Robertson were having on Canada's defence relations was the ambassador's long-held conviction that the Canadian-American alliance was "our most precious international asset."[17] As he confided to the prime minister in August 1960, the specter of the United States sliding into "isolationism" partly because of Canada's stand on defence, was a "nightmare":

[I said] my nightmare was that the US would revert to an isolationist policy under the buffetings and criticisms of her allies & what Americans regarded as the lack of support which other nations were displaying. Here Canadian attitudes were of importance because of our traditional friendship ... It would be tragic if this came about as a result of the disintegration of the alliance and doubly so if we – who not long ago had despaired of the US accepting international responsibilities – had any part in bringing about such a development.[18]

A close reading of the primary documents – drafts of speeches, personal letters, transcripts of commentary and interviews, diaries, and personal accounts – reveals that Douglas Harkness and Arnold Heeney were consistently susceptible to fears of abandonment. Diefenbaker was less fearful in this regard. George Pearkes and Charles Foulkes also feared abandonment, and their decision to refer to NORAD as a NATO Command may have been based, in part, on the fear that Canada would otherwise be left to fend for itself with its neighbour to the south. At the time of writing, however, supporting evidence from the National Archives of Canada remains inaccessible.[19] No evidence exists that other high-level decision-makers, whether within the centre, inner, or outer core of decision-making – people such as Sidney Smith, Howard Green, or Norman Robertson – believed the allies were in danger of abandoning Canada, or vice-versa.

Defenders believed Canada should pursue closer ties to the allies through established kinds of military commitments

Although Canadian decision-makers had suggested a variety of ways to pursue closer ties to the Alliance, the marked tendency among Defenders was to consider only established methods of fostering such ties, including commitments to maintain or increase the number of Canadian Forces earmarked for NATO purposes, particularly the number of military personnel deployed overseas in Europe. Promises to modernize or deploy more weapons systems and equipment to NATO were also typical ways of conveying support. Similarly, it was taken for granted that commitments to maintain or increase the percentage of the government's defence budget and the GNP directed toward NATO defence purposes would be highly valued.

This case study focuses on Canada's decision to modernize and deploy nuclear weapons systems. To some extent, because the Canadian government had not yet shouldered them, the commitments of the Diefenbaker government undertaken between 1957 and 1961 were non-traditional and unestablished. Nevertheless, from the perspective of the NATO Council and NATO's Military Committee, the Alliance's reliance on atomic and thermonuclear weapons had been recommended five years earlier, in 1952. In fact, the introduction of nuclear weapons for NATO's Forces in Europe was first recognized at NATO's Council meeting in Lisbon in February 1952. It was not until 1957, however, that SACEUR began to recommend, in SHAPE's official planning guidance, that Canada acquire and deploy weapons systems defined as having nuclear weapon delivery capability. Thus, NATO's decision to make defence preparations, on the assumption that nuclear weapons would be used from the outset, had already been established between 1952 and 1954. At least five years would intervene, however, before the Canadian government had to decide if Canada would follow orthodox practice in this regard.

To some extent, those who assumed Canada should contribute to NATO in such a traditional manner tended to adopt standard procedures. Diefenbaker and Pearkes refrained from querying the proposal to stockpile nuclear weapons in Europe at the first meeting of the NATO Heads of Government. According to Basil Robinson, Diefenbaker's aide, this was because it was their first visit to "the NATO club," a club which Diefenbaker "had joined but never visited and whose rules and procedures he would encounter for the first time."

Neither Diefenbaker nor the Defence minister took a major part in the 1957 discussions. Although a note of uncertainty could be detected regarding the nuclear issue, little was said.[20]

The Canadian tendency to accept established ways of thinking is further evidenced by these decision-makers' ready acquiescence to General Norstad's request that Canada provide a nuclear strike-reconnaissance role for the Canadian Air Division in Europe. By the time Cabinet was forced to make a decision about replacing the unworkable Lacrosse system, the Defence minister's explanation that the Honest John missile "was already in service with, or about to be introduced by," other NATO forces indicated that this was almost standard procedure. The Cabinet agreed without debate to the Defence minister's recommendation that Canada acquire the Honest John system.[21] The records of Cabinet discussions from 1957–60 indicate that the Cabinet did not conduct a comprehensive examination of all options to determine which would be most suitable. Rather, ministers agreed to whatever military commitment General George Pearkes, visiting SACEUR General Norstad, or the chairmen of the Chiefs of Staff Hugh Campbell and Frank Miller recommended.[22] In many instances, then, the tendency to follow orthodox procedure influenced the decision-making skills of high-level defence policy-makers.

Although decision-makers had a tendency to follow standard practice, many at the centre and inner core were truly convinced that Canada should pursue closer ties to the allies by acquiring nuclear weapons. Among the influential decision-makers in this case study, it was Minister of National Defence General George Pearkes; his successor Douglas Harkness; Chairmen of the Canadian Chiefs of Staff General Charles Foulkes, Hugh Campbell, and Frank Miller; as well as Prime Minister John Diefenbaker (until 1961) who firmly believed that Canada should foster closer allied ties by fulfilling its nuclear commitments. When Harkness wanted to make clear in speeches or letters that Canada was committed to strengthening NATO, he highlighted his determination to "proceed with the steps necessary" to strengthen the brigade group in Europe by "modernizing" its weapons; he also emphasized his intention to acquire Bomarc and Honest John missiles as well as CF-101 and CF-104 nuclear-armed aircraft.[23] Similarly, General Pearkes often expressed confidence in the government's willingness to arm Canadian troops with nuclear weapons as "efficiently" and "effectively" as the troops with which they were co-operating.[24] As well, General Foulkes assumed that the government was clearly obligated to acquire nuclear weapons. As he explained in a 1969 television interview:

I think in this problem of what nuclear weapons Canada should acquire we should clearly understand what weapons are necessary. Now the government has agreed to the Canadian Forces in Europe, in the North Atlantic and in Canada undertaking certain tasks. Some of these tasks indicate the necessity of nuclear weapons. And I would just point out what these tasks are; what the weapons are; how we expect to get them; and how they will be stored and how they will be controlled, and then we can look at the problem of whether we should acquire them or not when we know what we are after. Now for the brigade in Europe each brigade has a front-line task. It requires heavy support and for that heavy support, the government is planning to supply the Honest John rocket. Now the Honest John rocket requires a nuclear warhead. The Air Division you will recall had eight squadrons of F-86 day fighters. Now the day fighter is out of the picture and General Norstad has recommended to the government that we should replace them by a strike-reconnaissance – reconnaissance strike aircraft – and the Government decided to go into production of the F-104 ...[25]

Between 1957 and 1961, Prime Minister Diefenbaker assumed as well that Canada could signal its ties to the Alliance in a traditional fashion. At the 1957 NATO ministerial meeting, Diefenbaker endorsed the concept of acquiring nuclear weapons, reasoning that such a decision "follows logically from the decision taken in 1954 to organize our forces in Europe on the understanding that they would be able to use such weapons to repel attacks." Until at least 1961, the prime minister also tended to assume that the decisions to "re-equip" the brigade and the air division in Europe, and to acquire Bomarcs and Voodoos, were the most important symbols of his government's determination to strengthen NATO. Thus, within the inner circle of defence decision-making, all four – Harkness, Pearkes, Foulkes, and Diefenbaker (until 1961) – were convinced that Canada should modernize its weapons systems and equipment, particularly its forces in Europe, by acquiring nuclear weapons systems and equipment.[26]

Compared to Harkness, Foulkes, and Pearkes, however, the prime minister tended between 1957 and 1963 to place a greater emphasis on Canada's contribution of conventional forces to Europe. He saw this commitment as another symbol of Canada's allegiance to the allies. By 1959, Canada's overseas deployment of conventional forces in Europe was such an established commitment that most high-level decision-makers simply overlooked it. In drafts of speeches and notations he wrote to himself, however, Diefenbaker frequently equated the strengthening of Canada's conventional forces in Europe with the signalling of close Alliance ties.[27]

These decision-makers based their convictions about the imperative of re-equipping the Canadian Forces overseas and in Canada on typical "first-stream" and "second-stream" assumptions.[28] For example, Harkness, in arguing that Canada's contributions of nuclear-tipped Bomarcs and interceptors were important to the Alliance, made a first-stream assumption that these commitments were key to the continuing function of the Alliance:

Over the years Canada has made her contribution to the overall deterrent forces of the West. In comparison to some of our allies, particularly the United States, that contribution may be small, but it does have some significance taken in conjunction with the forces contributed by other member nations of NATO. On this continent, just as we rely on the retaliatory forces maintained by the United States to discourage an attack, so too does the United States rely on Canada to provide defensive forces to ensure the effectiveness of their part of the deterrent.[29]

Diefenbaker, on the other hand, tended to make second-stream assumptions, in that he usually assumed the overall balance of conventional forces in Europe would either prevent war or affect the outcome of war. Rather than emphasize Canada's key role in protecting the US nuclear deterrent, Diefenbaker drew attention to Canada's contribution to the balance of conventional forces in Europe. The prime minister's constant emphasis on Canada's conventional contribution to Europe, culminating in his much-criticized "Nassau speech" in January 1963, was based on a second-stream assumption: in case of war, the prior balance of conventional forces in Europe would heavily determine the outcome. Finally, in terms of third-stream assumptions, none of these decision-makers assumed that Canada's military commitments to NATO made little strategic difference, being important only insofar as they signalled a unified resolve and Alliance solidarity.

As we have seen in chapter 3, Defenders sometimes promoted military commitments that strengthened Alliance ties without assessing their strategic rationale or implications. For example, some espoused different weapons systems as an appropriate commitment to NATO, without appreciating their purported military purpose. In 1957, Diefenbaker committed the government to abide by NATO documents MC 14/2 and MC 48/2 because he seemed to want to belong to "the NATO club." He neither appreciated nor fully understood the implications of these documents for re-equipping the Canadian Forces. Then, in 1959, he announced that the government would acquire Bomarc missiles to replace the Canadian-made Avro Arrow;

however, he did not acknowledge or examine the Bomarc's strategic rationale. The Chiefs of Staff tried to advise him against simultaneously announcing the Arrow cancellation and the Bomarc acquisition, saying that Bomarcs were intended to complement, not replace, interceptors. Nevertheless, the prime minister, without military advice, wrote his speech announcing the new commitment.[30]

In another episode illustrating his tendency until 1961 to promote agreed-upon commitments that apparently strengthened Alliance ties, Diefenbaker consented to acquire the F-101 interceptor without fully exploring its nuclear capability. Although he had cancelled production of the Arrow interceptor in 1959, the Department of National Defence later advised him that they needed an air interceptor. Diefenbaker, however, emphatically drew a large question mark on the department's paper arguing for the F-101 Voodoos to meet the bomber threat and achieve "adequate deterrence." He was clearly perplexed by the sentence arguing that CINCNORAD had a stated requirement for a "supersonic" interceptor in the North American air defence system "for as far in the future as it is was possible to see."[31] Whether he was confused because he had recently cancelled production of the Arrow interceptor or because he doubted the military's recommendation is difficult to judge. Certainly, he knew there would be "criticism that we cancelled a Canadian program, thereby throwing people out of employment, and are now accepting American planes to do the job that the Canadian planes would have done."[32] Yet Diefenbaker did agree to acquire the Voodoos from the United States. It was only later, when the Defence department advised him that the Voodoos needed arming with MB1 nuclear missiles, that he began to direct a behind-the-scenes effort to acquire conventional warheads. The entire episode illustrates Diefenbaker's initial tendency to agree to commitments that augured well for Canada's defence relationship with the United States, without fully appreciating their strategic rationale or implications.

Although their occasional inconsistencies can be attributed to ignorance or disingenuousness, some Defenders' beliefs about the need to strengthen Alliance ties were so thoroughly entrenched that a coherent, strategic rationale to support a NATO commitment was not always necessary. For example, whether Diefenbaker was uninformed about strategic rationales or politically astute and deliberately ambiguous is still very much debated.[33] It is well known that the prime minister was disinclined to seek advice from advisers in Defence or External Affairs, and that he rarely called together the Cabinet Defence Committee while he was prime minister. As well, he was renowned for leaving RCAF presentations before decisions were taken and never seemed to want to take the time to debate defence-related issues.[34] Moreover, for at least his first eighteen months in office, Diefenbaker did not trust External's "Pearsonalities," especially "the intellectual" Norman Robertson. It took "a lot of hard work" before Diefenbaker could appreciate that he was no longer leader of the Opposition and might now consult more comfortably with External Affairs.[35] Indeed, until Green came to power and allied himself with Robertson, the prime minister relied almost entirely on his own beliefs and assumptions to guide him, although, to a lesser degree, he did listen to the advice of General Pearkes and General Foulkes. Until 1961, then, he often neither required a strategic rationale nor wanted information about possible defence implications before deciding in favour of another new Alliance commitment.

Defenders rarely put forward unconventional proposals about how Canada might pursue closer ties to its allies. The tendency was to reaffirm conventional wisdom and maintain the status quo. Harkness, for one, focused almost entirely on established methods of fostering closer ties, particularly on acquiring nuclear warheads. However, Diefenbaker and a few other influential decision-makers occasionally did put forward less traditional ideas. The prime minister first referred to NORAD as a multilateral NATO Command at the 1957 NATO ministerial meeting. This was initially interpreted as a diversionary tactic, to deflect criticisms by Pearson and others that the government was moving too closely toward defence integration with the United States.[36] However, Diefenbaker, Pearkes, and Foulkes continued to make this argument at secret NATO Council meetings, in speeches, and in private correspondence. They believed Canada's new commitment to NORAD could entail another military command for NATO.[37] Even though a flurry of memoranda from Jules Leger in External Affairs warned that NORAD could not be a NATO command – American reluctance to establish a multinational command in North America and the implications for American disclosure policy would not allow it – these three decision-makers continued to portray NORAD as part of the established military framework of NATO.[38] At NATO ministerial meetings, General Pearkes saw fit to remind other defence ministers: "To increase the effectiveness of the air defence of this continent, we have within the last year set up the joint air defence command known as NORAD. As the Prime Minister said in Paris, and as he reiterated in the House, we consider this to be an integral part of the NATO military structure."[39]

The belief that NORAD should be viewed as a NATO command seems to have been based on a first-stream assumption – namely, that the Canadian air-defence system was of primary importance in defending the entire Alliance. The *Sputnik* launch in 1957 heralded the development of Russian ICBMS, against which American and Canadian interceptors and missiles were powerless. Nevertheless, Diefenbaker, Foulkes, and Pearkes continued to assume Canada's air-defence system was essential to defending the US deterrent, and that the front line of battle would be on Canadian territory. As the prime minister noted in a 1959 television address, technological revolutions beginning with the *Sputnik* launch and the development of the long-range ballistic missile meant that "Canadians as a whole realize that, for the first time in history, this country will be one of the first to be attacked if war begins."[40] In fact, well before his government deployed nuclear-armed interceptors and Bomarcs, Diefenbaker assumed, in typical first-stream fashion, that Canada's contribution of conventional air interceptors to the balance of conventionally equipped forces substantially helped defend the Alliance. As he confidently told an American audience in 1959, "The United States of America cannot defend itself with full effectiveness without Canadian cooperation and without defence facilities on Canadian territory."[41]

Besides suggesting that NORAD become a NATO command, Diefenbaker, Smith, and Smith's successor Green sometimes made unconventional suggestions about fostering economic and political interdependence among the allies and opening up consultation channels as a way of strengthening the Alliance. During his short time in office, Smith often spoke about it not being enough to trust "military instruments of policy alone." He underlined the importance of NATO members "developing their political, economic and social partnership." He mentioned pursuing closer ties to the allies through "non-military fields" (although Smith admitted it was "too early a stage" in the development of these non-military forms of co-operation to be more specific.)[42]

The prime minister was a much more vigorous advocate of opening up consultation channels than most.[43] While Pearkes, Foulkes, Campbell, and Harkness focused exclusively on strengthening Canada's military commitments to the Alliance, Diefenbaker believed the first requirement for the Western nations was to strive for "Western unity," to "remain true to each other," and to work toward "perfect understanding."[44] Indeed, the problem of how to foster non-military ties with NATO so preoccupied Diefenbaker that he sometimes scribbled questions in the margins of speeches asking himself how he proposed to make NATO more than a military alliance. In one speech, his own answer was that Canadians could contribute to the Alliance's strength by obtaining more extensive knowledge of NATO's organization and by participating in NATO's consultative assembly of parliamentarians.[45] The prime minister's most unconventional suggestion, however, was his notion of "full and fair consultation."[46] From 1957 to 1963, the prime minister repeatedly suggested to the allies, especially the United States, that they consult on all decisions that could affect one another.[47] In his opinion, the "Basic NATO Principle" was increased consultation, and he did not hesitate to remind Americans of this obligation: "It needs constantly to be recalled that NATO is an alliance of sovereign states each bearing its own responsibility for the safeguarding of peace, each with its survival at stake. A special obligation falls on the larger, more powerful members to make a reality of consultation, and to reconcile the responsibilities of leadership with those of true partnership."[48]

Yet Diefenbaker – and to a lesser extent Pearkes, Smith, and Green – may have emphasized consultation not because they wanted to consult with the allies but because they wanted to be consulted on issues of importance. The emphasis Diefenbaker and Pearkes placed on their "distinctly beneficial" consultations with General Norstad, and Diefenbaker's wounded reaction in October 1962 to Kennedy's nationwide television address airing barely two hours after he himself was consulted, seem to indicate that they believed the allies should consult with Canada more extensively and more often on issues of great moment.[49] Whereas Pearkes, Foulkes, Harkness, and initially Diefenbaker believed that Canada should modernize its forces with nuclear weapons, they also assumed that the United States and the other allies should consult with Canada if and when the use of these weapons was contemplated.

Defenders believed the external threat to the Alliance
was opportunistic and aggressive

Between 1949 and 1959, Defenders tended to perceive the external threat to the Alliance as monolithic and inexorably bent on NATO's destruction. Through the 1960s and 1970s, the idea of a monolithic threat assumed a mythic stature which some Defenders realized was not necessarily based on reality, but which, nevertheless, remained potent. Although this threat appeared in various guises over the years, its chief manifestation was as an aggressive challenge to the Alliance from an adversary inexorably bent on expansion.

The first point to be made about the imagery of high-level Canadian decision-makers between 1957 and 1963 is that although their assumptions about the threat were seldom articulated, they nonetheless seemed to provide the context for decision-making. Among themselves, though, decision-makers rarely discussed the enemy's underlying motives or intentions and seldom concretely referred to their conception of the nature of the menace. Thus, when the prime minister spoke of the threat to the Alliance, he referred interchangeably to "Mr. Khrushchev," "the USSR" or "the Kremlin." Harkness, too, rarely referred in concrete terms to the threat, although when he did so he focused on the "expansionist" imperatives of the "Soviet Union" or the "Soviet Bloc." For Sidney Smith, though, the Soviet Union's "military machine" was the problem, while General Foulkes and General Pearkes saw little need to refer concretely to the threat from the Soviet Union, as it was omnipresent.[50]

From 1954 through 1961–62, Diefenbaker's imagery hardly changed at all. In 1954, he stated that "the responsibility for a continuation of the Cold War rests on the USSR."[51] In 1959, when the Soviet attitude seemed to give way to a measure of moderation and understanding, he continued to suggest that "nothing justifies the conclusion that any of the basic Soviet positions have been abandoned or modified."[52] During the Berlin Crisis, Diefenbaker was certain that "the Kremlin" created crises wherever and whenever it suited its purposes.[53] For Diefenbaker, the threat was inexorably resolved on destroying peace and creating crises.[54] Indeed, if Diefenbaker analysed the reasons for changes in Soviet policy, his musings often seemed to be the product of pure conjecture. As he told the Canadian Bar Association in a lengthy exposition on the nature of the Soviet threat:

One could speculate indefinitely on Soviet motives for desiring a relaxation of tension. It seems clear that one of Mr. Khrushchev's main concerns is to modernize Soviet society and to raise the standard of living of the Soviet people. To this end he no doubt requires the assurance of a long period of peace, with some relief from the burden of armaments production and with time to broaden and consolidate the Soviet economy ... The fresh look which Mr. Khrushchev has given to Soviet foreign policy ... arises primarily from a deep-seated Soviet fear of nuclear war and its consequences. It might be influenced by possible Soviet concern about the long-range implications of the policies of Communist China. It accords better with the image of benevolence and reasonableness which the Soviet Union hopes to project in the under-developed world. Of more direct concern to Canada, a Soviet policy of conciliation offers a better prospect of driving wedges into the ranks of his diplomatic adversaries, of creating slits [sic] among members of NATO.[55]

By 1961, Diefenbaker had recognized that the threat was no longer monolithic (e.g., he spoke of Soviet concern over China) and, by 1961–62, he had developed a more nuanced view of the USSR. Nevertheless, he continued to believe that an aggressive and opportunistic adversary threatened the Alliance.

Other high-level decision-makers were more reticent about naming the true nature of the threat. Evidence documenting Pearkes's and Foulkes's beliefs about "the threat" is, in fact, difficult to find. However, Ignatieff, years later, said, "Foulkes was in on the Pentagon view, that the enemy was the Soviet Union, that they were a direct threat to North America, and that for purposes of defending North America there could be no separation of authority or sovereignty."[56] Basil Robinson suggests, too, that Pearkes was "in the Harkness/ Foulkes school of thought," although it was widely understood at the time that "the military" presented its viewpoint to Pearkes and he accepted it unequivocally.[57]

As Defence minister, Harkness emphasized that "overriding all other considerations is the open threat of the Soviet Union to eventually achieve world domination." Harkness believed the Soviets were implementing their threat of world domination on all fronts – ideological, military, economic, and political – and gave little thought to the underlying tenets of Soviet military or communist doctrine.[58] In a classified speech delivered in 1961, he stated his conviction that, once the Soviet Union's reliance on force and the threat of force was realized, the true intentions of the Soviet bloc would be clear to everyone:

The present world situation is typified by a speech by Mr. Khrushchev published in Moscow exactly one month ago today. In that speech he spoke of peaceful co-existence but he also referred to the fact that the communists govern a vast area of the world and that they in turn will rule the whole globe. He termed this victory inevitable by the laws of historical development. While we can perhaps vary in our interpretation of such statements, there is no doubt that force, and the threat of force, unfortunately continue to be a declared factor of Soviet bloc policy.[59]

Pearkes, Foulkes, Harkness, and Diefenbaker may have projected harsh images of the external threat to the Alliance but their imagery was not much different from that of many other Conservative members of Parliament, military representatives, and Canadian citizens. It was fairly typical in the late 1950s to make categorical assertions, such as one member's comment to the prime minister that "the head of the Soviet Government can be compared with the typical schoolyard bully who understands only one language, calculated in terms of military strength."[60] It is important to appreciate the lengths to which these decision-makers would go in order to preserve their underlying beliefs about the nature of the threat.

In Harkness's case, as well as Diefenbaker's until 1961, any evidence demonstrating the threat as other than aggressive and opportunistic was generally ignored, overlooked, or rejected. Examples abound of this tendency to overlook or deny evidence that undermined these men's core beliefs about the external threat to the Alliance. In 1958, for instance, Diefenbaker disregarded Khrushchev's purported grounds for unilaterally suspending the Soviet nuclear-testing program. Instead, he attacked him in a personal letter for a decision that he saw not as "the product of negotiation and agreement among nations" but as one which "could be reversed overnight and without consultation by your Government."[61] Diefenbaker also denied any notion that Khrushchev's visit to the United States in 1959 heralded a basic change in Soviet policy. In his view, neither this visit nor any other gestures of accommodation warranted a change of attitude toward the Soviet Union:

On the Soviet side, threats, abuse and suspicion appear to have given way to an attitude of greater moderation and understanding. Many different interpretations have been placed on the new Soviet approach. There are those who see it as reliable evidence of a genuine determination on the part of the Soviet Union to negotiate settlements of outstanding differences. There are others who cannot bring themselves to believe [that] Mr. Khrushchov's [sic] words of moderation are anything but a deceitful cloak for continued Soviet pursuance of aggressive aims ... Nothing which emerged from Mr. Khrushchov's [sic] visit to the United States and nothing he has said publicly since that time justifies the conclusion that any of the basic Soviet positions have been abandoned or modified. The Soviet hold on Eastern Europe has not been relaxed. The German problem is as intractable as ever. There are no signs of falling-off in Soviet defence preparations. There is still much room for skepticism as to the real substance of Soviet disarmament proposals. We should not leap to the conclusion that the differences we have lived with for more than a decade are on the point of being swept away, or that trouble may not arise again in areas which are at present in a state of quiet.[62]

Initially, Diefenbaker explained the unexpected – the defused Berlin situation, the Soviet Union's disarmament proposals at the UN – as "certain modifications" in the Soviet approach but not a "basic change." As the prime minister wrote in a speech he himself drafted in 1959, "Past experience with the Soviet Union will warn us that we should not assume uncritically that ... [there is] a change of heart among Soviet leaders."[63] Indeed, Diefenbaker's reluctance to accept that there could be any kind of basic change in the Soviet Union continued until 1961–62.

Harkness also ignored any evidence that undermined his convictions. As he saw it, the situation of peaceful co-existence was simply a front. Mr. Khrushchev, he said, had an underlying plan. Even now he was developing "peace fronts throughout the world, including pacifists of all political beliefs."[64] Even after the Cuban missile crisis ended and Khrushchev retreated in the face of Kennedy's threat and a naval blockade, Harkness saw fit to warn Diefenbaker, "recent events in Cuba have, of course, provided further evidence of what a Soviet promise is worth."[65]

Notably, between 1957 and 1961, few leaders viewed the United States or the other NATO allies as a threat. Diefenbaker often referred to the allies as a "grand alliance" or the "Anglo-Canadian-American Community." The members of the "NATO family," he said, pose no threat to Canada or to each other, given their "unswerving dedication to freedom."[66] For General Pearkes and General Foulkes, who helped establish NORAD, the United States could not conceivably pose a threat and, comparatively speaking, the intentions of the other allies were of little significance. Indeed, for Pearkes, the Alliance leader was "the principal arsenal and bastion of the free world."[67] Certainly, from 1957 to 1961–62, few if any of these decision-makers were disconcerted about the capacity or propensity of the United States to use its own growing stockpile of tactical and strategic nuclear weapons.

If they perceived an internal threat to the Alliance at all, it emanated from the neutralists and pacifists within the general populace. Harkness utterly rejected "the pacifist position advocated by those who say there is no possible defence at the present time [and] we should throw up our hands in utter bewilderment and disband all our military forces."[68] On 1 March 1962 he wrote to a Mrs. Worrall about the Voice of Women. He was afraid, he wrote, that this group had "attracted to itself, a large number of pacifists, neutralists, and left-wingers, and that these people are making every effort to undermine public feeling as far as maintaining strong defences is concerned. They are, however a group which it is politically unwise to attack, I believe, as they play on the sympathy of individuals and gain the active support of a considerable number of well-meaning women who may not be too well informed as to the actualities of the world situation."[69] For Harkness, Pearkes, Foulkes, and Diefenbaker (until 1961), the external threat to Canada and NATO was single-mindedly aggressive and inexorably bent on expansion.

Defenders assumed both Canada's and the Alliance's weapons were necessary and non-threatening

Defenders were inclined to downplay the capabilities of Canada's weapons systems and view the Alliance's as non-threatening. Many

Defenders entirely overlooked Canada's conventionally equipped forces overseas, and it was left to aides such as Jules Leger and John Holmes to tally the real measure of Canada's conventional commitments to NATO.[70] The brigade group and the air division in Europe, along with the ocean escorts, were assumed to be so obviously necessary that they were almost entirely ignored. Thus, between 1957 and 1963, little, if any, debate occurred about whether to increase, withdraw, or reduce the number of Canadian Forces deployed overseas. Even after the Berlin crisis in September 1961, Diefenbaker decided, without discussion or fanfare, to nearly double the brigade group from 5,500 to 10,000 soldiers.[71]

As well, many Defenders downplayed the capabilities of the nuclear weapons systems Canada intended to acquire. As Douglas Harkness was careful to explain to the House of Commons: "[The] three weapons systems ... being obtained need a nuclear capability, but I should like to make it clear that their military role can in no way be compared to such strategic nuclear weapons as are maintained by the United Kingdom, the United States and the Soviet Union. Defensive weapons with a nuclear capability may be required to maintain the credibility of the deterrent and in the event that the worst happened, would be required to provide an effective defence against Soviet aggression."[72] Similarly, General Pearkes explained to Cabinet in 1958 that the "central question of policy was whether Canadian forces should be as well equipped as US forces alongside them."[73] He emphasized that the Canadian Forces should be equipped with "the best weapons available," and that "to refuse or to neglect to have these available when required would place an intolerable handicap on our defences."[74] According to Diefenbaker in 1959, the negotiations connected with the acquisition of nuclear warheads were motivated by "our intention to provide Canadian forces with modern and efficient weapons."[75] However, as minister of National Defence, Harkness was most firmly convinced that Canada's nuclear weapons were necessary. Indeed, in his view a world without nuclear weapons could increase the possibility of war: "I dare say that all of us wish that the atomic bomb had never been discovered. Yet its absence would not reduce the possibility of war. It might even heighten it. Man can destroy himself without the aid of nuclear weapons."[76] The Defence minister's conviction that Canadian nuclear weapons were necessary and defensive also prompted him to write what might be called "rationalizations" rather than "strategic justifications." He reasoned, for example, that Canada's deployment of nuclear-tipped missiles in Europe would be a measured response to the enemy's initially threatening provocation: "[The Honest John] would be used against concentrations of enemy forces in the battle area and it should be remembered that the Soviet field forces are also furnished with similar weapons. I do not think our troops should be required to face a potential enemy with inferior weapons and it is for this reason that our Army has been supplied with the Honest John. Several other armies of NATO members also have this weapon."[77]

The tendency to assume that the Alliance's own weapons were largely benign is illustrated, too, by these decision-makers' approach to the issue of fallout from nuclear explosions over Canada. In 1961 the Cabinet received "the best information available" so it might consider what was called the "dead man fuse" question.[78] The decision-makers were told that the Bomarc missiles could destroy the enemy's aircraft without causing the nuclear weapons they carried to explode, even if the warheads had been activated beforehand. As for the resulting fallout from the Bomarc missiles exploding on impact with the enemy's aircraft, they were told that these small nuclear explosions would not cause a great deal of fallout because of their explosion high in the air. However, it was added, there was a "strong probability" that the use of conventional warheads would result in the explosion of activated nuclear weapons carried by enemy aircraft.[79] Later, Harkness assured Green in a personal letter that the Bomarc missiles would destroy Soviet bombers and the bombs they were carrying with only a "minor" release of radioactive fallout.[80] Although Cabinet ministers seemed reassured by phrases such as "would not cause great fallout" and "strong probability," many Canadians were not as confident. The minister of National Defence continued to receive well-reasoned letters from citizens, asking, for example:

Although the atomic blast from our missile may not trigger the enemies' H-bomb, what about the blast of the atomic bomb in our Bomarc? No matter how small it is, it will liberate deadly radiation; if it is anywhere near a town or city, it could partially or completely destroy it and its inhabitants; and the flash could blind people for miles around ... It would seem to me, in this age of advanced technology, that it would be quite easy for an enemy, once he knows that his plane or missile is about to be destroyed, to set off his bomb before he is hit, thus still causing undue damage through blast, heat, and radiation.[81]

Harkness, in his personally written draft of a "standard reply," vigorously maintained that such concerns were unwarranted and "completely incorrect":

The Bomarc equipped with a nuclear warhead on contact with an aircraft or even exploded in close proximity to that aircraft would in all probability not only destroy the aircraft but also neutralize or "cook" the bomb thus preventing it being triggered. The size of the nuclear warhead designed for the Bomarc is relatively small as compared to the bomb or bombs carried in the aircraft and this, coupled with the fact that the explosion would occur several thousands of feet in the air, would have little affect [sic] at ground level.[82]

Moreover, Harkness's conviction that the explosions from the Bomarc missiles would not threaten Canadian lives was sufficiently firm that he expressed no concerns to the prime minister about possibly moving the line of defence northward. As he wrote in secret correspondence, the only foreseeable problem with moving the likely area of air battle was the possibility of negative newspaper articles written by so-called defence "experts": "From a Canadian point of view, I believe we would be at a disadvantage, although military opinion does not accept this, in moving the likely area of air battle from roughly along the 49th parallel to roughly a line through Calgary, Saskatoon and 100 miles north of Winnipeg. I would think it almost inevitable that some of the newspaper defence experts would finally get on to this idea and you are well aware of what the effect on people in Western Canada would be of articles along this line."[83] Rather than acknowledging the concerns about the dangerous effects of nuclear fallout from Soviet bombers and Bomarcs alike, Harkness worried about the predictably negative reactions of newspapers and Western Canadians.

Harkness insisted that Canadian nuclear weapons would be defensive and tactical, not offensive or strategic. As he wrote to his nephew, "In any discussion with regard to the acquisition of nuclear weapons, I think you must make a distinction between the strategic nuclear bombs or retaliatory forces, to which I have already referred, and the tactical and defensive nuclear weapons necessary for the ground forces in Europe and for the air defences here at home."[84] Once his colleagues in Cabinet and Canadians in general became agitated about whether to fulfill Canada's nuclear commitments, Harkness drew an even sharper distinction between the "offensive" nuclear weapons possessed by the United States and Britain, and soon to be possessed by France, and the "defensive" nuclear weapons sought by Canada. As he wrote to a constituent shortly after the Cuban missile crisis, Canada had no intention of either acquiring or manufacturing offensive nuclear weapons: "Although Britain has offensive nuclear weapons and France is in the process of developing them, we have no intention of either acquiring or manufacturing such weapons in Canada. As a partner in NATO, we rely on the strategic nuclear forces of the United States and there is no requirement for us to obtain an offensive nuclear arsenal similar to that possessed by members of the so-called 'nuclear club.'"[85] The Defence minister buttressed his claim with the argument that Canada's possession of nuclear weapons would be "entirely different from a military and moral standpoint, the fundamental difference being the fact that it was not physically possible to use these weapons unless an enemy had on his own initiative made their use imperative to the survival of a defender."[86] Harkness also asserted that the Bomarcs and Voodoos deployed in Canada could only be used in a defensive mode (i.e., they could not reach Russian or Eastern European territory). But he completely avoided the question of whether, as part of NATO's "forward strategy" in Western Europe, Canada's CF-104s, Lacrosse, and Honest John systems were defensive or offensive.[87] The CF-104s, in fact, were meant to strike as far forward as possible, and the Lacrosse and Honest John atomic weapons were intended to be used from the outset in forward areas. Nevertheless, Harkness consistently avoided any discussion of whether these systems were therefore defensive, like the Bomarcs and the CF-101s.

Unlike military experts such as Pearkes, Foulkes, and Harkness, Prime Minister Diefenbaker initially drew few distinctions among nuclear weapons. Judging from the lack of evidence indicating his views, the prime minister did not address these questions until 1961–62. As Basil Robinson explains, it may have been that, on assuming power, Diefenbaker never had to consider contrary arguments; only later, when the public, media, and Green began putting forward opposing ideas, was Diefenbaker forced to review any ideas and arguments contrary to the prevailing "pro-nuclear" view.[88] By 1961, however, the prime minister was suggesting that Canada would abide by the principle of "not spreading nuclear weapons" because all its nuclear weapons would be "defensive," and the warheads would be "neither manufactured nor tested in Canada."[89]

As already mentioned, high-level decision-makers during this time period nearly always referred to the nuclear weapons Canada planned on acquiring as "Honest John," "Little John," or the "Lacrosse" systems, not as nuclear missiles. As well, they consistently referred to the nuclear-equipped interceptors and missiles as "Voodoos" and "Bomarcs." The Chief of the Defence Staff wrote of the need to acquire interceptors to complement the "family" of nuclear weapons.[90] And Douglas Harkness likened the acquisition of nuclear weapons to buying a rifle: "The situation is much the same as a man living in a lonely cabin in the woods who fears that he may be attacked by a bear. He does not wait until the bear actually attacks him to buy a rifle, but secures it beforehand and has it ready in the event of need."[91]

In the 1950s and 1960s, many Defenders tended to contemplate the use of nuclear weapons with relative equanimity. Douglas Harkness, for example, assumed that those who advocated acquiring and using nuclear weapons were rational, while those who were opposed to nuclear arsenals or to contemplating their eventual use were irrational and emotional. The issue of whether or not to acquire nuclear weapons, he explained, "is a question which some people cannot face dispassionately. It gives rise to emotional disturbances which cloud the issue and preclude rational discussion."[92] Similarly, General Pearkes assumed that it was all right for Canada to have nuclear weapons, since it would never use them unreasonably (although other countries might). His remarks in one Cabinet meeting are instructive. He said it would be necessary to undertake complex negotiations with the United States to equip Canadian Forces with "the most effective weapons." At the same time, he praised the United States for having refrained from conducting similar negotiations with other countries outside the Alliance. In his view, "the rigid u.s. attitude with respect to nuclear weapons was understandable when one thought of what some countries outside the 'Iron Curtain' might have done in the last few years if they had had such weapons available to them."[93]

Such attitudes may have stemmed from a reluctance to accept disturbing new information about the dangers of nuclear weapons. For instance, Basil Robinson now believes that the true measure of the force of a hydrogen nuclear explosion had not yet been brought home to General Foulkes, Air Marshal Miller, or Douglas Harkness.[94] In Harkness's case, his reluctance to accept "nuclear reality" may have impelled him to defend the utility of nuclear weapons. Rather than confront the apocalyptic nature of nuclear weapons, he claimed he had faced up to the "hard fact" that a nuclear war could come about:

I believe that the basic reason for so much questioning on defence matters is the underlying fear of the nuclear weapon. Unfortunately the hydrogen bomb is with us and we have to accept this as a reality ... I am inclined to believe that this fear of the present nuclear stalemate leads some people into a "head in the sand" attitude. By that I mean a refusal to face the fact that a nuclear war could conceivably come about. This in turn leads to an irritation on the part of those individuals because the government is planning defence measures to meet such an awful possibility, remote as it may seem.[95]

The established point of view at the time was that it would be possible to survive a nuclear war. Although today the underground system designed in the 1950s to protect the prime minister and his aides – "the Diefenbunker" – has been converted into a museum, thirty years ago it symbolized the government's determination to protect Canada's leadership against nuclear attack. The view among defence policy-makers in the late 1950s was that the principal organs of government could survive a nuclear war relatively intact. Although comparatively little was known about the after-effects of nuclear warfare on people and the environment, the Department of National Defence engaged in intensive planning to put in place "survival operations" in the event of a nuclear attack. Preparations were also made for the "post-attack situation," so as to ensure continuity of government, emergency communications, shelter, and the maintenance of law and order. When Harkness was minister of National Defence, he too spent considerable time improving the "national survival program" in case of nuclear war. He ordered civil defence preparations, including the stockpiling of stores and the provision of a nuclear detonation-and-fallout reporting system. He also arranged a large national survival exercise, and called for the training of up to 100,000 militia in special nuclear survival courses.[96] He was provided with background information on the "Post-Attack Situation," indicating that "it is reasonable to assume that if an approximate balance in nuclear strength is achieved between EAST and WEST, the side having made the most efficient preparations for survival will possess a marked advantage."[97]

Defence decision-makers received detailed estimates about the number of Canadians who would be killed in "a heavy attack." The dead would number "many hundreds of thousands of people," while some 1.2 million people in sixteen Canadian cities would need to be "rescued." With few household shelters under construction, departmental estimates suggested that most Canadians could find some shelter from fallout in their basements. Arrangements to ensure some form of continuity of government at the federal and provincial levels were made as well.[98] Taken together, all these estimates and contingency plans probably contributed to the widespread assumption that the Alliance's weapons were necessary and that it would be possible to survive a nuclear war.

Defenders believed deterrence doctrine was suitable and reliable

Many Defenders expressed faith in deterrence, although the kinds of military commitments it required to be credible varied as technology and nuclear strategy evolved. In 1954, American Secretary of State John Foster Dulles announced what came to be called the doctrine of "massive retaliation," based on the American government's decision to depend on its capacity to retaliate, instantly, by means and in places of its own choosing. The NATO Council, in turn, revised its military doctrine by declaring that the Alliance would resort to atomic weapons whether the enemy did so or not. Despite the Soviet Union's development of the hydrogen bomb and the reality of mutual vulnerability, the main elements of deterrence, based on the strategy of massive retaliation, did not change. Indeed, the lesson learned by US strategists from the Korean War prevailed: that the allies should rely on nuclear weapons in preparation for future wars. As well, American interest in reducing the cost of armed personnel contributed to shifting the reliance from conventional to nuclear forces.

Although American doctrine changed little between 1954 and 1960, defence strategists were mindful of the essential ambiguity of the threat to resort to mutual destruction, and the implications of technological developments in the Soviet Union. The production of long-range Soviet bombers increased after 1955, and the Soviets began experimenting with medium-range ballistic missiles. The United States accordingly devoted more of its military expenditure than before to strengthening its Strategic Air Command (SAC) forces and developing nuclear missiles.

In 1957, owing to the Alliance's increasing reliance on nuclear systems to sustain the doctrine of deterrence, NATO military authorities decided to reduce the conventional forces in Europe – to the point where they were deemed inadequate to sustain a massive attack in the frontal sector of Europe. The spread of tactical atomic weapons, which were developed before the Korean War but were unavailable in sufficient numbers until 1955, then became the starting point for various theories of limited war. And American Secretary of State John Foster Dulles and SACEUR General Lauris Norstad became the two principal architects of American policies on limited war. According to defence analyst Albert Legault, "Their statements ... were not marked by precision and clarity, and it is difficult to give an opinion on the exact substance of American thought during this period."[99] In principle, however, the two Americans indicated that the use of atomic weapons in a limited conflict (possibly over Berlin in 1959) would be the prelude to full-scale thermonuclear warfare. For Dulles in particular, the prospect of a limited war, based on the danger of automatic escalation to full-scale nuclear warfare, was still a credible deterrent. The problem that became apparent to Norstad and others in the higher echelons, however, revolved around the double-edged sword of massive retaliation. Legault explains:

The policy of massive retaliation had the advantage of offering no alternative bargaining point. It was thus a double-edged weapon, for it created such a feeling of uncertainty in the mind of the enemy that he was compelled to think rationally about other means of procedure if he did not wish to precipitate a crisis of which he would have been the first victim. On the other hand, the dubious effectiveness of the West's conventional forces and the necessity of having recourse to atomic arms threatened to plunge the West into the very abyss it was trying to avoid.[100]

In order to limit the problems associated with massive retaliation, Norstad conceived the idea of creating an advance line of conventional and tactical nuclear forces to form a shield within Europe (MC/70). His ideas about stockpiling tactical atomic weapons and the forward deployment of conventional forces in Europe did not imply, however, that he was advocating a strategy of limited war in Europe for NATO. Norstad was always careful to be seen as supportive of Dulles's principal doctrine of massive retaliation.

Between 1960 and 1964, the main tenets of deterrence altered. Immediately on Kennedy's succession to power, the doctrine of "flexible response" or "controlled response" was officially endorsed. (Flexible response had been the unofficial doctrine of the USAF and the Navy since 1958). Known also as the "McNamara doctrine," after Defence Secretary Robert McNamara, deterrence was now based on the idea that, since nuclear parity was fully established, the United States could not reasonably resort to general nuclear warfare in order to defend limited goals. As Kennedy explained in 1961, "We intend to have a wider choice than humiliation or all-out nuclear action." The United States thus decided to strengthen its non-nuclear capability for limited war. The American administration reassured the allies, however, that this in no way weakened NATO's determination to resort to nuclear weapons in the event of a major aggression that could not be resisted by conventional weapons. The new concept was that in the event that NATO forces were about to be overwhelmed, the "shield" would force what Norstad called "a pause," thereby emphasizing the costs and consequences of continued aggression.

Thus, in the period between 1954 and 1963, deterrence doctrine evolved. Dependence on all-out retaliation using nuclear weapons gradually gave way to reliance on different levels of response, ranging from limited conventional and nuclear war (the shield), to full-scale intercontinental nuclear warfare (the sword).[101]

In the inner circle of defence decision-making in Canada, leaders seldom followed the various permutations of deterrence doctrine as it developed during these years. Most expressed faith in the credibility of massive retaliation and assumed that, to deter the threat, the allies simply had to ensure that the costs of attacking would be far greater than any conceivable benefits. Rarely, in fact, are more complicated concepts – the shield, the sword, and flexible response, or references to the underlying contradictions and ambiguities of deterrence – found in the available classified, declassified, and unclassified documents.[102]

Several of the decision-makers at the centre and core of policy-making – General Pearkes, General Foulkes, Douglas Harkness, Ambassador Arnold Heeney, and Prime Minister Diefenbaker – had a great deal of faith in the utility of nuclear weapons to deter war. As General Pearkes explained to Parliament in 1959, "The aim of the western alliance is, first of all, to deter the outbreak of war. Should this fail and an attack follow, we must be in a position to defend ourselves and to destroy the enemy's ability to wage war."[103] Pearkes also proved to be relatively prescient in 1959 about the implications for deterrence of stockpiling nuclear weapons in Europe. As he told his fellow Defence ministers at NATO headquarters, the Alliance's defence was based on "the concept of the deterrent." Therefore, he believed "advances" in the future, such as placing "intermediate range missiles" in "certain European countries" and maintaining stockpiles of nuclear warheads for the defence of the whole NATO area would "provide us in due course with an increasingly flexible deterrent power."[104] At this same meeting, Pearkes told the other ministers that, "should the Russians ever think that they were in a position to make a full-scale onslaught, we will be ready to unleash the nuclear striking force which is that sword of which I have spoken."[105]

Harkness also had a great deal of faith in the utility of nuclear deterrence to prevent war. Indeed, his reliance on the doctrine was almost religious. This faith was reflected in his personally developed standard reply to those who wrote to him opposing nuclear weapons:

It should be pointed out that the purpose in maintaining our defence force is to prevent a war rather than to start one. This we do, along with the Allies, by creating a situation wherein any potential aggressor knows that if he attacks us he would be destroyed. The only two weapons systems being obtained for our forces in Canada which have a nuclear capability are the Bomarc surface-to-air missile and the F101B interceptor aircraft. Neither of these can be used until after hostile aircraft have been over Canadian territory many hundreds of miles. Thus, they are incapable of starting a war but do contribute to the deterrence of war.[106]

By referring in his standard reply to the nuclear forces "in Canada" only, Harkness avoided dealing with the issue of whether the CF-104s and Honest John missiles in Europe buttressed or undermined the stability of nuclear deterrence.

Harkness was never reluctant to deal with the issue of whether, by acquiring nuclear weapons, Canada would deter or increase the risk of war. As he argued in personal correspondence, "The possession of such weapons [e.g., nuclear weapons for air defence] cannot be regarded as increasing the risk of war. On the contrary, the risk of failure which they present to an aggressor can represent a definite contribution to the deterrence of aggression."[107] The presence of peace, he explained, was attributable only to the workings of deterrence: "There is no doubt in my mind that the nuclear retaliatory power of the West has been the key to peace in the past few years. Atomic energy can be a force for good – a force to help maintain peace through fear of its almost incomprehensible power."[108] Harkness interpreted even the most ambiguous evidence as confirmation of the validity of deterrence. "I do not think," he said to students at the Royal Canadian Military Institute, "that there could be a single responsible student of defence in the Western world who would not admit that Soviet military aggression had been prevented in the past ten years by the nuclear deterrent in the hands of the United States and the United Kingdom."[109]

In each decade, different military commitments were deemed necessary to help ensure a credible deterrence posture. In this time period, most military officials were neither confused nor uncertain about the imperative of fulfilling Canada's nuclear commitments in order to render credible the Alliance's system of nuclear deterrence. The imperative of acquiring nuclear warheads so as not to abandon the allies in the face of the Soviet threat gave rise to frequent outbursts of frustration directed against the prime minister and Howard Green.[110] By 1962, many high-level officials shared Defence Minister Harkness's concern about the "woeful" inadequacy of continental air defence owing to the deployment of warhead-less Bomarcs and CF-101 aircraft, and were in agreement that Canada had to acquire weapons "equal or superior to those in the hands of the enemy they would have to fight."[111] The Joint Chiefs of Staff strongly recommended in 1961 that the government fulfill its commitments in order to protect the American deterrent and provide twenty percent of NATO's tactical nuclear strike force in Europe. As they saw it, acquiring nuclear weapons of a tactical nature and limited range would be neither provocative nor increase the risk of nuclear war.[112]

In contrast to such advisers, Prime Minister Diefenbaker experienced considerable unease about the issue of rendering Canada's defences credible and either deterring a nuclear war or prevailing in it. On the question of what would happen if deterrence failed, he stated in 1959 that the Alliance should be able to defend itself with conventional weapons. He also believed that nuclear war would result in either "total destruction for all or, at best, a victory over a shattered world."[113] By September 1961, he was waffling in favour of acquiring nuclear weapons for Canadian Forces in Europe, but believed that what was at stake during the Berlin crisis could be "the survival of mankind." It could be a question of "existence or non-existence," he said; "head-on collision" would be insane and suicidal.[114] By December 1962, Prime Minister Diefenbaker had utterly rejected the utility of nuclear weapons for deterring aggression or prevailing in the event of war.

Between 1954 and 1960, however, the prime minister had placed a great deal of faith in the basic principle of nuclear deterrence. Simply put, he recognized that "Canada, the United States, and the other nations of the free world must maintain sufficient military strength to deter an aggressor."[115] He also grasped the principle underlying Dulles's doctrine of mutual destruction early on. Even in 1954, he was able to explain that peace was finally obtainable now that the USSR understood the deterrent power of the nuclear bomb. In Diefenbaker's own words, with some assistance from Winston Churchill: "[T]he awful power of the H. bomb may mean man's survival and mankind's freedom from war. Mankind may be on the threshold of Peace because the USSR realizes what the free nations have contended since 1945, that war may spell the physical extinction of mankind. The prayer of Canadians and people everywhere is that the H. bomb, in the words of Churchill, may be the greatest deterrent to the outbreak of World War III and may well be the beginning of a new age of Peace."[116] The prime minister also understood nuclear deterrence well enough to realize that a policy of "no-first use" might undermine the threat of mutual destruction. In August 1960, he warned the House of Commons: "To declare in advance that we would never use such weapons would weaken immeasurably their deterrent effect. Do not let us overlook the importance of the deterrent ... if we announce that we are not going to use them we would be decreasing our ability to prevent war, which is the main object of all our defence preparations."[117]

Yet it is notable that, compared to other close colleagues like Pearkes, Foulkes, Harkness, and Heeney, the prime minister was much more concerned that the threat of nuclear retaliation would not necessarily prevent all kinds of nuclear war. Indeed, the danger of nuclear war breaking out by accident or miscalculation was such that Diefenbaker addressed these concerns in a personal letter written to Khrushchev in 1958.[118] This is not to say, however, that between 1957 and 1961 the prime minister paid a great deal of attention to alternative scenarios that could not be prevented by relying on deterrence doctrine. None of these decision-makers seemed to consider unconventional scenarios, though their American counterparts at the time were seeking to control the flexible and decentralized procedure the president relied on for authorizing the use of nuclear weapons in the field. Indeed, there is no record of Canadian ministers considering the dangers of a front-line commander resorting, without permission, to short-range atomic weapons such as the Honest John without presidential authority. In June 1962, the US Defence Department developed an electronic lock and key system for the remote control of tactical nuclear weapons from higher headquarters (now referred to as the Permissive Action Link, or PAL system).[119] In contrast, high-level Canadian decision-makers did not discuss whether the president would exercise final authority or whether the flexible, decentralized procedure the president relied on was dangerous. According to Cabinet records, neither did they consider whether massive retaliation could cope with the problem of a minor conflict escalating to a nuclear war. As well, the issue of whether accidental nuclear war was likely or controllable was hardly considered, and any ideas or suggestions that the Alliance could muster against amorphous, diffuse perils, such as environmental threats, human rights violations, and nuclear proliferation were inconceivable. In emergency meetings during the Cuban missile crisis, in fact, Cabinet ministers avoided discussing what the post-attack situation might look like in the event of a deterrence failure. During the emergency meeting of 25 October 1962, they agreed only that draft emergency orders should be sent out to "a lot of other departments affected." Rather than discuss how the general population might be affected in case of nuclear war, attention was focused on the shortcomings apparent in the "National Defence Warbook." Instead of discussing in concrete terms the foreseeable effects of a nuclear war on the North American population, Cabinet ministers focused on "certain revisions" to the Warbook that now seemed necessary.[120] With the exception of a few comments by Green about the dangers of nuclear proliferation, Cabinet ministers avoided considering threatening scenarios that could not be dealt with other than by relying on the workings of nuclear deterrence.[121]

CONCLUSION

Many Cabinet documents, memoranda, personal letters, diaries, original drafts of speeches, and transcripts of interviews indicate that the core beliefs of Defenders greatly influenced decision-making regarding Canada's nuclear commitments between 1957 and 1963. In particular, George Pearkes, Charles Foulkes, Douglas Harkness, Arnold Heeney, Frank Miller, and Hugh Campbell possessed belief systems typical of Defenders; moreover, until 1961–62, John Diefenbaker reflected many elements of this same belief system. Although these men differed somewhat in terms of the intensity with which they held certain core beliefs, all of them espoused elements of the same system. In secret discussions, debates, and correspondence, they feared that Canada might neglect the allies, and that the allies might abandon Canada, unless Canada fulfilled its nuclear and conventional commitments. They assumed that the country should pursue closer ties to its NATO allies through established military commitments, particularly by upgrading its weapons systems to nuclear capability. They believed that the external threat to the Alliance from the Soviet bloc was opportunistic and aggressive. They regarded both Canada's and the Alliance's weapons as necessary and non-threatening. And their faith in deterrence as a suitable and reliable doctrine led them to recommend retaining, if not modernizing, Canada's nuclear and conventional commitments to the Alliance. It was this adherence to the main elements of a belief system typical of Defenders that prompted these decision-makers to advocate the acquisition of five different types of nuclear weapons systems for the Canadian Forces.

Many ministers and defence advisers recommended modernizing Canada's weapons systems with nuclear weapons because of their beliefs about the dangers of abandonment, the nature of the threat, the utility of nuclear weapons, and the reliability and suitability of deterrence. Beginning in 1957, Defence Minister General Pearkes, supported by his senior adviser General Foulkes, argued in favour of acquiring these weapons systems for the Canadian Forces. Initially, the prime minister relied a great deal on their assessments. Although Diefenbaker was unsure of himself at the 1957 NATO Council meeting, and perhaps confused about the nature of the commitments he was undertaking, between 1957 and 1961 he undoubtedly favoured acquiring these weapons. Behind the scenes and in private conversations, Arnold Heeney, Frank Miller, Hugh Campbell, Pierre Sevigny, and George Hees were also vigorous advocates of the nation's nuclear commitments.

The presence of these influential Defenders in the inner circle of decision-making contributed greatly to the government's support for the acquisition of nuclear weapons. This is not to say, however, that it was solely Defenders who accounted for the government's pro-nuclear stand. Other factors – the climate of opinion among the NATO allies, technological developments, American pressure to acquire the CF-101s and Bomarcs – contributed to the outcome as well. Nevertheless, there can be no doubt that the main elements of the belief system of Defenders played an important contributory role.

In other words, we cannot attribute Canada's decision to acquire nuclear weapons to international, technological, and strategic developments beyond the government's control. The underlying belief systems of political leaders were important factors impelling the government to favour the acquisition of nuclear weapons. In fact, defence decision-making was affected by the 1957 NATO Council directives, General Norstad's briefing to Cabinet, Diefenbaker's cancellation of the Avro Arrow, and the launch of the *Sputnik*. However, key Canadian leaders supported the acquisition of nuclear weapons for the Canadian Forces because of their beliefs about the dangers of abandonment, the salience of the Soviet threat, the utility of nuclear weapons, and the importance of buttressing deterrence.

Finally, it is important to note that, within the inner circle, no high-level decision-makers initially opposed, or even criticized, Canada's nuclear commitments. The views of the first minister of External Affairs, Sidney Smith, had not yet crystallized and, until Howard Green assumed office, Deputy Minister Norman Robertson felt uncomfortable about putting forward his own growing concerns. The prime minister did not encourage debate and discussion among his advisers; indeed, with reference to defence matters, he initially preferred to rely on his own opinions and the advice of Pearkes and Foulkes rather than discuss the matter with External Affairs or submit the question to parliamentary debate. During this period, Howard Green was still a backbencher; he did not become minister of External Affairs until June 1959. And George Ignatieff, another potential critic of the government's stance, did not return to Ottawa from London, England, to act as Diefenbaker's adviser on nuclear issues until January 1961. The idea that it might be unnecessary to acquire nuclear warheads in order to demonstrate Canada's commitment to NATO was therefore an idea not yet considered. Indeed, it was not until Howard Green took office that the Prime Minister began to vacillate about whether or not to fulfill these commitments.

The Original Beliefs of Critics and the Onset of New Ways of Thinking, 1957–1963

In the period between 1959 and 1963, a few influential decision-makers held belief systems more typical of Critics than Defenders. This chapter documents these Critics' underlying assumptions regarding the dangers of entrapment, the nature of the threat, and the limitations of different weapons systems and strategies. It shows that their beliefs – which contrasted with and, at times, opposed those of Defenders – influenced defence decision-making in the direction of delaying and rejecting the fulfillment of Canada's nuclear commitments. Beginning in 1959, new ways of thinking about Canada's nuclear commitments began to affect defence policy-making and Canada's NATO commitments in major ways.

SUBSTANTIVE BELIEFS AND ASSUMPTIONS OF CRITICS

Critics feared entrapment

In contrast to Defenders, Critics were preoccupied with the dangers of entrapment. In different circumstances and with varying intensity, Critics were suspicious about the likelihood, and possible consequences, of the allies drawing Canada into an armed confrontation; they were also doubtful about NATO priorities, particularly American undertakings.

Prime Minister Diefenbaker's fears about entrapment first began to affect decision-making in 1960, about a year after he appointed Howard Green to External Affairs. Over time, these suspicions intensified. Diefenbaker expressed his strongest fears about the dangers and consequences of entrapment during the Cuban missile crisis, during the Cabinet debate about whether to alert the Canadian Forces.

From the time Howard Green took office in 1959, however, Green worried about the United States, fearing that the Alliance leader might draw Canada unwillingly into a dangerous confrontation.

In contrast to others, such as Minister of National Defence Douglas Harkness and Associate Defence Minister Pierre Sevigny, Diefenbaker and Green were unconcerned about the dangers of abandonment during the Cuban missile crisis. While Harkness saw fit to order (without the prime minister's permission) an immediate alert of the Canadian Forces, Diefenbaker and Green expressed no qualms about failing to come to America's aid during the crisis; nor did they worry about Kennedy's request to place Canadian Forces on alert falling on deaf ears. Instead, Diefenbaker and Green expressed concern that Canada was in danger of becoming entangled in "domestic" and "Cuban" affairs, and that Kennedy might involve Canada in a nuclear conflict.

At the emergency Cabinet meetings during the Cuban crisis, Diefenbaker and Green spearheaded the small group of ministers opposed to alerting the Canadian Forces and beginning Canada's scheduled troop rotation to Europe. They feared that alerting the forces and rotating the troops would exacerbate tensions, increase pressures, and draw Canada into the confrontation. Their comments during Cabinet meetings reflected their fears of entrapment. Over two days of discussions, they argued that "Canada was not automatically embroiled any time the US was," although they noted that, practically speaking, Canada was involved. They talked of the "great dangers in rushing in at this time" and argued that "quick action brought quick judgement." Furthermore, they said Canada should not appear to be "stampeded." Thus Diefenbaker and Green's fears about "embroilment" caused them to recommend that the government behave normally and deliberately, that the troop rotation to Europe be deferred, and that the government delay its decision to alert the Canadian Forces.[1]

Underlying these arguments about the dangers of rushing in was the assumption that alerting the forces would only increase the likelihood of war. In one emergency Cabinet meeting, Diefenbaker's concerns impelled him to caution his colleagues not only that "Canadian mothers did not want their sons to be killed in any foreign war," but that "the Cuba business was no affair of Canada's."[2] Indeed, his fear that the United States could drag Canada unwillingly into a nuclear confrontation was such that when British Prime Minister Harold Macmillan sent an urgent message, Diefenbaker misinterpreted it, reporting to Cabinet that Macmillan thought the Soviet Union was "balanced on the knife's edge of indecision" and "any hostile act might precipitate a Russian attack." Diefenbaker had taken this message to mean that alerting the Canadian Forces might be just enough to precipitate the outbreak of war.[3] After the crisis, it became apparent that Macmillan had strongly supported Kennedy throughout. The British prime minister scoffed at Diefenbaker for his "faint heart." But it was not Diefenbaker's fears about Khrushchev's intentions that provoked him to oppose alerting the forces. It was his belief about the escalatory tendencies of American military leaders that led him to reinterpret Macmillan's message.

Immediately after the Cuban missile crisis, and despite his heightened fears of entrapment, Diefenbaker ordered Harkness and Green to conduct secret negotiations with the United States. They were to arrange for the acquisition of nuclear warheads based on either the joint control or missing parts approaches.[4] The prime minister's decision to negotiate to acquire the nuclear warheads, despite his heightened fear of entrapment, seems inconsistent; that is, until his underlying assumptions about the term "joint control" are examined. Briefly then, by 1961 Diefenbaker was interpreting this nebulous concept to mean that Canada would accept joint control over all Canadian nuclear weapons systems as long as Kennedy used his executive powers to reinterpret the present law in such a way as to permit the necessary agreement with Canada.[5] Even during his first meeting with Kennedy, before their relationship turned sour, Diefenbaker referred to the imperative of obtaining "joint control and joint custody" over the nuclear weapons.[6] The evidence indicates that Diefenbaker insisted on some measure of joint control because he meant somehow to curtail, if not harness, any hasty American resort to the use of Canada's nuclear weapons.[7] In later years, Basil Robinson explained that, in his view, the prime minister's reason for seeking joint control was "to satisfy himself" that nuclear weapons would not be used, except with the agreement of the Canadian government. According to Robinson, Diefenbaker was not motivated simply by "crass politics," but believed that it was his "political responsibility" to acquire joint control. Indeed, the prime minister was "afraid" of being accused of not having ensured Canada an equal say in the decision to use nuclear weapons.[8] Diefenbaker's autobiography seems to confirm this assessment. As he explained, he had deemed it "essential that the Canadian government be in as strong a position as possible to bring its influence to bear on any decision to use nuclear weapons, and perhaps to deter the United States from any possible ill-considered decisions in this respect."[9]

Although Diefenbaker's concerns intensified while in office and contributed to his growing fear of entrapment, he retained considerable faith in Britain and the other allies. Even during the Berlin crisis in September 1961, the prime minister was unconcerned that the other NATO allies would draw Canada unwillingly into an armed confrontation. One possible explanation for this is that when Diefenbaker dwelled on the intentions of the other NATO allies, he tended to focus on the United Kingdom. In effect, his attachment to the British Crown may have disinclined him to suspect British motives. Over time, however, he became still more wary of entrapment in an American-led initiative.

Whereas Diefenbaker's suspicions grew during his term in office, Howard Green entered his position already concerned about American tendencies to escalate and entrap Canada.[10] Although Green prided himself on his harmonious interaction with individual Americans, he attributed the "different attitudes" of his American counterparts to "the very extent and complexity of their international responsibilities."[11] In keeping with his conviction that it was the extent of this powerful nation's worldwide interests which was problematic, Green occasionally confronted his US counterparts. At one meeting in 1960, he told the American secretary of state that the mounting criticism in Canada of the United States had more or less always been a feature of Canadian life. Green explained that the growing criticism could be largely attributed to Canada's status as a small nation living right up against the powerful United States, and to the resultant fear by Canadians of US domination.[12] Similarly, Green's assessment that "the USA would never meet our requirement for participation in the decision to use the weapon" reflected his own assumptions about the interests and imperatives of a powerful nation, not his beliefs about the intentions of particular individuals such as President Eisenhower.[13]

Although Green carefully attributed his suspicions about the United States to those of "Canadians" in general, his preoccupation with the idea that the United States could draw Canada into a nuclear confrontation became obvious early on, even to Americans. During a meeting with the US Ambassador to Canada in 1960, Green explained that among Canadians there was widespread anxiety about the possibility of nuclear war: "The US Defense Department were thought by some to be courting such disaster by provocative actions and words."[14] In another private discussion, Green explained to Ambassador Heeney that Canadians "simply did not want to get involved in the nuclear competition between the US and the Soviet Union."[15] Heeney quickly began to fret about his minister's tendency to speak frankly to high-level American officials and to the prime minister about "Canadian" anxiety regarding the United States and its "provocative" Defence department. He wrote in his diary that he thought Green was inclined to "pacific-isolationism."[16] But Green seemed not to harbour isolationist tendencies so much as frustration that Canada exerted so little influence over American defence policy. As well, Heeney's assessment that his minister was at heart an iso-lationist overlooked Green's internationalist leanings. For example, Green actively sought to involve Canada in other multilateral orga-nizations such as the UN and the Commonwealth, and consistently touted his devotion to the goals of the UN Charter and the North Atlantic Treaty. Perhaps, it was Heeney's own fears about Green's possible effect on American isolationist tendencies that led him to surmise that Green's attitude stemmed from pacific-isolationism.

Throughout his tenure, Green's fears about entrapment in an American-led nuclear war contributed to his strong disinclination to fulfill Canada's nuclear commitments. As the minister disclosed to Heeney, he believed "anxiety over the possibility of nuclear war and distrust of U.S. military policy and worries over American economic headway in Canada" were contributing to a "strong feeling" among Canadians that "we should have nothing to do with nuclear weapons in Canada." In fact, "this was at the root of the government's reluc-tance to sanction even storage on US bases."[17] Even during the 1961 Berlin crisis, when the prime minister wavered and said Canada's troops in Europe needed to be equipped with more than just "bows and arrows," Green remained convinced that fulfilling the nuclear commitments would only exacerbate tensions. In Cabinet meetings at the time, it was most likely Green who argued that "it would be especially bad for Canada to announce a decision to obtain these weapons during the present period of high international tension, when there was already danger of war. The worst of the Berlin crisis was perhaps over ... Canada should not do anything to worsen the situation."[18] It appears that Green also prompted the prime minister to speculate publicly about the attitude of the "average Canadian" toward Berlin. As Diefenbaker explained in a heavily underlined and annotated speech to the Canadian Bar Association in September 1961:

Some Canadians with the memory of two world wars are asking whether the Western nations should risk war over West Berlin, a war which in its fright-fulness would dwarf all the wars in history. The question is asked as to whether the Western nations are courting war over a (rubber-stamp) by their refusal to accept check-points en route to West Berlin bases signed by East Germans instead of by Russians. The average Canadian sees the problem of kaleidoscopic change – sees Soviet threats followed by Western counter-measures. He fears that some new incident in Berlin might eventually lead to the nuclear devastation of the world. He wants Canada to be heard speaking words of counsel with firmness but with calm moderation. He asks Canada to exert its influence to ensure that every possibility of finding a peaceful and honourable way out of this crisis is fully and patiently explored.[19]

Diefenbaker was echoing his close friend's sentiments in this speech. Certainly, Green was fearful that some incident might entrap Canada and the rest of world in a nuclear holocaust. He sought to prevent such an outcome by pressing, in Cabinet and at the United Nations, for nuclear disarmament.

Critics believed Canada's established military ties to the allies should be restructured and de-emphasized

Critics sought to revise and restructure Canada's traditional military ties to the other allies. In particular, they opposed increasing the number of Canadian Forces for NATO purposes, including the number of personnel deployed overseas. They were critical of the government's promises to modernize and deploy more weapons systems and equipment to NATO, and were generally intent on limiting the percentage of the federal government's defence budget and the percentage of GNP directed toward the Alliance.

Between 1957 and 1963, most high-level decision-makers, including John Diefenbaker and Howard Green, steadfastly rejected the severing of Canada's association with NATO – what they called "neutralism." In fact, Diefenbaker claimed that he could not abide neutralists and heaped scorn on James Minifie, "the reigning advocate of neutralism" and a "Washington-based journalist and expatriate for whom Canada wasn't good enough."[20] Green confided to Heeney that he himself could not be a neutralist like Minifie. To his mind, "it would not be in accordance with the Canadian tradition of 1914 and 1939," and "it would be bad for the Canadian character."[21] Nevertheless, among the decision-makers at the centre and core of defence policy-making, it was Green, Robertson, and George Ignatieff who consistently believed that the government should restructure its nuclear commitments to NATO. Beginning in 1960, Diefenbaker also sought to de-emphasize Canada's nuclear ties. He did this by wavering, and by advocating new proposals such as "joint control" and "missing parts" – propositions that seemed designed to delay negotiations interminably.[22]

According to the record of secret Cabinet discussions, Green based his belief that Canada should renege on the nuclear commitments partly on the idea that Canada, by taking such an initiative, would provide "moral leadership" to other nations. In Cabinet, he represented ministers who assumed, "if Canada stockpiled nuclear weapons its influence in world affairs and ability to provide leadership to other countries would be ended ... Canada had a position of moral leadership in the world that would be adversely affected by a decision to accept nuclear weapons, and this position should not be given up unless and until it was absolutely necessary to do so."[23] Cabinet ministers opposed to this argument told their colleagues not to overestimate the impact on world disarmament of changes in Canadian defence policy: "The position of Canada in the world [is] not so great that a decision to obtain nuclear weapons would affect the decision of the Soviet Union or the United States on whether they should permit the spread of these weapons to other countries such as the United Arab Republic. It [is] in the interest of the Soviet Union to restrict the spread of nuclear weapons at this time, and the fact that Canada [has] obtained them would not result in a reversal of the Soviet position."[24] Despite such arguments put forward by Harkness, Sevigny, Hees, and other ministers, Green remained adamant, even for years afterward, that Canada's acquisition of nuclear weapons would negatively affect the United Nations and the prospect of disarmament. As he later explained: "I'd been raising the devil in the United Nations ever since 1960 about nuclear testing and about disarmament and I thought that if Canada brought these weapons onto Canadian soil it would destroy any hope I had of having any effect in the UN on the question of disarmament and Diefenbaker came down on my side ... You couldn't be talking out of two sides of your mouth at the same time. I mean, we did a lot of work on disarmament."[25]

Green, Robertson, and eventually Diefenbaker sought to de-emphasize Canada's nuclear commitments and restructure the government's conventional contribution to NATO. None of them ever thought he could be accused of deliberately trying to undermine the Alliance. Those who opposed them in Cabinet, however, implied otherwise. Speaking in the House of Commons in September 1961, Harkness obliquely referred to "unilateral disarmers" who were ignorant of history and naive: "Presumably the thinking is that if Canada was completely disarmed there would be no provocation for attack. This theory, of course, ignores history; it ignores our geographical position, and it ignores the stated policy of the Soviet Union ... To suggest that such an action would have a profound effect on Russia, China or any other communist regime displays a naiveté that is beyond reasonable comprehension."[26] Green seemed not to take offence at these remarks; it was as if he did not appreciate that the minister of National Defence regarded him as representative of all the dangerous unilateral disarmers.

One explanation for Green and Diefenbaker's view of themselves as supporting, not undermining, the Alliance was that they believed NATO was held together by many kinds of ties, not simply military commitments. As Green once pointed out, the foundations of NATO were deep because they rested on a built-up spirit of comradeship, friendships that would last a lifetime, and an alliance of leaders on the very best of terms. He argued that NATO's strength derived in large measure not from its collective defence system but from "the freedom and independence which its members exercise and from the strong ties of history, culture and friendship, which the nations of Western Europe share with Canada and the United States."[27]

Another explanation for Green's de-emphasis of Canada's military contribution to NATO and his inability to recognize that Harkness and others saw him, so to speak, as a member of "the opposing team," is that he valued the Alliance much less than other international institutions such as the UN and the Commonwealth. As Basil Robinson points out, Green was "imbued with the climate of the UN" and "enchanted by the idea that men could collectively work toward peace."[28] During his lifetime, he was also concerned about preserving the Commonwealth (which at one time he advocated should be a "third superpower") and improving its capacity as a "bridge between the continents."[29] Compared to the UN and the Commonwealth, he characterized NATO as merely another means of multilateral consultation, and not the cornerstone of Canadian foreign and defence policy.[30]

In keeping with his conceptualization of NATO, Green emphasized the Alliance's function as a consulting body rather than its military purpose of collective defence. As the new minister of External Affairs explained to the NATO Council in 1959, frequent and frank consultations were critical: "One of the principles underlying the North Atlantic Alliance is that no state, however powerful, can guarantee its security and welfare in the nuclear age by national action alone ... In the Canadian view the most effective way of preserving our faith and trust in each other is through frequent and frank consultations."[31]

Yet another important characteristic of Green's approach to NATO was that he believed the chief problem facing the Alliance revolved around the question of worldwide disarmament, not the buildup of collective defences. As he put it, "Canada has felt that more importance should be placed in NATO on the activities of the United Nations."[32] In fact, Green viewed his work on the UN Disarmament Committee as a long-term contribution to NATO's eventual disarmament. As he explained in the House of Commons, "NATO is very much involved in the question of disarmament, because NATO has most of the forces which, of course, would be involved in disarmament and would have to work out many of the problems."[33]

The minister of External Affairs may not have thought that his efforts to promote disarmament at the UN in any way undermined the government's support for NATO or threatened allied ties, but Douglas Harkness saw a definite contradiction between Green's stand at the UN, which he portrayed as "unilateral disarmament," and his own support for NATO's "collective" approach to defence. Green's own line of logic on this question is evident in a memo, which he carefully underlined and retained, addressing the question of whether Canada should independently initiate disarmament:

[Should Canada independently initiate disarmament?]
(a) If this question means could Canada disarm unilaterally, the answer is "No" – not without scrapping our commitments under the United Nations Charter and the North Atlantic Treaty.
(b) [T]he government has no intention of acting in such a way, since this would weaken both the United Nations and NATO.
(c) [U]nilateral disarmament by a country with Canada's military strength would in any event be an ineffective gesture.
(d) If the question means can Canada exercise an independent influence in bringing about general disarmament, the answer is "yes".
(e) Canada's independent influence has, in fact, already been exerted on its allies in the development of the Western disarmament proposals.
(f) The Canadian delegation to the Ten Nation disarmament talks will continue to play a vigorous independent role ...[34]

Unlike Harkness, Green was convinced that his pursuit of disarmament under UN auspices in no way undermined NATO or threatened Canadian membership in the Alliance.

Between 1957 and 1963, a few influential decision-makers began to exhibit the different streams of thought identified in chapter 4 as features of the Critics' belief system.[35] Green, Robertson, and Diefenbaker (beginning in 1962) all made "first-stream" assumptions; that is, they believed that not fulfilling Canada's commitments of nuclear forces to NATO would be of little importance to the continuing function of the Alliance and to Canada's influence on the allies. They also made "second-stream" assumptions, in that they believed Canada's contribution of nuclear weapons to the Canadian Forces deployed in Canada and overseas would increase the likelihood of war, either by accident or miscalculation. As for "third-stream" assumptions, they assumed that fulfilling Canada's nuclear commitments would be relatively unimportant for signalling Alliance solidarity and resolve – indeed, that nuclear weapons were unnecessary and would only compound a difficult situation. As for Canada's contribution of a conventionally armed brigade and air division to Western Europe, this, they felt, was a relatively inconsequential commitment compared to the imperative of working toward nuclear disarmament.

While Critics recommended that Canada de-emphasize and restructure its traditional military ties to the Alliance, some did so without assessing the strategic rationale and implications of their counsel. Critics sometimes recommended, for instance, that certain weapons systems be cancelled, downsized, or simply not acquired, for they worried about the implications of signalling an escalation of the arms spiral. Critics frequently recommended options and alternative proposals to Canada's traditional military commitments to NATO because they wanted, above all, to depart from the government's previous policy direction.

There are a number of examples of Green, Robertson, Ignatieff, and Diefenbaker recommending that Canada not fulfill its NATO commitments without fully assessing their strategic purpose and implications. During the Cuban missile crisis, for example, Kennedy and Merchant were enraged by Diefenbaker's hesitation to alert the Canadian Forces and his impromptu proposal for an "on-site inspection team"; they felt it indicated that the Canadian prime minister distrusted both their intentions and their evidence.[36] However, Diefenbaker had not properly assessed his own proposal; as Green pointed out later that week in Cabinet, "The difficulty was that neither the Russians nor Cuba had denied that missile bases were established in Cuba."[37]

These decision-makers' advocacy of the "joint control" and "missing parts" approaches exemplifies their opposition to fulfilling the government's military commitments as well as their inclination to advocate alternative proposals. High-level military advisers such as General Charles Foulkes argued that the negotiations with the United States to acquire the nuclear weapons should be based on the principle that the United States supply nuclear warheads for the Canadian Forces in Europe and the interceptors in Canada, but that they would remain American property. They also maintained that NATO's soldiers would guard the nuclear weapons stockpiled in Europe, although custody and maintenance would remain with the United States.[38] Diefenbaker, Green, Robertson, and Ignatieff continued to push for joint control. As Diefenbaker explained, "We have made it equally clear that we shall not in any event consider nuclear weapons until, as a sovereign nation, we have equality of control – a joint control."[39]

Commentators such as Norstad, McIntosh, Lyon, Nash, and others argued that Diefenbaker was misunderstanding the American two-key system. He was, they said, presuming a liberalization of nuclear legislation to permit Canada more independent control over the nuclear weapons of the United States. Moreover, he was ignoring the international principles governing the transfer of nuclear weapons. In their view, even the missing parts approach seemed designed to delay the fulfillment of the nation's nuclear commitments.

It is unlikely, however, that Diefenbaker fully assessed the strategic rationale of rejecting nuclear weapons or the military implications of promoting the joint control and missing parts agenda. Together, Green and Robertson, with some assistance from Ignatieff, were the formulators of the joint control approach. As Ignatieff later explained, "We came up with our own formula for defusing the government's nuclear dilemma ... To the beleaguered Prime Minister, this compromise solution was a welcome peg on which to hang his own indecision, and he clung to it even after it became obvious that it wasn't strong enough to save his government."[40] The missing parts approach grew out of the trio's conversations as well.[41] Their suggestion that nuclear warheads be stored on American territory and delivered quickly in the event of an emergency seemed designed to bridge gaps among opposing viewpoints. Also, the missing parts approach sought to satisfy Diefenbaker's desire for joint control so as to deter American escalatory tendencies. It endeavoured not only to satisfy Green, who was fervently opposed to nuclear weapons, but also to mollify Harkness, who worried about Canada's defence of the deterrent.

Both the joint control and missing part approaches demonstrated the extent to which these decision-makers were prepared to advocate alternative strategies designed to delay or depart from the government's previous course of action. As Ignatieff later admitted, "We knew all along that the [joint control] proposal was no more than a holding action, that the Americans would never accept joint control with regard to the use of nuclear weapons. But in the meantime it did enable Howard Green to wage a number of successful campaigns on behalf of the one cause, which, in his mind, overshadowed all others in importance, namely arms control."[42]

Critics believed the external threat was exaggerated and misunderstood

Whereas Defenders portrayed the threat to the Alliance as opportunistic and aggressive, Green, Robertson, Ignatieff, and eventually Diefenbaker thought otherwise. The most striking evidence of the reversal in the prime minister's assessment of the threat is found in the declassified record of the Cabinet meetings during the Cuban missile crisis. Diefenbaker believed that American leaders were not only exaggerating, but misinterpreting the threat from Khrushchev. Beginning in 1961, the prime minister had begun to project a strikingly different image of the Soviet threat. During the Berlin crisis, he suddenly noted that the Soviet Union had fears, too. Although Soviet policies sometimes defied reason, he argued that it was important to seek to understand their vital interests, objectives, and fears.[43] A few months later, Diefenbaker referred to Mr. Khrushchev as a "realist" who supported "a course of peace – a course of realism – a course in keeping with the choice of the Canadian people."[44] By October 1962, Diefenbaker was so suspicious of the motives of President Kennedy and other "military leaders" that he hardly paused during Cabinet meetings to consider Khrushchev's intentions – and when he did so, he took a relatively benign view of Soviet motives. As he told ministers during the emergency meeting of Cabinet on 24 October 1962, the USSR had a similar reason to complain about American missile bases ringing Soviet territory: "Some years ago, when the USSR had complained about the establishment of US bases ringing Soviet territory, the US had responded that they had been invited to establish these bases by the countries concerned. The USSR could now use a similar argument to justify the establishment of bases in Cuba."[45] Indeed, years later, Diefenbaker still maintained that Khrushchev's behaviour during the crisis was cautious and relatively moderate: "Khrushchev went out of his way to cultivate a moderate and reasonable image."[46]

Whereas the threat Diefenbaker perceived from the Soviet Union and Khrushchev faded over time, his impression of the United States as a threat to international peace and security intensified. Instead of criticizing Khrushchev for secretly deploying missiles to Cuba, he lambasted American officials for emphasizing to him that the substance of their photographic evidence was confidential and, shortly afterwards, revealing it to the press.[47] The prime minister openly revealed his distrust of American intentions when he told reporters during the crisis that if his on-site inspection proposal was implemented, "the truth will be revealed."[48]

Diefenbaker also grew increasingly wary about American domestic politics and concerned that certain American leaders were bent on inciting war. As he and Green told the Cabinet in 1962, there were "domestic political overtones in the US decision" to confront the Soviet Union over Cuba. Instead of focusing on Khrushchev's provocations, they pointed out that the United States would be responsible for instigating war by imposing a selective blockade on Cuba.[49]

As the prime minister explained to Cabinet, certain military leaders in the United States appeared determined to fight the USSR. Indeed, he said, three years earlier, some of them had told him that the United States could defeat the Russians any time before the autumn of 1962, but that the outlook thereafter was less certain.[50]

Whereas Diefenbaker's perception of the threat to the Alliance from the USSR dissipated gradually from 1961 to 1963, Green's perception of the Soviet bloc was more consistent. For example, Green assumed that "the Eastern nations" were not necessarily inclined to aggression. As he told the House of Commons in 1962: "[NATO] was set up to prevent aggression by the Eastern nations. Whether or not they would have committed aggression no one can say but there has been no aggression during these ten years."[51] In discussions, Green regularly de-emphasized the Soviet threat, usually prefacing his remarks with the statement that his viewpoint reflected prevailing "Canadian opinion." In one meeting, he explained that part of the reason for the anti-Americanism in Canada was because Canadians did not perceive the threat of Soviet aggression as the Americans did. While both political parties in the United States campaigned for strengthened defences, the opposite, he stated, was the case in Canada.[52] Even an ornery American secretary of state could not deflect Green from expressing the "Canadian" point of view. As Green explained to Secretary Christian Herter, the current difficulties had arisen because Canadians were "not nearly so worried about the Russians as Americans." He then proceeded to point out that the American administration seemed to "anticipate Soviet aggression and the risk of war," while the Canadian government took a "more optimistic view." He concluded his provocative remarks by wondering aloud whether there was a distinction between the State Department's and the Pentagon's appreciations of the nature of the Soviet threat.[53]

Diefenbaker's change of heart regarding the Soviet threat seemed to stem in part from his gradual realization that, "as a matter of survival," it was important that the "freedom-loving nations" seek, through the processes of diplomacy, to build on the hope of international peace. The prime minister slowly came to recognize that, although Soviet foreign policy would not be transformed, it was possible "to identify and to welcome certain modifications in the Soviet approach to international problems." In particular, Diefenbaker felt he could not disregard the symbolic importance of the Soviet Union's participation on the UN's Special Disarmament Committee.[54] In fact, the prime minister's transformed perception of the threat altered the way he processed information about it. During the Cuban missile crisis, for instance, he thought Khrushchev's attempt to deploy nuclear missiles in Cuba was understandable, given the United States' prior deployment of nuclear missiles within striking distance of the Soviet Union. Whereas earlier Diefenbaker would have condemned Khrushchev, by 1962 he was trying to empathize and see the strategic situation from the Soviet premier's viewpoint.

Critics believed both sides' weapons were unnecessarily threatening

Critics tended to view the weapons and force structures of both NATO and the Warsaw Pact as problematic. They frequently pointed out that many of NATO's weapons systems were unnecessary, and could be perceived as overly menacing. In particular, Critics worried that both blocs would regard one another's forces and doctrine as provocative, thus prompting spiraling arms races.

As more information circulated in the mid-1950s about the dangers of nuclear war, some decision-makers began to recognize the drawbacks of nuclear weapons and to counsel disarmament. The opposition of Green, Robertson, and eventually Diefenbaker to nuclear weapons was partly based on their exposure to information and to disturbing facts about the dangers of nuclear war. As Arnold Heeney recorded in his diary, "My judgment is that this instinctive repulsion for nuclear involvement of any kind is at the base of Mr. G's [Green's] own negative attitude over all defence matters, espec. [especially] where the United States, the great nuclear power is involved."[55] Like his minister, Norman Robertson was also "absolutely horrified that mankind would seriously contemplate using the nuclear weapon."[56] As Basil Robinson explains, both Green and Robertson were exposed to the anti-nuclear arguments propounded in the mid-fifties by the peace movement, first in the United Kingdom and later in Canada. Robertson, particularly, took the anti-nuclear viewpoint to heart, believing that once one understood the effect of a nuclear explosion, the only course was to shun the weapons and put them outside humankind's experience.[57]

Undoubtedly, the peace movements that began in Britain in the 1950s and spreading throughout Western Europe and North America in the 1960s and 1980s stimulated many people to think about the dangers of nuclear war and question the doctrine of deterrence. Letters, marches, and public appeals made an overwhelming impact on some leaders. For some, dismantling and destroying nuclear, conventional, biological, and chemical weapons seemed the preferred option.

Prime Minister Diefenbaker's beliefs were profoundly influenced by impressions he received in the early 1960s, when people increasingly began to discuss the dangers of nuclear war. His claim in

January 1963 that "nuclear war is indivisible" and "nuclear weapons as a universal deterrent are a dangerous solution" was purportedly based on his reading of the Nassau communiqué and the ideas expressed by George W. Ball, the American under-secretary of state.[58] However, the prime minister was also influenced by the mail he received from anti-nuclear groups. Although swayed by Howard Green,[59] he claimed to be affected as well by the thousands of letters he received that reflected changes in the general climate of opinion. Although Diefenbaker reasoned that people rarely wrote letters except to express opposition, he regarded his letters as a useful cross-section of the public's understanding – and sometimes misunder-standing – of the goals the government had set for itself.[60] Yet it was also true that, at other times, if public opinion contradicted his own views, the prime minister seemed unaffected by it.[61] As Pierre Sevigny, associate minister of Defence and a strong NATO Defender, recalled later, Diefenbaker "was more and more influenced by what he thought was a political reaction throughout the nation to a policy that looked bellicose. Ban the Bomb movements, Voice of Women groups, and a great many intellectuals were growing vociferous in their demands that Canada remain outside the nuclear clubs and there were noisy manifestations in many cities aimed at preventing the Government from accepting nuclear armaments of any sort on Canadian soil."[62] No doubt the prime minister's finely honed politi-cal instincts, his proven ability to appraise public sentiment, and his many reliable sources helped him to gauge changes in the electorate's beliefs. Although the prime minister's "conversion" was not driven by electoral considerations, it is true that Diefenbaker adeptly used the trends in domestic public opinion to support his arguments; he quickly recognized that anti-American sentiments could be useful to him for electoral purposes; he knew how to capitalize on the memo he found for electoral gain; and he did not hesitate to use the State Department's press release to incite anti-American sentiment during the 1963 election. In other words, Diefenbaker tended to interpret letters, shifts in public opinion, and changes in the electorate's mood in light of his own gradually shifting belief system.[63]

An examination of the prime minister's own jottings reveal that, by 1961, Diefenbaker seemed to believe he himself would somehow be responsible if nuclear weapons were used in a third world war. As he scrawled on his notes for a radio speech, "the thought of a third world war, especially one in which nuclear weapons would be used is a constant companion of one who has the responsibility and trust which rests on me."[64] It may have been this sense of responsi-bility and trust that prompted him to begin cautioning that many

NATO weapons were unnecessary and might be perceived as an offensive threat to Warsaw Pact nations. Certainly by 1963, in his Nassau speech, Diefenbaker felt compelled to explain to the House of Commons that acquiring more nuclear weapons was a mistake:

So what should we do? Should we carry on with what we have done in the past, merely for the purpose of saying, "Well, we started, and having started and having proceeded, we will continue"? Should we do this in an area where mistakes are made? I am not dealing with those mistakes at the moment; but should we continue with such programs, in the light of changing circumstances? These were not mistakes in judgement at the time, but the failure to be able to look ahead and read the mind of Khrushchev and those associated with him in the presidium. More and more the nuclear deterrent is becoming of such a nature that more nuclear arms will add nothing materially to our defences.[65]

In part, while Diefenbaker's attitude seems to have been prompted by his personal sense of responsibility for the survival of millions of Canadians, it probably also grew out of his regular weekend conversations with Howard Green. The minister of External Affairs believed that any acquisition of nuclear arms by Canada might lead to arms proliferation in other regions of the world, including the Middle East, and thence to heightened dangers of unintentional escalation.[66] Although Diefenbaker initially assumed nuclear weapons for the Canadian Forces were necessary, near the end of his second mandate he believed, like Green and Robertson, that these weapons were a dangerous solution.

As he came to believe that both sides' weapons were offensive, Diefenbaker no longer refrained from referring to the possibility of nuclear war; he began putting forward vivid and grisly references to its consequences. He excelled at vivid metaphors – the Pentagon intended to make of Canada a "burnt sacrifice"; the Liberal party wanted to make Canada a "nuclear dump." The prime minister also calculated the destructive capacity of nuclear weapons. As he declared in May 1962: "The present day bomb, with the dimension of 100 million tons of T.N.T., would equal the explosive content of 10 million aircraft in the last war. That is why those of us who have the responsibility of leadership – this responsibility that remains with us day and night – carry this fear that through error or mistake we bring about a war that will destroy all mankind."[67] Diefenbaker's assertion that he might be responsible, through error or mistake, for bringing about a nuclear war is explicable only with reference to the concept of joint control. He was convinced that Canada had to play a more important role in harnessing the United States' possible resort to the use of these devastating weapons.

The perception of NATO's own weapons as unnecessarily threatening sometimes influenced the way in which Critics filed and interpreted other related information. For instance, once Diefenbaker came to believe nuclear weapons were undesirable, he conveniently overlooked the fact that he had previously favoured their acquisition. As Harkness later commented, "He convinced himself by some process of self-hypnosis that he had never favoured getting the nuclear weapons."[68] The prime minister's capacity to reinterpret the past is best illustrated, however, by his claim during the 1963 election campaign that he had always sought to acquire conventional warheads for the Bomarc missiles, and that "the Liberal party would have us put nuclear warheads on something hardly worth having."[69] Even his definition of "the nuclear club" was revised to reflect these new beliefs. In 1962, he interpreted Kennedy's disarmament plan, announced at the UN, to mean that Canada, by acquiring nuclear warheads, would contribute to a dangerous expansion of the nuclear club. In fact, Kennedy had said merely that there should be no expansion of independent nuclear capabilities to other nations; he had not referred to a reduced need for NATO's nuclear weapons systems. As well, Diefenbaker interpreted the Kennedy declaration to mean that Canada would now not need to join the nuclear club. Yet the Canadian Joint Chiefs of Staff, in their attempt to present a rationale in support of nuclear weapons, had pointed out that the only members of the so-called nuclear club were the four nations that had developed an independent nuclear capability. According to the Chiefs of Staff, Canada was really seeking an "interdependent capability," in conjunction with the United States and the NATO allies.[70] Again, Diefenbaker's reluctance to acquire nuclear weapons affected the way he interpreted related information, including President Kennedy's speeches and advice he received from the Canadian Joint Chiefs of Staff.

The convictions of high-level policy-makers about the danger of nuclear weapons affected the way in which they categorized incoming information. Green made no strong distinctions between strategic, tactical, defensive, or offensive nuclear weapons. As he pointed out to Cabinet, once the nuclear threshold was crossed, civilization would be destroyed: "A nuclear war would be quite unlike any wars previously known; it would destroy civilization. There were already enough nuclear weapons in the possession of the U.S. and the Soviet Union to destroy the world and there [is] no need for more in Canada."[71] Whereas the ministers of National Defence, George Pearkes and Douglas Harkness, distinguished between offensive and defensive nuclear weapons, Green, Robertson, and Diefenbaker refrained from using these categories. If they categorized Canadian nuclear weapons systems at all, they grouped them according to whether their deployment destination was on Western European or Canadian soil.[72] Even after Diefenbaker and Green reluctantly consented to begin negotiations to place future Canadian nuclear weapons systems in Europe under NATO's command, shortly after the Cuban missile crisis ended, they steadfastly opposed deploying nuclear warheads on Canadian soil. According to Knowlton Nash, their attitude puzzled high-level military representatives in Canada and the United States because Canada seemed about to acquiesce to an offensive nuclear strike role in Europe, while rejecting a defensive nuclear role in Canada.[73] It may have been, as Nash argues, that whereas Diefenbaker and Green countenanced nuclear weapons in Europe, which was far away, they were reluctant to accept them in their own backyard.[74] It is more likely, however, that the long delay preceding Diefenbaker and Green's agreement to pursue these negotiations, as well as Diefenbaker's subsequent obfuscation and refusal to sign the papers authorizing their acquisition, meant that they agreed to pursue discussions with the US as an unfortunate, yet necessary, compromise to satisfy the allies and the Defenders in Cabinet.[75] The Cabinet records show that, on 30 October 1962, Diefenbaker consented to pursue secret negotiations with the United States, led by Green and Harkness, toward "a general agreement," based not only on the storage of missing parts for the Bomarcs and the 101s in the United States but also on the storage of weapons on European bases for the Canadian Forces in Europe. There is no record that Diefenbaker and Green actually agreed, in the end, to acquire these nuclear warheads.[76]

In summary, then, the influential decision-makers who abhorred the idea of acquiring nuclear weapons were Diefenbaker (beginning in 1961), Green, and Robertson. Further removed from the centre of decision-making, one finds Ignatieff; possibly Basil Robinson; and General E.L.M. Burns, Canada's adviser to the UN's Eighteen-Nation Disarmament Committee.

Whereas Diefenbaker, in the end, could not countenance nuclear warheads for the Canadian Forces, he consistently supported the idea of conventional weapons systems. As his Nassau speech in 1963 indicated, he supported an increase in the Alliance's conventional strength so that, in the event of the failure of deterrence, the allies would not be faced with a stark choice. His argument was the following: "More and more the nuclear deterrent is becoming of such a nature that more nuclear arms will add nothing materially to our defences ... The purpose of increasing the conventional strength is to ensure that if the western alliance is ever faced with aggression from its enemies it will have sufficient strength in non-nuclear forces to avoid the disastrous choice between surrender and all-out nuclear war."[77] Howard Green generally supported Canada's conventional commitments as well. Indeed, as a member of Parliament during the Korean War, he called for a greater Canadian conventional commitment than the government was prepared to endorse. It seems Green countenanced strengthened conventional forces in Europe if only because he thought Canadians might some day have to fight another European war. As he explained to fellow MPS in 1962, Canada's commitments to a permanent-force army and air force stationed in Europe also served to strengthen NATO:

I think it would be worthwhile for Canadians to recognize the fact that in peacetime Canada has abroad a permanent-force army. How difficult it is for any old soldier from the First World War to realize that. I think back to those days when my one ambition was to fulfil the terms of the old song "When I get my civvy clothes, Oh how happy I will be." I remember how everybody wanted to get out of Europe by the first boat and what a job it was to get them sorted out because everybody thought he should be on the first boat. The same thing was true of the Second World War. We now have a permanent-force army and a permanent air force stationed in Europe. I repeat that Canada can hold her head high because of the contribution that is being made by her young men to the strength of NATO.[78]

Again, it may have been that both leaders countenanced conventional weapons because they sought a necessary political compromise to an otherwise unacceptable dilemma. However, it may also have been that World Wars I and II and the Korean War taught them to reappraise the utility of nuclear versus conventional weapons. As a native British Columbian, Green's only real acquaintance with Europe stemmed from his experience as a soldier during World War I. Green had fought in the trenches during World War I and his experience of war was, reportedly, horrific. According to Ignatieff, "having been a veteran in the First World War and wounded, and seen in his early age what a hell of a thing world war is, [Green] was a convinced pacifist and was absolutely against the nuclear commitment in any form. He was for the elimination of nuclear weapons. He would have been a leader in the peace movement if he had been given the chance. In fact, his closest friend and colleague in the House of Commons was the member for Kootenay, Mr. Herridge, who also had been a veteran and lost his arm."[79] While some veterans rejected further involvement in European affairs, Green continued to support the deployment of conventional forces in Europe, though he was "absolutely against the nuclear commitment in any form."

Critics believed deterrence doctrine was unsuitable and unreliable

Another important characteristic of Critics was their lack of faith in deterrence and a tendency to denigrate the assumptions underpinning this doctrine. Critics generally believed that relying on the Alliance's nuclear forces would increase, not reduce, the likelihood of war. Rather than depend on deterrence to prevent conflicts, they drew attention to threatening scenarios that they feared deterrence could not avert.

As early as 1961, during a secret Cabinet discussion, ministers argued that it would be misleading to give Canadians the impression that two Bomarc missile bases and sixty-six Voodoo interceptors could defend them against nuclear attack. They contended that the purpose of these weapons was to defend the SAC bases, and not Canada: "An attack might be made with missiles, against which these weapons were ineffective, and even if the attack was made with bombers, enough of them would get through the defences to do great damage. It was doubtful if these weapons would provide any defence against nuclear equipped submarines or against stand-off bombers that could launch missiles from several hundred miles away from the target."[80] Despite an unnamed minister's warning that there could be no defence against the enemy's weapons, many Cabinet ministers maintained that the Alliance would be able to defend itself in the event of war. Prime Minister Diefenbaker's problem was that he initially subscribed to the view that making preparations for civil defence against nuclear attack was necessary. However, by 1959–60, he believed that there would be "total destruction" and a "shattered world" if nations drifted into nuclear war. Owing to such disparate beliefs about the foreseeable outcome of nuclear war, it was probably easier for him to convert to the view that there could be no defence against nuclear weapons and no winner in a nuclear war. Whereas by 1961 he considered that there could be "no margin for doubt about the devastation which could be wreaked on mankind either by intent or by miscalculation," by 1963 he had no hesitation about making stronger references to nuclear war. As he put it, "The day the strike takes place, eighteen million people in North America will die in the first two hours, four million of them in Canada."[81]

From the beginning, it was readily apparent to Green that, in the event of a superpower conflict, "that would be the end of Canada."[82]

Even in private discussions with Defenders, Green did not waver from this conviction. "Total destruction of Canada" could be expected, he confided to Heeney in 1960, if we are "caught between the two protagonists."[83] Green was sufficiently convinced that it would be impossible to survive a nuclear war that he stood up in the House of Commons shortly after the Cuban missile crisis and stated: "If there is a nuclear war we are in for it. Our cities will be destroyed. On the Saturday night after the Cuban missile crisis arose I believed, and I have no doubt many other people did, that before morning Ottawa might be abolished, as well as Montreal, Toronto and my home city of Vancouver."[84] Green exhibited little, if any, faith in the capacity of nuclear deterrence to avert an armed conflict between the superpowers. On the Saturday night during the Cuban missile crisis, when he thought there would be war before morning, he retired with great foreboding and "in the middle of the night ... a transformer blew up outside the Roxborough Apartments ... [It] made an awful noise and I woke up and I thought, 'Oh, that's it. There's the first Russian bomb.'"[85] The minister fully expected the Cuban crisis would provoke a worldwide nuclear war.[86]

Prime Minister Diefenbaker's lack of faith in deterrence began to be evident in 1960. His fear that Canada could not survive a thermo-nuclear war fuelled his growing lack of confidence in the efficacy of nuclear deterrence. It is noteworthy that, by 1960, other defence policy-makers, such as Arnold Heeney, were carefully expressing their doubts about the credibility of the doctrine of massive retalia-tion.[87] The prime minister did not voice his own growing doubts about deterrence doctrine in strategic orthodoxy; instead he responded with his own ideas about joint control: "We took the stand that we would have them available if war ever came – that Canada would then be in a position to have available to her the best weapons possible."[88] Nevertheless, his explanation demonstrated a lack of faith in nuclear deterrence, which was based at that point on ready-to-shoot missiles and interceptors already in place.

Diefenbaker's insistence on the missing parts approach also defied conventional strategic logic. His primary objective seemed to be to delay, not deploy, nuclear warheads. Defenders argued that Diefenbaker's approach meant that the missing warheads would have to be flown to Canada during a crisis. They maintained that putting parts for nuclear warheads in place during an emergency, or once a war had already begun, undermined the survivability of the United States' second-strike capability. Such an approach also belied a lesson of the Cuban missile crisis, which was that a crisis could happen in a matter of hours, and there would be no time to install missing parts. Diefenbaker reasoned differently. He seemed to assume that Canada's espousal of the missing parts approach would contribute to decreasing, not exacerbating, tensions and slow down, if not prevent, hair-trigger readiness during a crisis. By 1963, when he decided that the "white rocketry" would be scrapped because no one had guessed four years earlier that the Soviet Union would develop intercontinental missiles, he seemed to understand that both sides' vulnerability meant that what was now important was that the Alliance strengthen its conventional forces.

Diefenbaker's unorthodox suggestions about joint control, missing parts, and strengthening the Alliance's stockpile of conventional weapons, seem to have been advanced in order to slow down escalatory tendencies, raise the nuclear threshold, and discourage the United States from any hasty resort to the use of nuclear weapons.

Presumably, the minister of External Affairs also lacked faith in deterrence, because he supported the prime minister in putting forward his joint control and missing parts proposals. Certainly, Green's references to the problems of nuclear deterrence were quite astute for that period. After attending the December 1962 NATO meeting, he pointed out that, since the United States was suggesting that there was now "ample deterrent capability on the Western side," it was unlikely that either of the great nuclear powers would wish to precipitate a nuclear war. Instead of concluding, therefore, that nuclear deterrence would prevent all limited wars, Green pointed out that, in the future, crises would likely not be quite serious enough to precipitate a nuclear war.[89] The minister's recognition that "ample deterrence" would not necessarily prevent future crises also led him to warn the Alliance to broaden its consultation about new types of threats. As he explained, "Many threats are of global nature, and furthermore, one can never be quite sure in what part of the world the next threat is going to come."[90]

Green's reluctance to rely solely on nuclear deterrence to prevent war led him to put forward a different foreseeable scenario, one that could arise out of Canada's decision to fulfill its nuclear commitments. As he explained to Cabinet in 1961, if ministers chose to stockpile nuclear weapons, Canada would be setting a bad example to other countries – that they, too, had an equal right to provide for their defence. This could result in a dozen other powers following Canada's example in dangerous parts of the world.[91] Green foresaw a frightening scenario stemming from rampant horizontal nuclear proliferation and uncontrollable escalation. It was an unusual scenario for a Canadian decision-maker to advance at the time. Most decision-makers that came to fear nuclear escalation envisioned nuclear war solely in terms of the prospect of deterrence failing between the two superpowers. Relatively few feared the consequences of horizontal nuclear proliferation. But the minister of External Affairs was willing to think independently about the logic of deterrence and to draw attention to alternative scenarios accorded little attention from strategists in NATO's upper echelons. As Ignatieff later recorded, "If Green's naiveté and lack of sophistication led to some embarrassing incidents, these shrank in significance beside his selfless pursuit of world peace and the determined, often imaginative way in which he explored solutions to international conflicts."[92]

CONCLUSION

Belief systems played a major role in the decision-making regarding Canada's nuclear commitments. Some high-level decision-makers interpreted events and developments quite differently, based on their core beliefs and assumptions related to the dangers of entrapment, the salience of the threat, and the dangers of relying solely on the Alliance's weapons and strategy.

The previous chapter demonstrated that a substantial group of decision-makers – George Pearkes, Charles Foulkes, Douglas Harkness, Arnold Heeney, Hugh Campbell, Frank Miller, and George Hees – possessed beliefs typical of Defenders, beliefs which led them to advocate the acquisition of nuclear weapons. Initially, the prime minister was also convinced that Canada should acquire these weapon systems, although he became less sure beginning in 1959, after Howard Green's appointment as minister of External Affairs. In the early years, however, the presence in the inner circle of these Defenders helped lead the government toward acquisition of nuclear weapons.

At the centre and inner core of decision-making stood Howard Green and Norman Robertson; both adhered to belief systems typical of Critics – beliefs which led them between 1959 and 1963 to oppose the acquisition of nuclear weapons. In effect, Green and Robertson, with the assistance of George Ignatieff, sought to delay the acquisition process and counselled the prime minister against acquiring nuclear weapons. Although the growing peace movement and the public's increasingly anti-American stance also pushed the prime minister to rethink the nuclear issue, there is no doubt that it was "the trio" that sought to delay, if not reverse, the prime minister's stated policy in favour of obtaining nuclear weapons.

General Pearkes's appointment as lieutenant governor of British Columbia in 1960, and his replacement in Cabinet by Douglas Harkness, was also a significant contributing factor. Whereas the prime minister had accorded Pearkes a great deal of authority and influence, Harkness was neither as close to the prime minister nor as highly esteemed. Moreover, although he proved to be a vigorous NATO Defender, Harkness was not able to convince the prime minister and the Cabinet of his views. General Foulkes's resignation in 1960, in opposition to the government's vacillating policy regarding nuclear weapons, and Arnold Heeney's ill health in 1961, forcing his eventual replacement by Charles Ritchie in January 1962, also weakened the force of the arguments put forward by Defenders in favour of acquiring nuclear weapons. In the inner circles of defence decision-making, Douglas Harkness, Pierre Sevigny, George Hees, Hugh Campbell, and Frank Miller found themselves confronted with an increasingly indecisive prime minister and a vociferous External Affairs minister, backed by a strongly motivated deputy minister and a determined assistant deputy minister.

As for the prime minister himself, between 1960 and 1962 his views gradually changed from those of a Defender to those of a Critic. This shift partly accounted for his initial advocacy of nuclear weapons between June 1957 and August 1960, his indecisiveness until October 1962, and his subsequent rejection of the nuclear commitments in the period between December 1962 and April 1963. Although the prime minister wanted to remain a member of NATO in good standing, he questioned the necessity of acquiring nuclear weapons as part of Canada's commitment to the Alliance. Despite pressures from authorities in the United States, the media, and military personnel, Diefenbaker became more inclined to the Critics' viewpoint. He realized that Canada's acquisition of nuclear weapons could contribute to international tensions and increase the likelihood of entrapment in a global holocaust. Although he never questioned the necessity of deploying Canadian Forces in Europe, he equivocated on the nuclear issue. His attitudes toward President Kennedy, the Cuban missile crisis, Kennedy's memorandum, and the US State Department's press release all contributed to his growing fear of entrapment and his reluctance to authorize the acquisition of nuclear weapons. Although Diefenbaker's new belief system was not the only factor impelling the government to oppose the acquisition of nuclear weapons, it was significant. Allied with Green, Robertson, and Ignatieff, the beliefs of Critics eventually overrode the convictions of Defenders.

Many influential decision-makers in the inner circle possessed interlocking belief structures typical of Defenders or Critics. These belief systems shaped and constrained decision-making with regard to the fulfillment of Canada's Alliance commitments. Although there can be no doubt that a variety of other systemic- and domestic-level factors interacted to push the government toward acquiring nuclear weapons – and eventually away from previous commitments – the beliefs of important decision-makers played a significant role in affecting policy outcomes.

Finally, it is interesting to consider that Canada was the only country during this period that rejected nuclear systems.[93] Despite the opportunity, capability, and even the knowledge base required to produce its own nuclear weapons, the strong convictions of a few politicians helped bring about a Canadian anti-nuclear stance. Although the opposition was short-lived – incoming Prime Minister Lester Pearson acted quickly to fulfill the government's commitments – a few years later the same prime minister who ordered the phasing-out of Canada's nuclear systems, Pierre Elliott Trudeau, held many of the same underlying beliefs and convictions as Green, Robertson, and Ignatieff. Thus whereas "the trio" members were among the first influential Canadian decision-makers to criticize and oppose nuclear weapons, the main elements of their beliefs resurfaced in later years with respect to nuclear weapons as well as other NATO commitments, particularly vis-à-vis Canadian land forces stationed overseas. This oscillating pattern of support and opposition among influential Canadian decision-makers for select NATO commitments has repeated itself continually over the years. Most politicians and senior advisers have wanted Canada to remain a member of NATO in good standing. However, owing in large part to their conflicting belief systems, they have frequently differed as to the way in which Canada should continue to contribute to the Alliance.

The Root Causes of Confrontation: Reasons for Defenders' and Critics' Belief Systems, 1930s to 1980s

Belief systems are generally rooted in a range of first-hand observations and early experiences. They can be shaped both before an individual assumes office and while in power. They can stem from the shared experiences of participating in government – the lessons learned from international events, for example, or from different interpretations of domestic crises – or a particular military or bureaucratic structure.

Explanations abound as to why certain belief systems predominate. Studies suggest that people learn largely from first-hand experiences, from incidents in their adult life or career, and from events with important personal or national consequences.[1] The person who fought in the trenches during World War I will come to hold different beliefs than the person who has never experienced combat. Early events – those "powerful, formative experiences of a young person in his twenties or early thirties or during highly structured professional training" – influence emerging beliefs.[2] A nation's important events such as war or economic depression will likewise shape a person's worldview.[3]

It is always difficult, though, to ascertain exactly which experiences and events shaped a particular individual's belief system. Undoubtedly, it is combination of many different experiences and events that accounts for peculiar or idiosyncratic beliefs. Knowlton Nash, for example, blames Prime Minister Diefenbaker's dislike of President Kennedy for precipitating the crisis in Canadian-American relations. "If only" Donald Fleming had been named minister of External Affairs, rather than Green, writes Nash, "the clash between Diefenbaker and Kennedy would probably have been less ferocious and the dangerous collapse of Canada-American relations might never have happened."[4] Whereas Peter Newman argues that it was

Diefenbaker's indecisiveness and lack of leadership skills that accounted for the government's fall,[5] Douglas Harkness assigns some blame to Diefenbaker's pathological hatred of making a hard decision as well as to his intransigence and hypocrisy.[6] Basil Robinson cites Diefenbaker's "anti-establishmentism" – his jealousy of establishment figures such as Robertson, Pearson, and Kennedy – and his "push-resistant nationalism."[7] Peyton Lyon cites a lack of firm leadership and Green's magnificent obsession with disarmament as explanations for the government's record.[8] Although each author focuses on the characteristics of one or two decision-makers to explain the Diefenbaker government's record, analyses based on idiosyncrasies provide, at best, a one-time explanation of events.

It is easier to analyse the roots of a set of beliefs when the beliefs are shared by many individuals. Thus far, this study has focused on discerning the common elements of different leaders' belief systems over different time periods. As we have seen, certain patterns of thought appeared repeatedly. While some leaders feared abandonment, others feared entrapment. Many believed Canada should de-emphasize and restructure its military ties to NATO, while others argued the opposite. Leaders who projected an aggressive and relentless threat to the Alliance were contradicted by others who argued that this image was exaggerated and mistaken. Many believed that the Alliance and Canada's weapons systems were fundamentally defensive; others saw both sides' weapons systems and strategies as dangerously offensive. Defenders believed in deterrence, while Critics rejected different permutations of this doctrine. This chapter considers the sources of these beliefs and assumptions – what might be called their antecedent causes.[9] As such, it is necessarily conjectural, based not on psychological testing or techniques of content analysis, but on the impressions formed during the course of my research.[10]

WHY DID DEFENDERS FEAR ABANDONMENT?

There can be little doubt that one of the main reasons for the Defenders' tendency to project fears of abandonment was their personal experience of war. Generals Pearkes and Foulkes and Prime Ministers Pearson and Diefenbaker all trained for, or served in, World War I. Pearkes, Douglas Harkness, Associate Defence Minister Pierre Sevigny, and Defence Minister Paul Hellyer served in World War II. In fact, Harkness was under Pearkes's command in the First Division during World War II, and Pearkes, Harkness, and Sevigny all served with distinction during extended periods of military service. After fighting in Italy during World War II, General Jean Allard commanded a brigade during the Korean War, going on to become Chief of the Defence Staff in 1966. Robert Cameron served in the officers' training corps in Germany during the last few months of World War II, before volunteering to join the Canadian troops sent to fight the Japanese in 1945. Charles Nixon, a naval officer, escorted American aircraft carriers attacking North Korea. John Halstead worked in naval intelligence throughout World War II. And Ross Campbell served in numerous naval campaigns during World War II. For decision-makers such as these, memories of war-torn Europe and of family members and friends lost to war instilled a life-long conviction that Canada could not abandon its NATO allies. The Canadian government's prompt decisions to enter the world wars, the nation's generous response to the allies' need for troops and supplies, and the experience of forging close military bonds with the British and American allies – all exerted a powerful impact on the thinking of these individuals. Such experiences formed the basis of many Defenders' later positions vis-à-vis Canada's North American and Western European allies.[11]

After World War II and the Korean War, many Defenders felt that Canada should play a prominent role in the reconstruction of Western Europe. "In the 1950s Europe was destitute," Charles Nixon, a former deputy minister of National Defence, recalled:

Keep in mind that at the end of the war we had the third largest navy in the world, and that was obviously overtaken by all kinds of events. It was the same thing at first in NATO; we had 300 Sabre aircraft over there because nobody else had them then. The Brits could not afford them. So I think that we would be out of line to think that we could ever come back into the same position we had in world affairs at that time. That doesn't imply that we shouldn't produce or contribute more in various ways, not only in the defence field, but also in terms of economic aid, for example ... My concern is that I look on the deterrence/defence contribution as a prerequisite to achieving some of the other things ...[12]

Defenders such as Nixon recognized that Canada was no longer the major power it had been during World War II. They nevertheless believed that not contributing more, particularly in the defence field, would be tantamount to abandoning Western Europe.

Defenders feared abandonment because of a parallel conviction that the close military bonds forged among the allies during and after World War II should not be allowed to wither. For many veterans, it was imperative to strengthen and consolidate the military ties among Canada, the United States, and Western Europe. For Douglas Harkness, the experience of building military ties with the United States during World War II was exhilarating. As Robinson has suggested, this may have rendered World War II a "heady," not a sobering experience for Harkness.[13] Apparently, Harkness learned three powerful lessons from the war and the immediate post-war period. In a letter to his nephew, the Defence minister emphasized, first, that NATO was "a defensive organization which came into being as a result of the Soviet Union taking over a large area of eastern Europe following World War II ... The purpose of NATO was, through unity, to prevent any further expansion on the part of the Communists."[14] Second, Harkness stated that "history showed ... if the coalitions that won the last two world wars had been in existence and firmly united before the wars, these wars might well have been avoided." NATO, consequently, was for him "the cornerstone of our defence policy."[15] Third, Harkness remained convinced that the defence of North America was a "single problem" that could not be separated by boundary lines or territorial limits. In his opinion, the speed of modern aircraft and increasingly shorter reaction times meant that the "two partner nations" had to co-operate in North American defence.[16]

The attempt by Canadian diplomats in 1948–49 to establish NATO seems to have been based as well on the conviction that Canada had a responsibility to promote stronger ties in the Atlantic community.[17] As Lester Pearson stated in 1948: "A North Atlantic treaty ... will create a new living international institution which will have within itself possibilities of growth and of adaptation to changing conditions. The North Atlantic Community is a real commonwealth of nations which share the same democratic and cultural traditions. If a movement towards its political and economic unification can be started this year, none of us can forecast the extent of the unity which may exist five, ten or fifteen years from now."[18] The efforts of diplomats such as Pearson to establish the Alliance were premised on the recognition that Canada could not desert its Western European allies in the North Atlantic Community.[19] Indeed, during the 1961 Berlin crisis, when Diefenbaker came closest to deciding to fulfill Canada's nuclear commitments, it was his memories of the 1948 Berlin Blockade that played a key role in explaining his position. In 1948, he recalled, Berlin had been "saved by an airlift unique in history," without which he was certain Berlin, and freedom itself, would have been "strangled." He urged the other allies to remain unified, and indicated in Cabinet that his government would pursue negotiations to acquire nuclear warheads.[20] Diefenbaker's recollection of the allies' determination not to abandon Berlin in 1948 led him to support, at least temporarily, the acquisition of nuclear warheads.

The tendency among Defenders to predict dire consequences if Canada abandoned its allies stemmed, in part, from the experiences of war and of European post-war reconstruction. But some Defenders were also motivated by allied reaction to previous decisions to cut back Canadian NATO commitments. Ross Campbell, for one, was greatly disturbed by the allies' reaction to the Diefenbaker government's hesitancy to alert Canadian Forces during the Cuban missile crisis. He was further upset by the allies' response to the Trudeau government's initial decision to cut Canadian Forces in Europe by two-thirds. As he later explained, "The cutting of our forces in 1968 and the throwing away of the nuclear responsibility, unilaterally, not in concert with our allies has very severely undermined our voice in NATO." According to Campbell, Canada "never really recovered" from its "wobbling on nuclear weapons," and from the "real trouble" around 1968–69 that both created and compounded a weaker Canadian presence in NATO. Twenty years later Campbell recalled:

We made the announcement of our intention to cut our forces by this huge amount in the wake of the Czech crisis. Two defence ministers, one Dutch, one Belgian, wept, burst into tears if you can imagine, grown men who were politicians, with tears running down their faces saying, how could this country, this Canada to which they twice owed their liberation, be so insensitive to the lessons of history, of World Wars I and II, not to mention the Czech crisis that had just passed. They said that we could undo the Alliance by this action, that they couldn't credit that we would do so and if we went ahead with it they would never forgive us. And they never have. The beginning of Canada's decline in Europe dates precisely from that day. We said to Europe, we don't care about you in the area that is most vital to you, your security when you are in danger. They said back to us, in effect, therefore, we don't give a damn about you when you come knocking economically on our door. Buzz off! You've had it with us. To me that's coloured the whole period since 1968 in our relations with Europe, and it's twenty years now. And I think we are still paying for it.[21]

Other Defenders feared abandonment because they witnessed the reaction among the NATO allies to reductions in Canadian defence spending. As one high-level official recalled in 1982, "Canada's decision to reduce our contingent in Europe in the early 1970s was criticized on the grounds that we were weakening NATO's strength in Europe. Subsequently, we continued to draw criticism because of the low percentage of our GNP spent on defence, compared to most other members of the Alliance."[22] From such criticism, some Defenders learned that there could be negative consequences if Canada did not meet its NATO commitments.[23] In 1980, after witnessing recent "severe criticisms," particularly by the United States, of Canada's defence efforts, one senior adviser expressed grave concern to the Privy Council Office about the "adverse effect in foreign policy terms that a failure by Canada to make every effort to achieve the 3% real growth rate in defence expenditures" could have.[24] For many Defenders, further negative consequences could well result from the government's failure to live up to its financial commitments to NATO.

Still another reason for the Defenders' fear of abandonment stemmed from their deep-seated loyalty to the United States. It was Generals Pearkes and Foulkes, Harkness, and Air Marshal Frank Miller, in particular, who felt a strong allegiance to the United States. Pearkes and Foulkes wanted to establish NORAD in response to Canada's defence being irrevocably tied in future to the United States. The initiatives these two veterans took to establish NORAD bolstered their confidence that Canada-American defence relations would be immeasurably strengthened. In their view, it was ultimately to Canada's advantage to grant the United States the use of Canadian airspace and facilities.[25] Foulkes's successor, Air Marshal Hugh Campbell, was similarly reassured that, "although we can expect to surrender some degree of national sovereignty in the interests of national survival," the newly strengthened relationship was to Canada's advantage – "particularly so when we cannot afford to meet the weapon requirements ourselves."[26] All these men presumed a common interest in strengthening Canadian-American defence ties. As Douglas Harkness reasoned, "Canada belonged to the NATO alliance whose policy was based on nuclear strategy; Canada relied on the nuclear deterrent maintained by the United States and the United Kingdom to prevent aggression; and Canada had sold uranium to the United States and the United Kingdom for the production of nuclear weapons."[27]

Defenders feared abandonment because of a wide range of first-hand and early experiences, learned images, and lessons of history. They had observed and experienced war first-hand. They also retained images of a destitute Europe, which they thought it was Canada's duty to aid and defend. They had learned the lessons of forging bonds of defence with the United States and Western Europe. As well, they remained convinced that Canada had a responsibility to promote closer ties within the Atlantic Community. Finally, they had closely observed the allies' reaction to the announcement of previous cutbacks and, in many cases, felt a strong sense of loyalty to the United States.

WHY DID CRITICS FEAR ENTRAPMENT?

Some Critics feared entrapment because of their different understanding of war. Howard Green's combat experience, for example, led him to counsel against Canada becoming enmeshed in another European war. His chief experience of Europe was as a soldier in World War I, where he fought in the trenches – it was, reportedly, hellish.[28] However, while some veterans rejected any further involvement in European affairs,[29] Green continued to support the deployment of conventional forces in Europe. He opposed the deployment of nuclear weapons because he saw even a limited nuclear war in Europe escalating to a global holocaust.

The Cuban missile crisis taught many Critics to be alert to spirals of hostility and, thus, to search for alternatives. As Paul McRae wrote to Pierre Trudeau: "It is my belief that if the Soviets were weak, as they were during the period of the Cuban Missile crisis, they might well respond by backing down. However, in a world where most observers concede that there is general parity between both sides, the response is more likely to be to deploy more weapons, and to continue to deploy them in more troublesome areas."[30] McRae interpreted the Cuban crisis to mean that leaders should be alert to the possibility of arms races escalating out of control. Whereas Defenders concluded from the Cuban crisis that the acquisition of nuclear weapons was imperative, Critics advised that such armaments were more likely to result in arms races than in immediate co-operation and concessions.

Another reason that Critics warned about entrapment stemmed from their underlying frustration that Canada exerted so little influence over American decision-making, particularly decisions related to defence and security. Indeed, some saw the Alliance leader as confrontational, and deemed it Canada's responsibility to "harness" the United States. Green, for example, before he took office, believed that Canada had sided too easily with the Americans during the Suez Crisis (Canada chose to vote at the UN with the United States, against Britain and France). Thirty years later, Green remained adamant that Canada should have abstained, like Australia and New Zealand; the problem, he contended, was that Canada tended to follow the United States' lead unquestioningly.[31] As soon as Green became minister of External Affairs, Arnold Heeney began to fret about his tendency to speak frankly, both to high-level American officials and to the prime minister, about "Canadian" anxiety vis-à-vis the United States and its "provocative" Defence department. Heeney wrote in his diary that he thought Green was inclined to "pacific-isolationism."[32] But Green was not isolationist so much as frustrated that Canada exerted so little influence over US defence policy. Heeney's assessment also overlooked Green's internationalist leanings. The minister's long-held image of the United States as a powerful nation dominated by the Pentagon, combined with the lessons he had learned in the trenches about the horrors of war, all contributed to his fear of entrapment.

On the other hand, Prime Minister Diefenbaker's growing belief that Canada was in danger of entrapment stemmed primarily from his experience in office. At about the same time as he began wavering about nuclear acquisitions, his closest advisers began to worry about his growing "anti-Americanism." When Heeney questioned Diefenbaker closely in 1960, for example, the prime minister explained that "the avalanche of anti-Americanism" in Canada stemmed from the widespread impression that the United States was pushing other people around; from distrust of the American military; from the economic aggressiveness of American interests; and, he added almost as an afterthought, from Canada's adverse trading position.[33] Diefenbaker's imagery of the American leadership began to affect his decision-making in 1960, well before Kennedy became president. His growing impression that the United States' political leadership was aggressive and its military leaders untrustworthy seems to have been influenced by first-hand experiences as well. After establishing NORAD, he decided that the 1957 agreement had been presented under false pretences.[34] Diefenbaker was frustrated by his failure to sell the Avro Arrow to the United States, doubly so because he had to acquire American-made interceptors afterward. As George Ignatieff later explained: "He was told by National Defence after he had signed NORAD, there was no need for such an aircraft, because the United States would take care of all that and they would not buy the Arrow in any shape or form; they had all kinds of aircraft and missiles and we were going into the missile age anyway. And in his fury, I think, Diefenbaker not only made the decision to scrap the Arrow, but he said that every Arrow plane, even the few models that had been made, had to be destroyed."[35] Diefenbaker also did not want to admit that he had been obliged to intervene to ensure reinstatement of the Bomarc program.[36] With the inauguration in 1961 of a young and seemingly impetuous American president, Diefenbaker's suspicions grew. Although in April 1961 they were strengthened by the Bay of Pigs incident, it was only after he found the memo "What We Want from Ottawa Trip" that they began to preoccupy him entirely.[37] By 1963, according to Ignatieff, the prime minister's distrust of the United States had grown to the point that he truly believed he had been tricked into accepting a defence policy for Canada that was subordinate to a certain type of weapons program and to the interest of a foreign government. As Ignatieff recalled, "It affected his whole attitude in relation to the United States. I mean a lot has been said about his personal antipathy to a young President such as Kennedy. But it had this background in the defence issues, where he felt he had been cornered into a subordinate position and contrary to all his convictions."[38]

Critics, then, feared entrapment because of differing personal experiences, acquired imagery, and historical lessons. Some were fearful because of their own wartime experiences, others because of the lessons they had learned about the consequences of war. Most had surmised from their observations of international crises that Canada would hardly be consulted before being dragged into another war. As well, the impression some Critics gained, both before and after assuming office, of the United States as unnecessarily confrontational contributed to their fear that Canada was in danger of becoming embroiled in another deadly conflict.

WHY DID DEFENDERS BELIEVE CANADA SHOULD PURSUE CLOSER TIES TO ITS ALLIES THROUGH ESTABLISHED KINDS OF COMMITMENTS?

Defenders were generally convinced that, by contributing to the allied war effort, Canada had earned the right to be heard by the other allies. As John Holmes explained, perceptions of Canada's performance during World War II as a great military power only contributed to the view that Canada should continue making commitments to NATO appropriate to that status:

It seems to me, certainly when looking at the record, that the illusions of grandeur persisted about ourselves as a military power based on our performance during the war … It was a curious illusion, because it was based on thinking of ourselves as a great military power – because of the past – while we were in fact disarming and demobilizing and clearly had no intention of remaining an important military power… So you get this kind of illusion of our importance, and it carries over into NATO. Of course it was reinforced in NATO by the fact that we really were in at the ground floor. Those secret tripartite discussions in Washington confirmed a view that we were pretty important, and you could see the illusion again. We knew we were not a great power, but we weren't Luxembourg. I suppose there were again those who wanted to press our position and those who were nervous of the commitments in which we would be involved. It was the old dichotomy in Canadian policy.[39]

According to many Defenders, Canada's considerable contribution to Western European defence in the immediate post-war period had earned its citizens a continuing voice in the higher councils. As the former ambassador to NATO, James Taylor, explained in 1984:

By the end of both wars, Canada was able to assert a right to be heard because Canadians had so convincingly earned that right by what they had contributed to the allied war effort. The history of our participation in NATO demonstrates that the same principle operates in a peacetime alliance. Quite apart from its military value, our defence contribution in Europe earns us the right to be heard by our European allies. And since the defence of Europe is to be a vital interest of the US, it earns us a right to be heard by our American ally as well.[40]

Many Defenders continued to assume that, by maintaining traditional military commitments to NATO, Canada would be accorded a "seat at the table" during important NATO consultations.

Another reason Defenders favoured traditional commitments was that they assumed less orthodox contributions would be regarded as neither appropriate nor acceptable. The Ad Hoc Defence Committee, for example, dismissed the argument that alternative contributions, non-NATO contributions such as to the UN or foreign aid, could be made to justify the withdrawal of Canada's Forces from Europe. The Committee concluded in 1963 that the issue was not whether alternatives were reasonable, but whether they would "carry weight" with the allies:

One can argue that Canada's contribution to the UN should also be regarded as a contribution to the maintenance of world security and the defence of Western interests ... It is therefore conceivable that increased contributions outside the NATO area, including contributions made in the form of foreign aid, could be cited in order to justify the withdrawal of Canadian Forces from Europe. The issue, however, is not whether plausible arguments can be found, but whether such arguments might reasonably be expected to carry weight with our allies.[41]

Their conviction that less orthodox commitments to NATO would be inappropriate was supported by historical precedent and standard operating procedures.[42] Many assumed that stationing Canadian Forces on the Central Front was acceptable proof of our commitment to defending Europe; this, after all, was the historical standard for Canada's commitment. Indeed, Defenders were inclined to cite historical example and recommend standard procedure. As the Ad Hoc Defence Committee suggested in 1963: "Although the threat of Soviet aggression is less menacing today than in 1949 the test of will and resolution continues. The presence of Canadian Forces on the Central Front is the proof of Canada's commitment. As long as Canadian Forces, and especially Canadian troops, are physically present on this front Canada's credentials within NATO can never be seriously challenged."[43] Or as a secret high-level memo recommended in 1968:

"Our need for NATO is substantial: it is perhaps the most important manifestation of our cooperation with the Europeans; and we have no other politically significant institutional links which could serve a similar function. Therefore, if we expect to participate in NATO's affairs other than on a nominal basis and wish to continue to derive the direct benefits which membership brings us, we shall be expected to make a contribution to NATO's military forces."[44]

"Satisficing" – the concept of settling for the first satisfactory option – is also a useful concept for understanding the Defenders' tendency to advocate traditional commitments to NATO.[45] Some did not compare strategies and commitments to see which was most suitable, but adopted the first acceptable alternative, usually preferring the status quo. Charles Nixon, former deputy minister of National Defence, recalls that when the question of whether Canada should acquire new tanks for Canadian Forces in Europe came up, decision-makers concluded: "Look, with the commitments we've got, we can't really change the formations that we have."[46] In another example of satisficing, the 1969 STAFEUR report acknowledged that "a large Canadian force contribution might be needed elsewhere for a peacekeeping mission which might be regarded temporarily as important enough to warrant a reduction of Canadian forces in Europe," but it was "difficult to do more than speculate on the possibility of such a requirement at this stage." Furthermore, "the possibility of future large UN peacekeeping operations involving armed forces is, in any case, increasingly doubtful."[47]

Thus, the assumption that Canada should pursue closer ties to the allies through traditional military commitments appeared to stem from the "lesson" that Canada had earned a right to be consulted by contributing military personnel, equipment, and resources to the allied war effort. Defenders presumed that alternative methods of signalling a commitment would be regarded by the other allies as inappropriate. Moreover, they tended to follow historical example, resort to standard operating procedures, and satisfice.

WHY DID CRITICS BELIEVE CANADA'S ESTABLISHED MILITARY TIES TO THE ALLIES SHOULD BE RESTRUCTURED AND DE-EMPHASIZED?

Some Critics ran contrary to conventional wisdom because they were not themselves regular participants in incremental decision-making processes about NATO and, hence, were not swayed by shared practices and ways of thinking.[48] Many were willing both to challenge previous policy and to propose unorthodox options. Howard Green, Walter Gordon, Pierre Trudeau, Eric Kierans, Ivan Head, Donald Macdonald, and Paul McRae, all appointed from different decision-making environments, seemed particularly inclined to see problems in a new light and recommend non-incremental changes. Head, for instance, doubted that there existed "a probable, direct and credible threat to Canadian territorial integrity." He reasoned that this left the Canadian government "free to make the major decisions concerning Canadian defence policy solely on political considerations."[49] Another senior Ottawa mandarin from the PCO, Gordon Robertson, viewed NATO with less attention to the military's perspective than to political considerations. According to Robertson, "broad political considerations" were more important than military factors in determining Canadian defence policy; therefore, "the size, role and structure of our forces should be developed in the future primarily as a function of our relations with the United States and Canadian internal security."[50] Critics, in part because they were newly appointed from a different decision-making environment and were not directly connected to the institutions affected, argued that the government could revise its traditional defence commitments. Moreover, they themselves were not inclined to be swayed by prevailing wisdom.[51]

Prime Minister Trudeau considered it the responsibility of a newly elected government to re-examine the basic assumptions and principles undergirding its foreign policy. As Trudeau advised Cabinet in 1968, until such time as firm decisions are reached concerning Canada's defence policy, every minister should be cautious in statements on the subject lest it be interpreted that Canada has agreed to remain in NATO for an indefinite period. It was to be made clear that "the continuing thing is the reassessment of defence and foreign policy." Until the reassessment was complete, there was to be no basic policy change which could be interpreted as supporting a continuing commitment to NATO.[52] As one who had been elected on a platform of change and renewal, Trudeau considered it incumbent on his government to examine all the options, to question the assumptions underlying defence policy, and, if necessary, to reject historical precedent. Before the end of 1968, in fact, Trudeau had already posed the following fundamental questions to high-level officials, including the secretary of state for External Affairs and the minister of National Defence:

Is the Soviet Union not as afraid of us as we are of it?
Will the US sacrifice Europe and NATO before resorting to the use of nuclear weapons? Where does Canada fit in?

When are we going to start trying to de-escalate? When are we going to
arrive at a plan to achieve peace by not getting stronger militarily?

If NATO should engage in a conventional war with the Warsaw Pact, NATO
would eventually lose because of the Warsaw Pact's superior conventional
forces. If NATO resorted to nuclear weapons everything would be lost. In
these circumstances, what is the point of NATO maintaining substantial military forces?

Can NATO influence US and Soviet decisions about issues of war and peace
including the use of nuclear weapons?[53]

Trudeau believed that Canadian Forces stationed in Europe might be
withdrawn because, at least at the beginning of his mandate, he
doubted the established rationale for such a troop presence. Moreover, he was disinclined to follow standard defence decision-making
processes.[54]

Critics believed Canada's established military ties to the Alliance
had to be restructured and de-emphasized owing to a wide range of
factors. Frequently, Critics were newly appointed decision-makers,
unconstrained by direct institutional ties. They opposed the government's traditional military commitments to NATO, arguing that these
commitments made no real difference to the allies, either in terms of
the strategic balance or with respect to other areas such as trade.
Prone to rejecting established ways of analysing issues, they tended
to press for a thorough re-examination of the traditional assumptions
and practices underlying Canadian defence policy, and to put forward alternatives.

WHY DID DEFENDERS PROJECT A BELIEF THAT THE EXTERNAL THREAT TO THE ALLIANCE WAS OPPORTUNISTIC AND AGGRESSIVE?

Defenders saw the enemy as a monolithic threat both because of
shared experiences and events that tended to reinforce their perceptions. Such events included the problems in Canadian-Soviet relations
between 1943 and 1948, the Gouzenko affair in 1945, the Czech coups
in 1948 and 1968, the Berlin crises in 1948 and 1961, the Korean War
between 1950 and 1953, the Cuban missile crisis in 1962, the invasion
of Afghanistan in 1979, and the downing of the KAL airliner in 1983.[55]
In Ross Campbell's words, there was "a whole series of crises, in fact,
starting in 1948 with the Czech putsch, to the Berlin crises and failures
of summits. I have got somewhere … a checklist of the dreadful things
that were happening from 1948 onwards with monotonous regularity

about once a year to 1962, the Cuban missile crisis. Just one critical situation with the Soviets after another. No matter what we did on our side always it ended up in failure and renewed tension."[56] According to Defenders' perception of events, it was the Soviet Union's intransigence that had provoked the allies into establishing the Alliance. Indeed, their shared version of events was so salient and widely held that they felt entirely justified in their impression of the threat. As Diefenbaker explained to an American audience in 1959, NATO was established because of "the concern for security, the determination to resist the encroachment of tyranny, and the judgement that only a collective defence effort by nations of the West could preserve the peace threatened by Soviet military power."[57]

Although vivid memories and profound life experiences played a role in shaping many Defenders' imagery, it is difficult to discern whether some Defenders perceived the peril to the Alliance because of lessons they had learned personally or because they had adopted their colleagues' beliefs.[58] Some seemed to portray the Soviet Union as malign, based not on their own recollections of Soviet intransigence, but on acquired rhetoric. According to Associate Minister of National Defence Paul Dick, a strong defender of Canada's NATO commitments:

I know this will sound a little like cold war rhetoric, and I do not wish it to sound that way, but why did we go into NATO? One historian has stated that you have to understand and believe your history, otherwise you are about to repeat it. For the sake of going through it, let me record that there were a group of forces in the world of countries which did not concur in our free democratic philosophy and the way that we would like to run our society and our country. Of course, that group has been headed by a country referred to as Russia or the Union of Soviet Socialist Republics. Let us look at the record it has. We could start back in 1939–40. It invaded Finland, Latvia, Lithuania, Estonia. It moved into the Balkans and into its sphere of influence. It moved into Czechoslovakia and took it over, and it moved into Germany. After that there was a pause, and perhaps everybody in the cold war was standing off and saying that that was the way it was going to be. But Hungary tried to break away, so Russia ruthlessly came in and crushed it. Then Czechoslovakia had a breath of fresh air, and the Russians and their colleagues came in and ruthlessly crushed them. In more recent years, just to show that perhaps they have not always changed over the 50 years in which they have been using their muscle, they invaded Afghanistan, and now are involved heavily in Ethiopia, Angola, and Cuba. Over 50 years, Russia does not have a great record in which we can have a lot of faith or a reason for laying down our arms and believing that it wants peace.[59]

In some cases, convictions about the threat to NATO were shaped by historical and word-of-mouth accounts rather than first-hand experience.

Another reason Defenders perceived an overwhelming threat may have stemmed from the human tendency to see "the enemy" as unjust and untrustworthy, whereas "we" are democratic and conciliatory.[60] Defenders had a marked inclination to view the enemy in we/they terms. Whereas "they" were totalitarian, expansionist, and aggressive, "we" were democratic, legitimate, and peace loving. Many Defenders resisted the argument that parallels could be drawn between NATO and the Warsaw Pact. In the words of one prominent Defender: "It must be made clear that NATO is a free association of sovereign states voluntarily gathered together for genuine collective defence and mutual political support; [the] Warsaw Pact is an instrument of Soviet hegemony, of communist domination within member states and, as shown by Czechoslovakia, is employed by the Soviet Union as a means of arresting the decomposition of its empire."[61] As is characteristic of we/they kinds of thinking, "we" were assumed to be just and trustworthy, while "they" were believed to be illegitimate and irrational. As J. Gilles Lamontagne, minister of National Defence put it in 1983 regarding the Soviet Union's intentions: "I just wanted to illustrate that when the Soviets decide to have their way, making people submit who would not do that voluntarily, they do what they want by force. That is contrary to the manner on our side which always tries to act as democratically as possible."[62] Or as Lieutenant-General Charles Belzile, former commander of Mobile Command and chief of Land Doctrine and Operations, explained in 1987 when he was asked about his own attitudes and beliefs as a young military soldier: "I think about the two ideologies confronting each other at that time. Most of us, certainly me again as a Jesuit graduate, did not believe in the other side at all, and we didn't want any part of it."[63] A common assumption in Diefenbaker's thinking was his conviction that Canada was part of the "we": the "freedom-loving nations," the "Free World nations," and the "leaders of the Free World."[64] Harkness also believed this, saying "it is not we who have resorted to sabre rattling and military threats."[65] Again, in a fashion typical of we/they thinking, Sidney Smith in 1958 spoke of the enemy as having left Canada with no alternative but to arm itself. As he saw it, the "Soviet military machine looms before us in an outline and with a motive power which leaves us no alternative but to be vigilant and strong ourselves."[66]

Possible threats from the others in the Alliance alarmed Defenders hardly at all. The capacity of the United States to unilaterally use force beyond its borders, for instance, was rarely mentioned. Moreover, there was little, if any, inclination to perceive American foreign policy as a potential menace. According to the Ad Hoc Defence Committee in 1963: "The identity of security interests between Canada and the United States is nearly complete, and there is no possible hope of disentanglement ... The USA is bound to defend Canada against external aggression in all conceivable circumstances. It is equally true that Canada has no possible hope of distinguishing her security interests from those of the United States."[67] Shared national interests were also assumed by Paul Martin, minister of External Affairs, when he stated in 1965: "For Canadians to offer ill-informed criticism of United States foreign policy, without recognizing the enormous responsibilities which go with American power, and without recognizing the degree to which our interests coincide with those of the United States, would be a sign of immaturity and could have unfortunate consequences."[68] Consequently, Defenders often condemned protestors who portrayed Canada's dominant ally as a potential threat. In 1983, in the words of J. Gilles Lamontagne, minister of National Defence:

The United States has been and remains essential to our security and that of Europe. NATO policies and determination have brought about changes in Soviet attitudes, not those of the peace movements or the unilateralists. It is NATO which is proposing radical solutions in arms negotiations and the Soviet Union which is holding things up. Popular protest should be directed at the Soviet Union, not at the United States. If one had only two choices, to live in one or the other country as a pacifist, which one would be chosen – to live in the United States with its freedoms or in Soviet Russia which incarcerates pacifists or anyone who wants to petition their Government?[69]

The tendency among Defenders to believe the adversary was aggressive and illegitimate may have been due, as well, to the human propensity to see one's adversaries as similar.[70] Dealing with one type of enemy, such as Hitler during World War II or Khruschev during the Cuban missile crisis, may have increased the propensity among Defenders to view other East bloc leaders, such as Leonid Brezhnev or Mikhail Gorbachev, in a similar fashion. Former Deputy Minister of National Defence Charles Nixon recalls that the older officers who had served in the war against Germany saw the world quite clearly as divided into two competing camps: "After the war they just shifted the focus to the Soviet Union, particularly as we came to see more and more confrontation during the latter part of the 1940s, leading up to the first Western defence arrangements."[71] Another telling example of the tendency among Defenders to see adversaries as similar arose during a meeting in 1982 of the Standing Committee on External Affairs and National Defence, when Defence Minister Lamontagne referred three times to Mr. Brezhnev, the current Soviet leader, as "Mr. Khrushchev."[72]

Examples are legion of Defenders concluding that the communist threat was unlikely to change in the future. As the Ad Hoc Defence Committee predicted in 1963, "International Communism is ... almost certain to remain an important political force." According to the committee, thirty years hence, communism would continue to be a threat: "Marxist-Leninism provides a rationale and blueprint for revolution. More than this, it provides a whole arsenal of proven revolutionary techniques ... As an article for export, Communism is much like any other form of weaponry ... This is one of the lessons of Soviet foreign policy since 1945."[73] Following a similar line of reasoning, the STAFEUR report of 1969 asserted that the Soviet Union's institutions and policy had not changed since 1917:

In fact, one of the major constants in the East-West equation is the deep-seated Soviet conviction that the rest of the world, and not only the "capitalist" world, is implacably hostile to the USSR and bound by class interest to seek the destruction of what communists persist in believing is its "revolutionary" society. This siege mentality has, perhaps more than any other single factor, shaped Soviet institutions and policy since 1917. It is essential to bear in mind that this has always been so, irrespective of the real behaviour of other countries, and that those few attempts which have been made to break out of the pattern, such as those of Khrushchev, have so threatened the Soviet edifice that they have had to be abandoned.[74]

Indeed, according to one of Canada's most senior diplomats and a foremost expert on Soviet policy, Russian leaders retained many "simplistic" concepts dating from as far back as the nineteenth century. He stated that "in recent years it has become ever more apparent that the Soviet leaders (and presumably the schools of diplomacy) retain many 19th Century concepts, which tend to be reinforced by the existence of only two superpowers, each with its clients. The Russians appear to interpret the international system in terms of simplistic formulations such as balance of power, spheres of influence, and the basic hostility of capitalist states, with other similarly obsolete doctrines of antagonism."[75] For many Defenders, the fundamental nature of the Russian threat had changed little since 1945, 1917, or even the previous century.

Defenders believed the threat was malign and relentless, in part because of collective experience, in part because of long-standing preconceptions and myths. Some assessed the threat based on personal and shared interpretations of salient events, but also on truisms they had absorbed from colleagues and allies about the enemy. Psychological tendencies to see the enemy in we/they terms, and to regard adversaries as similar and unchanging, also contributed to the tendency among Defenders to warn about a serious and unyielding peril to the Alliance.

WHY DID CRITICS BELIEVE THE EXTERNAL THREAT WAS EXAGGERATED AND MISUNDERSTOOD?

The Critics' imagery of NATO's traditional adversary differed from that of Defenders, partly because they did not ignore or discount evidence of the Soviet threat posing a limited threat to the Alliance. Little research has been done on how beliefs systems alter in response to new information. It is clear that people tend to maintain their beliefs even in the face of discrepant evidence, but it is unclear why some decision-makers alter their perceptions of rival states while others do not. As Robert Jervis points out, "Once a new image of another state is established, the other's actions appear very different than they had before. New bits of behaviour are noticed, some old ones are dismissed, and other bits are reinterpreted."[76] It appears that Critics who reassessed the traditional view of the threat to the Alliance, or underwent a gradual change in their imagery of the peril, did so because they processed incoming information differently than did Defenders. They paid greater attention to new evidence and proffered different interpretations of events. Once Diefenbaker began to perceive Khrushchev as a "realist" intent on disarmament and world peace, for example, he interpreted the Russian leader's deployment of nuclear missiles to Cuba in 1962 far more benignly than did other world leaders. The USSR, he reasoned, had had a similar reason to complain about American missile bases ringing Soviet territory some years before.[77] In another example of the inclination among Critics to reinterpret events and challenge conventional wisdom, Paul McRae disputed American assessments of the Soviet threat in his secret report to the prime minister: "The internal problems, including a weak economy having to sustain very large defence expenditures, strains produced by the relations between the Russians and other Soviet peoples, including those of the Moslem faith, and the insecurity of living surrounded by enemies, both real and imagined, would seem to me to make any idea of invading the NATO powers rather ridiculous."[78] Even when faced with evidence of Soviet intransigence, Critics frequently held to the position that the Soviet threat was misunderstood. While some ministers were concerned about the new "element of military risk" owing to the Soviet invasion of Czechoslovakia in 1968, for instance, Donald Macdonald and Eric Kierans interpreted the invasion as a sign of weakness, not strength, and certainly not directed against the West.[79] Similarly, Pierre Trudeau interpreted the Soviet downing of a Korean airliner as an aberration of the normal progression of East-West relations. In like fashion, Paul McRae saw the invasion of Aghanistan as an unfortunate outcome, not of expansionism, but of the Soviet Union's own insecurity.[80]

Some Critics viewed the Soviet threat within the context of a structural problem arising from the competition between two, heavily armed superpowers. Green, Trudeau, and McRae all warned that Canada was in danger of being entrapped, and subject to, great power ambitions, conflicting ideologies, and ominous military capabilities. From their perspective, the Soviet threat was simply part of a larger threat system dominated by opposing military alliances and an ongoing arms race. Consequently, Critics were not averse to drawing comparisons, suggesting that the United States was also provocative and dangerous. As McRae reasoned in the early 1980s, American deployment of the Pershing missile would lead the Soviets not to back down but, more likely, to World War III: "Thus the deployment of a Pershing II missile with a 6 to 8 minute run from Europe to a Soviet silo, evoking a launch-on-warning situation, could result in the deployment of a missile off the u.s. shore, with a comparable flight period. A computer error, due to the short time for verification left under such a situation, would, or could, bring about World War III. The world would move from the balance of terror to the balance of error, a scenario that should give us all a great deal of genuine concern."[81] For some, the prospect of American unilateral military initiatives was fearsome, along with the prospect of the United States manipulating the Soviet threat to justify such actions. These worries about the larger threat system, and the escalatory intentions and capabilities of both superpowers, were often exacerbated by American behaviour in an array of domestic, continental, and international incidents, ranging from the Cuban missile crisis in the 1960s to Ronald Reagan's "dangerous downplay" of America's might in the 1980s. Whether it was the "determination of certain leaders in the United States to fight the ussr," the propensity of the United States to possibly undertake a "first-strike," or President Reagan's "constant belittling of his own military" and "enhancement of the Soviet threat," a number of Critics focused on the threatening behaviour of the United States.[82]

Of course, younger Critics experienced a different international environment from those who had fought in World War II and come to power in the immediate post-war years. The younger generation of decision-makers was conceivably influenced as much by American behaviour in Vietnam and Cambodia, as by Soviet intrusions into Berlin and Czechoslovakia. American behaviour during the Vietnam War, for example, was probably more relevant to shaping their belief systems than Soviet behaviour during the Korean War. Also, Canada's opening up to Communist China in 1971 may have been more salient for these Critics than diplomatic revelations dating from the 1940s about a Soviet spy ring in Canada. In effect, Ronald Reagan's bellicose reaction to the downing of the Korean airliner in 1987 may have seemed more threatening to younger Critics than their dimly remembered recollection of the Soviet Union's downing in 1962 of an American u2 spy plane. On the other hand, there is no denying that many Critics were from the older generation. But Green, Robertson, Ignatieff, and Kierans, all of whom lived through many of the same international events as other high-level Defenders, still developed radically different belief systems. For this reason, explanations based primarily on decision-makers' generational cohorts are difficult to pin down.

Critics challenged traditional assessments of the Soviet threat for different reasons. It appears many were inclined to search for and accept evidence that the menace was limited. A few viewed the Soviet challenge as part of a larger threat system in which a superpower's behaviour and intentions had the potential to be both provocative and dangerous. Some had not lived through the same disturbing events in the first half of the twentieth century as had their elders. So while Critics often put forward plausible evidence that the threat was misunderstood and exaggerated, their assessments of the Soviet threat seemed premised on their desire to rebuild international confidence and restore the conditions necessary for peaceful East-West dialogue and arms control.

WHY DID DEFENDERS BELIEVE CANADA'S AND THE ALLIANCE'S WEAPONS WERE NECESSARY AND NON-THREATENING?

Many Defenders were reticent to accept disturbing information about the consequences of using nuclear and conventional weapons of mass destruction. They tended to assume that the aftermath of war would be survivable. Indeed, in the 1940s, '50s, and '60s, the government put in place civil defence plans on the premise that it would be possible to survive a nuclear war. In 1962, Arthur Menzies, former head of the Defence Liaison Division in the Department of External Affairs, was responsible for dealing with the survival of the government in case of nuclear attack. He comments:

I was allocated the External Affairs responsibility for dealing with the survival of government in Ottawa in the event that some of the missiles planted in Cuba were to land in the Ottawa area. We had a team of special persons picked out, with the most beautiful stenographers, who were to go down a hole near Carp and provide some continuity of government. This was just an added strain at a time of international crisis, and gave one to understand that the whole mechanism for crisis management requires a very, very elaborate structure of planning and of communications and of contingency arrangements and so on.[83]

Given that considerable time and money was spent in the 1950s and '60s preparing and rehearsing elaborate contingency plans, some policy-makers may have tended to see any future war as resembling the situation they were contemplating and as calling for the plans they had developed.[84] Even in the 1970s and '80s, as information about the effects of nuclear, biological, chemical, and conventional war became more widespread, some decision-makers continued to assume that nuclear war would be survivable.

Some Defenders viewed the Alliance's weapons as relatively benign because of their propensity to regard "our side" as good and "the other side" as evil. Robert Jervis points out that, "a state may take as evidence of another's hostility actions that, if it had carried them out itself, it would have believed were consistent with its own peacefulness."[85] And as Douglas Harkness explained in 1962, "I do not think our troops should be required to face a potential enemy with inferior weapons and it is for this reason that our Army has been supplied with the Honest John."[86] Even as Defenders tended to see their side as good and the other side as hostile, they also viewed Canada's capabilities as defensive and similar systems and strategies on the other side as offensive.

As well, some Canadian leaders seemed to need to make the potential use of nuclear weapons into a viable defence strategy. Their psychological need to believe that nuclear deterrence kept them safe led them to deny that such weapons were inherently dangerous.[87] Faced with new and conflicting information about the effects of nuclear weapons, other denial mechanisms came into play. For example, by dismissing new information and discrediting alternative sources, some Defenders denied nuclear reality and engaged in "bolstering."[88]

There is a great deal of evidence that Defenders ignored new information, sought opinions that supported their beliefs, and drowned out contradictory evidence. Defenders in Cabinet, for example, generally refused to deal with Trudeau's warning that Canadian systems such as the CF-104s could be perceived by the Soviet Union as first-strike weapons. Confronted with disturbing information about nuclear fallout, ministers in Diefenbaker's Cabinet unquestioningly accepted the USAF's argument that the fallout from exploding Soviet and Bomarc weapons over Canadian territory would be relatively less harmful in comparison to full-scale nuclear war. In short, the presumption that resorting to the use of the Alliance's weapons could be a credible and rational course of action seemed to be buttressed by different denial mechanisms such as "premature cognitive closure" and bolstering.[89]

The widespread tendency to view the Alliance's own weapons and strategies as non-threatening and defensive may have stemmed as well from the universal tendency to deal with guilt by "projection." Sometimes, instead of accepting guilt, people project their anger and irrational feelings onto the adversary. As one psychoanalyst has explained, although the Americans and the British were the first to produce an atomic weapon and the only ones to use it, "the belief of the majority of US and British people [was] that it is all right for us to have atomic weapons since we would never use them unreasonably – not like those 'others' which could be Russians, Arabs or Israelis."[90] In this regard, there are some disturbing examples of Defenders projecting hatred and irrational motivation onto the enemy even as they assumed that the NATO allies would never use similar weapons systems out of hatred or irrationality. As General Pearkes pointed out to Cabinet in 1958, it was all right for Canada to begin negotiations to acquire nuclear weapons, since Canada would never use them unreasonably – but the United States should be praised for having refrained in the past from conducting similar negotiations with countries outside the Alliance, because of what they might have done in the past few years if they had had such weapons available to them.[91]

It seems that various human tendencies led Defenders to present the Alliance's weapons and strategies as necessary and defensive. They were disinclined to accept disturbing information about the consequences of both nuclear and conventional war, although many had lived through the latter. Many tended to see any future nuclear or conventional war as survivable. There was a propensity to regard "our side's" weapons as good, and the other side's as hostile. As well, Defenders seemed to have psychological needs to make nuclear

weapons a rational defence strategy, and to deny evidence that neither nuclear nor conventional weapons could guarantee their safety.
Respectful of established practices and traditional military doctrine,
desirous of implementing some measure of a "defensive" defence
policy, and disposed to believe that nuclear war was conceivable,
Defenders widely assumed that Canada and NATO's weapons systems were imperative.

WHY DID CRITICS BELIEVE BOTH SIDES' WEAPONS WERE UNNECESSARILY THREATENING?

Critics were more inclined than Defenders to question conventional
wisdom concerning weapons systems and to challenge established
doctrine. During one Cabinet briefing, Prime Minister Trudeau
rejected the accepted grounds for Canada's continued contribution
to NATO's submarine surveillance program. Instead, he asked a series
of logical questions undermining the military's traditional assumptions for supporting Canada's role in NATO's anti-submarine warfare
strategy.[92] Another illustration of Trudeau's tendency to question
traditional assumptions was his criticism of the logic of maintaining
an active anti-bomber defence system: "If the USSR was to launch a
first strike on the USA, all nuclear systems – the ICBMS, the SLBMS
and the bombers – would be used. By the time the USSR bombers
were detected over Canada the nuclear holocaust would have begun.
What then was the point of being able to shoot down Russian bombers? ... Detection and warning of the approach of USSR bombers was
necessary but the scenario envisaged which attempted to justify the
need for an interception and destruction capability against Soviet
bombers was marginal ..."[93] Trudeau was typical of many Critics in
that he seldom shrank from questioning or rejecting military doctrine. Critics seemed more inclined to question authority, reject the
rules, and query established thinking.[94]

Exposure to information about the dangers of limited nuclear war
and the effects of nuclear and conventional weapons of mass destruction impelled many Critics to oppose the buildup of both sides'
defence systems. Such exposure included belated reports about the
aftermath of Hiroshima and Nagasaki, scientific studies about the
global effects of "nuclear winter," and revelations about the inadequacy of civilian defences in case of a nuclear, chemical, or biological
war. Critics found information surfacing about the effects of a nuclear
explosion difficult to ignore. Many recognized that nuclear weapons
were a qualitatively different means of destructive force, and that

resorting to first use in any conflict would result in uncontrollable escalation. As Ivan Head wrote in 1969: "What must be understood is that the dissemination of nuclear weapons has served to introduce a qualitatively different means of destruction. A tactical nuclear weapon cannot be equated with the firepower of X infantrymen or Y batteries of artillery, anymore than the educational value of a colour television program can be equated with Z radio programs."[95] Similarly, Paul McRae felt compelled to point out in the 1980s: "What must be remembered is that 400 missiles, whether they be ss-20s or ss-4's and ss-5's, would completely destroy meaningful existence in Europe in a war. It would be insane to use such weapons in a strike as part of a conventional invasion of Western Europe, because the occupied land would be uninhabitable."[96] As more information about the dangers of nuclear war became available, decision-makers began to recognize the drawbacks of such weapons and counsel disarmament. The opposition of Howard Green and Norman Robertson to nuclear weapons was partly based on their exposure in the late 1950s to disturbing facts about the dangers of nuclear war. As Basil Robinson explains, both Green and Robertson were exposed to the anti-nuclear arguments propounded in the mid-fifties by the peace movement, first in the United Kingdom and later in Canada. Robertson took the anti-nuclear viewpoint to heart, believing that once one understood the effect of a nuclear explosion, the only course was to shun nuclear weapons and put them outside humankind's experience.[97]

Perceptions about the climate of opinion also seemed to prompt some decision-makers to oppose both sides' buildups and postures. The peace movements beginning in Britain in the 1950s and spreading throughout Western Europe and North America in the 1960s and 1980s incited many Canadian citizens to think about the dangers of nuclear war and to question the assumptions supporting deterrence. Letters, marches, and appeals drawing attention to the dangers of war had an overwhelming impact on some leaders. For some, dismantling and destroying nuclear, conventional, biological, and chemical weapons became the preferred option.[98] Diefenbaker's beliefs seemed profoundly influenced, for example, by impressions he received in the early 1960s, as more people began to discuss the dangers of nuclear war.[99] His assertion in January 1963 that "nuclear weapons as a universal deterrent are a dangerous solution" was purportedly based on his reading of the Nassau communiqué and ideas expressed by George W. Ball, American under-secretary of state.[100] But the prime minister was also influenced by the mail he received from anti-nuclear groups such as the Voice of Women, by Stanley Kramer's movie *On the Beach*, and by arguments put forward by James Minifie in *Peacemaker or Powdermonkey*. Diefenbaker, although largely influenced by Green, was swayed, too, by the mail he received reflecting changes in the general climate of opinion.

Prime Minister Trudeau appeared similarly affected by the general climate of opinion in the early 1980s. In Trudeau's opinion, the field of nuclear strategy had begun to be penetrated by people like himself who openly questioned the basic assumptions of strategic thought in the nuclear age. As he argued: "This is a period of deep questioning of many of the strategic concepts which have dominated the post-war world. New-school strategists, and critics from left and right, are probing the fundamentals of strategic thought in the nuclear age from many points of view. They are in agreement, however, when they point to changing realities, to evolution in the psychology of those who live constantly with the spectre of nuclear war, and to the importance of weeding out obsolete ideas."[101] Indeed, Trudeau's decision to undertake a peace initiative in 1983–84, visiting fifteen world capitals to initiate a dialogue about nuclear disarmament, can be partly attributed to the climate of opinion on nuclear testing and cruise missile deployment. As he told a group of American journalists: "It is, in reality, the politicization of the disarmament question, which maybe our various populations have brought us to. As usual, the people often send the signals and catch the reality before their leaders do." [102] The prime minister was convinced of the need to do something, while in power, to slow down the arms race.[103]

We have seen that Critics were concerned that modern weapons and force structures posed an unacceptable risk to the fragile peace between East and West. For these decision-makers, it was imperative that the government oppose destabilizing and provocative technologies. They were particularly concerned that both sides' weapons contributed to international tension, undermining the chance of constructive dialogue. Critics tended both to accept disturbing information and to question conventional wisdom, and they were swayed by perceived shifts in the general climate of opinion against nuclear weapons, nuclear weapons testing, or overseas forces. Less authoritarian, less rule-bound, and more disdainful of tradition and hierarchy than Defenders, Critics were more likely to reject established opinion about each side's weapons systems.

WHY DID DEFENDERS BELIEVE DETERRENCE DOCTRINE WAS SUITABLE AND RELIABLE?

During the late 1950s and early 1960s, Defenders relied on pre-nuclear thinking about war. General Foulkes, for example, thought of the "front-line" nuclear weapons in Europe in terms of the "heavy support" they would provide and the "prestige" and "morale" they would accord Canadian Forces.[104] In their secret Cabinet discussions in 1958, General Pearkes referred to nuclear weapons in terms of the financial costs of acquiring them, not the human costs of actually using them. As he explained, when the time came to use nuclear warheads, "the Canadian expense" would be restricted to replacing their storage facilities: "Ownership of the weapons would remain with the u.s. and hence the cost could be expected to be borne by the u.s., at least until the time came to use the warheads. The Canadian expense would be restricted to the cost of constructing storage facilities for Canadian use or on bases for joint use by Canada and the u.s.[105] Cabinet records confirm that some ministers relied on conventional war concepts to explain what would happen if nuclear war occurred. According to some ministers in August 1961, lives and property could be "defended," the "best" weapons would help defend Canada, and a Soviet nuclear strike would merely be the "first blow." As they noted, "Not all attacking aircraft would be destroyed, but an effective air defence would save many lives and much property. If war occurred, Canada would want to have the best weapons and equipment available to defend itself. If it did not occur, the fact of having acquired nuclear weapons would not matter ... The Soviet Union which had legitimate reason to fear Germany could possibly strike the first blow."[106] Some Defenders even resisted the concept of mutual vulnerability in favour of the idea that it would be possible for the Alliance to erect a defence against nuclear weapons. As Prime Minister Diefenbaker told other NATO heads of government in 1957, "We must see how we can organize our collective resources to render impregnable the defensive capacity of the Atlantic Community in the nuclear era."[107]

In keeping with the tendency not to closely examine their use of conventional war concepts, many Defenders "overgeneralized" lessons drawn from conventional war. The wartime experience of General Pearkes, General Foulkes, and Douglas Harkness taught them to be wary of an all-out attack. Similarly, Diefenbaker's willingness to open Canadian territory to international inspection – an "Open Skies" agreement with the Soviets – reflected his early preoccupation with preventing a surprise onslaught. Until President Kennedy officially promulgated the doctrine of flexible response, it was generally assumed that the enemy could be deterred at all levels by threatening all-out retaliation, including the use of nuclear weapons.

In the 1960s, '70s, and '80s, Defenders continued to recall the lessons of deterrence from World War II. They often argued, for example, that war might have been avoided if Chamberlain had chosen to deter rather than appease Hitler. As Mitchell Sharp explained to Cabinet in 1969, "The reason we had the last war was because the Germans were tempted to attack because of our weakness."[108] For many Defenders, one of the main lessons of World War II was that, to prevent another world war, all the allies had to contribute to "collective security" and a united front. Again, as Mitchell Sharp stated:

I have yet to hear any convincing argument that, if Canada wants to play a part in ensuring its own security, in the resolution of the security problems of Europe that directly affect our own fate, and in mitigating the confrontation between the super-powers, we could do so as effectively as within some such collective effort as NATO. We could opt out, of course. That is an alternative. We could decide not to participate with our NATO partners in the search for collective security and a settlement in Europe. But the problems of a divided Europe will not disappear if we opt out. In or out of NATO, Canada cannot isolate itself from the consequences of failure to establish a stable order in Europe.[109]

Any inclination of the Canadian government not to support efforts to enhance "collective defence" – withdrawing Canadian Forces from Europe, for example, or refusing to test the cruise missile – would indicate to the Soviets that the West was not united in deterring this "expansionist totalitarian" power.[110]

Since many of those profoundly influenced by World War II were too young to affect decision-making processes until the 1950s and '60s, the lessons they learned had a protracted impact. As Robert Jervis explains, "The lessons learned from a major war may have less impact on policy in the immediate postwar years than they will 20 years later when those people who were most strongly stamped by the war take power."[111] Many of the generation most affected by World War II embraced deterrence as a credible strategy to help avoid war. The contradictory lessons learned from the Korean War – that the Alliance should rely on tactical nuclear weapons, not conventional forces, and that conventional rearmament was necessary during peacetime – helped strengthen, not undermine, deterrence doctrine.[112] The paradoxical lessons of the Vietnam War – that, on the one hand, small-scale "out-of-area" incursions could be deterred and, on the other hand, that they could not – also helped buttress, rather than fundamentally undermine, deterrence doctrine.[113] Because perceptions were slow to change, and decision-makers assimilated information according to their existing beliefs about deterrence, the stability of this doctrine increased as time went by. Indeed, Defenders at times interpreted all but the most ambiguous evidence as a confirmation of the validity of this policy. As Mitchell Sharp, minister of External Affairs said in 1969: "I am often asked how one can be sure that the 20 years of peace Europe has enjoyed are due to the existence of NATO. I suppose in the end there is no substantive proof, but I can tell you this. The question is one which is easily asked in Calgary, 6,000 miles from the Iron Curtain. But it is a question that simply is not asked by those who live their daily lives in the shadow of massive Soviet forces."[114] Or as J. Gilles Lamontagne, minister of National Defence, said in 1983: "I mentioned that the nuclear deterrent is essential in order to prevent war and preserve peace. I do not want to imply that every country should have nuclear weapons in order to prevent invasion. I just say that if Afghanistan had been a nuclear power, I do not think Soviet Russia would have dared risk a nuclear war by invading it."[115]

Over time, some Defenders became increasingly convinced that deterrence was an appropriate strategy precisely because NATO had never had to use its nuclear or conventional weapons. As Lamontagne explained, "Deterrence is not an attractive way of ensuring peace, but it has worked."[116] And according to Robert Jervis, the human tendency to believe that the enemy's intentions have been thwarted owing to one's own actions may have played a role. As he stated: "Not having the historian's knowledge of the other side's intentions, the decision-maker is relatively free to select a pleasing interpretation of why the adversary has not harmed him. He is more apt to believe that deterrence worked than it was not necessary. And if, in spite of the actor's threats, the other does take hostile action, the actor can believe that the other would have taken even more damaging steps had it not been for his stance."[117]

Some Defenders' resistance to questions about the reliability of deterrence could also have been caused by shared practices in the military and the civil service. Alistair Mackie notes that military personnel share distinctive values and practices. They believe in discipline and obedience, as manifested in the rituals of saluting, marching, and combat training. They value uniformity and conformity, as shown by their dress. And they respect rules and hierarchy, as demonstrated by the military's hierarchical structure.[118] The ingrained military code of those Defenders who shared a military background (such as Foulkes, Pearkes, Miller, Campbell, Harkness, Sevigny, Allard, Hellyer, Halstead, Campbell, and Nixon) may have made it difficult for them to question or reject deterrence doctrine, or to imagine scenarios that could not be solved with military force.

Indeed, few active or retired military personnel have ever openly questioned the underlying tenets of nuclear deterrence doctrine.[119] For the most part, senior military personnel placed a heavy reliance on the various permutations of evolving NATO doctrine. Nuclear weapons were the central components of NATO's deterrent strategy; because this was the established view, military personnel were disinclined to accept disturbing information or to portray Alliance strategy as unsuitable.

A parallel explanation for the tendency among Defenders to place their faith in deterrence is that the belief systems of senior bureaucrats were highly resistant to change. John Steinbrunner argues that by the time bureaucrats rise to powerful positions in government, they tend to believe in tradition, to value precedent, and to be guided by standard operating procedures.[120] To question whether the traditional threat to the Alliance was salient, to consider setting new precedents regarding Canadian NATO commitments, and to question NATO's established doctrine, may not only have gone against the grain but also jeopardized career prospects and invoked the risk of losing the respect of one's colleagues. Some high-level bureaucrats in the Departments of External Affairs and National Defence were concerned in May 1968, for example, that incoming Prime Minister Trudeau would order a comprehensive study of the grounds for withdrawing Canadian Forces from Europe. By this time, former Prime Minister Pearson, appearing on the American program *Face the Nation* after he left office in April 1968, also supported the idea of withdrawing Canadian Forces from Europe. According to a memo written by one senior bureaucrat, "I think we must accept the fact that many senior officials in the Privy Council and in the financial departments have largely made up their minds that Canadian Forces in Europe are no longer necessary and therefore that they can be disbanded without serious damage to Canada's interests." Faced with the prospect of discouraging the prime minister from setting such a precedent, the memo advised Marcel Cadieux, under-secretary of External Affairs (and a strong Defender) that:

Our first objective should be to persuade Mr. Sharp to attend the NATO Ministerial Meeting. After the election, we might also try to arrange a couple of meetings in his office where he could go into the underlying foreign policy considerations involved in the defence review. If he were impressed by our arguments, he might think it advisable in advance of the Cabinet Committee meeting to seek to persuade some of his colleagues who hold key positions, including the Prime Minister of course. It might be that at that stage we could prepare material as we did last year at Mr. Martin's request for Mr. Gordon and some of his colleagues.[121]

In another example of senior bureaucrats' tendencies to be guided by precedent, Ambassador Heeney reported to Howard Green about the US congressional debate in 1960 concerning "the adequacy of the deterrent." If Heeney had doubts about whether it would be possible to defend Canadian territory against bombers and missiles, however, he was careful not to express them, except in a roundabout fashion:

With ever-increasing evidence that the threat from manned bombers is receding as the Soviets progress in the ICBM field, and will within a few years probably be minimal, is it wise to proceed with billion dollar programs – SAGE and Bomarc, for instance – which are effective only against bombers and useless against missiles? Would not the money be more wisely spent in accelerating the missile program, providing for "hard-site" deployment, producing more missile launching submarines which will be virtually invulnerable to surprise attack? Is even the fixed "hard site" concept of missile deployment tenable now, in views of current estimates of Soviet missile accuracy, or should it be abandoned in favour of random-dispersal rail- and road-mobile deployment? It is very unlikely that anyone has full answers to these questions.[122]

Rather than openly question the direction of North American strategic doctrine, Heeney reasoned that it was unlikely that anyone had full answers. For this senior bureaucrat, it went against the grain to openly query whether deterrence was a suitable and reliable doctrine for Canada to support.

Yet another reason Defenders firmly espoused deterrence doctrine and resisted alternative strategies may have been that they wanted to believe that decision-makers, in a crisis, would remain rational and in control. It was simply unpalatable that the American president, NATO and SHAPE headquarters, or the Alliance's Command, Control and Intelligence System would be unable to control the crisis at every level. The idea that deterrence could fail, or that an unintended, uncontrollable war might happen because humans were not always completely rational had to be resisted. Defence Minister Harkness very much believed that, in a crisis, the president of the United States would control the possible use of nuclear weapons at every level of confrontation. The only dangerous scenario Harkness foresaw was if countries other than "the United States and several of our NATO allies" exercised "unilateral control" over the use of nuclear weapons.

As Harkness personally replied to a woman who wrote him after the Cuban missile crisis, suggesting that the fewer the number of countries with nuclear arms, the less risk there would be of accidental war:

I agree, but with one qualification. The fewer countries which have *unilateral control* of the use of nuclear arms, the less risk of accidental war. The agreements entered into by the United States and several of our NATO allies conform to present United States law. The United States retains control of the nuclear warheads until such time as the President of that country releases them. Then, and only then, can the participating country to the agreement decide whether to use such weapons or not. Thus, under such agreements, there is no immediate or direct increase in the number of countries which might by accident or otherwise employ nuclear weapons.[123]

The fact that the president exercised unilateral control of decision-making authority was not a worry for Harkness; in effect, he presumed the president would act rationally and control a crisis at every level of escalation.

Some Defenders relied on deterrence doctrine simply because the possibility of a nuclear attack occurring by accident was unthinkable. Morris Bradley explains:

Nuclear war is so terrifying a possibility that denial is ubiquitous, even though this terror is partly assuaged by the belief – not necessarily plausible – that nobody could be so insane as to attack if there are sufficiently terrible weapons with which to retaliate. However, when the possibility of nuclear war happening by accident is considered, it must be even more emotionally shocking and subject to denial. The possibility that civilization could end through blunder is incompatible with the system of beliefs that most people hold about the meaning of life. Our cultural traditions make such a possibility unimaginable for many people. It is easier to deny such an appalling reality than to face the anguish of reconstructing a belief system to accommodate it, and to act upon the implications.[124]

Rather than face the terrifying implications of accidental nuclear war and uncontrollable escalation, many Defenders resorted to denial mechanisms, such as "defensive avoidance."[125] In emergency meetings during the Cuban missile crisis, for example, ministers avoided discussing what the "post-attack" situation might look like, and how the general population might be affected in case of a nuclear war. Instead, they focused on the shortcomings now apparent with the "National Defence Warbook." Rather than discuss the foreseeable effects of a nuclear war on the Canadian population, ministers focused on "certain revisions" to the Warbook which were now deemed necessary. Cabinet resolved that "a thorough review should be made of the National Defence Warbook over the next six weeks and any necessary changes made to it, after which it should be submitted again to the [Cabinet Defence] Committee for approval."[126] Harkness similarly engaged in denial and wishful thinking in the months prior to Diefenbaker's famous Nassau speech of January 1963. His own account of the events leading up to his resignation demonstrates that, for months, he ignored mounting evidence that the prime minister seriously doubted the necessity of nuclear weapons. In fact, Harkness was flabbergasted by the newspaper reports of Diefenbaker's Nassau speech. He had listened to the speech and rejoiced because he thought the prime minister was finally announcing that Canada would acquire nuclear warheads. Reports to the contrary astonished him, and he issued a clarification of Diefenbaker's remarks. During the subsequent Cabinet meeting that took Harkness to task for his press release, the Defence minister finally realized that Diefenbaker did not intend to acquire nuclear warheads, and promptly resigned. His handwritten account, penned shortly afterwards, defended his own conviction that Canada had to acquire nuclear weapons to contribute to the Alliance's deterrence strategy. It also illustrated that in the months preceding his resignation, Harkness had engaged in wishful thinking, defensive avoidance, and bolstering.[127]

One of the principal findings of this study has been that many Defenders held interlocking belief systems, of which their beliefs about the merits of deterrence doctrine were only one element. It is likely that many defended deterrence because their belief system impelled them to perceive and interpret reality in a certain way. Since they were particularly fearful of abandonment, they had to portray the Alliance's strategic doctrine as reliable. Because they perceived the external threat to the Alliance as aggressive and opportunistic, deterrence was deemed eminently suitable. Moreover, because they saw the Alliance's weapons and strategies as necessary and defensive, they considered deterrence doctrine appropriate. Confronted with information that conflicted with their belief system, they resorted to various kinds of denial.

WHY DID CRITICS BELIEVE DETERRENCE DOCTRINE WAS UNSUITABLE AND UNRELIABLE?

Some Critics questioned deterrence from an underlying conviction that stockpiling armaments had never guaranteed peace and security. Ivan Head unequivocally declared in his secret 1969 study: "In all

history, arms by themselves have never guaranteed security for long
… The present balance of deterrents is an absurdly unsatisfactory
substitute for real security. A more stable alternative is necessary. Yet
through history, there is always recurring resistance to arms control
and the avoidance of violence as a means of change. For nothing has
ever arisen to challenge the primacy of war as a means of doing evil
while at the same time feeling good. War is socially approved violence."[128] Some Critics believed that threatening to use nuclear or
conventional weapons of mass destruction to prevent attack had
fundamentally undermined national and global security. As Trudeau
remarked in 1984, "Canadians, and people everywhere, believe their
security has been diminished, not enhanced, by a generation of work
spent on perfecting the theories and instruments of human annihilation."[129] Similarly, McRae concluded that new technological developments in weaponry had increased, not decreased, the likelihood of
any conflict escalating into a major war: "The fate of civilization is
rapidly passing from the control of humans to control by a computer."[130] For most Critics, the lesson of history was that deterrence
had imperilled, rather than ensured, Canadian security and the
future of human civilization.

Another reason Critics questioned deterrence arose out of their
suspicion that other countries, including the NATO allies, might mismanage a crisis, setting off a limited nuclear war which might, in
turn, lead to global conflagration. Ivan Head challenged the premise
underlying the Alliance's doctrine of flexible response – that the use
of tactical nuclear weapons would not escalate into a nuclear holocaust – on the grounds that there were no "provable criteria" for it.[131]
Similarly, McRae advised the Prime Minister in 1983: "I find it impossible to believe that a war in the European theatre involving ss-20's
etc., would not immediately become a global conflict, even if comparable weapons like Cruise missiles were involved. Counterforce, and
the idea of limited nuclear war is not a credible option."[132] For some
Critics, it was doubtful that other nuclear powers, including the
United States, would be able to control a crisis and prevent Canada
and the other allies from becoming entrapped in a nuclear holocaust.

Many decision-makers had little confidence in the arguments put
forward by Defenders. Some Critics disbelieved, confronted, or
pointedly ignored those they considered to be downplaying "nuclear
reality." According to Basil Robinson, Norman Robertson had no
patience with those who talked "war-game language" about how to
minimize the impact of the bomb or whether the use of tactical
nuclear weapons might lead to nuclear war.[133] Howard Green was
similarly reluctant to engage in debates about deterrence; if he was
confronted with arguments contrary to his own belief system, he

tended to listen but not change his mind. This practice is noticeable in another of Heeney's diary entries:

Apart from specific items in joint defence arrangements, I said, my anxiety derives from the fact that we continued to support the principle of joint N. Am. defence with the US; we proclaimed that the US nuclear capability (SAC) was the deterrent upon which we, and the rest of the free world depended; our contribution to the joint defence was a contribution in the first instance to the protection of the deterrent. It therefore seemed to follow that we shd [should] do what was necessary to maintain our defences, with the US, in good order. Did this not imply, in due course, the arming of Cdn forces with nuclear defensive weapons? and meantime their preparation, equipment & training on this assumption? ... The Minister would not accept this proposition. He said there wd. [would] be total destruction of Canada if we were caught between the two protagonists.[134]

For many Critics, the arguments Defenders put forward about deterrence were arcane and far removed from reality. As Paul McRae wrote Trudeau, he was surprised and worried to meet people who applied pre-World War I and II ways of thinking, as well as the Munich syndrome, and who seemed to have no concept of what was in store for civilization if the two superpowers ever went beyond the brink.[135]

Another reason Critics lacked faith in deterrence may have been owing to their tendency to question established practice and reject conventional thinking. Critics seemed more inclined to confront, rather than dismiss or ignore, unpalatable scenarios, ranging from the risk of deterrence failing, to the danger of accidental nuclear war, to the problem of human irrationality in a crisis. Because they already held one or more elements of an entirely different, yet interrelated, belief system that impelled them to interpret information and events differently, some of the contradictions and paradoxes of deterrence may have seemed more apparent to them. In part, they may have regarded deterrence as unreliable because they greatly feared entrapment in an interalliance war. Threatening all-out or controlled retaliation was deemed inappropriate because the threat to the Alliance was both exaggerated and misunderstood. Stockpiling weapons was unsuitable for ensuring national and global security because both sides' offensive weapons and strategies were already overly threatening and unnecessary.

CONCLUSION

This chapter has explored some of the antecedent reasons for the prevalence of the belief systems of Defenders and Critics. Defenders tended to warn about the dire consequences of abandonment because they had observed and experienced war firsthand. They also retained images of a destitute Europe which they considered it was Canada's duty to aid and defend. As well, they had learned about the imperative of forging close defence bonds with the United States and Britain, and remained convinced that Canada had a responsibility to promote closer ties in the Atlantic Community. They had observed, moreover, the allies' reaction to the announcement of previous cutbacks and, in some cases, shared strong feelings of loyalty toward the United States or the United Kingdom. Critics, on the other hand, after observing the horrible consequences of war, tended to be more wary of being dragged into another bloody conflict. Many were concerned about the possibility of entrapment because of lessons they had learned from international crises, indicating that Canada would hardly be consulted before another war. The impression that the United States as the Alliance leader was unnecessarily confrontational also contributed to their fear that Canada was in danger of entrapment.

Some of the reasons Defenders assumed that Canada should pursue closer ties to the allies through traditional commitments stemmed from their conviction that Canada had earned the right to be consulted by contributing military personnel, equipment, and resources to the allied war effort. They also bought into the widespread assumption that alternative or less traditional methods of signalling Canada's national commitment would be regarded by the allies as implausible and inappropriate. Defenders shared tendencies to follow historical example, adopt standard operating procedures, and resort to psychological shortcuts. Critics, on the other hand, believed that Canada should de-emphasize its traditional military commitments to NATO. They assumed that these commitments made no real difference to the allies, either in terms of the overall strategic balance or with respect to other areas such as trade. In many cases, they were newly appointed and unfamiliar with NATO issues, or prone to rejecting established ways of analysing issues. Most tended to eschew traditional approaches to problems and issues in favour of a thorough re-examination of the underlying assumptions for implementing a policy in the first place.

My research has suggested that Defenders believed the external threat was monolithic and inexorable because of their shared interpretation of salient experiences and incidents, or because of lessons they had absorbed from colleagues and allies about the enemy. They may also have had psychological tendencies to see the enemy in "we/they" terms, and to see all adversaries as similar and unchanging. Critics, however, believed the external threat was exaggerated and misunderstood precisely because they were inclined to search for – or at least not reject – evidence that the threat was exaggerated and misunderstood. Preoccupied with both superpowers' behaviour, they sought to demonstrate that, compared with the USSR, the United States was also provocative. Some Critics, furthermore, had not lived through the same events of the first half of the twentieth century as had their elders and those who often interpreted salient events and crises very differently.

I have suggested, too, that Defenders presented the Alliance's weapons and strategies as necessary and defensive because of a disinclination to accept disturbing information about the consequences of nuclear and conventional war, and a shared tendency to see future nuclear or conventional wars as survivable. There seemed to be a propensity among Defenders to regard Canada's weapons and strategies as good and the other side's as hostile. Their psychological needs to make nuclear weapons a "rational" defence strategy and to deny information indicating that nuclear deterrence did not guarantee international security also exerted an impact. Certainly, Defenders tended to be more respectful of established practices and traditional military doctrine, more desirous of implementing some measure of a rational defence policy, and less disposed to believe nuclear war was inconceivable. On the other hand, the tendency among Critics to believe that both sides' weapons and strategies were unnecessarily threatening was buttressed by their inclination to search for, and accept, disturbing information and to question conventional wisdom. Perceived shifts in the general climate of opinion often affected their beliefs. Less authoritarian, less rule-bound, and less respectful of tradition and hierarchy, Critics were more likely than Defenders to reject established opinion about both sides' weapons systems and strategies.

Many antecedent factors contributed to the belief among Defenders that deterrence was a suitable and reliable doctrine. Some continued to use pre-nuclear war concepts without examining their relevance in the nuclear era. The stability of this doctrine increased over time as all but the most ambiguous evidence was interpreted as a confirmation of the validity of this policy. Some Defenders also supposed that deterrence had worked because nuclear weapons had never been used and no war had taken place in Europe. As well, shared practices within the military and the civil service made high-ranking officials unwilling to question established military doctrine. For example, for many, the idea that deterrence could fail because of human irrationality, broken lines of communication, miscalculation, or accident was profoundly disturbing, and therefore resisted. In contrast to

Defenders, Critics lacked confidence in deterrence and tended to question the doctrine's underlying tenets. They believed that history showed that stockpiling weapons never guaranteed peace and security, and that threats to use weapons of such immense destructive potential to guarantee the Alliance's security were shortsighted and misguided. Most Critics suspected that other countries, including NATO allies, might mismanage a crisis, leading to Canada's possible entrapment in a limited nuclear or conventional war in Europe. Moreover, they thought those who defended deterrence in effect downplayed nuclear reality and the consequences of nuclear war.

We have seen that the principal elements of these two competing belief systems were rooted in various personal experiences and human characteristics, in different historical lessons learned and absorbed from others, in contrasting images about the source and salience of the threat, and in alternative ways of approaching problems and participating in shared practices. Many Canadian leaders approached the issue of deciding about the nature and extent of the country's NATO commitments from opposing perspectives because of different firsthand and early experiences, shared historical lessons, common interpretations of international and domestic practices, and ingrained bureaucratic and military procedures. By exploring some of the underlying reasons that leaders advocated change, or consistency, with respect to Canada's past role in NATO, we have deepened our understanding of the factors that have shaped past Canadian defence policy – while broadening our appreciation of the types of variables that could shape future Canadian policy in all sorts of multilateral security arrangements, including NATO.

The Dilemma of Alliance Membership

It is hoped that the reader's understanding of defence policy-making and Canada's support – or lack of support – for its NATO commitments has been broadened and deepened by this presentation, in a conceptual framework, of the belief systems of influential policy-makers. This study shows that certain underlying beliefs significantly contributed to the variation of support among influential decision-makers for some of Canada's military commitments. It also pursues a new approach to the study of Canadian decision-making, with the concepts of "Defender" and "Critic," as well as "abandonment" and "entrapment," shedding fresh light on the assumptions and decisions of those who formulated Canadian defence policy in the nuclear era.

A PATTERN OF SHIFTING SUPPORT FOR CANADA'S NATO COMMITMENTS

Canadian defence policy-makers have often contemplated and pursued significant changes in Canada's NATO commitments. For example, Diefenbaker's government, having decided initially to expand Canada's Alliance commitments, made plans to obtain nuclear missiles for five different weapons systems to be deployed on Canadian and Western European soil. The process of acquiring the nuclear warheads was delayed, however, by acrimonious debate within Cabinet and the federal bureaucracy. Finally, the prime minister and his minister of External Affairs opposed the very commitments the government had undertaken. Next, Pearson, before becoming prime minister, reversed his party's avowed opposition to acquiring nuclear weapons for the Canadian Forces. However, by the time he stepped down from power, he opposed retaining Canada's NATO commitment of overseas-stationed forces. Then, in 1969, Prime Minister

Trudeau reformulated his initial intention to cut and possibly with-draw Canadian Forces from Europe, and the Cabinet eventually compromised by halving the forces. Under Trudeau, too, Canada's nuclear weapons systems were converted to perform a conventional role in the Alliance. The prime minister's 1978 speech at the United Nations General Assembly calling for a "strategy of suffocation" and the cessation of nuclear weapons testing was followed, in 1979, by his government's decision to allow cruise missile testing as part of Canada's commitment to NATO. Trudeau's "peace initiative" fol-lowed shortly thereafter, in 1984. The subsequent lessening of ten-sions between the superpowers was followed by an unprecedented set of unilateral and multilateral arms-control initiatives. By 1989, with the fall of the Berlin Wall, the Cold War was officially over.

THE DILEMMA OF ALLIANCE MEMBERSHIP

In many respects, this pattern of contrasting support for Canada's NATO commitments reflected a longstanding dilemma for Canadian decision-makers vis-à-vis Alliance membership. Membership entailed dues and obligations. But while most decision-makers wanted to remain in the NATO club, there was little consensus as to the means whereby, and the extent to which, Canada should contribute. It is clear that the lack of consensus regarding Canada's NATO commitments stemmed in large measure from opposing belief systems. Although a variety of other factors affected defence decision-making, beliefs typ-ical of Defenders and Critics exerted considerable influence between 1957 and 1989. Certain competing beliefs and assumptions of influen-tial policy-makers led many to recommend maintaining, if not strengthening, Canada's NATO commitments; others, however, advo-cated de-emphasizing and restructuring select commitments.

From chapters 3 and 4, which documented these beliefs and assumptions using evidence from across a considerable time period, we saw that decision-makers who possessed belief systems typical of Defenders feared the consequences – possible isolation and aban-donment – of deserting the NATO allies. They feared that the close ties among the allies were in danger of dissipating, and that the government was in danger of forgetting its friends and suffering from an array of unpleasant consequences. Defenders tended to worry that Canada might not make a sufficient military contribution to the Alliance; that the Alliance's security, close ties, and solidarity would thereby be jeopardized; and that, if the government failed to fulfill its NATO commitments, Canada could suffer an array of neg-ative outcomes.

Other decision-makers, those whose belief systems were more reflective of Critics, focused on the dangers of entrapment. They were suspicious of the likelihood and possible consequences of the allies drawing Canada into a dangerous confrontation. Some distrusted American intentions and capabilities. Many felt that, in the nuclear era, Canadian policies should enhance the prospects of constructive East-West dialogue, mutual confidence, arms control, and disarmament. Accordingly, among Critics it was widely assumed that the previous emphasis on traditional military solutions had to be replaced by alternative approaches to war prevention. Critics therefore advocated that the government de-emphasize, if not restructure, its NATO commitments in order to signal Canada's intention to reduce international tensions.

Whereas Defenders believed Canada should retain and, where possible, enhance its NATO ties by modernizing military equipment, strengthening the overseas Canadian Forces, and increasing defence spending, Critics frequently perceived such an expanded role as entailing unnecessary risks, and proposed alternatives to established military ties. While Defenders warned that Canada should strengthen its NATO commitments because of an aggressive and opportunistic threat from the USSR, Critics pointed out that this imagery was exaggerated and misunderstood. Whereas Defenders portrayed Canada and the Alliance's weapons systems as necessary and non-threatening, Critics warned that both blocs' weapons could be perceived as dangerously offensive. Moreover, while Defenders based their support for Canada's NATO commitments on the different requirements of deterrence strategy, Critics feared that reliance on this doctrine would fuel a perilous arms race.

Thus, the analysis in chapters 3 and 4 indicated that contrasting beliefs among influential decision-makers led Defenders to recommend sustaining, if not increasing, the level of resources Canada contributed to NATO. Critics, on the other hand, suggested reducing or withdrawing select NATO commitments.

The case study of defence decision-making in the Diefenbaker government showed that underlying beliefs typical of Defenders and Critics affected Canada's changing support apropos its nuclear commitments to NATO. In the inner circle of defence decision-making, the Defenders comprised Defence Ministers General George Pearkes and Douglas Harkness; Ambassador Arnold Heeney; and the Chiefs of the Defence Staff, General Charles Foulkes, Hugh Campbell, and Frank Miller. Their beliefs led them during their terms in office to advocate the acquisition of nuclear weapons. In contrast, Critics included Minister of External Affairs Howard Green, Deputy Minister

Norman Robertson, and Assistant Deputy Minister George Ignatieff. Their underlying belief systems led them, between 1959 and 1963, to oppose the acquisition of nuclear weapons. As for Prime Minister Diefenbaker, between 1960 and 1961 his belief system gradually changed from that of a Defender to that of a Critic. This shift accounts for his initial advocacy of the nuclear commitments between 1957 and 1960; his subsequent vacillation and search for options; and, finally, his outright rejection of the nuclear commitments between 1962 and 1963. The case study demonstrates that it was the onset of opposing belief systems within the inner circle of decision-makers that significantly influenced defence policy-making between 1957 and 1963, resulting in Canada's oscillating record of nuclear commitments.

The case study indicates, moreover, that, contrary to conventional wisdom, senior officials within the Diefenbaker government, including the prime minister after 1961, were not necessarily confused by the strategic environment, nor naive about their defence responsibilities and NATO obligations. Some deliberately attempted to buy time and to seek options that would delay the acquisition of nuclear weapons. Whereas Defenders within the government worked to fulfill the NATO commitments, Critics pursued alternatives that they deemed to be in the best interests of war prevention. They seem to have established a precedent during this period, with the assumptions, tactics, and outcomes reflected, at various times, in the beliefs and policy directions of the Trudeau government.

TWO COMMON SETS OF BELIEFS REGARDING A LONG-STANDING DILEMMA

This study suggests that two competing belief systems, with their attendant elements, provide a satisfactory explanation for the variation in support among defence decision-makers regarding Canada's NATO commitments. It acknowledges that typecasting decision-makers into two categories may well oversimplify the complexity of these leaders' beliefs. Yet, for the sake of increased understanding and a parsimonious conceptual framework, the descriptive labels of Defender and Critic have proved both illuminating and explanatory.

Many influential decision-makers based their support, or lack of support, for Canada's defence commitments on beliefs typical of Defenders or Critics. One wonders, however, whether some leaders' beliefs were not considerably more nuanced than indicated by the profiles. Witness the fact that neither Prime Minister Pearson nor Prime Minister Trudeau could be unequivocally categorized. As well, since the conceptual framework does not easily accommodate indecision and vacillation, Prime Minister Diefenbaker's gradual conversion from one belief system to another is difficult to explain. One might well ask if this research project needed an additional belief system – one more typical of "ambivalents".

However, rather than posit other belief systems reflective of the prime ministers' evolving viewpoints, we must first appreciate the unique duties of a prime minister. The overall evidence suggests that the responsibility of being prime minister contributed to these leaders' equivocal decision-making styles. Clearly, Diefenbaker, Pearson, and Trudeau were often engaged in arranging political compromises, adjudicating between ministers, and chairing Cabinet discussions. Although by the end of their time in office, they each held underlying beliefs more typical of Critics than Defenders, for much of the time their responsibilities may have taken precedence over their own convictions. Perhaps this is one reason why the beliefs of Pearson and Trudeau, and to a lesser extent Diefenbaker, defy easy categorization.

Questions nevertheless remain about the advisability of positing only two mind-sets, each comprising five core assumptions. Admittedly, there is a tendency to "squeeze" policy-makers into analytical compartments. Moreover, although some leaders possessed coherent belief systems, with their beliefs about the dangers of abandonment or entrapment as important sub-elements, some apparently had less coherent worldviews. Would it have been advisable, therefore, to postulate the existence of other belief systems and core assumptions, reflective of the more complex or less coherent thinking patterns of a few decision-makers?

It should be noted that the greater the number of categories introduced to reflect the nuances of different decision-makers' belief systems, the faster the dissipation of the explanatory power of this line of analysis would be. Certainly lengthy analyses could be written about the views of each of these decision-makers regarding a variety of defence issues. In fact, lengthy monographs have been (or could be) written about the idiosyncratic ideas and convictions of Prime Ministers John Diefenbaker, Lester Pearson, Pierre Elliott Trudeau; External Affairs Ministers Howard Green, Paul Martin, Mitchell Sharp; Defence Ministers George Pearkes, Douglas Harkness, Paul Hellyer, Leo Cadieux, J. Gilles Lamontagne, Paul Dick; Cabinet Ministers Walter Gordon, Eric Kierans, Donald Macdonald, Gerard Pelletier; and of powerful civil servants Norman Robertson, George Ignatieff, Charles Foulkes, Ivan Head, Marcel Cadieux, Gordon Robertson, Robert Cameron, John Halstead, and so on. This book was premised, however, on the supposition that when leaders share a common set of beliefs regarding a long-standing dilemma, it is more helpful to develop an informed analysis of the significance of these beliefs for policy-making. The focus here was on discerning the shared elements of different leaders' belief systems. Instead of attributing different decision-makers' support – or lack thereof – for Canada's defence commitments to a host of beliefs and convictions, the research attempted to discern two sets of commonly held beliefs and assumptions. As a result, and most importantly, it was possible to ascertain that there were two competing patterns of thinking about NATO that were repeatedly evident.

OTHER RESEARCH PROBLEMS CONCERNING NATO

One problem worth noting was the insufficiency of available documentation concerning some influential decision-makers' perceptions of the Soviet threat. Part of the problem in analysing Prime Minister Diefenbaker's imagery of the external threat to the Alliance, for instance, was that many of his statements were blatantly rhetorical. Indeed, the prime minister's handwritten amendments to his speeches often seemed more intended for domestic consumption than reflective of his own underlying convictions. In addition, final perusal of many of the relevant papers of the Chiefs of Staff was denied, despite the thirty-year rule. In future, when more information is released, it may be possible to collect further evidence documenting leaders' imagery of the Soviet threat. On the basis of the body of evidence examined for this study, however, it appears that specific references to the nature of the threat were infrequent because Defenders' and Critics' perceptions of the menace formed the backdrop of their thinking. Rather than dwell on the threat, their principal concerns revolved around the allies' foreseeable reactions, especially the United States' intentions and capabilities.

Other research problems related to obtaining documented information stemmed from Canada's regulations preventing access to information related to issues of national security, particularly information concerning defence policy, nuclear weapons, NATO, and Canadian attitudes toward the other NATO allies. For these reasons, the case study as well as much of the published evidence in this book had to focus on decision-making prior to 1978. Not all avenues of analysis could be explored, despite the twenty- and thirty-year rules. For this reason it will be interesting to learn, as more classified documents are released, whether the main findings of this book are corroborated by new sources of evidence.

Another notable problem with this book's findings is my reliance on a wide variety of confidential sources. Frequent references to confidential sources make it difficult for other researchers to pursue a similar line of inquiry. The fact that there is limited funding in various governmental departments and institutions (e.g., DND, DFAIT, NA, PCO) for declassifying documents also means that it can take months, even years, to obtain requested items. Added to these stumbling blocks is the necessity to obtain security clearance in order to peruse files selected from DFAIT's departmental records. This process takes a minimum of six months. Taken together, these hurdles mean that it would be impossible for another researcher to gather the same data and analyse it exactly as in this study.

Most importantly, it is critical to recall that the information pool shrinks considerably in the late 1970s and '80s. Although I was able to see screened files at the Department of Foreign Affairs relating to the decision to test the cruise missile, these papers did not contain many references to the underlying beliefs of influential decision-makers such as Pierre Trudeau, Defence Minister J. Gilles Lamontagne, or Minister of External Affairs Alan MacEachen. As a result, this book relies overmuch on transcripts of Trudeau's speeches and comments to the press and on MP Paul McRae's confidential study, written for Trudeau's perusal. Although McRae was considered to be quite influential personally, this present project would have been improved if reference could have been made to the underlying beliefs of other influential decision-makers critical of the testing (e.g., Cabinet Ministers Lloyd Axworthy and Warren Allmand). It should also be pointed out with reference to the lack of primary documentation pertaining to Trudeau's peace initiative that, according to John Fowell, director, Defence Relations Division, many papers collected by the Department of External Affairs were mistakenly discarded. As well, due to financial constraints, the Historical Section of the Department of Foreign Affairs did not make available files relevant to this recent time period.

Faced with these kinds of problems, I am inclined to make two recommendations. First, researchers and journalists should use the Access to Information Act to obtain information rather than depend on the resources of such institutions as the National Archives of Canada. A significant consideration in this regard, however, is that access requests must be of a specific nature (e.g., location, author, title, date, subject) if they are to be successful and not prohibitively expensive. Second, researchers should rely more extensively on *ex post-facto* interviews for information related to defence and foreign policy-making. Increasingly, defence decisions are being made by personnel using the telephone, email, and facsimile. Ottawa civil servants are more wary, too, about putting ideas and convictions on paper, given the powers of the Access to Information Act. As a result, it will become increasingly difficult to document high-level decision-makers' beliefs and convictions. In future, transcribed interviews similar to the CIIPS transcripts, but available on the public record, could become an extremely valuable research tool.

BELIEF SYSTEMS AFFECT DEFENCE POLICY-MAKING

While this study provides new insights into Canadian defence decision-making, it also draws attention to wide gaps in the literature concerning the role of beliefs and assumptions in affecting defence policy. In future, it might be possible to relax the methodology that was outlined in chapter 2 so as to explore later time periods. Perhaps analysis could focus on the beliefs and assumptions of today's Canadian defence decision-making élite, as evidenced through in-depth interviews rather than on another historical case study. As well, future research could explore whether current defence debates in Canada are still based on similar beliefs and assumptions.

Further research might also identify other increasingly influential factors affecting defence decision-making. For example, defence industry interests and the 1980s' emergence of a military-industrial complex may well have strengthened the Defenders' arguments. Conversely, the issues advanced by the arms control and disarmament community, as well as the interests of fiscal conservatives, may have strengthened the Critics' inclination to limit or at least de-emphasize Canada's participation in various defence initiatives. Last but not least, as the documents related to Cabinet decision-making and high-level defence policy-making become accessible (1998–2019), it should be possible to discern whether the belief systems of Defenders and Critics continued to influence different governments' approaches to Canada's NATO commitments.

As I have emphasized, this study's attention to heretofore classified materials provides considerable new evidence confirming that beliefs were a significant influence on defence decision-making. It also provides new insights into the various competing pressures on defence policy-makers. In future, international relations theorists and defence policy analysts will need to pay greater attention to previously classified evidence taken from past decision-making processes. Now that many of the original documents pertaining to behind-the-scenes negotiations and discussions are being made available, researchers have a responsibility to further explore the ways in which leaders' beliefs and convictions affected all kinds of defence decision-making.

IMPLICATIONS FOR CANADIAN DEFENCE POLICY

Although the ideas and opinions of individual policy-makers have previously been accorded little attention and importance in the literature, my findings indicate that beliefs are important to overall defence policy-making and Canada's approach to collective defence. In broader terms, this book also reveals something about the basic objectives toward which Canadian defence policy was directed. What, for example, can be said about Canadian motives during the Cold War? Undoubtedly, many Canadian policy-makers were preoccupied with the possible reactions and intentions of both the United States and the other NATO allies. Indeed, the high-level debates of the time indicate that the intentions and capabilities of the Soviet Union were less significant than the concerns about what the NATO allies might do or say. The actual deliberations of Canadian leaders about Canada's military commitments had much more to do, then, with their perceptions of what the United States and the other NATO allies expected. Keeping this in mind, it is not surprising that even though the USSR has disappeared, the debate continues about what should be the extent and measure of Canada's NATO commitments.

The evidence also suggests that many of the Defenders' underlying beliefs reflected certain major tenets underpinning the "realist" school of thought. Critics, on the other hand, tended to reflect concerns that arose among proponents of the "idealist" school in international relations. Although this point should not be overstated, parallels do seem to emerge between the high-level discussions in Cabinet and the debate between these two schools of thought in the academic community. It is unlikely that Canadian leaders took their arguments from scholarly analyses arising out of either school. Rather, they reflected the ongoing debates in the United States and NATO's higher decision-making echelons as well as the debates within political and academic circles. Suffice it to say, however, that competition within the inner circles of defence decision-making between these two belief systems was paralleled by a paradigm debate in international relations theory.

Finally, my findings indicate that, in high-level discussions, Canada's NATO commitments took on a symbolic importance far exceeding their operational significance. Relative to NATO's actual

force structure and the United States' possession of the strategic
deterrent, Canada's nuclear and conventional contributions to NATO
were militarily insignificant. However, Canadian leaders often extensively debated proposed changes in Canada's Alliance commitments.
Rather than discuss larger issues, such as the advantages of outright
withdrawal from the Alliance or the foreseeable disadvantages of
non-alignment, leaders focused their attention on presumably less
objectionable alternatives. The perimeters of the debate were limited,
perhaps because politicians and bureaucrats assumed there was not
much room during the Cold War for a middle power such as Canada
to manoeuvre. Instead, Canada's certainty or ambivalence about
being part of this military alliance – the dilemma of Alliance membership – coalesced around the issue of what should be the measure
and extent of Canada's Alliance commitments. Now that the Cold
War is over, it is time to put aside old belief systems and forge new
ways of thinking. Traditional thought patterns will not fall by the
wayside, however, until we understand them. As H.G. Wells wrote,
"Human history becomes more and more a race between education
and catastrophe."[1]

Notes

CHAPTER ONE

1 Richard Gwyn, "NATO's World Obsolete," *Toronto Star*, 7 May 1989; editorial, "Deciding How Best to Bury the Cold War," *Globe and Mail*, 24 November 1990; "Warsaw Pact Dies," *Globe and Mail*, 26 February 1991. On the prospect of a peace dividend, see, for example, the Citizens' Inquiry into Peace and Security, *Transformation Moment: A Canadian Vision of Common Security*; "Pearson Urges Troop Withdrawal," *Globe and Mail*, 31 October 1991; editorial, "Paving the Way for the End of NATO," *Globe and Mail*, 5 July 1990; comments by New Democratic Party (NDP) external affairs critic, Svend Robinson, "Reaction Mixed to Canadian Troop Policy," *Globe and Mail*, 15 June 1991.

2 Department of National Defence (DND), Statement by the Honourable Marcel Masse, September 17, 1991 ("Statement on Defence Policy"). Alex Morrison, executive director of the Canadian Institute for Strategic Studies, for example, applauded the gradual withdrawal as entirely appropriate and John Lamb, from the Canadian Centre for Arms Control and Disarmament, called the step important, "Canada to Shut Bases in Europe, Slash Military," *Toronto Star*, 18 September 1991. See also John Hay, "Masse's Plan Takes Aim at Defence, but Who are Canada's enemies?" *Ottawa Citizen*, 18 September 1991.

3 "Canada Speeds Pace to Pull 6,000 Troops from Europe," *Defense News*, 2 March 1992. At that time, the annual commitment of $1.2 billion to Europe was estimated to cost nearly 10 cents out of every defence dollar. Editorial, "Mulroney is Right on Troop Withdrawal," *Toronto Star*, 22 March 1992.

4 For brief comments on the "battle" between the "Atlanticists" in government and the "military isolationists," see John Best, "Canada and NATO," *Winnipeg Free Press*, 5 July 1991. On Canada's role in NATO's

new Strategic Concept, see "Flexible Fighting Forces," *Defense News*, 13 May 1991, and George Reay, "The Canadian Army and Atlantic Security," in *A Continuing Commitment: Canada and North Atlantic Security*, 91. Notably, by the fall of 1992, it had not been established how Canada might contribute to NATO's "rapid reaction forces" but developing plans were that the country would earmark North American-based "main" and "augmentation" forces to the Alliance's new "Strategic Concept." Interview with Erwin Sippert, defence counsellor, Defence Policy and Planning, NATO Headquarters (NATO HQS), October 1992.

5 DND, Minister of National Defence Marcel Masse, "Statement on Defence Policy," Ottawa, 17 September 1991 and comments by Masse quoted in Sylvia Strojek, "Canada Insists Troops to Leave NATO Bases," *Edmonton Journal*, 19 May 1992.

6 For example, see comments by Alex Morrison in "Cuts Ordered to Military Bases, Programs," *Ottawa Citizen*, 26 February 1992; Bob Hicks, chairman of the North Atlantic Assembly's parliamentary wing in "Troop Pullout Decried," *Calgary Herald*, 2 March 1992; "Troops Question Pullout from Unstable Europe," *Halifax Chronicle-Herald*, 25 April 1992; and editorial, "A Shocking About-face in our Defence Policy," *Regina Leader-Post*, 20 May 1992.

7 Confidential interviews at NATO and SHAPE headquarters, October 1992; "NATO Greets Troop Pullout from Europe 'with Regret,'" *Montreal Gazette*, 27 February 1992; "Canadian Pullout from Europe Worries British," *Ottawa Citizen*, 3 March 1992; "Canadian Troop Pullout Upsets Allies in NATO," *Globe and Mail*, 5 March 1992; "NATO Wants Canada to Drop Troop Withdrawal," *Ottawa Citizen*, 25 March 1992; and "NATO Members Gang Up on Canada over Pullout," *Globe and Mail*, 9 April 1992.

8 Briefing by Ralph Lysyshyn, deputy ambassador to the North Atlantic Council, NATO HQS, October, 1992 on NACC and interviews by author with Angela Bogden, Canadian delegation, and Glen Brown, Canadian liaison officer, NATO HQS, Brussels, October 1992. On Canada's growing commitment to European security through peacekeeping in Europe in 1992, see comments by Colonel Tony Anderson, "NATO Members Gang Up on Canada over Pullout," *Globe and Mail*, 9 April 1992.

9 Prime Minister's Office (PMO), Prime Minister Brian Mulroney, speech to Stanford University, 29 September 1991. See also "Throw Soviets a 'Lifeline,' Mulroney Says," *Globe and Mail*, 30 September 1991. Interviews by author with Angela Bogden and Glen Brown, Canadian delegation, NATO HQS, Brussels, October 1992.

10 Confidential interviews by author, NATO and SHAPE headquarters, October 1992. See also "Masse Tells NATO Troop Withdrawal Decision is Final," *Ottawa Citizen*, 2 April 1992.

11 Interview by author with John Barrett, Disarmament, Arms Control and Cooperation Section, Political Affairs Division, NATO HQS, October 1992. See also "Germans Plan to Expand UN Role," *Globe and Mail*, 10 July 1992.

12 See criticisms by German and British NATO officials in "Troop Withdrawal Plan Comes Under Fire," *Halifax Chronicle-Herald*, 7 November 1992. On the effect of a shift to peacekeeping on Canada's NATO image, sources include confidential interviews, NATO HQS, October 1992; and off-record commentary at the seminar "A New Generation of Peacekeeping," sponsored by the Parliamentary Centre for Foreign Affairs and Foreign Trade, Ottawa, 21 April 1993.

13 Confidential interviews at NATO HQS, October 1992; see also "Newly Isolationist U.S. Poised to Withdraw from NATO," *Winnipeg Free Press*, 10 February 1992.

14 DND, Statements and Speeches 1957–99, Associate Minister of National Defence Mary Collins, "Canada and North Atlantic Security," National Security Studies Course, National Defence College, Kingston, 7 April 1992, 4–7.

15 "NATO Greets Troop Pullout from Europe 'with Regret,'" *Montreal Gazette*, 27 February 1992. Despite Woerner's comments, a classified report was apparently issued at NATO HQS that took Canada to task for the withdrawal. Confidential interview, NATO HQS, October 1992.

16 According to Parliament, Special Joint Committee Reviewing Canadian Foreign Policy, *Canada's Foreign Policy: Principles and Priorities for the Future*, 21; DND, Minister of National Defence Marcel Masse, "Statement on Defence Policy," Ottawa, September 1991, 18; DND, Statements and Speeches 1957–99, Associate Minister of National Defence, Mary Collins, "Canada and North Atlantic Security," 5; and Alex Morrison, "Canadian Defence Policy and Burden-Sharing in NATO," in *Canada and NATO: The Forgotten Ally?* ed. Barbara McDougall, et al., 49.

17 According to comments by Dr. Erika Bruce, Office of Information and Press, NATO HQS, Brussels, 19 October 1992 and a report by the NATO Defence Planning Committee, "Enhancing Alliance Collective Security," December 1988, cited by Alex Morrison in "Canadian Defence Policy and Burden-Sharing in NATO," in *Canada and NATO: The Forgotten Ally?*, 41. Notably, in 1994, in testimony before the Special Joint Committee of the Senate and the House of Commons on Canada's Defence Policy (Special Joint Committee on Defence Policy),

representatives of the Council of 21, a group of prominent Canadians, criticized the fact that Canada was continuing to pay a significant sum of NATO's infrastructure budget. See, for example, the testimony of Maurice Archdeacon, Parliament, Special Joint Committee of the Senate, *Minutes of Proceedings of Evidence*, no. 3 (20 April 1994), 18–19 and Admiral Robert Falls (ret.), no. 4 (26 April 1994) 28–29.

18 Interview with Lieutenant-Colonel J. van Boeschoten, deputy, national military representative, NATO HQS, Brussels, October 1992; DND, *Statements and Press Releases*, AFN: 61/92, 10 December 1992; and on Goose Bay and the grounds for the American withdrawal, see "Germany aims for peace role," *Globe and Mail*, 12 July 1994 and "Ottawa lost Goose Bay duel," *Globe and Mail*, 9 July 1991.

19 On retaining a symbolic commitment of land forces, see Barbara McDougall, et al., *Canada and NATO: The Forgotten Ally?*, and Alex Morrison, ed., *A Continuing Commitment: Canada and North Atlantic Security*. On possibly using Lahr as a forward-staging base for peacekeeping operations and a peacekeeping training centre, see Axworthy and Stewart, "The Liberal Foreign Policy Handbook"; Michel Rossignol, "Peacekeeping Training Centres"; and Office of the Leader of the Opposition, Press Release, "Turn Lahr Base into International Peacekeeping Centre Liberals Propose," 8 October 1992. On converting CFB Cornwallis, not Lahr, into a Canadian and multinational peacekeeping training centre, see Common Security Consultants (H. Peter Langille and Erika Simpson) and Stratman Consulting Inc. (Brigadier-General Clayton Beattie), CFB *Cornwallis: Canada's Peacekeeping Training Centre – A Blueprint for a Peacekeeping Training Centre of Excellence*, and Common Security Consultants, CFB *Cornwallis: Canada's Peacekeeping Training Centre*. The notion of establishing an "airhead capacity" in Germany was put forward by Lieutenant-Colonel J. van Boeschoten, deputy, national military representative in an interview at NATO HQS, Brussels, October 1992. The "tongue-in-cheek" commentary is from an interview by the author with Gordon Smith, ambassador to the European Community and former ambassador to NATO, European Community, Brussels, October 1992.

20 Briefing by Ralph Lysyshyn, deputy ambassador to the North Atlantic Council, NATO HQS, October 1992.

21 For example, defence policy planners at NATO HQS such as Erwin Sippert pointed to the need to strengthen the equipment for Canada's "augmentation forces"; at SHAPE Headquarters, military representatives such as Lieutenant-Colonel van Boeschoten recommended enhancing Canada's diplomatic and consultative profile at NATO HQS. As well, in 1994, in testimony before the Special Joint Committee Reviewing Canadian Defence Policy, a number of witnesses

recommended maintaining Canada's commitment to NATO in other ways. Professor Albert Legault recommended that by conducting joint exercises and joint training through NATO and other collective organizations, Canada's peacekeeping troops would be better protected. Parliament, Special Joint Committee of the Senate and the House of Commons on Canada's Defence Policy, *Minutes and Proceedings of Evidence (Minutes and Proceedings)*, issue no. 7 (3 May 1994), 15. Professor Joel Sokolsky suggested that Canada maintain its existing air and maritime forces in order to maintain a discretionary overseas capability. He also advised that the government obtain a replacement for the EH-101 and that DND rely on more lightly armed forces but refrain from placing a higher priority on UN peacekeeping obligations. *Minutes and Proceedings*, issue no. 7 (3 May 1994), 22–23, 34. The late Professor John Halstead, a former ambassador to NATO, suggested that the Canadian Forces' commitments to NATO be used for collective security operations – that is, "peacekeeping operations," which Halstead broadly defined to include different roles from peace-making through crisis management to peacebuilding. *Minutes and Proceedings*, issue no. 5 (27 April 1994), 7–8.

22 Although this is a generalization of different positions, it is evident in various presentations to the Special Joint Committee on Canada's Defence Policy. For example, see the testimony of Professor Michael Hennessy and Professor Greg Kennedy in *Minutes and Proceedings*, issue no. 2 (19 April 1994); the testimony of Vice Admiral Daniel Mainguy (ret.) of the Defence Associations National Network, *Minutes and Proceedings*, issue no. 4 (26 April 1994); Lt. Col Ernest Wesson (ret.) and Col. Sean Henry (ret.) of the Conference of Defence Associations *Minutes and Proceedings*, issue no. 3 (20 April 1994); and the testimony of Professor David Haglund, Professor Robert Spencer, and Lt. Col. John Marteinson, *Minutes and Proceedings*, issue no. 5 (27 April 1994).

23 Once again, this is an approximation of various arguments and proposals. For testimony which reflects this approach, however, see, for example, the testimony of those affiliated with the Canada 21 Council, including Donald Macdonald, Professor Janice Stein, and Maurice Archdeacon, in *Minutes and Proceedings*, issue no. 3 (20 April 1994). See also the analysis put forward by Professor Harriet Critchley, *Minutes and Proceedings*, issue no. 10 (9 May 1994); Admiral Robert Falls (ret.), *Minutes and Proceedings*, issue no. 4 (26 April 1994); and H. Peter Langille, *Minutes and Proceedings*, issue no. 26 (21 June 1994). On the detailed recommendations of the Canada 21 Council, see *Canada 21 Council: Canada and Common Security in the Twenty-First Century*. On the *Agenda for Peace*, see Boutros Boutros-Ghali, *An*

Agenda for Peace: Preventive Diplomacy, Peacemaking and Peace-keeping,
report of the Secretary-General, 31 January 1992.

24 PMO, Prime Minister Jean Chrétien, "Speech to the United Nations
Association in Canada," 24 October 1994, Ottawa, 4; DFAIT, *State-*
ments and Speeches, Minister of Foreign Affairs and International Trade
André Ouellet, "Notes for an Address to the 49th General Assembly
of the United Nations," New York, 29 September 1994, 7; and DND,
Press release, "Cornwallis: A Canadian International Peacekeeping
Training Centre." For details, see DND, *1994 Defence White Paper,* 34,
37, 38; Common Security Consultants, *A 1994 Blueprint for a Canadian*
and Multinational Peacekeeping Training Centre at CFB *Cornwallis;* Common
Security Consultants and Stratman Consulting Inc. (Brigadier-General
Clayton), CFB *Cornwallis: Canada's Peacekeeping Training Centre – A Blue-*
print for a Peacekeeping Training Centre of Excellence; H. Peter Langille
and Erika Simpson, "Combat Skill isn't Enough for Canada's Peacekeepers," *Globe and Mail,* 10 September 1993; and Common Security
Consultants, CFB *Cornwallis: Canada's Peacekeeping Training Centre.*"

25 DND, *1994 Defence White Paper,* 30, 36.

26 Ibid., 36

27 It is noteworthy that the White Paper consistently makes reference to
Canada's NATO defence commitments after pointing out the country's United Nations obligations. This may herald a fundamental
reordering of Canadian defence priorities. See, for example, ibid.,
27–39.

28 Ibid., 38–9, 23. Notably, the White Paper stated that, given changed
geostrategic circumstances, plans were to maintain Canada's NORAD
commitments (e.g., aerospace surveillance, missile warning, and air
defence capabilities) at a significantly reduced level but to "preserve
the ability of Canada and the US to regenerate forces should a strategic threat to the continent arise in the future." 23.

29 For more information, see Erika Simpson, "The Looming Costs
of NATO Expansion in the 21st Century," *International Journal;*
"Canada's Defence Costs will Jump with NATO Expansion," *Peace*
Research; and "The Costs of NATO Expansion for Canada," *Globe and*
Mail, 25 July 1997.

30 Department of Foreign Affairs and International Trade, *Government*
Response to the Recommendations, 1999; available at
http://www.dfait-maeci.gc.ca/nucchallenge/ANNEXB-e.htm

31 Report of the Standing Committee on Foreign Affairs and
International Trade, *Canada and the Nuclear Challenge: Reducing the*
Political Value of Nuclear Weapons for the Twenty-First Century,
December 1998; available at
http://www.parl.gc.ca/InfoComDoc/36/1/FAIT/Studies/Reports/faitrp07-e.htm

32 DFAIT, *Government Response to the Recommendations.*

33 Senator Douglas Roche, chairman, Middle Powers Initiative, "Analysis of NATO Action on Nuclear Weapons," 28 April 1999; available at *http://sen.parl.gc.ca/droche/9*

34 Ibid.

35 Diana McCaffrey and Katherine Starr, eds., "Consequences of Kosovo – Views from Western Europe and Canada," United States Information Agency, Office of Research and Media Reaction, 9 July 1999, available at *http://www.usia.gov/admin/005/wwwh9709.html*; and "Canada on the attack: daily military updates," CBC, *News Online*, available at *http://www.cbcnews.cbc.ca/news/indepth/canadaattack/updates.html*

36 For example, for comprehensive coverage of the parliamentary and national debate, see "Canada on the Attack: The Debate," CBC, *News Online*; available at *http://cbcnews.cbc.ca/news/indepth/canadaattack/debate.html.* See also "The Question of Ground Troops," CBC TV *The National*, 7 April 1999; online transcript available at *http://tv.cbc.ca/national/pgminfo/kosovo2/eggleton990407.html*

37 "NATO Rejects Serb Ceasefire, Steps up Air Attacks: Chrétien Gathers Cabinet for Special Meeting as Crisis Deepens," *Globe and Mail*, 7 April 1999; on Axworthy's reservations about the war, see "Mission to Moscow," CBC TV *The National Online*; online transcript of Axworthy's comments available at *http://tv.cbc.ca/national/pgminfo/kosovo2/axworthy990426.html.* And see "Lloyd Axworthy's Biggest Test," *Globe and Mail*, 16 June 1999; for some Canadian reservations about Canada's NATO commitments, see "Canadians against war on Yugoslavia"; available at *http://www.stopwar.net/.* Most recently, it has come to light that NATO was itself internally divided and fractured. For example, see "The Dilemmas of War: What Went Wrong for NATO?" CBC TV, *The National Online*, 11 June 1999; online transcript available at *http://tv.cbc.ca/national/pgminfo/kosovo3/nato.html.* See also "NATO's Inner Kosovo Conflict," BBC Two program, 20 August 1999; online transcript at *http://news.bbc.co.uk/hi/english/world/europe/newsid_425000/425468.stm.*

38 Many of the primary documents relevant to this period are individually cited in chaps. 5, 6, and 7 of this study (e.g., the Cabinet documents, memoranda, and records of discussion as well as the original speeches, letters, and notes of Prime Minister Diefenbaker and other Cabinet ministers). Notably, the 'secret' records of meetings of the Diefenbaker Cabinet were obtained under the Access to Information Act from the Privy Council Office (PCO). Permission to examine the original speeches and notes of Prime Minister John Diefenbaker was originally granted from the John G. Diefenbaker Centre (JGD Centre). However, these Cabinet Conclusions and Diefenbaker papers (on microfiche) are now on deposit at the National Archives of Canada (NA).

Secondary sources which describe and analyse the events of the Diefenbaker era include: Peter C. Newman, *Renegade in Power*; Jon B. McLin, *Canada's Changing Defense Policy, 1957–1963: The Problems of a Middle Power in Alliance*; Peyton V. Lyon, *Canada in World Affairs, 1961–1963*, chap. 3; John G. Diefenbaker, *One Canada: The Years of Achievement, 1956–1962*, vol. 2.; and John Diefenbaker, *One Canada: The Tumultuous Years, 1962–1967*; Peter Stursberg, *Diefenbaker: Leadership Lost, 1962–67*; J.L. Granatstein, *A Man of Influence: Norman Robertson and Canadian Statecraft 1929–1968*; John F. Hilliker, "The Politicians and the 'Pearsonalities': The Diefenbaker Government and the Conduct of Canadian External Relations," in *Canadian Foreign Policy: Historical Readings*, ed. J.L. Granatstein, 223–39; George Ignatieff, *The Making of a Peacemonger*; David McIntosh, *Ottawa Unbuttoned*; Basil Robinson, *Diefenbaker's World*; Knowlton Nash, *Kennedy and Diefenbaker: Fear and Loathing Across the Canadian Border*; Peter Haydon, *The Cuban Missile Crisis*; Denis Smith, *Rogue Tory: The Life and Legend of John G. Diefenbaker*; and D.C. Story and R. Bruce Shepard, eds., *Diefenbaker's Legacy*.

39 Pearson's *volte-face* is briefly described in Peter C. Newman, *Renegade in Power*, 395–7; Judy LaMarsh, *Memoirs of a Bird in a Gilded Cage*, 25–31; Patrick Nicholson, *Vision and Indecision*, 212–15; Marilyn Eustace, *Canada's European Force, 1964–1971: Canada's Commitment to Europe*, National Security Series no. 4/82, 15; and Paul Hellyer, *Damn the Torpedoes: My Fight to Save the Canadian Forces*, 25.

40 NA, L.B. Pearson Papers, Leader of the Opposition Correspondence Series, 1958–63, Manuscript Group (MG) 26, N2, vol. 54, file 830, letter to Bob Abrahams, treasurer of the Liberal Club at Sir George Williams University, 7 January 1963.

41 On whether Pearson's *volte-face* was electorally motivated, see comments by Howard Green in Peter Stursberg, *Diefenbaker: Leadership Lost*, 25; Judy LaMarsh, *Memoirs of a Bird in a Gilded Cage*, 28–31; and Walter Gordon, "The Liberal Leadership and Nuclear Weapons," in *Canada and the Nuclear Arms Race*, eds. Ernie Regehr and Simon Rosenblum, 200.

42 Many of the primary documents relevant to understanding the reasons for Pearson's *volte-face* are available in the restricted L.B. Pearson Papers at the NA. Pearson's son, Geoffrey Pearson, kindly accorded me access to some of the relevant documents and papers regarding Pearson's attitude toward the nuclear weapons issue; not enough documented information was available, however, to undertake a comprehensive analysis of Pearson's beliefs about nuclear weapons. Most importantly, Pearson was not an "influential" defence decision-maker when, as leader of the Opposition, he

opposed the acquisition of nuclear weapons. As well, because this study focuses on influential leaders within the inner circles of defence decision-making, I did not study Pearson's beliefs between 1957 and 1963. For my analysis of Pearson's general political philosophy, not merely his attitude toward defence issues and NATO, see Erika Simpson, "The Principles of Liberal Internationalism according to Lester Pearson," *Journal of Canadian Studies*.

43 On the hold Pearson and Paul Martin exerted over the defence policy-making process, see Walter Gordon, "The Liberal Leadership and Nuclear Weapons," in *Canada and the Nuclear Arms Race*, eds. Ernie Regehr and Simon Rosenblum, 201.

44 J.L. Granatstein and Robert Bothwell, *Pirouette*, 11.

45 Jerome D. Davis, "To the NATO Review: Constancy and Change in Canadian NATO Policy, 1949–1969," (PhD dissertation submitted to The Johns Hopkins University, Washington, D.C., 1973), 206–7, 215.

46 On whether Trudeau consulted Pearson, see the conflicting accounts in Peter Stursberg, *Lester Pearson and the American Dilemma*, and J.L. Granatstein and Robert Bothwell, *Pirouette*, introduction.

47 For example, see the report of Trudeau's speech to the Liberal convention in Moncton, *Globe and Mail*, 14 March 1968.

48 *Globe and Mail*, 30 May 1968.

49 Many of the primary documents relevant to this period are cited in chaps. 3 and 4 of this study or listed as confidential sources. Many of the records of the meetings of the Cabinet and the Cabinet Committee on Defence Policy, as well as the various reports by governmental advisory groups that studied the issue, were obtained under the Access to Information Act from the PCO and the Department of National Defence, Directorate of History (DHist). Permission to examine classified files from the Department of External Affairs (DEA) from between 1967 and 1983 was also granted after selected files were screened by foreign service officers and this author obtained security clearance.

50 The discussions within Cabinet and the Cabinet Committee on defence policy, as well as the various reports by Cabinet ministers, special advisers, and different governmental advisory groups, are individually cited in chaps. 3 and 4. The Standing Committee on External Affairs and National Defence, *Fifth Report to the House Respecting Defence and External Affairs Policy* ['Wahn Committee Report'], 25 March 1969 and the testimony in the *Minutes and Proceedings of Evidence*, First Session, 28th Parliament, nos. 19–35 also indicate the contrasting viewpoints of academics and non-governmental representatives. However, their viewpoints were accorded very little importance by Cabinet ministers and their government advisers. For

example, see the Cabinet ministers' comments in PCO, Cabinet Conclusions, 29 March 1969, 3. As the under-secretary of External Affairs, Marcel Cadieux wrote in his briefing papers for the Cabinet sessions: "Note that views expressed by academics cover [a] very wide range, though almost none advocate immediate withdrawal from NATO Problem; each has pet theme; views tend to be put as negative criticisms rather than well thought out positive proposals; frequent lack of internal consistency; many seem to think world is waiting to be told what to do by Canada ." Confidential source, 28 March 1969.

51 For a flavour of the discussion, see House of Commons Debates, *Hansard*, 23–24 April, 2 June 1969. Synopses of the behind-the-scenes reactions of the NATO allies, USSR, and foreign press are in the DEA, 27–1–15, memo regarding "Foreign and press reaction," 23 April 1969, (RESTRICTED); 27–1–1–11, telegram from Moscow, 3 June 1969, (CONFIDENTIAL); 27–1–1–11, "Memo by HBR [H. Basil Robinson] for the Secretary of State of External Affairs regarding Leo Cadieux's Conversation with US Secretary of Defense Laird," 6 May 1969; 27–1–1–11, R. Lyman, "Summary of Arguments Advanced by Canada's Allies in Opposition to the Proposed Canadian Troop Reduction in NATO," 17 June 1969; and telegram from Washington to External Affairs, 25 June 1969. The secretary-general of NATO also called the permanent representatives of the Defence Planning Council to a restricted meeting on 8 and 28 May to discuss the results of the Canadian defence review; he also considered flying to Canada for urgent consultations with ministers. Confidential source.

52 Some of the principal secondary sources that describe and analyse the defence policy review process between April 1968 and September 1969, and the reaction of Cabinet ministers such as Eric Kierans, include: Bruce Thordarson, *Trudeau and Foreign Policy*; Peter C. Dobell, *Canada's Search for New Roles*; Jerome D. Davis, "To the NATO Review: Constancy and Change in Canadian NATO Policy, 1949–1969"; Peter Stursberg, *Lester Pearson and the American Dilemma*, 298–318; Marilyn Eustace, *Canada's European Force, 1964–1971: Canada's Commitment to Europe*; and J.L. Granatstein and Robert Bothwell, *Pirouette*, chap. 1.

53 Confidential source. See also DEA, files 27–1–1-USA; 27–1–1–29; and 27–1–1–3.

54 On the CAST commitment, see Howard Peter Langille, *Changing the Guard: Canada's Defence in a World in Transition*, 68–75 and Joseph T. Jockel, *Canada and NATO's Northern Flank*.

55 Prime Minister Pierre Elliott Trudeau, "Speech to the United Nations General Assembly Special Session on Disarmament," New York, 26 May 1978, reprinted in Pierre Elliott Trudeau, *Lifting the Shadow of War*, ed. C. David Crenna, chap. 2.

56 Howard Peter Langille, *Changing the Guard*, ch. 2, 38–58. The Conservative government of Joe Clark was in power when it was decided at the 1979 NATO ministerial meeting that, as part of a "two-track strategy," the allies would deploy Pershing and cruise missiles if the arms control track of the strategy was unsuccessful after four years. The secretary of state for External Affairs at that time, Flora MacDonald, later maintained, however, that, "we should be quite clear, though, that throughout those meetings which resulted in the decision in 1979 at Brussels the decision in no way constituted a commitment by Canada to test the Cruise missile, nor was any such discussion entered into at the time of the NATO agreement. It never came up for agreement." *Hansard,* 14 June 1983, 26356.

57 On these questions, see, for example: Howard Peter Langille, *Changing the Guard*, 45; David Cox, "The Cruise Testing Agreement," *International Perspectives*; M.V. Naidu, "Canada, NATO and the Cruise Missile," *Peace Research*; David Macfarlane, "In the Shadow of the Cruise," *Saturday Night*, December 1984; and Simon Rosenblum, *Misguided Missiles: Canada, the Cruise and Star Wars.*

58 Howard Peter Langille, *Changing the Guard*, 46; "Canada agrees to test U.S. cruise missile," *Globe and Mail*, 16 July 1983; and DEA, 27–8-USA-3, transcript of a CTV *Canada AM* interview with Pauline Jewitt, 7 February 1983.

59 Confidential source, 20 March 1983.

60 DEA, *Statements and Speeches*, no. 83/8, Prime Minister Trudeau, "Canada's Position on Testing Cruise Missiles and Disarmament: An Open Letter to All Canadians," 9 May 1983.

61 A thick binder of conflicting statements by members of Parliament (MPs) in the House of Commons regarding the cruise missile debate was compiled for CIIPS and is now available through the Toronto Staff College Library. See also R.B. Byers, "Canadian Defence: The Genesis of a Debate," *Current History.*

62 Some transcripts that reveal Trudeau's motives for undertaking a "peace initiative" are found in the Library of Parliament, "Transcript of the Prime Minister's Scrum following a Meeting with the Representatives of the Government of Bangladesh," 21 November 1983; and, "Transcript of the Prime Minister's Interview with a Group of American Journalists," Washington, 15 December 1983. The peace initiative was referred to as Trudeau's "last hurrah" in J.L. Granatstein and Robert Bothwell, *Pirouette,* chap. 14.

63 Secondary sources describing and analysing the Trudeau peace initiative include: Christopher Sapardanis, "'The World is Entitled to Ask Questions': The Trudeau Peace Initiative Reconsidered," *International Journal*; Geoffrey Pearson, "Trudeau Peace Initiative Reflections,"

International Perspectives; Adam Bromke and Kim Richard Nossal, "Trudeau Rides the 'Third Rail,'" *International Perspectives*; Harald von Riekhoff and John Sigler, "The Trudeau Peace Initiative: The Politics of Reversing the Arms Race," in *Canada Among Nations 1988*, eds. Brian Tomlin and Maureen Appel Molot, 50–69; and J. L. Granatstein and Robert Bothwell, *Pirouette*, chap. 14.

64 See Pierre Elliott Trudeau, "Statements by Prime Minister Trudeau and President Reagan, Following Their Meeting," Washington, 15 December 1983, in *Lifting the Shadow of War*, 91.

65 According to Howard Peter Langille, *Changing the* Guard, 92–8; Tom Keating and Larry Pratt, *Canada, NATO and the Bomb: The Western Alliance in Crisis*, 44–5. For example, see the address by President Thomas d'Aquino of the Business Council of National Issues, Royal Military College, 15 June 1984.

66 DND, *Challenge and Commitment: A Defence Policy for Canada* (White Paper on National Defence). See also Joel K. Sokolsky, "Trends in United States Strategy and the 1987 White Paper on Defence," *International Journal*, and D.W. Middlemiss and J.J. Sokolsky, *Canadian Defence: Decisions and Determinants*.

67 Quoted in Howard Peter Langille, *Changing the Guard*, 96.

68 According to an interview by the author with a member of DND, Directorate of Policy Planning, Ottawa, 4 May 1989. Brief outlines and analyses of these cuts are available in Ross Howard, "Defence Analysts See New Foreign Policy in Military Cutbacks," *Globe and Mail*, 3 May 1989; "Allies Will Help Us Protect Arctic, McKnight Says," *Toronto Star*, 28 April 1989; *The Wednesday Report: Canada's Defence News Bulletin*, 3, 10, 24 May 1989; David Langille, "Defence Cuts Camouflage a Spending Increase," *Toronto Star*, 18 May 1989; Joseph T. Jockel and Joel J. Sokolsky, "Defence White Paper Lives Again," *International Perspectives*; and D.W. Middlemiss and J.J. Sokolsky, *Canadian Defence: Decisions and Determinants*.

69 For example, see Gérard Thériault, et al., "What is to be Done: Canada's Military Security in the 1990s," *Peace and Security*, 2–6; Desmond Morton, "Defence Policy for a Nice Country," *Peace and Security*, 2–3; Bernard Wood, "The Gulf Crisis and the Future World Order" and Reg Whitaker, "Prisoner of the American Dream: Canada, the Gulf and the New World Order," in *International Relations in the Post-Cold War Era*, eds. Mark Charlton and Elizabeth Riddell-Dixon.

70 Some commentary by those opposed to the rumoured cutbacks and the 17 September 1991 announcement includes Mike O'Brien, ed., "Comment: October Answers," *Wednesday Report*, 14 August 1991; Colonel Bujold, "Canadians Need Something to Do," *Globe and Mail*, 15 August 1991; "Canadian Troops to Stay in NATO But There Will Be

Fewer Soldiers, PM says," *Montreal Gazette*, 15 June 1991; Nick
Stetham, "Virtues and Vices of Decisions Delayed" and W.G. Kinsman,
"Has DND Lost Sight of One of its Roles?," *The Defence Associations'
National Network News*, no. 13 (15 October 1991). For comments by
those who greeted the cutbacks with equanimity, see General de
Chastelain, Alex Morrison, and John Lamb quoted in "Canada to
Shut Bases in Europe, Slash Military," *Toronto Star*, 18 September 1991.

71 "PM Lends an Ear to German Arguments," *Globe and Mail*, 14 June
1991 and "Canada Urged to Keep Troops in Europe," *Globe and Mail*,
20 May 1991.

72 Interview with Geoffrey Pearson by Roger Hill, senior research fellow, Canadian Institute for International Peace and Security, "Canadian Institute for International Peace and Security Transcripts" (CIIPS
transcripts) (unpublished transcripts, Ottawa, 1987), 175–6. Note that
these are verbatim transcripts of interviews conducted by Roger Hill,
David Cox, Nancy Gordon, et al. Excerpts from these transcripts are
cited with the permission of Roger Hill.

73 Admiral Robert Falls (ret.), "Canada Should Rethink Military Role in
NATO, Says Retired Admiral," *Ottawa Citizen*, 9 December 1989.

74 Leonard V. Johnson, "Canada and NATO: What Price Symbolism?" in
Defending Europe: Options for Security, ed. Derek Paul, 57–9.

CHAPTER TWO

1 This definition and the accompanying example are from Scilla
Elworthy, John Hamwee, and Hugh Miall, "The Assumptions of
Nuclear Weapons Decision-Makers," in *The Nuclear Mentality: A Psy-
chosocial Analysis of the Arms Race*, eds. Lynn Barnett and Ian Lee, 72.

2 As Denis Stairs points out, "Many observers have regarded Canada's
cold war alignment as context rather than essence, as a background
'given' rather than as an intrinsically significant characteristic." "The
Political Culture of Canadian Foreign Policy," *Canadian Journal of
Political Science*, 676. Some methodological problems related in this
case to the resulting lack of evidence are discussed in chaps. 6 and 8.

3 This definition is an amalgamation of various points made by by
Herbert C. Kelman, *International Behaviour: A Social Psychological Anal-
ysis*; Richard Snyder, H.B. Bruick, and Burton Sapin, *Foreign Policy
Decision-Making*; and, Margaret G. Hermann and Charles F. Hermann,
"Who Makes Foreign Policy Decisions and How: An Empirical
Inquiry." *International Studies Quarterly* 33 (1989).

4 For analysis and a diagram of Pross's "policy community," see
A. Paul Pross, *Group Politics and Public Policy*, particularly figure 4-1,
100.

5 Although the effect of beliefs, mindsets or world views on Canadian policy-making has hardly been explored, research in international relations on the importance of belief systems to interpreting information and making decisions has grown steadily. In the literature, the concept of a belief system is often used interchangeably with terms such as world view, ideology, schema, mindset, and discourse. For example, on belief systems and belief structures, see Richard Little and Steve Smith, *Belief Systems and International Relations*; and Robert Jervis, *Perception and Misperception in International Politics*, chap. 4. On the psychological processes involved in making defence policy, see Steven Kull, *Minds at War: Nuclear Reality and the Inner Conflicts of Defense Policymakers*. On old mindsets, see Ken Booth, "New Challenges and Old Mindsets: Ten Rules for Empirical Realists," in *The Uncertain Course: New Weapons, Strategies and Mindsets*, ed. Carl Jacobsen. On mindsets functioning as filters for processing information, see Irving Janis, *Crucial Decisions: Leadership in Policymaking and Crisis*, 98–9. On the forms of discourse in the nuclear arms debate, see James V. Wertsch, "Modes of Discourse in the Nuclear Arms Debate," *Current Research on Peace and Violence*. On initial belief systems, see Glen H. Snyder and Paul Diesing, *Conflict Among Nations*. On psychological explanations of threat perception including schemata, see Janice Gross Stein, "Building Politics into Psychology: The Misperception of Threat," *Political Psychology*, 245.

6 Kim Richard Nossal, for example, divides policy-makers into "Atlanticists" and those less enamoured of the Atlantic ideal ("hard-headed instrumentalists") in "A European Nation? The Life and Times of Atlanticism in Canada," in *Making a Difference? Canada's Foreign Policy in a Changing World Order*, eds. John English and Norman Hillmer, 79–102. And Douglas Ross divides officials from the Department of External Affairs into left liberals, liberal moderates, and conservatives in *In the Interests of Peace: Canada and Vietnam, 1954–1973*. The tendency to ease understanding by typecasting decision-makers is not peculiar to Canada, as evidenced by the huge variety of articles in the general literature that divide people into such categories as old mindsets and empirical realists, Ken Booth, "New Challenges and Old Mindsets"; peace, power, and security types of thinkers, Barry Buzan, *People, States & Fear*; hard-liners and soft-liners, Glen Snyder and Diesing, *Conflict among Nations*; and hawks, doves, and owls, G.T. Allison, A. Carnesale and Joseph Nye, *Hawks, Doves, and Owls: An Agenda for Avoiding Nuclear War*.

7 For a discussion of "representational" versus "instrumental" models of communication, and methodological problems encountered when inferring the world views of key leaders, see Albert S. Yee, "The

causal effect of ideas on policies," *International Organization*; Deborah Welch Larson, "Problems of Content Analysis in Foreign-Policy Research: Notes from the Study of the Origins of Cold War Belief Systems," *International Studies Quarterly*; and Richard K. Hermann, "Analyzing Soviet Images of the United States," *Journal of Conflict Resolution*.

8 For this reason, the original classification of a document (e.g., top secret) is noted, although in most cases the original document has now been declassified.

9 Deductions about core assumptions related to "abandonment" and "entrapment" at the individual level of analysis were, to some extent, extrapolations of the original concepts developed by Michael Mandelbaum, *The Nuclear Revolution: International Politics Before and After Hiroshima*, where Mandelbaum coined these terms to describe systemic-level relations between the superpowers. Subsequently, Glen H. Snyder uses them to analyse state behaviour using game theory concepts in "The Security Dilemma in Alliance Politics," and Jane Sharp uses them to describe Western European fears in "After Reykjavik: Arms Control and the Allies," *International Affairs* and "Arms Control and Alliance Commitments," *Political Science Quarterly*. My other deductions concerning different images of the threat were partly based on work by Ken Booth, "New Challenges and Old Mindsets"; Robert Jervis, *Perception and Misperception in International Politics*; Steven Kull, *Minds at War*, 29, 38; and Elworthy, Hamwee, and Miall, "The Assumptions of Nuclear Weapons Decision-makers." The deductively and inductively derived questions were also based on primary and secondary material related to Canadian decision-making about NATO between 1957 and 1989. In the chapters to follow, some of this evidence is presented. For more theoretical background, see Erika Simpson, "Canada's Contrasting Alliance Commitments and the Underlying Beliefs and Assumptions of NATO Defenders and Critics," (PhD dissertation, University of Toronto, 1995), chap. 1, 37–77, chap. 2, 78–105. For a similar "inductive" approach, see Denis Stairs, "The Political Culture of Canadian Foreign Policy," *Canadian Journal of Political Science*, 678–83, in which Stairs analyses the explicit and consistent set of assumptions that Canadian statesmen and diplomats have held, based not on a formal survey, but on an examination of their behaviour and arguments. Whereas Stairs focuses on the assumptions of the "liberal-internationalists" prominent in the "Golden Age" of Canadian diplomacy, such as John Holmes and Lester Pearson, this present book focuses on the periods of contrasting NATO commitment that occurred between 1957 and 1963, 1968 and 1974, and 1978 and 1989.

10 Although much of the historical evidence is cited in the notes, some sources of information and authors of documents could not be published. Chapter 9 discuss in greater detail the problem this non-disclosure poses for replication of the findings, as well as for other researchers pursuing a similar line of inquiry.

11 On the objectives of undertaking a historical case study, see Arend Lijphart, "Comparative Politics and the Comparative Method," *American Political Science Review*, 691–3; and Earl Babbie, *The Practice of Social Research*, 3rd ed., 244.

12 At various times, the government committed albeit narrowly, to provide territory, such as the Suffield chemical-testing range in Alberta. It contributed to ensuring territorial surveillance through, for example, the Distant Early Warning (DEW) line. Promises to provide weapons-testing facilities and weapons parts – including, for instance, parts for the cruise missile tested over Canada – were carried out. Pledges to channel a certain amount of money, such as a percentage of GNP, to NATO were also made. Offers to share the costs of a capital project, such as the North Warning System, were made as well. Even commitments to provide a measure of consultation and expertise to NATO, including advice on arms control, verification or peacekeeping, were conceivable.

13 The thirty-year rule concerning declassification and the twenty-year rule concerning access to the official Cabinet Conclusions were factors in selecting the case studies. However, even when a case occurred outside the twenty- or thirty-year periods, a great deal of evidence remained classified because of Sections 13 (1) and 15 (1) under the Access to Information Act. In particular, Section 13 (1), pertaining to information obtained in confidence, stipulates that the head of a government institution shall refuse to disclose any record requested under the Act that contains information obtained in confidence from the government of a foreign state or an institution thereof or from an international organization of states or an institution thereof. Section 15 (1), pertaining to international affairs and defence, rules that the government may refuse to disclose any information

"which could reasonably be expected to be injurious to the conduct of international affairs, the defence of Canada or any state allied or associated with Canada or the detection, prevention or suppression of subversive or hostile activities including, without restricting the generality of the foregoing, any such information relating to military tactics or strategy … military exercises or operations … weapons or other defence equipment … relating to the characteristics, capabilities, performance, potential, deployment, functions or role of any defence establishment, of any military force, unit or personnel or of any organization or person responsible for the detection, prevention or suppression of subversive or hostile activities ... [and including any such information] obtained or prepared for the purpose of intelligence respecting foreign states, international organizations of states or citizens of foreign states used by the Government of Canada in the process of deliberation and consultation or in the conduct of international affairs."

14 For example, when Gordan Smith was asked in 1992 about whether he thought Ivan Head's top-secret assessment in 1969 of the nature of the Canadian-American-Soviet relationship reflected his own concerns, when he himself was a high-level member of the Canadian delegation to NATO, Smith admitted to a great deal of difficulty recalling his own imagery of the United States and the Soviet Union in 1969, especially because of the kinds of positions he had since held (i.e., as the Canadian Ambassador to NATO he had observed the dissolution of the Soviet threat).

15 The case study could have focused on Canada's record of shifting commitment under Prime Minister Diefenbaker. Between 1957 and 1963, the government's various decisions to commit Canada to NATO by acquiring five different nuclear weapons systems were followed by acrimony within Cabinet, a growing disinclination to acquire nuclear warheads for the weapons, and eventual outright rejection of the nuclear commitments. Similarly, the case study could have focused on Canada's record of contrasting commitment under Prime Minister Trudeau from 1968 to 1971. The government's initial intention in 1968 to withdraw the Canadian Forces from Europe was reformulated; it was decided, first, to cut the forces by two-thirds and later, to halve the forces instead.

16 For example, recently opened collections include DND's "Raymont Series," the PCO Cabinet Conclusions, and the Prime Minister's papers at the J.G. Diefenbaker Centre. New books and memoirs include Knowlton Nash, *Kennedy & Diefenbaker: Fear and Loathing Across the Undefended Border*, 1990; Basil Robinson, *Diefenbaker's World: A Populist in Foreign Affairs*, 1989; Peter Haydon, *The 1962 Cuban Missile Crisis: Canadian Involvement Reconsidered*, 1993; Denis Stairs, *Rogue Tory*, 1995; and D.C. Story and R. Bruce Shepard, eds., *Diefenbaker's Legacy*, 1998.

CHAPTER THREE

1 The research questions used to draw out the principal elements of the belief system of Defenders are summarized on 36–7.

2 Confidential source, 1969.

3 PCO, Cabinet Documents, Department of National Defence Paper for Special Task Force Europe (STAFEUR), "Canadian Military Interest in Europe," V 2390–1 (STAFEUR), 1 November 1968, 12, [secret].

4 DHist, General Records, R.J. Sutherland (chairman), A.C. Grant (deputy minister's staff), Captain V.J. Wilgress (Royal Canadian Navy), Brigadier D.A.G. Waldock (Army) and C.C.H. Mussels (Royal Canadian Air Force), "Report of the Ad Hoc Committee on Defence Policy" (Ad Hoc Committee on Defence Policy), 1963, 68, [secret – Canadian eyes only]. Notably, the Ad Hoc Committee on Defence Policy reported directly to the minister of National Defence, Paul Hellyer, and was instructed to provide Hellyer with a series of options available to Canada.

5 Confidential source, 10 April 1968 [secret].

6 PCO, Cabinet document 165–550, H.H.W. [probably Mr. Wright], memorandum for Mr. Crowe describing meeting of the Cabinet Committee on External Policy and Defence to consider the "Defence Policy Review," 11 March 1969, 1 [secret].

7 DHist, Ad Hoc Committee on Defence Policy, 24, [secret – Canadian eyes only].

8 Ross Campbell, CIIPS transcripts, 1987, 658.

9 PCO, Cabinet Conclusions, 9 May 1963, 13 [secret].

10 PCO, Cabinet Conclusions, 10 March 1969, 2 [secret].

11 DHist, "Defence Policy Review," February 1969, 20 [secret – Canadian eyes only].

12 Ibid., 20–2. The "Defence Policy Review" was an intradepartmental report prepared for the Cabinet Committee on External Affairs and Defence. It was written in 1969 by anonymous members of the Departments of External Affairs, National Defence, Transportation, Immigration, and Commerce.

13 Confidential source, Paul Martin, minister of External Affairs, 1966 [secret].

14 Confidential source, 1964 [secret].

15 Confidential source, May 1968.

16 PCO, Cabinet document 165–550, H.H.W. [probably Mr. Wright], memorandum for Mr. Crowe describing meeting of the Cabinet Committee on External Policy and Defence to consider the "Defence Policy Review," 11 March 1969, 2 [secret].

17 Confidential source [secret – Canadian eyes only].

18 Confidential source, memorandum regarding "Unilateral deployment of CF committed to the Defence of Western Europe," May 1984 [restricted].

19 DHist, "Defence Policy Review," February 1969, 33 [secret – Canadian eyes only].

20 Confidential source, 1969 [secret]. Similar comments by Mitchell Sharp are found in PCO, Cabinet document 165–550, H.H.W. [probably Mr. Wright], memorandum for Mr. Crowe describing meeting of the Cabinet Committee on External Policy and Defence to consider the "Defence Policy Review," 11 March 1969, 3–4 [secret].

21 DHist, Department of National Defence Paper for Special Task Force Europe (STAFEUR), "Canadian Military Interest in Europe," V 2390–1 (STAFEUR), 1 November 1968, 28 [secret].

22 These comments were made by the Canadian ambassador to NATO, Gordon Smith, in a briefing at NATO headquarters, Brussels, 19 June 1990.

23 Paul Dick, associate minister of National Defence, *Hansard*, 4 March 1988, 13422.

24 Confidential source, October 1968 [secret]. In another example, a letter written to John Halstead in the European Division of the Department of External Affairs warned that withdrawal from the Western Alliance and refusal to co-operate in continental defence "would greatly alter the American public's basic view of Canada ... [cause] serious concern to the US authorities ... [and] there would undoubtedly be an adverse effect on the USA's attitude towards economic cooperation with us." Confidential source, 31 October 1968.

25 Confidential source, 17 November 1982.

26 The "flagging" Canadian performance was criticized by representatives from the United States, the United Kingdom, the Federal Republic of Germany, the Netherlands, the NATO Military Committee, SHAPE, and the Supreme Allied Commander (SACLANT) at a meeting on 27 October 1980. It was pointed out that, at a time when the need to modernize the Canadian Forces was becoming increasingly urgent, postponement and procrastination seemed to be the dominant characteristics of the Canadian decision-making process. Confidential sources. For the attitude of high-level Canadian representatives to this sort of criticism, see DEA, 27–1–1-USA and DEA, 27–1–1-29.

27 Confidential source, 9 April 1980.

28 Arthur Menzies, CIIPS transcripts, 1987, 759.

29 Ross Campbell, CIIPS transcripts, 1987, 673–4. As Campbell explains, "The lesson had been learned [from the Vietnam War] that the United States could be a pretty ruthless military actor. And I think at that stage the Europeans thought: 'Well, we'd better pull ourselves together and see whether we can't assume responsibility for a bit

more of European defence than we have done up to now without
pulling the Alliance apart; do it within NATO'. And again, this was
absolutely deadly for Canada ... Where did it leave us? You know we
didn't want to be left on the shelf with the Americans, and yet that's
really what has been the consequence of the growth of this European
centre within NATO."

30 Confidential source [secret– Canadian eyes only].

31 Also according to this high-level adviser, "There is a pervading con-
sciousness in Washington of the heavy burden of responsibility now
being carried by the US. This stems predominantly from Vietnam but
spills over into other fields, such as external aid and NATO. They feel
very keenly that US capacity and willingness to share generously in
the burdens of providing global security may be circumscribed by the
unwillingness of its allies to accept responsibility for proportionate
shares." Confidential memorandum, June 1966 [secret].

32 For more discussion of the impact of lessons learned during World
War II and the Korean War, see chap. 8, pp. 186-7. On the best way of
indicating Canada's support of the allies, see comments, for example,
by Robert Cameron, a former assistant under-secretary of state for
External Affairs, CIIPS transcripts, 1987, 201 and DEA, 27–1–1, memorandum on "Defence Evaluation Group Papers: Paper 1, Canadian
Industrial Defence Base," 22 May 1984 [restricted].

33 John Holmes, CIIPS transcripts, 49–50.

34 DHist, Department of National Defence Paper for Special Task Force
Europe (STAFEUR), "Canadian Military Interest in Europe," V 2390–1
(STAFEUR), 1 November 1968, 3 [secret].

35 The close contacts among decision-makers from Canada and those
from the Western European countries were fostered through the
NATO Parliamentarians Association, briefing trips for Canadian MPS
and policy-makers sponsored by NATO headquarters, as well as meetings in Canada of various NATO committees (e.g., the Nuclear Planning Group). Descriptions of the close contacts abound. See, for
example, the reference by Lieutenant-General Charles Belzile, former
commander of Mobile Command and chief, Land Doctrine and Operations, as to the effect on policy-making in the 1970s of the close ties
among General Dextraze, Chief of the Defence Staff; John Halstead,
ambassador to Germany; and himself, as commander of Canadian
Forces Europe. CIIPS transcripts, 1987, 494. As Geoffrey Pearson
explained in 1987, "NATO does have this familiarity, and informal
capacity for the Allies to meet, in various different guises, whether it
is policy-planning or regional conflicts or relations with the Soviets,
which gives it a continuing vitality." CIIPS transcripts, 1987, 182.

36 PCO, Cabinet Committee on External Policy and Defence, Conclusions, 10 March 1969, 2 [secret].

37 Confidential high-level source, July 1984 [confidential]. Another former ambassador to NATO, George Ignatieff, also complained about the lack of recognition "certain countries, particularly those which have interests and contacts in the Arctic" had in accepting "specific commitments for the defence of the Canadian North as we have accepted in support of Norway." George Ignatieff, CIIPS transcripts, 1987, 131.

38 DHist, "Defence Policy Review," February 1969, 104 [secret – Canadian eyes only]. Similarly, six years earlier in 1963, the Ad Hoc Committee on Defence Policy dismissed the argument that alternative contributions outside the NATO area could be made to justify the withdrawal of Canada's Forces from Europe (such as contributions to the UN and foreign aid). It was pointed out that the important issue was not whether alternatives were reasonable, but whether they would "carry weight" with the allies. DHist, Ad Hoc Committee on Defence Policy, 74 [secret – Canadian Eyes Only].

39 Confidential source, memorandum regarding "Unilateral deployment of CF committed to the Defence of Western Europe," May 1984 [restricted].

40 Ad Hoc Committee on Defence Policy, 170 [secret – Canadian eyes only]. In a similar vein, according to DND's 1968 Basic Paper for STAFEUR:

It can be assumed that a Canadian commitment which is neither recognized by the Europeans as a significant and meaningful military force nor seen by Canadians as an identifiable Canadian contribution would represent a pointless and unacceptable expenditure of scarce resources … Under [this] assumption regarding minimum meaningful contributions, the options open for reducing forces on the Central Front are withdrawal of either the Air Division or the Mechanized Brigade Group. Withdrawal of either formation in the near future would seriously weaken the NATO defence structure at a time when the military imperatives seem to demand at least no weakening and possibly a strengthening of the Alliance's defence capabilities. In this context, no force element, however small, is insignificant.

DHist, DND Basic Paper for STAFEUR, "Canadian Military Interest in Europe," V-2390 (STAFEUR), 1 November 1968, 28–9 [secret]. Similarly, according to another secret defence policy review written in 1969, Canada's traditional defence posture in Western Europe had to be maintained because "politically, identifiable Canadian forces physically present" in Europe were "the most tangible and, from the European point of view, the most acceptable evidence of Canadian interest and involvement in the problems of European security." DHist, "Defence Policy Review," February 1969, 45 [secret – Canadian eyes only].

41 The controversy behind the scenes concerning how to fairly measure GNP is referred to in DHist, Department of National Defence Paper for Special Task Force Europe (STAFEUR), "Canadian Military Interest in Europe," V 2390–1 (STAFEUR), 1 November 1968, 21 [secret]; Confidential sources, letter from Alan Gotlieb to Michael Pitfield, secretary to the Cabinet, PCO, 9 April 1980 [secret]; letter from Harold Brown, US secretary of Defense, Washington, 10 April 1980; and note for the undersecretary of External Affairs, August 1981. For more on the assumption that Canada was not pulling its weight in the Alliance because the defence budget as a proportion of GNP was one of the smallest in the Alliance, see comments by John Halstead, CIIPS transcripts, 1987, 830.

42 Confidential source, June 1968 [secret].

43 Confidential source, 18 November 1974.

44 Confidential source, April 1980 [restricted].

45 Confidential source, April 1980 [secret].

46 Notably, NATO's sixteen members officially pledged in 1978 to maintain a three-percent real increase in defence spending each year. The Stockholm International Peace Research Institute reported in 1987 that "the 3 per cent goal was followed with some consistency by only four NATO countries: Canada, Italy, the U.K. and the USA. The latter two have now, in practice, abandoned it." Cited in Howard Peter Langille, *Changing the Guard*, 128.

47 Steven Kull shows that, among American defence policy-makers, three "streams" of thought developed regarding military commitments and force structures. The three streams referring to Canadian assumptions are, in part, modelled on Kull's analysis. See *Minds at War*, 296.

48 Confidential source, March 1969.

49 The propensity to see ourselves as the central point of reference when explaining the actions of others is referred to in the psychological literature as an egocentric bias. For further elaboration, see Janice Gross Stein, "The Misperception of Threat: Building Politics into Psychology," *Political Psychology*, 253. As Robert Jervis points out, actors have a propensity "to see themselves as central to others' behaviour. An actor's knowledge of what he wants, what he fears, and what he has done sets the framework for his perceptions." *Perception and Misperception in International Politics*, 212.

50 Confidential source, January, 1969. Similarly, a senior Canadian official pointed out in 1982 that Canada's contribution to the conventional balance of forces in Europe played a role in preventing war and in the potential outcome of interalliance warfare. According to his letter, "We and our allies have been seriously concerned about NATO's weakness in conventional forces [in central Europe], both in numbers and state of readiness, compared to those of the Warsaw Pact. NATO Commanders have repeatedly warned that by failing to match the Pact's improvements we would be seriously compromising our ability to withstand a conventional attack, and would risk having to consider escalation to a nuclear level at an early stage ... Recent decisions to re-equip both the land and air elements of the CFE have been welcomed because of the real improvement they would make to the Allies' conventional capabilities." Confidential source, November 1982 [secret].

51 Steven Kull shows that outdated beliefs about conventional warfare undergirded American defence policy-makers' rationales about a possible nuclear war in Europe. For more analysis of the way in which beliefs about conventional warfare were manifested in the nuclear era, see Kull's interviews and discussion in *Minds at War*.

52 DHist, Ad Hoc Committee on Defence Policy, 1963, 7 [secret – Canadian eyes only].

53 Confidential source, memorandum regarding "Unilateral deployment of CF committed to the Defence of Western Europe," May 1984 [restricted].

54 Ross Campbell, CIIPS transcripts, 1987, 652.

55 PCO, Cabinet Conclusions, 9 May 1963, 15–17 [secret].

56 See PCO, Cabinet Conclusions, 1 November 1968, 2–5 [secret]. With respect to their strategic rationale, Hellyer advised that the CF-104s were "redundant"; "they made a contribution where the west has far more power than necessary," and "they performed a role which was more strategic than tactical and two or three weapons were often assigned to the same target." He concluded that "the maintenance of our Air Division at 108 aircraft would be for show and symbolic." The Cabinet Conclusions do not indicate whether Hellyer nevertheless supported maintaining the CF-104s. Notably, Hellyer had originally recommended acquisition of the CF-5s to replace the CF-104s. The CF-5 squadrons were to be considered part of Canada's CAST commitment to defend Norway.

57 Further evidence of some Cabinet Ministers' tendency to support traditional commitments without assessing their strategic rationale and implications is found in the Trudeau Cabinet's discussion of the problem of interpreting weapons systems as either "offensive" or

"defensive". PCO, Cabinet Conclusions, 20 November 1969. Other notes which "give the flavour of the discussion in a way that a more formal record doesn't" are contained in a memorandum describing a meeting of the Cabinet Committee on External Policy and Defence, during which ministers put forward their reasons for opposing or maintaining Canada's troops in Europe. PCO, Cabinet document 165–550, H.H.W. [probably Mr. Wright], memorandum for Mr. Crowe describing meeting of the Cabinet Committee on External Policy and Defence, "Defence Policy Review," 11 March 1969, 1–5 [secret].

58 This definition is based on Raymond Cohen's definition of threat in *Threat Perception in International Crisis*, 4.

59 As John Holmes later explained, "Not many people argued whether or not there was a Soviet threat during this time period, but was it immutable, was there any change? Perhaps the biggest arguments were over the question of whether the Communist world was monolithic. I was rather anti-monolith and I think it had to do with my experience in Moscow." On the other hand, he stated, "then this thing happened in June in Korea, and I can't pretend for a moment that I expected it, and we just had to face this question: 'Maybe they are all working together, maybe this is monolithic.'" CIIPS transcripts, 1987, 43. For further documentation and discussion considering whether prominent Canadian decision-makers tended, during the 1940s and 1950s, to perceive a monolithic threat, see the comments by Mackenzie King and Louis St. Laurent in James Eayrs, *In Defence of Canada: Growing Up Allied*, 58–60 and the comments in 1946 by Lester Pearson and others on the objectives of Soviet foreign policy in Denis Smith, *Diplomacy of Fear: Canada and the Cold War 1941–1948*, 167, 173–4.

60 Arthur Menzies, CIIPS transcripts, 1987, 703.

61 DHist, file 74/426, Air Marshall Campbell Speeches, speech to RCAF Staff College, "Farewell for A/C Orr," 24 June 1960 [classified].

62 For example, see DHist, "Defence Policy Review," February 1969, 127 [secret – Canadian eyes only].

63 For example, see PCO, Cabinet Conclusions, Mitchell Sharp, minister of External Affairs, 10 March 1969, 2 [secret].

64 For example, see DHist, Ad Hoc Committee on Defence Policy, 1963, 165 [secret – Canadian eyes only].

65 For example, see DEA, 20–1–2-STAFEUR 8, statement of under-secretary of state for External Affairs, Marcel Cadieux, at interdepartmental meeting to consider implications of possible restrictions on defence spending in 1969–70, 1970–71, 2 [secret – Canadian eyes only].

66 For example, see DHist, Raymont Papers, 73/1223, file 848, speech by Secretary of State for External Affairs Paul Martin to the Atlantic

Treaty Organization, 15 September 1964, 4; for analysis, see also John
Holmes on the great fear of the threat of communism compared to
the lesser fear of the Soviet Union in CIIPS transcripts, 1987, 24.

67 For example, see DHist, "Defence Policy Review," February 1969, 128
[secret – Canadian eyes only].

68 For example, see DHist, Ad Hoc Committee on Defence Policy, 1963,
45 [secret – Canadian eyes only].

69 Confidential source, secret high-level memorandum, April 1968
[secret].

70 For example, see DEA, 20–1–2-STAFEUR-8, J.A. Andrew to the under-
secretary of state for External Affairs, memorandum regarding the
"Review of Canadian Foreign Policy," Stockholm Embassy, 25 June
1968, 2.

71 For example, see Robert Cameron interview, CIIPS transcripts, 1987,
199.

72 For example, see PCO, Cabinet document, no. 724–68, Mitchell Sharp,
minister of External Affairs, memorandum to the Cabinet, "Special
NATO Ministerial Meeting – Proposed Canadian Position," 24 October 1968 [secret].

73 For example, see PCO, Cabinet Documents, STAFEUR report, 44, [con-
fidential – Canadian eyes only]. The STAFEUR report was co-chaired
by Paul Tremblay, Canadian ambassador to NATO and Robert Ford,
Canadian ambassador to Moscow. To a great extent, it was super-
vised and written by Deputy Chair John Halstead, head of the European Division of the Department of External Affairs.

74 There were few high-level references during the 1950s, '60s, and '70s
to amorphous or internal threats. The threat of spreading communism within Canada among Canadian citizens was referred to only
once. Although DND's highly classified "Defence Review" briefly
referred to the threat of Communist Party activities within Canadian
society, this prospect was not a major preoccupation of high-level
policy-makers. According to brief comments in that review, "Although
there is no prospect in the foreseeable future of a communist seizure
of power in Canada, the Communist Party's activities are increasingly widespread. Trade unions have been viewed as the main channels for exerting influence, and several are communist-led at the
senior executive level. Communists and sympathizers have made
inroads in other sections of Canadian society, notably, local government, education, cultural fields and some parts of the communications media, and have thus improved the Party's ability to
disseminate propaganda and further its own ends." Relative to
spreading communism within Canada, the problem of "nationalism

in Quebec and student unrest," was more frequently referred to as a potential threat. See DHist, "Defence Policy Review," February 1969, 64 [secret – Canadian eyes only].

75 DEA, *Statements and Speeches*, no. 67/35, Secretary of State for External Affairs Paul Martin to the Canadian Club, 13 November 1967, 2.

76 DEA, 20–1–2-STAFEUR 8, statement by the under-secretary of state for External Affairs, Marcel Cadieux, at interdepartmental meeting to consider implications of possible restrictions on defence spending in 1969–70, 1970–71, 2 [secret – Canadian eyes only].

77 Perrin Beatty, *Hansard*, 5 June 1987, 6777.

78 DND, *Challenge and Commitment: A Defence Policy for Canada* (1987 White Paper on Defence), 1987, 9.

79 Ad Hoc Committee on Defence Policy, 166, [secret – Canadian eyes only].

80 Quoted in PCO, M.A.C. [Marcel Cadieux], memorandum for the prime minister regarding "Defence and Foreign Policy Review," 4 March 1969, 2 [secret].

81 Confidential high-level source, 5 July 1984 [confidential].

82 Paul Dick, associate minister of National Defence, *Hansard*, 4 March 1988, 13424.

83 Indeed, in 1990 Canada's Ambassador to NATO maintained, after the events of 1989, that it was as yet inappropriate to entirely rethink Canada's definition of the Soviet threat. As he pointed out, "We Canadians tend to think of the Soviet Union from a European perspective, not an Asian one. They don't see much change in the Soviet Union." Briefing, NATO headquarters, 19 June 1990. In a similar fashion, according to another representative of the Canadian delegation to NATO headquarters, "if we have a democratized Russia without the Soviet Union, it would still be good to have a balancer [e.g., NATO] against Russia." Confidential briefing, Toronto, 7 February 1990. Despite the end of the Cold War, this high-level representative continued to reject evidence that contradicted his convictions about the nature of the "Russian threat."

84 For further discussion of the problems inherent in distinguishing offensive and threatening weapons and postures from defensive weapons and force structures, see, for example, Johan Galtung, *There are Alternatives! Four Roads to Peace and Security*, 172–80 and Dietrich Fisher, *Preventing War in the Nuclear Age*, chap. 5. On Canada's options with respect to establishing a non-offensive defence posture, see Howard Peter Langille, *Changing the Guard*, chap. 6.

85 Minister of National Defence, George Pearkes, *Hansard*, 2 July 1959, 5352.

86 Reprinted in DEA, *Statements and Speeches*, no. 69/8, Pierre Elliott
   Trudeau, "The Relation of Defence Policy to Foreign Policy," Speech
   to the Alberta Liberal Association, 12 April 1969, 5. Evidence of the
   opposition by civil servants within DEA and DND is found in DEA,
   27-1-1, 1 May 1968 [confidential]; 27-1-1-1-USA, 1 May 1968; and DEA,
   27-1-1-1-5, 12 April 1969.

87 Confidential source, 10 April 1968 [secret].

88 A comprehensive DND study concerning "Canada's Military Interest
   in Europe" and the purpose for deploying the Air Division and Brigade Group in Europe dealt with the issue of whether the "nuclear
   bombers of the Air Division" could be "destabilizing" in one short
   paragraph. As this lengthy report cursorily pointed out: "A consideration that applies to Canada as well as to some other countries is that
   the nuclear bombers of the Air Division are highly vulnerable to
   nuclear atttack. It must be assumed that among the priority targets of
   the 700 medium and intermediate-range ballistic missiles in Eastern
   Europe are the bases of the NATO strike air forces, and since the
   warning time against an attack by these missiles would be extremely
   short, it is problematic whether any significant proportion of NATO's
   nuclear strike force would survive. This vulnerability could in itself
   be de-stabilizing in a crisis, since it provides both sides with a strong
   incentive to strike first." Although by this time the Prime Minister
   was asking whether the Soviets might therefore perceive these aircraft as provocative and offensive, DND advisers immediately proceeded to argue in this brief that "the question of influence also has
   some bearing on Canadian nuclear equipment. The fact that Canada's
   NATO forces are equipped with nuclear weapons increases Canada's
   ability to participate in the formulation of the nuclear policies of the
   Alliance ... there is no logic to the claim that Canada would somehow be better off if it dissociated itself from the decisions that must
   in any case be taken." DHist, "Canadian Military Interest in Europe,"
   V 2390–1 (STAFEUR), 1 November 1968, 28–29 [SECRET].

89 Lieutenant-General Charles Belzile, CIIPS transcripts, 1987, 445.

90 Confidential source, 1965 [secret].

91 *Hansard*, 14 June 1983, 26359. In another example, during the same
   debate another MP told the House of Commons that the air-launched
   cruise missile was not a dedicated nuclear weapons system but a
   simple conventional vehicle put together with rivets, and designed to
   be a slightly upgraded version of a drone, which flew over the skies
   of Alberta 25 years ago. J.M. Forrestall, 26349.

92 Charles Nixon, deputy minister of National Defence, CIIPS transcripts, 1987, 593–4.

93 Confidential source, comments in Cabinet by Leo Cadieux, minister of National Defence, and Bud Drury, September 1968 [secret]. In an aside, Drury added that sometimes second-hand Cadillacs were as good as new ones.

94 In 1983 the Department of External Affairs maintained that, "Canada and its allies would prefer not to deploy new missiles. They are convinced, however, that the INF negotiations will not succeed if the Western Alliance shows signs of weakness. They cannot accept a result which would require NATO to abandon the modernization of its forces in Europe while the Soviet Union maintains its missiles." DEA, press release, "Agreement with the United States of America on Test and Evaluation of US Defence Systems in Canada," no. 15, 10 February 1983, 2. See also the transcript of a CBC radio interview with Secretary of State for External Affairs Alan MacEachen, CBC *Sunday Morning*, 13 February 1983 and similar comments by Garnet Bloomfield, parliamentary secretary to the minister of National Revenue, *Hansard*, 14 June 1983, 26360.

95 See DND, 1987 White Paper on Defence, 9.

96 According to the analysis of the Ad Hoc Committee on Defence Policy, one of the most important "negative decisions" made by a previous Canadian government was that Canada elected not to undertake a nuclear weapons program. "This meant, in effect, that as a matter of deliberate choice Canada did not stake out a claim to Great Power status. Canada renounced the ability and the aspiration to participate in the mission of strategic nuclear deterrence, and by doing so accepted a position of strategic subordination to the United States." DHist, Ad Hoc Committee on Defence Policy, 1963, 9 [secret – Canadian eyes only].

97 *Ibid.*, 83.

98 The Working Group went on to write, "In Europe, on the other hand, the numbers of tactical nuclear weapons disposed by the NATO forces may now be excessive to foreseeable requirements, and it might lend more balance to NATO's defences if Canada were to convert to a conventional role." DHist, Raymont Series 73/1223, series 2, file 832, Canadian Defence Policy Rationale, 11/20/67–02/10/69, Working Group from DND and DEA, Rationale for Canadian Forces, 3 May 1968, 2 [confidential].

99 Lieutenant-General Charles Belzile, CIIPS transcripts, 1987, 445.

100 Minister of National Defence, J. Gilles Lamontagne, *Hansard*, 14 June 1983, 26321.

101 DEA, 27-1-1-USA (DEA), press release and information for members of the press accompanying the "Exchange of Notes" signed in Washington by Alan Gotlieb, Canada's ambassador to the US and Thomas

Niles, deputy assistant secretary of state for Canadian Affairs, section on "Anticipated Questions and Suggested Answers," 1983.

102 Confidential source, 8 February 1983.

103 According to Lieutenant-General Charles Belzile, CIIPS transcripts, 1987, 447.

104 See comments by the former minister of External Affairs, Flora MacDonald, regarding the "defensive system" of Pershing and cruise missiles, and comments by Gerard Pelletier that the cruise missile was not a nuclear or atomic missile, but merely a delivery system, *Hansard*, 14 June 1983, 26359, 26345.

105 The Ad Hoc Committee on Defence Policy pointed out in 1963:

> Since 1939, Canadian maritime programs have been heavily concentrated upon the defence of North Atlantic sea communications against submarine attack. This concentration has been based on sound strategic grounds, the importance of these communications to the entire North Atlantic community. It has produced a most desirable concentration in the focus of Canada's maritime programs and it has also had the effect of establishing a strong Canadian presence in the approaches to the Gulf of St. Lawrence and in the waters off the Eastern Atlantic coast. There is the further point that an attack submarine force would involve Canada in an 'offensive' naval role which might be opposed by some segments of Canadian public opinion. It is concluded that Canada's principal interest is likely to lie in hunter-killer submarines. This is an option within the ASW mission rather than an extension of this mission. 84, 87 [secret – Canadian eyes only].

> See also the comments by Charles Nixon regarding the legacies and lessons of the Second World War in terms of "anti-submarine tactics" and "sanitized corridors," CIIPS transcripts, 1987, 540, 546; as well as the comments by Mitchell Sharp regarding Robert Kennedy's book in PCO, Cabinet document 165–606, H.H.W. [probably Mr. Wright], memorandum for Mr. Crowe regarding "Special Cabinet meeting this afternoon," 20 May 1969, 1 [secret].

106 Until 1949, only the United States had developed thermonuclear weapons. The first Soviet explosion of an atomic bomb in 1949 was followed four years later by the development of a hydrogen bomb. But it was not until 1957, with the launch of the Russian artificial earth satellite *Sputnik*, that military strategists in the United States and Canada generally recognized that there now existed a "balance of terror" between the US and the USSR. This balance also had attendant implications for deterrence strategy – implications that came to

be appreciated around 1959–60. This topic is explained in further detail in forthcoming chapters.

107 John Foster Dulles promulgated the doctrine of massive retaliation in 1954. The doctrine suggested that the United States would retaliate with considerable force, possibly including nuclear weapons, anywhere in the world. According to James Eayrs, Canadian diplomats did not begin to challenge this doctrine until Lester Pearson stated his reservations in a series of lectures to Princeton University in 1955; *In Defence of Canada: Growing Up Allied*, 259. The beliefs Defenders had about "mutual assured destruction" during the 1950s are explored in greater detail in chapter 6.

108 The strategy of flexible response was officially adopted by the Alliance in 1967; however, it had been unofficial doctrine since the early 1960s. According to the Ad Hoc Committee on Defence Policy in 1963, "Flexible response is in a sense a generalization of the concept of a limited war. It is based upon the proposition that the Western Alliance as a whole and the United States in particular should not be placed in a position of excessive reliance upon nuclear weapons or, more generally, of requiring to employ force in a manner incompatible with Western aims and objectives. The principle of flexible response places increased emphasis upon the provision of conventional forces. It involves reduced *dependence* upon strategic and tactical nuclear weapons although it does not reduce the *requirement* for these capabilities"; 14 [secret – Canadian eyes only]. Similarly, according to DND's 1970 "Defence Planning Guidance": "Thus, by maintaining a broad range of military capabilities the West is able, not only to ensure that hostile acts fail to achieve their objectives, but also to reduce the risk they will be attempted. The strategy of flexible response is commonly thought of in the context of Western Europe. In fact, however, it is equally valid in relation to other aspects of the West's defence"; DHist, DND, "Defence Planning Guidance," 1970, section 1, 6–7 [restricted].

109 For example, regarding the need to deploy tactical nuclear weapons such as cruise missiles in Western Europe, see comments by the minister of National Defence, J. Gilles Lamontagne, *Hansard*, 14 June 1983, 26321. Lamontagne also argued that credible deterrence required flexible response, intercontinental missiles, short- and long-range nuclear forces, and conventional forces. See, for example, his comments in DEA, telegram from NATO to External Ottawa, "Edited text of interview of the Minister of National Defence [J. Gilles Lamontagne] by Associated Press on December 1, 1982," 3 December 1982.

110 According to an interview, for example, with Erwin Sippert, Canadian defence counsellor, Defence Policy and Planning, NATO

Headquarters, Brussels, October 1992. On NATO's Strategic Concept, see NATO Office of Information and Press, "The Alliance's Strategic Concept," Brussels, Belgium, November 1991. Notably, the 1994 Report of the Special Joint Committee Reviewing Canadian Foreign Policy grouped Canada's current NATO commitments into four categories: immediate reaction forces, rapid reaction forces, main defence forces, and augmentation forces. On Canada's specific force commitments to each category, see "Canada's Foreign Policy: Principles and Priorities for the Future," 21.

111 DHist, no. 82/80, DND, "Defence Planning Guidance (U), (Shortened Version), Section II, 2 December 1970, 6 [restricted].

112 DND, Directorate of Strategic Analysis, Operational Research and Analysis Establishment, Lawrence Hagan, "Air-launched cruise missiles: implications for deterrence stability, arms control, and Canadian security," project report no. 114, October 1993, 18–19.

113 Quoted in DEA, 27-1-1-16, memorandum by A.E.R., [?] to the minister of External Affairs, "Summary of Mr. Hellyer's statement before the House of Commons Special Committee on Defence of 27 June 1963," 18 May 1971.

114 Confidential source, 18 May 1971.

115 DEA, telegram from NATO to External Ottawa, "Edited text of interview of the Minister of National Defence [J. Gilles Lamontagne] by Associated Press on December 1, 1982," 3 December 1982.

116 Ad Hoc Committee on Defence Policy, 1963, 16 [secret – Canadian eyes only].

117 George Ignatieff recalled that, while he was ambassador to NATO, "there was the shift from the massive retaliation schemes of Foster Dulles to the strategy of flexible response under MacNamara, but we were never happy then, nor happy now, with really what the basic strategy of NATO is, namely the forward strategy to have a thin red line which would trigger a nuclear response." Indeed, Ignatieff claimed that during his time at NATO headquarters in the mid-1960s: "Mountbatten was the head of defence and Lord Zuckerman was his scientific advisor. One of the interesting things was that, while the Americans talked about flexible response and forward defence and triggering this kind of nuclear response, Zuckerman, both in NATO and in visits to Ottawa, was saying that it was totally unrealistic, that the use of nuclear weapons on a tactical level would create such havoc in the battlefield as well as resulting in massive casualties in the civil population in the areas in which the fighting took place, that it would not be feasible to conduct a 'limited' nuclear battle ... Zuckerman's theories were pretty well confirmed." George Ignatieff, CIIPS transcripts, 1987, 138–9.

118 Robert Falls, CIIPS transcripts, 1987, 399.

119 For example, at one time some members of the Canadian delegation
    at NATO headquarters differed with the interpretation of flexible
    response put forward by British Secretary of Defence Denis Healey.
    They advanced their understanding of the new concept, which was
    that conventional forces in Europe should be expected to properly
    defend European territory. But the British secretary's interpretation of
    the role of conventional forces in Europe as a tripwire that could inev-
    itably lead to nuclear war ultimately gained greater momentum. Soon
    these Canadians were also defending the doctrine of flexible response
    using Healey's strategic rationale. Confidential sources, 1969.

120 Ross Campbell, CIIPS transcripts, 1987, 683.

121 J. Gilles Lamontagne, *Hansard*, 14 June 1983, 26321.

122 Charles Nixon, CIIPS transcripts, 1987, 561–2. Nixon was deputy min-
    ister of National Defence in 1974 when Cabinet proposed, in Nixon's
    words, a defence structure review "to look at what equipment there
    was and what could be done about commitments." 560.

123 As explained by Lieutenant-General Charles Belzile, CIIPS tran-
    scripts, 1987, 483.

124 Interview with John Halstead, CIIPS transcripts, 1987. He added:

    [General Rogers] said that what he wanted, as Supreme Allied Com-
    mander Europe, was sufficient conventional force to halt the initial,
    any initial, Soviet attack and to break up any follow-on forces, and
    thereby to put the onus for the first use of nuclear weapons on the
    Soviets' back rather than upon the Western back. He had very clearly
    in his mind what he wanted to do; he did not want to see NATO put
    in the position of having to use nuclear forces first. He thought the
    decision for the first use of nuclear forces was in itself a deterrent.
    The man, the President, the Commander, the side that had to make
    that decision on the first use of nuclear weapons, was going to be
    under enormous deterrence. So he wanted the conventional situation
    to be such that we would force the Soviets to bear that responsibility,
    we would put that monkey on the Soviets' back. I think this was
    very sound. 844–5.

125 Minister of National Defence J. Gilles Lamontagne, *Hansard*, 14 June
    1983, 26321. In a similar fashion, Lieutenant-General Belzile explained
    that, "we felt very strongly about the tank, not only for its power,
    and for its weapons system," but because, "if it was removed, we
    would be left with an army that would not be able to fight in a high
    intensity battlefield because it would not be balanced." Without bal-
    anced forces, this former commander of Canada's Mobile Forces

feared that, "we would then have had to revert to much lesser roles and probably not have been able to survive very well in a high intensity battlefield." CIIPS transcripts, 1987, 485.

126 James Taylor, former under-secretary of state for External Affairs and ambassador to NATO, CIIPS transcripts, 1987, 912.

127 A detailed study, for instance, written in 1968 by the Department of National Defence concerning Canada's military interest in Europe considered the question of whether nuclear escalation could be controlled only in passing:

More recently, however, there has been some reason for believing that the nuclear strength of the forces in Europe may have become excessive to any foreseeable requirement short of general nuclear war. Expert opinions differ widely on the question of whether a conflict could in fact be controlled once any kind of nuclear weapons have been invoked; presumably there are some kinds of circumstances in which this would be possible, but the chances are probably not very good. There is, on the other hand, a continuing requirement to strengthen NATO's conventional forces in order to control the Alliance's capability to meet limited aggression without the use of nuclear weapons. In consequence, it is obviously desirable that NATO's conventional forces should be as strong as possible.

DHist, Department of National Defence Paper for Special Task Force Europe (STAFEUR), "Canadian Military Interest in Europe," v 2390–1 (STAFEUR), 1 November 1968, 27 [secret].

128 For example, despite the Soviet invasion of Czechoslovakia in 1968, only brief commentary was accorded in Cabinet as to the possibility of unrest and conflict within the Soviet bloc "spilling over into Western European borders by accident or miscalculation," and a DND paper for STAFEUR on "Canadian Military Interest in Europe" concluded that the possibility of escalation was unlikely. PCO, Cabinet Conclusions, 1 November 1968 [secret] and DHist, DND Paper for STAFEUR, "Canadian Military Interest in Europe," 1 November 1968, 3.

129 The possibility of nuclear war occurring as a result of accident or miscalculation was only briefly mentioned, for instance, in the STAFEUR report, the most comprehensive report submitted to Cabinet. See PCO, Cabinet document 158/69, STAFEUR report, February 1969, 57–8 [secret – Canadian eyes only].

130 At one point, however, it was acknowledged that an immediate menace to NATO was the threatened conflict between two of NATO's members: Greece and Turkey. As Prime Minister Pearson emphasized, "Armed conflict between two NATO members, using military

equipment provided by other members for other collective defence purposes, could have a fatal effect on the NATO alliance." DEA, *Statements and Speeches*, no. 67/40, Prime Minister Lester Pearson, "An Era of Change for the UN and NATO," Mansion House, London, England, 27 November 1967.

131 For example, "Annex A" of DND's 137-page "Defence Policy Review" of 1969 advised Cabinet ministers as to the nature of the "Military Threat." This secret report for the Cabinet Defence Committee asserted that the principal threat to North America for the next ten years related only to the possibility of nuclear war between the United States and Soviet Russia: "The Soviet Union will be the only state capable of mounting a substantial nuclear attack against North America." Apart from the "small nuclear threat from Communist China" and the "remote" possibility of a non-nuclear attack against North America, or attacks against commercial maritime activities, other kinds of threats such as nuclear proliferation, terrorism, and threats to the environment were typically not mentioned in detailed analyses as to the nature of the military threat. DHist, "Defence Policy Review," no. 82/128, February 1969, annex A, 127–9 [secret].

CHAPTER FOUR

1 The research questions used to draw out the principal elements of the belief system of Critics are summarized on pp. 36–7.

2 PCO, Cabinet document 165–550, H.H.W. [probably Mr. Wright], memorandum for Mr. Crowe describing meeting of the Cabinet Committee on External Policy and Defence, "Defence Policy Review," 11 March 1969, 2 [secret].

3 Kierans added: "Rather we should be devoting our energies to persuading our allies that we have major domestic problems to solve and from their point of view it would be far better to have a strong and unified Canada as a prior condition to being able to contribute to the resolution of international problems." In turn, according to the Cabinet Conclusions, ministers opposed to Kierans's view pointed out, "the consequences of such a policy, emphasizing the loss of Canadian influence in European affairs, the possibility of adverse effects on our economic and trade relations, and the harmful effect on Canada-United States relations." PCO, Cabinet Committee on External Policy and Defence, 10 March 1969, 3 [secret].

4 DEA, *Statements and Speeches*, no. 69/8, Pierre Elliott Trudeau, "The Relation of Defence Policy to Foreign Policy," speech to the Alberta Liberal Association, 12 April 1969, 4.

5 PCO, Cabinet document 165-S42, G.H.D. [?], memorandum for Mr. Wright regarding "Defence Review," 5 March 1969, 2 [confidential].

6 PCO, Cabinet document 165–550, H.H.W. [probably Mr. Wright], memorandum for Mr. Crowe describing meeting of the Cabinet Committee on External Policy and Defence to consider "Defence Policy Review," 11 March 1969, 2 [secret].

7 PCO, Cabinet document 310/69 (165–461), Ivan Head, et al. "Canada Defence Policy: A Study," 28 March 1969 (hereafter Ivan Head's study), 13 [secret – Canadian eyes only]. Notably, this study was written by Ivan Head and other unspecified members of the PCO and the Treasury Board at the request of Prime Minister Trudeau. Dissatisfied with reviews conducted by the Departments of External Affairs and National Defence (e.g., the STAFEUR report), Trudeau asked Head to chair a committee that would secretly consult with experts from different departments in order to make recommendations to Cabinet. It appears much of Head's report was based on an analysis written by Gordon Robertson, clerk of the Privy Council Office and secretary to the Cabinet. See PCO, Cabinet document 165–558, R.G. Robertson, Memorandum for the Prime Minister regarding the Defence Policy Review and the Report of the Special Task Force on Europe, 25 March 1969, 3 [secret].

8 NA, Lester B. Pearson Papers, Leader of the Opposition Series 1957–1963, MG 26, N2, vol. 54, file 830, letter in reply to Ron Lander, Saskatoon, Saskatchewan, 1 June 1961.

9 DHist, Raymont Papers, 73/1223, series 2, file 848, "Canadian Foreign and Domestic Policy, 09/15/64–06/16/65," excerpts from Prime Minister Pearson's private lecture to the Institute for Strategic Studies, London, England, 16 June 1965, 3. The ambassador to the United States at that time, Arnold Heeney, was a strong NATO Defender, but he, too, commented on the difficulty of assessing the United States' military position due to, "partisan claims and statements, inter-service rivalries, and competing demands on the military budget" that resulted in "a babel of voices and opinions in which deliberate attempts are often made to exaggerate Soviet military might in this or that direction ..." DEA, file 4901-Y-40, vol. 58, dispatch from Arnold Heeney, ambassador to Washington regarding "The Defence Debate II: The Relative Strengths of the United States and the Soviet Union," 14 March 1960, 1 [confidential].

10 Confidential source, 15 November 1982.

11 Author's files, MP Paul McRae, untitled report for Prime Minister Trudeau (Paul McRae's study), n.d. [circa 1982].

12 Eric Kierans, transcript of speech to fundraising dinner for the Liberal association, Nanaimo, B.C., 25 January 1969. According to Kierans's

biographer, Jamie Swift, Trudeau reviewed the transcript of this speech beforehand and counselled Kierans to give the speech so as to provoke a national debate. Jamie Swift, *Odd Man Out: The Life and Times of Eric Kierans*, chap. 10.

13 PCO, Cabinet Conclusions, 1 April 1, 1969, 4 [secret].

14 Confidential source, 9 December 1968.

15 Confidential source, telegram reporting on bilateral discussions between Harold Wilson and Pierre Trudeau, 7 January 1969 [confidential].

16 PCO, Cabinet document 309/69, report by President of the Privy Council Donald Macdonald to the Cabinet, 25 March 1969, 4 [secret]; and Cabinet document 165–541, M.A.C. [Marcel Cadieux], "Memorandum for the Prime Minister: Defence and Foreign Policy Review," 4 March 1969, 3 [secret].

17 In this regard, the journalist Richard Gwyn advised Eric Kierans during his bid for the Liberal leadership in 1968 "not to be negative, never to state his opposition to Canadian membership in NATO and NORAD in negative terms, but to phrase such positions in the form of positive, constructive alternatives." Jamie Swift, *Odd Man Out: The Life and Times of Eric Kierans*, 28.

18 On the new order of priorities, see DND, *Defence in the 70s: White Paper on Defence*, 1971, 16.

19 On Trudeau's clarification of the allocation of resources toward these new priorities, see PCO, Cabinet Conclusions, 22 July 1970 [secret]. For a flavour of the Cabinet's debates concerning sovereignty and its importance, see PCO, Cabinet Conclusions, 18 June 1970 [secret]. On the difficulties experienced by personnel in identifying DND's role in the protection of sovereignty due to the ambiguity of the word "sovereignty" and the interlocking responsibilities of many federal departments and agencies, see, for example, DHist, 73/1223, series 2, file 832, "Canadian Defence Policy Rationale 11/20/67–02/10/69" correspondence from J.F. Anderson, director of Program Analysis, deputy minister of National Defence, 23 July 1970 [confidential].

20 Confidential source, letter from Prime Minister Trudeau to NATO Secretary-General Manlio Brosio, 29 July 1969.

21 PCO, Cabinet Conclusions, 22 July 1970 [secret].

22 Lester B. Pearson, *Mike: The Memoirs of the Right Honourable Lester B. Pearson*, vol. 2, 92–7.

23 John Holmes, CIIPS transcripts, 1987, 52.

24 Lester Pearson, *Mike: The Memoirs of the Right Honourable Lester B. Pearson*, vol. 3, 286; see also his speech, "An Era of Change for the Commonwealth and NATO," Mansion House, London, England, 27 November 1967, reprinted in Lester B. Pearson, *Words and Occasions*, 3.

25 Confidential source, telegram reporting Trudeau's comments, 22 May 1971. These comments met with consternation in Ottawa and provoked a firm rebuttal from American representatives.

26 Library of Parliament, transcript of the prime minister's news conference following the NATO Summit in Bonn, 10 June 1982.

27 Confidential source, 1980.

28 DEA, *Statements and Speeches*, no. 69/8, speech to the Alberta Liberal Association, 12 April 1969, 4.

29 Lester B. Pearson, *Mike*, vol. 2, 92. He also added that "an improvement in relations with the USSR was beginning to lessen the common fears which were the cement that held us together." See also similar comments in Lester Pearson, "An Era of Change for the Commonwealth and NATO," 3.

30 DEA, 27-1-1, Prime Minister Trudeau, "Transcript of remarks to press," Canada House, 25 January 1969.

31 Admiral Robert Falls, CIIPS transcripts, 375.

32 DEA, 20-CDA-9, Trudeau-Europe, transcript of the Prime Minister's press conference on October 23, 1974, 15.

33 For example, as we have seen, he expressed dissatisfaction with the NATO summits, especially the practice of "rubber-stamping" communiqués. He also questioned the need for new Leopard II tanks for the brigade in Europe, as opposed to retrofitted Centurion tanks or rented tanks (although he allowed German Chancellor Helmut Schmidt to pressure him into acquiring German-made heavy tanks, contrary to *Defence in the 1970s*). It will also be documented in this chapter that he queried the utility of NATO's ASW strategy and the Alliance's reliance on the "necessary evil" of "mutual assured destruction." Furthermore, Trudeau questioned American authorities as to whether cruise testing was a NATO obligation. The evidence in this chapter of his critical attitude toward NATO is garnered from Cabinet Conclusions and Cabinet-related documents and memoranda between 1968 and 1972, from a variety of primary and confidential documents prior to 1983, and from selected off-record comments and correspondence by a few policy-makers close to the prime minister. Until Trudeau's papers at the National Archives of Canada are opened to researchers, however, it may be too early to arrive at firm conclusions about Trudeau's overall attitude toward NATO between 1974 and 1984.

34 Confidential source, 26 March 1969 [secret].

35 *Ibid.*

36 DEA, 20-CDA-9, Trudeau-Europe, transcript of the prime minister's press conference on 23 October 1974, 15–17.

37 According to General John de Chastelain, Chief of the Defence Staff, briefing to the Association of Foreign Service Officers, "The Canadian Forces: Yesterday, Today and Tomorrow," DEA, Ottawa, 12 June 1991.

38 PCO, Cabinet Conclusions, 10 March 1969, 2 [secret]. Some ministers proceeded to argue that, "since our military contribution was of minimal significance and since our influence in political decisions in NATO was slight, then consideration should be given to retaining the Forces in North America to return to Europe if a crisis reached an alert status."

39 PCO, Cabinet document 309–69, President of the Privy Council Donald Macdonald, 25 March 1969, 2–3 [secret]. See also PCO, Cabinet document 165–541, in which Macdonald concluded it was a gross exaggeration to argue that Canada had any influence in NATO – he thought that evidence of any influence was "lean indeed." 4 March 1969, 3 [secret].

40 PCO, Cabinet document 310/69, Ivan Head's study, 28 March 1969, 5 [secret]. And Head added, further, that "one is inclined to ask to what extent the hard-currency profit-motive stimulates the desire of our NATO allies to retain full Canadian membership including, as is so often repeated, the stationing in Europe of Canadian Forces (with dependents)." 16.

41 PCO, Cabinet document 165–550, memorandum describing meeting of the Cabinet Committee on External Policy and Defence regarding "Defence Policy Review," 11 March 1969 [secret], 4.

42 PCO, Cabinet document 165/456, Macdonald's submission to Cabinet, Ottawa, 25 March 1969, 3 [secret]. Twenty-five years later, in testimony before the Special Joint Committee of the Senate and of the House of Commons on Canada's Defence Policy, Macdonald again pointed out: "I have a feeling that by now the Europeans should be mature enough to be able to look after their own affairs. We really don't have to go over there and solve their problems for them. They should do it for themselves." *Minutes and Proceedings of Evidence*, issue no. 3, 20 April 1994, 9.

43 Confidential source, December 1968.

44 As this high-level official wrote:

It is often thought that NATO embodies the concept of collective security which, if applied in the 30's would have stopped Hitler. In essence this concept was that by irrevocably committing themselves in advance to defend each other if attacked, potential victims of German aggression could deter Hitler. The position is very different today because the main deterrent consists of the bilateral nuclear balance of terror and not the collective strength of Western conventional forces. The conventional defence system in Europe, except in a case of the original occupying powers in Germany, is an arrangement to link together the forces of European members of the Alliance, which are stationed in their own territories and which would probably be maintained in any case. In the case of the United States, a primary purpose of stationing forces in Europe is to make the nuclear guarantee credible. It is often contended that Canada should continue to participate militarily in NATO Europe until an alternative is found. This contention seems to miss a central consideration which is whether our military participation is any longer meaningful in present circumstances.

PCO, Cabinet document 165–558, R.G. Robertson "Memorandum for the Prime Minister: The Defence Policy Review and the Report of the Special Task Force on Europe," 25 March 1969, 7.

45 PCO, Cabinet document 310/69, Ivan Head's study, 28 March 1969, 6–7.

46 PCO, Cabinet Conclusions, 1, 7, 21 November 1968 [secret]; and Cabinet document 164–83, "Canadian Position at Special NATO Ministerial Meeting," 17 November 1968 [secret].

47 PCO, Cabinet document 310/69, Ivan Head's study, March 1969, 6–7 [secret – Canadian eyes only].

48 PCO, Cabinet document 165–558, R.G. Robertson, "Memorandum for the Prime Minister: The Defence Policy Review and the Report of the Special Task Force on Europe," 25 March 1969, 3 [secret].

49 Paul McRae's study, 17.

50 Confidential source, December 1968.

51 PCO, Cabinet Committee on External Policy and Defence, Conclusions, 10 March 1969, 3. See similar comments by Donald Macdonald reported in PCO, M.C. [Marcel Cadieux], "Memorandum for the Prime Minister: Defence and Foreign Policy Review," 4 March 1969, 3 [secret].

52 For example, Paul McRae drew the prime minister's attention to these examples of downplaying "America's might" in his study and advised Trudeau that President Reagan was constantly belittling the power of his own military at the same time as he falsely enhanced the Soviet threat, 12.

53 After the Soviet invasion of Czechoslovakia in 1968, for example, Eric Kierans, James Richardson, and Secretary of State Gerard Pelletier continued to argue in Cabinet that the Russian invasion had not been directed against the West and no reciprocal action should be taken. Kierans and Macdonald concluded the invasion posed a "new risk" but was not itself "directed against the West," while Pelletier

reasoned that the crisis arising from Czechoslovakia related "largely
to the stability of the Soviet Bloc." PCO, Cabinet Conclusions,
1 November 1968, 3 [secret]. See also the comments in Cabinet by
Pierre Trudeau, Bud Drury, and Eric Kierans of 7 November 1968, 2–3
[secret]. NATO member states finally agreed that the threat to the Alliance resulting from Soviet action in Czechoslovakia was an indirect
one. The immediate problem was not one of responding to premeditated aggression, but rather of coping with the uncertainty and the
possibility of miscalculation which the recent Russian conduct had
fostered. See PCO, Cabinet document 164–71, telegram from NATO
delegation to External Affairs, 15 November 1968, 2–3. In a similar
fashion, Paul McRae interpreted the invasion of Afghanistan in 1979
as an aberration, not as an outcome of the Soviet Union's expansionist tendencies but rather of its insecurity. Paul McRae's study, 17.

54 For example, see Eric Kierans, transcript of speech to fundraising
dinner for the Liberal association, Nanaimo, B.C., 25 January 1969;
and Paul McRae's study, 17.

55 As Prime Minister Trudeau privately told Hans Dietrich Genscher, for
example, he suspected that President Reagan's view of the USSR
derived not so much from deep ideological conviction as from his
perception of American domestic realities and his relatively naive
views inspired by unsophisticated Californian advisers. Confidential
source, 15 November 1982.

56 DEA, Eric Kierans, transcript of speech to fundraising dinner for the
Liberal association, Nanaimo, B.C., 25 January 1969.

57 Library of Parliament, transcript of the prime minister's address to
the Second United Nations Special Session on Disarmament, New
York, 18 June 1982. See also Trudeau's comments on the need to
break the escalating arms spiral, "Transcript of the Prime Minister's
Remarks at a Question-and-Answer Session at the Davos Symposium," 28 January 1984, reprinted in *Lifting the Shadow of War*, 101.

58 Walter Gordon, *Walter Gordon: A Political Memoir*, 277–8. In his memoir, Gordon quotes from a memorandum he wrote the prime minister on 12 February 1964 regarding Paul Hellyer's first draft of a
White Paper on Canadian defence policy.

59 PCO, Cabinet document 165–592, "Draft of a general policy statement
to be made by the Government regarding the 'Defence Review,'"
31 March 1969, 4 [secret]. Although this draft reflects Trudeau's reasoning on defence issues, it is not clear whether he wrote or edited it.

60 Paul McRae's study, 14.

61 Library of Parliament, transcript of remarks by the prime minister on
peace and security, Montreal, Quebec, 13 November 1983.

62 For example, for brief remarks on the way in which McCarthyism seemed to sour Lester Pearson's attitude toward the United States, see John English, *Shadow of Heaven: The Life of Lester Pearson*, vol. 2, 88–9; see Trudeau's comments in Cabinet in 1969 (after the Soviet invasion of Czechoslovakia) that, "it should be the primary concern of the Canadian Government to ensure that Canadian soil was not used to assist or abet a first strike by United States military forces." PCO, Cabinet Conclusions, 20 November 1969, 2 [secret]; and see Paul McRae's commentary to Trudeau that President Reagan "constantly belittles the power of his own military and, at the same time, enhances the Soviet threat." As McRae saw it, Reagan dangerously downplayed "America's might" compared to the Soviet Union's military capabilities, and the president's ideas (e.g., about a "window of vulnerability") were "dangerous nonsense." Paul McRae's study, 12.

63 PCO, Cabinet document 310/69, Ivan Head's study, 28 March 1969, 9–10 [secret – Canadian eyes only].

64 PCO, Cabinet document 165–558, R.G. Robertson, "Memorandum for the Prime Minister: The Defence Policy Review and the Report of the Special Task Force on Europe," 25 March 1969, 3 [secret].

65 Confidential source, 26 March 1969.

66 Paul McRae's study, 8, 10.

67 PCO, Cabinet document 1075–69, Prime Minister Trudeau, "Memorandum for Cabinet: North American Defence Policy," 13 November 1969, 1–2 [secret].

68 The Cabinet's criticisms of these hypotheses are in PCO, Cabinet Conclusions, 20 November 1969, 3 [secret] and PCO, Cabinet document 166–68, M.A. Crowe, memorandum for the prime minister, "North American Defence Policy," 25 November 1969.

69 The 1971 White Paper stressed: "A constant criterion for evaluating all aspects of policy is the determination to avoid any suggestion of the offensive use of Canadian Forces to commit aggression, or to contribute to such action by another state. Such a possibility would be unthinkable and unacceptable. With a view to ensuring the protection of Canada and contributing to the maintenance of stable mutual deterrence, Canada's resource, its territory, and its Armed Forces will be used solely for purposes which are defensive in the judgment of the Government of Canada." DND, *Defence in the 1970s: White Paper on Defence*, 7.

70 PCO, Cabinet document 1075–69, Prime Minister Trudeau, "Memorandum for Cabinet: North American Defence Policy," 13 November 1969, 3 [secret].

71 PCO, Cabinet Conclusions, 20 May 1969, 3 [secret].

72 Admiral Robert Falls, CIIPS transcripts, 375–376. SSBN is the acronym
    for ballistic missile-firing nuclear powered submarines. Falls added:
    "I don't think perhaps he was quite as well informed about the fact
    that we needed ASW capabilities for other reasons, if we were in fact
    to maintain our NATO commitment of supporting a supply to Europe
    and that kind of thing, where you need a capability against the attack
    submarines. But you know he was very conscious of that difference
    then, to an extent that a lot of modern day naval officers are not."

73 Paul McRae referred to the "nuclear accountants" in his study, 16.
    Pierre Trudeau referred to "technical spaghetti" and the "spaghetti
    factory" in his remarks to the American press; Library of Parliament,
    "Transcript of Prime Minister Trudeau's Interview with a Group of
    American Journalists," Washington, 15 December 1983.

74 For example, McRae argued that the Soviet's SS-4 and SS-5 missiles
    could be justified, since "Poseidon submarine missiles, and the Brit-
    ish and French missiles and other ICBM's in place around the world
    are much improved over older models." Paul McRae's study, 3.
    Similarly, one source indicates that Prime Minister Trudeau told
    Hans-Dietrich Genscher that he himself wondered whether the
    United States was using the Russian SS-20 as an excuse to justify
    deploying cruise and Pershing missiles. Confidential source,
    15 November 1982.

75 Pierre Elliott Trudeau, "Speech to the United Nations General Assem-
    bly Special Session on Disarmament," New York, 26 May 1978, in
    Lifting the Shadow of War, 31.

76 PCO, Cabinet document 310/69, Ivan Head's study, 28 March 1969, 9
    [secret – Canadian eyes only].

77 PCO, Cabinet document 310/69, Ivan Head's study, 28 March 1969, 18
    [secret – Canadian eyes only]. The secretary to the Cabinet, Gordon
    Robertson, also had doubts about the strategy of flexible response,
    "because, for one thing, it is very doubtful whether NATO has the
    capacity to effectively carry out a strategy of flexible conventional
    response in the first place." PCO, Cabinet document 165–558,
    R.G. Robertson, "Memorandum for the prime minister: The Defence
    Policy Review and the Report of the Special Task Force on Europe,"
    25 March 1969, 6 [secret].

78 PCO, Cabinet Conclusions, 1 November 1968, 4. As Prime Minister
    Trudeau told Cabinet:

    The government wanted neither to escalate or de-escalate or to preju-
    dice the defence review. This eliminated suggestions for earmarking
    for NATO the Airborne Regiment at present or the CF-5 squadrons in
    the future. The real question was whether the Air Division should

consist of 108 or 88 aircraft. A reduction to 88 aircraft might be interpreted as de-escalation. On the other hand, there were budgetary and psychological considerations involved in a departure from the original decision to reduce to 88 aircraft. A difficult decision had to be made … The government should not be interested in adopting measures just for show and there was a need for a basic re-assessment of the role of the middle power. In the event of hostilities in Europe, the French would retaliate with an atomic bomb and it was illusory to think otherwise. The question of Canadian policy towards NATO went beyond questions of cost and involved deep considerations relating to peace and our international role. 4.

79 Transcript of the prime minister's address to the Second United Nations Special Session on Disarmament, New York, 18 June 1982, reprinted in Pierre Elliott Trudeau, *Lifting the Shadow of War*, 45.

80 Trudeau's views about the unsuitability of deterrence, especially given the dangerous effects of rapidly developing technology, are further expounded in the transcript of the prime minister's address to the Second United Nations Special Session on Disarmament, New York, June 18, 1982, reprinted in Pierre Elliott Trudeau, *Lifting the Shadow of War*, 27–36. As Trudeau concluded, "All this suggests that stable deterrence remains an inadequate concept … a poor substitute for genuine world security." 30.

81 Trudeau, "Text of the Prime Minister's Remarks in the House of Commons on Peace and Security," Ottawa, February 9, 1984, 1, reprinted in Pierre Elliott Trudeau, *Lifting the Shadow of War*, 106.

82 Paul McRae's study, 14.

83 PCO, Cabinet document 310/69, Ivan Head's study, 9, 12 [secret – Canadian eyes only].

84 DEA, *Statements and Speeches*, no. 69/8, Prime Minister Trudeau, "The Relation of Defence Policy to Foreign Policy," speech to the Alberta Liberal Association, Calgary, 12 April 1969, 5–6.

85 For example, see Gordon Robertson's comments in PCO, Cabinet document 165–558, R.G. Robertson, "Memorandum for the Prime Minister: The Defence Policy Review and the Report of the Special Task Force on Europe," 25 March 1969, 7.

86 Paul McRae's study, 17.

87 For example, see Ivan Head's study, 18 and Paul McRae's study, 14.

88 See Trudeau's comments that "the present balance of deterrents is an absurdly unsatisfactory substitute for real security," that a "more stable alternative is necessary," and that the challenge of future events will not be met "by a stagnant, cautious attitude," in PCO, Cabinet document 165–592, draft of a general policy statement to be made by the government, "Defence Review," March 31, 1969, 11–12

[secret]. Trudeau continued along these lines in 1983, when he spoke to American reporters about the outdated mentality of those who still thought in terms of military superiority: "Look, there will always be people on our side, in the Pentagon, in the Kremlin, who believe that military superiority is the only way and that we would be fools if we didn't research every possible technology and test it and deploy it to make sure that our side was ahead. You know, I cannot deny that that exists. I know there are people doing that and that there is probably a weight of advisors in the Administration who weigh heavily in that direction." Library of Parliament, "Transcript of Prime Minister Trudeau's Interview with a Group of American Journalists," Washington, 15 December 1983.

89 According to unnamed ministers quoted in PCO, Cabinet Committee on External Policy and Defence Conclusions, 10 March 1969, 2 [secret]. These ministers proceeded to recommend that, "since our military contribution was of minimal military significance and since our influence in political decisions in NATO was slight, then consideration should be given to retaining the forces in North America to return to Europe if a crisis reached an alert status."

90 PCO, Cabinet document 165–558, R.G. Robertson, "Memorandum for the Prime Minister: The Defence Policy Review and the Report of the Special Task Force on Europe," 25 March 1969, 5–6 [secret].

91 Library of Parliament, transcript of Prime Minister Trudeau's remarks on "Peace and Security," Queen Elizabeth Hotel, Montreal, 13 November 1983. See also his comments, "Transcript of the Prime Minister's Remarks at a Question-and-Answer Session at the Davos Symposium," 28 January 1984, reprinted in Lifting the Shadow of War, 101.

92 As early as 1965, for example, Prime Minister Lester Pearson drew attention to the problem of what could be done to give non-nuclear powers in the developing world (e.g., India) some guarantee of protection against attack by nuclear powers during a private lecture to the Institute for Strategic Studies, London, U.K., 16 June 1965. A copy of the speech is in DHist, Raymont Papers, 73/1223, series 2, file 848, "Canadian Policy – Foreign and Domestic 09/15/64–06/16/65." Trudeau frequently drew attention to the problem of nuclear and conventional arms races in the Third World. For example, see "Transcript of the Prime Minister's Address to the Second United Nations Special Session on Disarmament," New York, 18 June 1982, reprinted in Pierre Elliott Trudeau, Lifting the Shadow of War, 28.

93 For instance, see PCO, Cabinet document 165–558, R.G. Robertson, "Memorandum for the Prime Minister: The Defence Policy Review and the Report of the Special Task Force on Europe," 25 March 1969,

6 [secret]; and PCO, Cabinet document 309/69, president of the Privy Council, Donald Macdonald report, 25 March 1969, 2 [secret].

94 See, for example, DEA, Eric Kierans, Speech to the Liberal association in Nanaimo, B.C., 25 January 1969, in which Kierans stated that, "the real battle is not the waning ideology of imperial communism versus consumer capitalism; it is the waxing tensions in a world which, in a mirror image of our own society, is increasingly divided into haves and have-nots." See also Ivan Head's comments on the failure of the balance of deterrents to prevent world poverty in PCO, Cabinet document 310/69, Ivan Head's study, March 1969, 19 [secret – Canadian eyes only]; and Trudeau's reference to arms races which cost $400 billion in resources year by year in a world in which basic human needs remained unsatisfied. "Transcript of the Prime Minister's Address to the Second United Nations Special Session on Disarmament," New York, 18 June 1982, reprinted in Pierre Elliott Trudeau, *Lifting the Shadow of War*, 28.

95 For more analysis of Lester Pearson's particular belief system, see Erika Simpson, "The Principles of Liberal Internationalism according to Lester Pearson," *Journal of Canadian Studies*, 64–77.

96 This succinct assessment of Macdonald, Richardson, and Pelletier's beliefs is corroborated by comments written by Marcel Cadieux, under-secretary of state for External Affairs. In a secret memorandum written for the prime minister, Cadieux briefly summarized these Cabinet ministers' viewpoints in a similar fashion. PCO, Cabinet document 165–554, "Memorandum for the Prime Minister: Ministers' Views on Defence Policy," 18 March 1969, 3 [secret].

97 According to Jamie Swift, *Odd Man Out: The Life and Times of Eric Kierans*, chap. 10.

98 Walter Stewart, *Shrug: Trudeau in Power*, 163.

CHAPTER FIVE

1 For a detailed explanation of the circumstances under which Diefenbaker committed his government to approve NORAD, see Basil Robinson, *Diefenbaker's World*, 4–23 and Trevor Lloyd, *Canada in World Affairs 1957–1959*, 25–39.

2 For a flavour of the emotional fervour this announcement ignited, see James Dow, *The Arrow*, and Murray Peden, *Fall of an Arrow*, chap. 9.

3 The use and introduction of nuclear weapons for the NATO Forces in Europe was first acknowledged during NATO discussions in February 1952, five years previously. At that time, it was agreed that "new weapons and techniques" should be taken into account in determining force requirements. (The words "new weapons and techniques"

referred at that time directly to atomic weapons, as it was felt at that early stage that this wording would be "more palatable and secure"). The NATO Council at Lisbon also approved in 1952 the concept of a "forward strategy" for the defence of Europe – holding the enemy as far to the east in Germany as feasible. It was recognized that the basic NATO undertaking should be to ensure allied ability to carry out strategic air attacks promptly, by all means possible and with all types of weapons. Beginning in 1952, the NATO Military Committee also recommended that NATO military authorities be authorized to plan and make preparations on the assumption that atomic and thermonuclear weapons would be used in defence from the outset. It was not until 1957, however, that these planning directives were brought up to date and approved as MC 14/2 and MC 48/2.

4 According to George Ignatieff:

> During the last months of the St.Laurent/Pearson regime … Pearson had argued with Dulles and the State Department that he did not see why one of the commands of the Alliance should be bilateral and confined to North America, while all the others were subject to the North Atlantic Council and the consultative machinery which was involved. And of course he was faced with the adamant position that the Americans had that they would not allow any other ally to have a finger on the nuclear trigger. That was the key issue, and they were insistent that this should be, therefore, a separate command structure and that it would be related to NATO only nominally, being described for NATO purposes as the 'North American Regional Planning Group'. But in fact they did not report to NATO and did not submit any of their plans and so on.

George Ignatieff interview, CIIPS transcripts, 116–17.

5 DHist, Raymont Papers, 73/1223, series 2, file 879, "Answers to Questions by Cabinet and Public" 07/25/57–05/26/58, Jules Leger, undersecretary of state for External Affairs, "Memorandum to the Minister on 'NORAD – Points of Special Interest to External Affairs,'" 2 December 1957 [secret]. See also Basil Robinson, *Diefenbaker's World*, 22–3.

6 *Ibid.* Basil Robinson also points out that Diefenbaker endeavoured to make it clear with these words that the Liberal government had originally been a party to the process, and his government was simply acquiescing to the consequences of a collective decision taken three years before. *Diefenbaker's World*, 33.

7 "The Bomarc Missile," *Aviation Week*, 11 August 1958, 11.

8 In later years, Diefenbaker denied having committed the government to acquiring nuclear weapons: "You know the things that have

happened in recent months. You remember how they criticized us most bitterly alleging a commitment for nuclear weapons. They have examined all the records and they have never been able to find any such thing. Finally I asked them to produce it and Mr. Pearson said they wouldn't produce things like that." JGD Centre, Diefenbaker Speech Series Collection, vol. 97, file 1254, untitled draft of speech to House of Commons, 16 November 1963, 2.

9 *Hansard*, 20 February 1959, 1223.

10 See the contrasting explanations in John G. Diefenbaker, *One Canada 1956–1962*, vol. 2; and Jon B. McLin, *Canada's Changing Defense Policy 1957–1963*. Whether Diefenbaker understood the Bomarc's strategic rationale is discussed further in chapter 6.

11 PCO, Cabinet Conclusions, May 3, 1960, 14; see also DHist, Raymont Papers, 73/1223, file 767, "Canadian Defence Policy 02/05/59–07/14/59," paper on "Defence Achievements 1961," n.d.

12 In his autobiography, Diefenbaker was careful not to make reference to pressure he may have exerted on Eisenhower to re-establish the Bomarc program because he wanted, for the record, to downplay his earlier strong commitment to the Bomarc missiles. See *One Canada 1956–1962*, 60.

13 DEA, 4901-Y-40, no. 33, telegram 1546 from Arnold Heeney, Washington, D.C. to the Department of External Affairs regarding "Defence Appropriations: Bomarc," 17 June 1960 [secret].

14 For example, see Jon McLin, *Canada's Changing Defense Policy, 1957–1963*, in which McLin concludes, on the basis of interviews with Herman Kahn and American defence officials, that the United States administration reinstated the program because of Canada's commitment to the Bomarc and, in particular, because of one American Senator's assertion that the cancellation might result in the defeat of the Canadian government and Canada's departure from NATO; also see Nash, *Kennedy and Diefenbaker*, 77.

15 Editorial, *Globe and Mail*, 6 May 1960.

16 DHist, Raymont Papers, 73/1223, series 1, file 303, Douglas Harkness, draft of letter to the secretary of state for External Affairs, Howard Green, n.d., 1.

17 Peter C. Newman, *Renegade in Power*, 341.

18 PCO, Cabinet Conclusions, August 23, 1961, 8 [secret].

19 NA, Douglas Harkness Papers, MG 32, B19, vol. 57, "'The Nuclear Arms Question,' Background Correspondence, memoranda, etc.," F.R. Miller, Air Marshal, chairman, Chiefs of Staff, "Air Defence Review," 23 December 1960, 4.

20 Dave McIntosh, "Four-Year Debate on Canadian Nuclear Arms Stand Reviewed," *New Glasgow News* (Nova Scotia), 1 December 1962.

21 JGD Centre, vol. 59, file 966, "Prime Minister's Statement in the House of Commons," June 1961, 3.

22 For further reference to a debate between the minister of Defence and the minister of External Affairs about obtaining nuclear warheads for the CF-101 interceptors, see DHist, Raymont Papers, 73/1223, series 1, file 303, draft of letter from Douglas Harkness to Howard Green (n.d. but written in reply to Green's letter of 30 March 1961), 1 [secret]. Note that excised text in the Cabinet Conclusions presumably refers to secret discussions about this commitment; however, public debate about the question of nuclear weapons for the Voodoos died down with Diefenbaker's statement of June 1961.

23 PCO, Cabinet Conclusions, 23 August 1961, 6–8 [secret].

24 George Ignatieff interview, CIIPS transcripts, 119.

25 Dhist, Raymont Papers 73/1223, series 2, File 997, "Nuclear Stockpiling of Weapons at Goose Bay," 02/16/60–08/09/65.

26 NA, Arnold Heeney Papers, MG 30, ₃144, vol. 2, file "Memoir, 1960, chapter 15, diary #2," 17 November 1960 entry.

27 At one point, General Charles Foulkes mentioned this commitment in an aside, CBC TV interview on the *Citizen's Forum*, 6 November 1960, transcribed in *News and Views*, no. 92, 22 November 1960. According to the declassified Cabinet Conclusions of 1963, however, Prime Minister Lester Pearson and his minister of National Defence thought this "fifth" commitment concerning nuclear weapons for anti-submarine forces was "almost a commitment comparable with the others" but "had not been identified publicly as a commitment." PCO, Cabinet Conclusions, 16 August 1963, 3.

28 *Hansard*, 2 July 1959, 5321; see also ₅352, 5401; PCO, Cabinet Conclusions, 19 June, 2 July 1959 and Record of Cabinet Decision, 10 July 1959. General Charles Foulkes also mentioned that General Norstad's recommendation was the primary factor leading to the decision in his interview for CBC TV on the *Citizen's Forum*, 6 November 1960, 10.

29 DHist, Raymont Papers 73/1223, series 1, file 309, "Cabinet Decisions and Hansard References," 02/20/59 to 02/26/63, letter from John G. Diefenbaker to General Norstad, 30 July 1959 [personal].

30 DHist, Raymont Papers 73/1223, series 1, file 309, "Cabinet Decisions and Hansard References," 02/20/59 to 02/26/63, letter from General Lauris Norstad to John Diefenbaker, SHAPE, Paris, 23 July 1959.

31 George Pearkes, *Hansard*, 29 March 1960, 2549.

32 PCO, Record of Cabinet Defence Committee Decision, 25 March 1960 [confidential].

33 George Pearkes, *Hansard*, 29 March 1960, 2549.

34 This basic conclusion is echoed in Robinson's account. See *Diefenbaker's World*, 86.

35 *Hansard*, 2 July 1959, 5393.

36 Diefenbaker first appointed Sidney Smith, the former president of the University of Toronto, as his minister of External Affairs. According to Basil Robinson, Smith had little impact on decision-making, primarily because of his inexperience; as well, he died suddenly before his view on the nuclear weapons issue had "crystallized." Robinson points out, however, that "temperamentally" Smith seemed to be inclining toward rejection of the nuclear weapons. Interview by author with Basil Robinson, 14 September 1992.

37 Interview by author with Basil Robinson, 14 September 1992. For more on Norman Robertson's views, see also Robinson, *Diefenbaker's World*, 108; Nash, *Kennedy and Diefenbaker*, 84; and J. L. Granatstein, *A Man of Influence: Norman Robertson and Canadian Statecraft, 1929–1968*, 336–63.

38 NA, Arnold Heeney Papers, MG 30, E 144, vol. 2, file "Memoir, 1962, chapter 15: diary #4," 4 February 1962.

39 A sentiment referred to by Basil Robinson in an interview, 14 September 1992 and also voiced by George Ignatieff in an interview, CIIPS transcripts, 115.

40 Dave McIntosh, "Four-Year Debate on Canadian Nuclear Arms Stand Reviewed," *New Glasgow News*, 1 December 1962.

41 DEA, *Statements and Speeches*, no. 60/41, John Diefenbaker, "Speech to the Canadian Club of Ottawa," Ottawa, 24 November 1960.

42 NA, Arnold Heeney Papers, MG 30, E 144, vol. 2, file "Memoir, 1960, chapter 15, diary #2," 17 November 1960.

43 *Ibid.*

44 PCO, Cabinet Conclusions, 6 December 1960, 6 [SECRET].

45 The record of Cabinet meetings written by the secretary to the Cabinet, Robert Bryce, attributes points made by ministers not to specific individuals but to "some Ministers" or to "the Cabinet." However, comments made by the prime minister, the minister of External Affairs, and the minister of National Defence were usually specifically attributed.

46 PCO, Cabinet Conclusions, 6 December 1960, 7 [secret].

47 *Ibid.*, 8.

48 *Ibid.*

49 *Ibid.*, 8–9.

50 PCO, Cabinet Conclusions, "Report on discussions with President Kennedy," 21 February 1961; see also Nash, *Kennedy and Diefenbaker*, 94–5. Nash points out that, according to one aide, Diefenbaker's ideas about Canadian control of the nuclear weapons "confused the hell" out of Kennedy. Canadian journalists were confused as well, for, the next day, Diefenbaker told a reporter that all rumours of his

indicating to Kennedy that he would take the warheads were "totally unfounded."

51 *Toronto Telegram*, 6 October 1961.

52 *Globe and Mail*, 2 October 1961.

53 See JGD Centre, Diefenbaker Speech Collection Series, vol. 74, file 10385, drafts of speeches for Prince George, B.C. and Red Deer, Alta., 1 September 1961, 4.

54 DEA, *Statements and Speeches*, no. 61/11, Prime Minister John Diefenbaker, 15 August 1961.

55 PCO, Cabinet Conclusions, 23 August 1961, 7 [secret].

56 PCO, Cabinet Conclusions, 25 August 1961, 4 [secret].

57 *Ibid.*, 4

58 Dave McIntosh, "Four-Year Debate on Canadian Nuclear Arms Stand Reviewed," *New Glasgow News*, 1 December 1962.

59 NA, Douglas Harkness Papers, MG 32, B19, vol. 57, letter from Air Chief Marshal F.R. Miller, chairman, Chiefs of Staff to Douglas Harkness, 17 August 1962, 1. Miller argued that, under the best of conditions, approximately fifteen hours would be needed to transport warheads from the US bases and then fit them into Canadian carriers at Canadian bases. On the other hand, in normal conditions, he thought the air defence system afforded no more than two hours' warning time.

60 As Basil Robinson explains, "Experience in the Cuban crisis, when the Canadian response in an emergency had been ambiguous, had weakened the theory that stand-by procedures for bringing nuclear equipment across the Canadian border could be relied on in a future crisis. Instead the Americans suggested that missing parts might be stored separately in Canada and thus might be more quickly united in case of need. Not surprisingly, this idea had no appeal for Diefenbaker or Green. If the missing parts were already on Canadian soil, the government could hardly claim that nuclear weapons were not present in Canada." *Diefenbaker's World*, 299–300.

61 NA, Douglas Harkness Papers, MG 32, B19, vol. 57, file " 'The Nuclear Arms Question,' Background Correspondence, memoranda, etc., 1958–1962," memorandum from Frank Miller, chairman, Chiefs of Staff to Douglas Harkness, stamped 18 September 1962. Miller was referring to Peyton Lyon's article, "Independent Control of Nuclear Weapons?" *Canadian Commentator* (September 1962): 2. Lyon argued that Diefenbaker was clouding the issue by stating that Canada would not take nuclear warheads because this would expand the 'family' of nuclear powers at the same time as he contended that Canada should refuse the weapons until American legislation was amended to permit joint control. Lyon argued that since the US had

already permitted joint control "to a degree satisfactory to most of the NATO allies," Diefenbaker's comments were baffling. Lyon went on, "If anything it means that he wants to loosen up the American law to allow other countries greater control over nuclear arms, but this runs directly counter to his expressed concern to restrict the size of the nuclear family. What does he want? Is he trying to please both the Canadian jingos and the 'Ban the Bomb' groups?"

62 NA, Arnold Heeney Papers, MG 30, E 144, vol. 2, file "Memoir, 1962, chapter 15: diary #4," 18 March 1962.

63 The offending memo is reprinted in Nash, *Kennedy and Diefenbaker*, 121.

64 Quoted in Patrick Nicholson, *Vision and Indecision*, 151.

65 According to Patrick Nicholson, *Vision and Indecision*, 56–157.

66 Harkness had gone ahead and put the Canadian Forces on equivalent alert status to US Defcon 2 without receiving Diefenbaker's approval. See his account in the *Ottawa Citizen*, "The Harkness Papers," 22–25 October 1977. See also his admittance in a letter to Brigadier-General J.A. Clark that, within an hour of President Kennedy's television speech, "we began immediately to take precautionary military actions and within approximately forty hours of the President's announcement, we had reached the same state of readiness in our air defence forces as those of the United States, although they had had some six days to make preparation prior to the President's statement –" NA, MG 32, B19, vol. 28, file 42–66, letter from Douglas Harkness to Brigadier-General J.A. Clark, November 1962 [personal and confidential].

67 See Newman, *Renegade in Power*, 341 and Nash, *Kennedy and Diefenbaker*, 194. Although the nuclear weapons systems were deemed to be an ineffective contribution to nuclear deterrence, Canadian naval forces at that time were present throughout the crisis in the waters allocated to Canadian command by NATO. See W.A.B. Douglas, "Why does Canada have armed forces?" *International Journal*, 277. On the role of Canadian naval forces, see also Peter Haydon, *The Cuban Missile Crisis: Canadian Involvement Reconsidered*.

68 See his ninety-page account of his actions in NA, Douglas Harkness Papers, MG 32, B 19, vol. 57, unnumbered file, "The Nuclear Arms Question and the Political Crisis which Arose from it in January and February, 1963." This was Harkness's version of events, written ten months later.

69 PCO, Cabinet Conclusions, October 23, 1962, 4 [secret].

70 *Ibid.*, 4–5

71 Kennedy sent Secretary of State Dean Acheson to Europe to pass on the same message as Canada had received to the British, French, and

West German governments. Acheson also briefed the NATO Council in Paris. Although Charles de Gaulle complained that he was merely "being informed," all these countries pledged their full support to the United States. Later, Canada's Ambassador to NATO, George Ignatieff, recalled, "I have seldom felt more uncomfortable or isolated." Nash, *Kennedy and Diefenbaker*, 197. According to another account by George Ignatieff, however, when Kennedy ordered the NORAD alert, which only affected the US and Canada, "we were still discussing in NATO what the allied response to the Soviet action should be." Ignatieff interview, CIIPS transcripts, 125.

72 According to Nash, *Kennedy and Diefenbaker*, 200. For detailed accounts of the Canadian reaction to the crisis, see Nash, 180–208 and Peter Haydon, *The Cuban Missile Crisis: Canadian Involvement Reconsidered*. Diefenbaker claimed not to have known at the time, and never to subsequently believe, that Harkness had already clandestinely authorized a full alert on October 22. The Cabinet had endured a three-day debate over an issue which had been arbitrarily decided beforehand by Harkness. Diefenbaker's consent was, therefore, only a formality.

73 Diefenbaker, *One Canada: 1962–1967*, vol. 2, 78.

74 JGD Centre, Prime Minister's Office, vol. 53, letter to John Diefenbaker from Brigadier N.A. Gianelli [ret.], armoured adviser to Army Comdr., First Canadian Army 1944, 10 December 1962 [stamped "seen by John Diefenbaker"].

75 Dave McIntosh, "Four-Year Debate on Canadian Nuclear Arms Stand Reviewed," *New Glasgow News* (Nova Scotia), 1 December 1962.

76 Yet the fact was that for weeks before the crisis, published newspaper reports warned that the "warheadless" Bomarc missiles were already in place and "stood useless." See, for example, Dave McIntosh, "New Bomarc Debate Probable When Parliament Meets Again," *Montreal Gazette*, 25 September 1962. High-level American representatives had protested for months about Canada's "lackadaisical" attitude. In fact, the chairman of the United States Section of the Permanent Joint Board on Defence had outlined the adverse military consequences for continental defence months before in May:

The inadequacy of our continental air defence has been of serious concern for a considerable time. It has only become more dramatically apparent with the deployment to North Bay of a BOMARC squadron lacking armament and the deployment in Canada of 66 F-101B aircraft not armed for maximum effectiveness. Forward deployment of these weapons without nuclear armament not only foregoes planned improvements in North American air defence; it actually degrades our air defence capability below the levels we would have achieved by deployment just below the Canadian border. Because we are not capable of employing our full military capabilities, we cannot be confident of preventing heavy damage, in the event of attack, to important industrial and administrative centres in both our countries. Further, we are not providing the maximum available protection to the Strategic Air Command and to the retaliatory forces of the Navy. These deterrent forces are important to the entire free world and the basic free world strategy is based upon them. It must be assumed that the potential assailant understands the nature and location of this weakness in our air defences, consequently, the credibility of the deterrent is thereby degraded.

NA, RG 25/90–91/001, vol.42, file 1415–40 pt. 11, "Visit of Mr. Rusk: Nuclear Weapons Questions," 23 August 1962, 1 [secret].

77 PCO, Cabinet Conclusions, 30 October 1962, 10–11. According to the Conclusions, the Cabinet agreed that "negotiations be undertaken with the U.S. Government to work out an agreement ... [under which] nuclear warheads would be held in bases in the United States to be moved to Canada to be available to the R.C.A.F. for use in Bomarc missiles and interceptor aircraft, on request by the Canadian government when war appears imminent ..." 11.

78 Quoted in Nash, *Kennedy and Diefenbaker*, 212.

79 PCO, Cabinet Conclusions, 30 October 1962, 10–11.

80 PCO, Cabinet Conclusions, 30 October 1962, 11 [top secret].

81 This was the estimation of Paul Nitze, U.S. assistant secretary of Defence (International Security Affairs). See DHist, Raymont Papers, 73/1223, series 2, file 828, "Canada-US Defence Planning," 01/22/63–10/29/63, telegram from CJS (W) to CCOS regarding 45-minute meeting between CCJS (W) [Ambassador Charles Ritchie?] and Paul Nitze, 14 February 1962 [secret]; see also Nash, *Kennedy and Diefenbaker*, 13.

82 DEA, *Statements and Speeches*, no. 62/17, Howard Green, "NATO's most harmonious meeting," 17 December 1962, 4.

83 Diefenbaker's announcement on 7 September 1961 of a 15,000-man increase in the armed forces – to 135,000 – and a strengthening of the brigade and 12-squadron RCAF air division in Europe was barely mentioned in the newspapers. See Dave McIntosh, "Nuclear Weapons – We Must Decide," *Halifax Chronicle-Herald*, 26 December 1961. The press, the opposition, and the government were entirely preoccupied with the nuclear weapons issue.

84 "NATO gives high marks to Canada," *Montreal Star*, 14 December 1962 and quoted in Peyton Lyon, *Canada in World Affairs*, 127.

85 According to DND's transcript of General Norstad's remarks repro-
duced in Lyon, *Canada in World Affairs*, 135. Norstad also pointed out
that when he referred to joint control, he was thinking of something
quite different from what the Canadian government had in mind.
Were Norstad's visit to Canada and his meeting with Harkness and
Sevigny undertaken so as to expedite the fulfilment of Canada's
NATO obligations? Journalist David McIntosh found it "hard to
believe that a general as astute as Norstad, and knowledgeable about
all the political vagaries of all alliance members, would not have
known what he was getting into," McIntosh, *Ottawa Unbuttoned*, 104.
Others like Pierre Trudeau and Charles Ritchie had similar concerns.
For a more detailed analysis, see Nash, *Kennedy and Diefenbaker*, 223–5.

86 Pearson's speech of 12 January 1963, "On Canadian Defence Policy,"
announcing the Liberal party's change of policy toward nuclear
weapons, is reprinted in *Words and Occasions*. As Pearson wrote in a
letter a few days before announcing his decision, "I feel very strongly
that commitments made for Canada by a Canadian government
should be honoured, until there is an opportunity to renegotiate and
alter those commitments. This requires discussions with our allies in
NATO and Washington." NA, L.B. Pearson Papers, leader of the Opposition Correspondence Series 1958–63, MG 26, N2, vol. 54, file 830,
letter to Bob Abrahams, treasurer of the Liberal Club at Sir George
Williams University, 7 January 1963.

87 *Hansard*, 25 January 1963, 3128–3137.

88 On the debate in Cabinet, see Harkness's account in NA, MG 32, B19,
vol. 57, "Unnumbered Series, 'The Nuclear Arms Crisis.'"

89 U.S. State Department Press Release, "US and Canadian Negotiations
Regarding Nuclear Weapons," reprinted in John McLin, *Canada's
Changing Defense Policy*, Appendix 4, 235.

90 Diefenbaker, *One Canada, 1956–1962*, 106.

91 Lyon, *Canada in World Affairs*, 205.

92 Newman, *Renegade in Power*, 389.

93 From the transcript of McNamara's remarks quoted in Lyon, *Canada
in World Affairs*, 203.

94 *Ibid.*, 203–5.

95 Once Pearson became prime minister, the aforementioned possibility
that the commitments might be "renegotiated and altered" was not
discussed in Cabinet. The principal question Cabinet considered was
whether the government should agree in the negotiations with the
United States to acquire either four or five different nuclear systems,
and allow the United States to store nuclear weapons at Argentia
in Newfoundland. PCO, Cabinet Conclusions, 9, 14 May 1963 and
16 August 1963 [secret].

96 Howard Lentner also analyses the Diefenbaker government's decision-making regarding nuclear weapons in "Foreign Policy Decision-making: The Case of Canada and Nuclear Weapons," *World Politics*. He writes that the ministers involved in developing the principles governing the use of nuclear weapons in Canada were John Diefenbaker, Minister of Finance Donald Fleming, Douglas Harkness, and Sidney Smith. However, little reference is made in the original documents or secondary literature to Fleming's involvement in defence decision-making, and Sidney Smith died 17 March 1959.

97 See also the historical accounts by Newman, *Renegade in Power*; Lyon, *Canada in World Affairs*; McLin, *Canada's Changing Defense Policy*; Robinson, *Diefenbaker's World*; Nash, *Kennedy and Diefenbaker*; Lentner, "Foreign Policy Decision-Making"; and McIntosh, *Ottawa Unbuttoned*. This assessment is confirmed by Basil Robinson and Robert Cameron. Interview by author with Basil Robinson, 14 September 1992 and discussion with Robert Cameron, 1 January 1993. Note that for thirty years Robinson was closely involved in the defence policy-making process, retiring in 1977 as under-secretary of External Affairs, while Cameron was active in defence and arms control policy-making from 1958 to 1985, retiring as assistant under-secretary of External Affairs.

CHAPTER SIX

1 DHist, Raymont Papers, 73/1223, file 767, "Canadian Defence Policy 02/05/59–07/14/59," Minister of National Defence Douglas Harkness, "Defence in a Changing World," Royal Canadian Military Institute, 17 February 1961, 5 [declassified].

2 *Ibid.*, 18.

3 NA, Douglas Harkness Papers, MG 32, B19, vol. 57, "'The Nuclear Arms Question,' Background Correspondence, memoranda, etc.," Douglas Harkness, "Disarmament Implications," n.d. [secret].

4 Diefenbaker also initially assumed that the Alliance should negotiate from a position of nuclear superiority. See JGD Centre, Prime Minister's Papers, vol. 52, "Extract from Mr. Diefenbaker's Statement to the NATO Heads of Government Meeting," 16 December 1957, 1 [secret].

5 NA, Douglas Harkness Papers, MG 32, B19, vol. 57, "'The Nuclear Arms Question,' Background Correspondence, memoranda, etc.," memorandum for the prime minister from Douglas Harkness, "Air Defence Problem," n.d. [secret].

6 Harkness decided to delete his reference to "a result patently distasteful to the United States" in the final draft of this letter. DHist, Raymont Papers, 73/1223, series 1, file 303, draft of letter from Douglas Harkness to Howard Green, n.d., 2 [secret].

7 NA, Douglas Harkness Papers, MG 32, B19, vol. 57, file "'The Nuclear Arms Question,' Background Correspondence; memoranda, etc., 1958–1962," letter from Minister of National Defence Douglas Harkness to Prime Minister Diefenbaker, 26 October 1962, 2 [confidential].

8 JGD Centre, Diefenbaker Speech Series Collection, vol. 27, file 751, text of speech for delivery on CBC TV series, *The Nation's Business*, 9 March 1959, 2. See also vol. 30, file 779, draft of speech to Michigan University, Lansing, USA, 7 June 1959, 7.

9 JGD Centre, Diefenbaker Speech Series Collection, vol. 15, file 558, n.d., 2. Because of Diefenbaker's habit of personally coordinating and editing his own speeches, the recently opened collection of original speeches at the John G. Diefenbaker Centre provides a rich source of research material. Diefenbaker habitually scrawled all over the original drafts of his speeches and vigorously edited subsequent drafts so as to accurately reflect his own strong opinions. The original speeches at the JGD Centre illustrate, as Basil Robinson points out, that "almost invariably the final product was arrived at by a sort of quilting process, the pieces assembled and stitched together only at the last minute and in a design that no one else would have predicted, and only the right honourable craftsman himself could have achieved." *Diefenbaker's World*, 40.

10 JGD Centre, Diefenbaker Speech Series Collection, vol. 15, file 558, n.d., 2.

11 JGD Centre, Diefenbaker Speech Series Collection, vol. 65, file 996, "Partial notes for an address to the Canadian Bar Association," Winnipeg, 1 September 1961, 15, 18, 19.

12 According to Robinson, *Diefenbaker's World*, 4.

13 For example, see JGD Centre, Diefenbaker Speech Series Collection, vol. 30, file 779, speech to Michigan University, Lansing, USA, 7 June 1959, 9–10.

14 DHist, Raymont Papers, 73/1223, series 1, file 771, "Canadian Security 1960–1970, Possible International Trends 05/13/60–06/12/61," R.B.B. [?], "Memorandum for the Prime Minister," 13 May 1960, 1, 3 [top secret]. At this time, Diefenbaker also confided to Macmillan his personal concern about the United States drifting back toward "isolationism."

15 That these sentiments were more than mere rhetoric is evidenced by Diefenbaker's forcefully written scribbles in the margins. See JGD Centre, Diefenbaker Speech Series Collection, vol. 30, file 779, speech to Michigan University, Lansing, US, June 7, 1959, 19. For similar sentiments in 1961 see DHist, Raymont Papers 73/1223, file 767, "Canadian Defence Policy 02/05/59–07/14/59," John Diefenbaker, "Notes

for an Address to the Canada-Israel Friendship Award Dinner,"
Toronto, 24 January 1961.

16 NA, Arnold Heeney Papers, MG 30, E144, vol. 2, file "Memoir, 1962,
chapter 15: diary #4," 4 February 1962.

17 NA, Arnold Heeney Papers, MG 30, E144, vol. 2, file "Memoir, 1960,
chapter 15, diary #2," 30 August 1960.

18 *Ibid.*

19 Final perusal of the relevant files at the PAC was denied, despite the
thirty-year rule. However, for further analysis of Pearkes's and
Foulkes's attitude toward NORAD as a NATO Command, see p. 138.

20 Basil Robinson interview, 14 September 1992; see also Robinson,
Diefenbaker's World, 30–1.

21 PCO, Record of Cabinet Defence Committee Decision, 25 March 1960
[confidential].

22 After Pearkes recommended to Cabinet on 15 October 1958 that negotiations begin with the United States to equip Canadian forces "with
the most effective weapons," there was very little Cabinet discussion
before it was recommended that the negotiations begin and "a minimum of other persons be informed of them." As well, Pearkes's recommendation that the Lacrosse missile be replaced with the Honest
John was also hardly discussed, let alone debated. See PCO, Cabinet
Conclusions, 15 October 1958, 10–12 for the brief discussion about
beginning negotiations with the United States; see PCO, Cabinet Conclusions, 9 December 1958, 2–5 for additional discussion; see PCO,
Cabinet Conclusions, "Record of Cabinet Decision," 2 July 1958 on
the choice of aircraft to replace the F-86 for the Air Division in
Europe; see PCO, Cabinet Conclusions, "Record of Cabinet Defence
Committee Decision," 25 March 1960 on the procurement of the
Honest John rockets in lieu of the Lacrosse system.

23 See DHist, Raymont Papers, 73/1223, series 1, file 768, "Canadian
Defence Policy 07/29/63–03/23/64," Douglas Harkness, draft of
speech to House of Commons, 13 September 1961, 18; and NA,
Douglas Harkness Papers, MG 32, B19, vol. 57, "'The Nuclear Arms
Question,' Background Correspondence, Memoranda, etc.," Douglas
Harkness, "Disarmament Implications" [secret].

24 See *Hansard*, 2 July 1959, 5393; and NA, Douglas Harkness Papers,
MG 32, B19, vol. 70, "Pearkes, G.R. NATO Ministerial Meeting, 'Draft
of speech to NATO Ministerial Meeting,'" 13 January 1959, 9–11.

25 General Foulkes, CBC TV interview on the *Citizen's Forum*, 6 November 1969, transcribed in *News and Views*, no. 92, 22 November 1960.

26 In his first statement to the NATO Council, the incoming minister of
External Affairs Howard Green expressed his support as well for the

recent decision to re-equip the Canadian Air Division "with the most modern aircraft," and pointed out that the maintenance of the Canadian Forces in Europe was a contribution to NATO "over and above heavy commitments" undertaken in the defence of the Canada-United States region. These published comments seem inconsistent, given his strong stand against nuclear weapons, and it seems fair to conclude that this maiden speech was written by someone else in the Department of External Affairs. See DEA, *Statements and Speeches*, no. 59/38, Howard Green, "A Canadian View of NATO," 28 October 1959, 1.

27 For example, see JGD Centre, Diefenbaker Speech Series Collection, vol. 31, file 784, untitled draft of a speech, 11 July 1959, 16; and vol. 87, file 11275, memorandum for the minister from Escott Reid with annotations by Diefenbaker, "Speech to the Canadian Bar Association," 28 August 1961, 5.

28 The differences between "first-," "second-," and "third-stream" assumptions were explained in chapter 3, pp. 53–5. By way of summary, among Defenders the first stream of thought assumed that the country's traditional contributions of forces, equipment, and money for the defence of Western European territory were of key importance to the continuing function of the Alliance. The second stream assumed that the Alliance's overall conventional balance in Western Europe would help prevent war and could also potentially affect the outcome of war. The third stream assumed Canada's military commitments to NATO made no strategic difference but were important insofar as they signalled the appearance of unified resolve and Alliance solidarity. And it was also explained that Defenders sometimes promoted traditional commitments, which appeared to strengthen Alliance ties, without assessing their strategic rationale and implications.

29 NA, MG 32, B19, Douglas Harkness Papers, vol. 28, file 42–66, Douglas Harkness, draft of letter to Joan Buffey, 13 December 1962, 4.

30 Jon B. McLin, *Canada's Changing Defense Policy*, 76.

31 NA, Douglas Harkness Papers, MG 32, B19, vol. 57, "'The Nuclear Arms Question,' Background Correspondence, memoranda, etc.," F.R. Miller, Air Marshal, chairman, Chiefs of Staff, "Air Defence Review," 23 December 1960, 7 [secret]. Note that this was Harkness's copy of the letter with personal notations added beforehand by Diefenbaker.

32 NA, Douglas Harkness Papers, MG 32, B19, vol. 57, "'The Nuclear Arms Question,' Background Correspondence, memoranda, etc.," Douglas Harkness, memorandum for the prime minister regarding the "Air Defence Problem," n.d., 2 [secret].

33 Personal correspondence from Knowlton Nash, 17 January 1991; Interview by author with Basil Robinson, 14 September 1992. According to Tom Keating, the commitment to acquire the Bomarcs was made "out of sincere confusion or deliberate obfuscation, the government never made this clear to Canadians." *Canada and World Order*, 156.

34 According to an interview by Douglas Breithaupter of David Golden, deputy minister in the Department of Defence Production, cited in Breithaupter, "The Bomarc Procurement" (research essay submitted to Carleton University), September 1980, 71. See also the record of confidential interviews conducted by Howard Lentner, "Foreign Policy Decision-Making," *World Politics*, 58; and the interview of George Ignatieff, CIIPS transcripts, 116.

35 Basil Robinson interview, 14 September 1992; see also George Ignatieff, *The Making of a Peacemonger*, 184, 189.

36 Robinson, *Diefenbaker's World*, 22.

37 The extent to which these three continued to make this argument, despite criticism from such civil servants as Jules Leger, John Holmes, and others, is exemplified in PCO, Cabinet document 908017-02, letter from General Charles Foulkes, chairman, Chiefs of Staff to Jules Leger, under-secretary of state for External Affairs, 26 November 1957, 1 [secret]; and DHist, Raymont Papers, 73/1223, series 2, file 879, "Answers to Questions by Cabinet and Public," 07/25/57–05/26/58, General Charles Foulkes, memorandum regarding "NATO Defence Arrangements in North America," 10 January 1958 [confidential]. Notably, in 1961–1962 Defence Minister Harkness also remembered, belatedly, to include NORAD under NATO in his speeches. For example, see the scribbled annotation in his draft, "World Political Changes and Their Effect on Defence," NA, MG 32, B19, vol. 70, Empire Club of Canada, 14 November 1963, 6.

38 DHist, Raymont Papers, 73/1223, series 2, file 879, "Answers to Questions by Cabinet and Public," 07/25/57–05/26/58, Jules Leger, under-secretary of state for External Affairs, "Memorandum to the Minister on 'NORAD – Points of Special Interest to External Affairs,'" 2 December 1957 [secret]; and General Charles Foulkes, chairman, Office of the Chairman Chiefs of Staff, "NATO Defence Arrangements in North America," 19 January 1958, 2 [confidential].

39 NA, Douglas Harkness Papers, MG 32, B19, file "Pearkes, G. NATO Ministerial Meeting, 13 January 1959," 10–11.

40 JGD Centre, Diefenbaker Speech Series Collection, vol. 27, file 751, text of speech for delivery on CBC TV series, *The Nation's Business*, 9 March 1959, 1.

41 JGD Centre, Diefenbaker Speech Series Collection, vol. 30, file 779, speech to Michigan University, Lansing, USA, 7 June 1959, 8.

42 DEA, *Statements and Speeches*, no. 58/19, minister of External Affairs, Sydney Smith, "Canada and NATO," Life Insurance Officers Association, Seignory Club, 27 May 1958, 2.

43 JGD Centre, Diefenbaker Speech Series Collection, vol. 74, file 10385, draft of speeches to Prince George, B.C. and Red Deer, Alta., 1 September 1961, 5.

44 JGD Centre, Diefenbaker Speech Series Collection, vol. 38, file 818, draft of untitled speech, 14 November 1959, 27.

45 JGD Centre, Diefenbaker Speech Series Collection, vol. 14, file 523, untitled speech to the House of Commons, Ottawa, 20 January 1955, 5, 12.

46 JGD Centre, Diefenbaker Speech Series Collection, vol. 30, file 7795, "Draft of Untitled Speech," 7 June 1959, 11.

47 For example, see his idea that "the process of consultation must be a constantly flowing stream" in JGD Centre, Diefenbaker Speech Series Collection, vol. 38, file 818, untitled speech, 14 November 1959, 28–9; similarly, see vol. 30, file 779, speech to Michigan University, Lansing, USA, 7 June 1959, 11; and vol. 44, file 865, "Western Policy Reexamined," Depauw University, Indiana, 5 June 1960.

48 DEA, *Statements and Speeches*, no. 60/21, John Diefenbaker "Western Policy Reexamined," Depauw University, Indiana, 5 June 1960, 2. The original draft of this speech is found in JGD Centre, Diefenbaker Speech Series Collection, vol. 44, file 865, 5 June 1960.

49 DHist, Raymont Papers 73/1223, series 1, file 309, "Cabinet Decisions and Hansard References," 02/20/59 to 02/26/63, letter from John G. Diefenbaker to General Norstad, 30 July 1959 [personal]; and *Hansard*, 2 July 1959, 5321. The vestiges of Diefenbaker's anger about the lack of consultation during the Cuban missile crisis remained for years. As he wrote in his memoirs, the purpose of Merchant's visit "was to convey President Kennedy's demand that my government should give carte blanche in support of unilateral action by the United States ... [but I] considered it unacceptable that every agreed requirement for consultation between our two counties should be ignored ..." Diefenbaker, *One Canada: 1962–1967*, vol. 3, 71–2.

50 None of these decision-makers equated the threat with "socialist" or "Marxist doctrine" or with "Communist China" – in fact, Diefenbaker was sympathetic toward Communist China.

51 JGD Centre, Diefenbaker Speech Series Collection, box 14, file 5075, untitled speech to the House of Commons, Ottawa, 6 April 1954, 13.

52 The atmosphere of moderation was a result of talks held by President Eisenhower and President Khrushchev at Camp David in

September 1959. See JGD Centre, Diefenbaker Speech Series Collection, vol. 38, file 318, 14 November 1959, 17.

53 JGD Centre, vol. 65, file 996, "Partial notes for an address to the Canadian Bar Association," Winnipeg, 1 September 1961, 19.

54 Diefenbaker's references to the threat need to be interpreted with an appreciation for his natural rhetorical tendency. For example, when he spoke of the USSR's intention to "extend the spinning of its worldwide spider web of tyranny in palatable form," he probably intended to impress his audience as much as express an opinion. JGD Centre, Diefenbaker Speech Series Collection, vol. 15, file 558, n.d., 2.

55 JGD Centre, Diefenbaker Speech Series Collection, vol. 65, file 996, "Partial notes for an address to the Canadian Bar Association," Winnipeg, 1 September 1961, 24–6. For virtually the same sentiments, see vol. 38, file 310, 14 November 1959, 24.

56 George Ignatieff interview, CIIPS transcripts, 118.

57 Basil Robinson interview, 14 September 1992.

58 DHist, Raymont Papers, 73/1223, series 2, file 768, "Canadian Defence Policy 07/29/63–03/23/64," draft of speech by Douglas Harkness, minister of National Defence, to the House of Commons, 13 September 1961, 2.

59 DHist, Raymont Papers, series 2, file 767, "Canadian Defence Policy 02/05/59–07/14/59," Minister of National Defence Douglas Harkness, "Defence in a Changing World," Royal Canadian Military Institute, 17 February 1961, 2 [declassified].

60 NA, Douglas Harkness Papers, MG 32, B19, vol. 57, "'The Nuclear Arms Crisis,' Background Correspondence, memoranda, etc.," letter from MP Arthur R. Smith to Prime Minister Diefenbaker, 20 September 1961 [personal].

61 JGD Centre, Prime Minister's Office Papers, vol. 52, draft of letter to Mr. Khrushchev, Ottawa, 9 May 1958, 1.

62 JGD Centre, Diefenbaker Speech Series Collection, vol. 38, file 818, untitled draft of speech on "International Affairs," 14 November 1959, 17, 18.

63 Ibid., 22.

64 DHist, Raymont Papers, 73/1223, series 2, file 768, "Canadian Defence Policy 07/29/63–03/23/64," draft of speech by Douglas Harkness, minister of National Defence, to the House of Commons, 13 September 1961, 2.

65 NA, Douglas Harkness Papers, MG 32, B19, vol. 57, file "'The Nuclear Arms Question,' Background Correspondence; memoranda, etc., 1958–1962," letter from Douglas Harkness to Prime Minister Diefenbaker, 26 October 1962, 2 [confidential].

66 See his assertion in 1959 that "the Anglo-Canadian-American Community constitutes a grand alliance for freedom, in partnership with

others of the NATO family, in the defence of democracy against the
Red Menace." JGD Centre, vol. 18, file 619, notes for a speech, 1959.

67 NA, Douglas Harkness Papers, MG 32, B19, vol. 70, "Draft of Speech
by General G.R. Pearkes to the NATO Ministerial Meeting," 13 January 1959, 9.

68 NA, Douglas Harkness Papers, MG 32, B19, vol. 28, file 42–66, letter
from Douglas Harkness to Mrs. Worrall, 1 March 1962. See also
DHist, Raymont Papers, 73/1223, series 2, file 767, "Canadian
Defence Policy 02/05/59–07/14/59," Douglas Harkness, "Defence in
a Changing World," Royal Canadian Military Institute, 17 February
1961, 5 [declassified].

69 NA, MG 32, B19, Douglas Harkness Papers, vol. 28, file 42–66, letter
from Douglas Harkness to Mrs. Worrall, 1 March 1962.

70 In 1957, the civil servants responsible for tallying Canada's NATO
contribution reckoned that it consisted of one brigade group, including an armoured regiment and the necessary administrative troops,
comprising a maximum of 5,500 soldiers; one air division and its supporting elements comprising four wings, including eight interceptor
day-fighter squadrons with 200 F-86 aircraft and four all-weather
fighter squadrons with 72 CF-100 aircraft, for a maximum total air
force commitment of 6,500 soldiers; and a navy commitment to provide by 31 June 1959 one light fleet carrier and aircraft with 42 ocean
escorts. DHist, Raymont Papers, series 2, file 826, "Canada's International Commitments Exclusive of NATO 06/13/53–09/04/57," Jules
Leger and John Holmes, "Canadian International Defence Commitments" for the Department of External Affairs and the Department of
National Defence, submitted through the office of Air Marshal
F.R. Miller, 13 June 1957, 2.

71 Dave McIntosh, "Nuclear Weapons – We Must Decide," *Halifax
Chronicle-Herald*, 26 December 1961.

72 DHist, Raymont Papers, 73/1223, series 2, file 768, "Canadian
Defence Policy 07/29/63–03/23/64," "Speech by the Honourable
Douglas Harkness, Minister of National Defence in the House of
Commons," 9. Harkness's understanding of a "defensive" force posture is further revealed by his comment in this speech: "I would like
to stress again that the NORAD agreement is a purely defensive agreement. Military action can only be taken if North America comes
under attack from the air. In other words, it cannot by conceivable
circumstance start a war." 6.

73 PCO, Cabinet Conclusions, 9 December 1958, 3.

74 For example, see his comments in PCO, Cabinet Conclusions, 15 October 1958, 11; and *Hansard*, 4 August 1960, 7556–7557.

75 *Hansard*, 20 February 1959, 1223.

76 JGD Centre, Prime Minister's Office, vol. 74, file 10385, "Public Statements by Members of the Government Regarding the Acquisition and
Storage of Nuclear Weapons," minister of National Defence speaking
to the Air Industries & Transport Association, 1 November 1961.

77 NA, MG 32, B19, Douglas Harkness Papers, vol. 28, file 42–66, draft of
letter from Douglas Harkness to Joan Buffey, 13 December 1962, 4.
Harkness was writing a rationalization rather than a strategic justifi-
cation. The original directive (from SACEUR in his SHAPE planning
guidance for 1957) recommended to Canada that one Honest John
rocket battalion be included in support of the Infantry Brigade Group
in Europe; this, in turn, arose from the decision taken at the NATO
Council meeting in December 1957 to establish stocks of nuclear warheads for the defence of the Alliance as well as the 1952–54 decisions
to organize NATO's forces in Europe on the understanding that these
weapons would be used to repel attacks. Although "recent Soviet
advances in the field of military technology" were of concern to
Diefenbaker at the NATO Heads of Government meeting in December 1957, evidently Diefenbaker, Pearkes, and Foulkes did not originally decide to acquire these weapons because, as Harkness later
reasoned, "the Soviet field forces are also furnished with similar
weapons." For the Cabinet's original discussion concerning the
grounds for acquiring Lacrosse, and later replacement Honest John
missiles, see PCO, Cabinet Conclusions, 15 October 1958 and 25 March
1960. Diefenbaker's vague reference to recent Soviet advances in military technology is in DHist, Raymont Papers, 73/1223, series 2, file 879,
"Answers to Questions by Cabinet and Public," 07/25/57–05/26/58,
"Extract from Mr. Diefenbaker's Statement to the NATO Heads of
Government Meeting," 16 December 1957 [secret].

78 The fear was that Soviet bombers would carry "dead man fuses"
preset for certain altitudes, at which they would detonate regardless
of whether the bomber's crew was dead or alive. An argument in
support of the Bomarc B missile by the USAF was that its nuclear
warhead could destroy all the nuclear warheads on the Soviet carrier
vehicle. To counter arguments that the nuclear explosion from the
Bomarc B would cause nuclear fallout over Canada, American experts
pointed out that the level of fallout would be insignificant compared
to the fallout showered down on Canada by the release of a high-
yield conventional bomb.

79 PCO, Cabinet Conclusions, 23 August 1961, 6 [secret]. See also NA,
RG 25/90–91/001, vol. 42, file 1415–40 pt. 11, "Visit of Mr. Rusk:
Nuclear Weapons Questions," 23 August 1962, 2 [secret].

80 DHist, Raymont Papers, 73/1223, series 1, file 303, draft of letter from
Douglas Harkness to Howard Green, n.d., 1 [secret].

81 NA, Douglas Harkness Papers, MG 32, B19, vol. 28, file 42–66, letter from Peter Light to Douglas Harkness, 29 October 1962, 4.

82 NA, Douglas Harkness Papers, MG 32, B19, vol. 28, file 42–66, letter from Douglas Harkness to Joan Buffey, 13 December 1962, 3.

83 NA, Douglas Harkness Papers, MG 32, B19, vol. 57, "'The Nuclear Arms Question,' Background Correspondence, memoranda, etc.," Douglas Harkness, memorandum for the prime minister, "Air Defence Problem," n.d., 4 [secret].

84 NA, Douglas Harkness Papers, MG 32, B19, vol. 28, file 42–66, letter from Douglas Harkness to Master Peter Macmillan, 26 January 1962, 2.

85 NA, MG 32, B19, vol. 28, file 42–66, Douglas Harkness, draft of letter to Joan Buffey, 13 December 1962, 1.

86 NA, Douglas Harkness Papers, MG 32, B19, vol. 57, "'The Nuclear Arms Question,' Background Correspondence, memoranda, etc.," Douglas Harkness, "Draft," n.d., 2.

87 For example, see DHist, Raymont Papers, 73/1223, file 768, "Canadian Defence Policy 07/29/63–03/23/64," "Speech by the Honourable Douglas Harkness, Minister of National Defence in the House of Commons," 9.

88 Basil Robinson interview by author, 14 September 1992.

89 See JGD Centre, Diefenbaker Speech Collection Series, vol. 74, file 10385, draft of speeches for Prince George, B.C. and Red Deer, Alta., 1 September 1961, 4; and, vol. 87, file 11275, memorandum for the minister from Escott Reid with annotations by Diefenbaker regarding "Speech to the Canadian Bar Association," 28 August 1961, 4.

90 For the Cabinet's brief discussion about beginning negotiations to acquire the Honest John, see PCO, Cabinet Conclusions, 15 October 1958, 10–12. On the "family" of nuclear weapons, see NA, Douglas Harkness Papers, MG 32, B19, vol. 57, "'The Nuclear Arms Question,' Background Correspondence, memoranda, etc.," F.R. Miller, Air Marshal, chairman, Chiefs of Staff, "Air Defence Review," 23 December 1960, 4.

91 DHist, Raymont Papers, 73/1223, file 768, "Canadian Defence Policy 07/29/63–03/23/64," draft of speech by Douglas Harkness, minister of National Defence in the House of Commons, 13 September 1961, 9.

92 JGD Centre, Prime Minister's Office, vol. 74, file 10385, "Public Statements by Members of the Government Regarding the Acquisition and Storage of Nuclear Weapons," minister of National Defence, speech to the Air Industries & Transport Association, 1 November 1961. Once Harkness realized the prime minister was opposed to nuclear weapons and once he had resigned, he portrayed Diefenbaker, in his written account of the nuclear missile crisis, as completely irrational. See

NA, Douglas Harkness Papers, MG 32, B19, vol. 57, "Unnumbered Series, 'The Nuclear Arms Crisis.'"

93 PCO, Cabinet Conclusions, 15 October 1958, 11.
94 Interview by author with Basil Robinson, 14 September 1992.
95 DHist, Raymont Papers, 73/1223, file 767, "Canadian Defence Policy 02/05/59–07/14/59," Douglas Harkness "Defence in a Changing World," Royal Canadian Military Institute, 17 February 1961, 17.
96 DHist, Raymont Papers, 73/1223, file 768, "Canadian Defence Policy 07/29/63–03/23/64," Douglas Harkness, minister of National Defence, draft of speech to the House of Commons, 13 September 1961, 118.
97 NA, Douglas Harkness Papers, MG 32, B19, vol. 55, file 87–0, "Civil Defence 1960–1965"; and vol. 3, "Post- Attack Situation," Annex A, TO HQC 2426–31, November 1960, 1 [confidential].
98 Ibid., 1–3.
99 Albert Legault, Deterrence and the Atlantic Alliance, 45.
100 Ibid., 47.
101 For an in-depth survey of the evolution of strategic thinking among high-level American and NATO decision-makers regarding nuclear deterrence during this time period, see Legault, Deterrence and the Atlantic Alliance; John Lewis Gaddis, Strategies of Containment: A Critical Appraisal of Postwar American National Security Policy, chaps. 6–7; Harald von Riekhoff, NATO: Issues and Prospects; and Lawrence Freedman, The Evolution of Nuclear Strategy.
102 On 25 January 1963, during his Nassau speech in the House of Commons, Diefenbaker did refer in passing to the importance of the "non-nuclear shield" and the "non-nuclear sword." But his reference was only to the last paragraph of an American communiqué which Diefenbaker had read. In fact, there are no references to complicated strategic terms such as "the shield" or to the underlying contradictions of deterrence doctrine in any of the Cabinet Conclusions accessed through the PCO. Furthermore, the discussion in the few papers of the Chiefs of Staff that have been made available is also similarly vague. A somewhat detailed analysis of NATO's concept of the shield was provided in 1960, however, by Dewar of the PCO for the chairman, Chiefs of Staff General Charles Foulkes. See DHist, Raymont Papers, 73/1223, file 767, "Canadian Defence Policy 05/02/59–14/07/59," letter from R.B. Bryce, PCO, to General Charles Foulkes with report by Dewar, 4 [secret]. And a rather detailed analysis of NATO's "deterrence-plus-defence" versus "deterrence-only" argument is found in a speech by R.J. Sutherland, Defence Research Board, DND to a restricted defence seminar. See DHist, R.J. Sutherland,

"The Military Problems of NATO," CSC 2195-4-A (JS/DSS), 26 October 1962 [restricted]. As Dewar and Sutherland were considered the Defence department's "experts" in strategic thinking, however, it cannot be surmised that those sections of the Cabinet Conclusions that continue to be excised and the Chiefs of Staff documents that are being kept closed (despite the thirty-year rule) contain any more complicated kinds of reasoning.

103 *Hansard*, 2 July 1959, 5353.

104 NA, Douglas Harkness Papers, MG 32, B19, vol. 70, draft of speech by General G.R. Pearkes to the NATO Ministerial Meeting, 13 January 1959, 9.

105 *Ibid.*, 10.

106 See NA, MG 32, B19, vol. 28, file 42–66, letter from Douglas Harkness to Peter Light, 22 October 1962, 1.

107 NA, Douglas Harkness Papers, MG 32, B19, vol. 57, "'The Nuclear Arms Question,' Background Correspondence, memoranda, etc.," Douglas Harkness, "Draft," n.d., 2.

108 Douglas Harkness "Speech to the Air Industries & Transport Association," 1 November 1961, reprinted in JGD Centre, vol. 74, file 10385, "Public Statements by Members of the Government regarding the Acquisition and Storage of Nuclear Weapons."

109 DHist, Raymont Papers, 73/1223, file 767, "Canadian Defence Policy 02/05/59–07/14/59," Douglas Harkness, "Defence in a Changing World," Royal Canadian Military Institute, 17 February 1961, 18.

110 As one forthright brigadier-general wrote in a personal letter to Diefenbaker, Canada had, by failing to accept the responsibility of accepting and being prepared to use nuclear weapons, reached "an all-time low as a member of the NATO team." JGD Centre, Prime Minister's Office Collection, vol. 53, letter from Brigadier N.A. Gianelli (ret.) to John Diefenbaker, 10 December 1962.

111 NA, Douglas Harkness Papers, MG 32, B19, vol. 57, file "'The Nuclear Arms Question,' Background, Correspondence, memoranda, etc.," letter from Douglas Harkness to Howard Green, 19 December 1961, 2 [secret]; and vol. 28 (16), file 42–66, letter from Douglas Harkness to Brigader-General J. A. Clark, 7 November 1962, 1 [personal & confidential].

112 DHist, Raymont Papers, 73/1223 series 1, file 303, Joint Staff Working Paper, "Nuclear Weapons for Canadian Forces," 11 October 1961, 2. There is also evidence that Ambassador Heeney, among others, believed the Alliance's present buildup of forces, even without the Canadian nuclear weapons, would still be able to deter a Soviet attack, unless the Soviets developed an anti-missile system. In 1960 Heeney wrote a detailed outline of the American defence debate concerning "the adequacy of the deterrent." In it, he himself accepted the

American military's major premise (which he asserted had been confirmed by the Canadian chairman of the Joint Chiefs of Staff) that the Soviet Union did not in 1960, nor in the foreseeable future, deliberately plan to initiate a general war. As Heeney explained, according to the American's own intelligence estimates and despite what some critics in the United States had been insisting, there was no danger of a "missile gap." He stated: "Contrary to the public impression which has been created, intelligence estimates do not give the Soviet Union a really significant lead over the United States in ICBM's. The striking power of SAC is believed to be more than adequate to cover the missile gap, if any, during the next two years." In Ambassador Heeney's opinion, the Alliance would be able to deter the Soviet Union from attacking "as long as there is no evident significant tipping of the scales in favour of the Soviet Union, such as, for example, the acquisition by the Soviets of an effective anti-missile defence." In the unlikely event of deterrence failing, Heeney and Harkness, along with the Canadian Joint Chiefs of Staff, believed that "Soviet advances in the nuclear weapons field and their fundamental military advantage derived from geography and numerically superior forces" meant that NATO would clearly have to rely on its "nuclear defence strategy". See DEA, file 4901-Y-40, vol. 58, Ambassador Heeney to the secretary of state for External Affairs, "The Defence Debate I: Adequacy of the Deterrent," Washington, 8 March 1960, 3 [secret]; DEA, file 4901-Y-40, vol. 58, Ambassador Heeney to the secretary of state for External Affairs, "The Defence Debate: The Relative Strengths of the United States and the Soviet Union," Washington, 14 March 1960, 3 [confidential]; and DHist, Raymont Papers, 73/1223, series 1, file 303, Joint Staff Working Paper, "Nuclear Weapons for Canadian Forces," 1.

113 JGD Centre, Diefenbaker Speech Series Collection, vol. 30, file 779, speech to Michigan University, Lansing, USA, 7 June 1959, 17.

114 JGD Centre, Diefenbaker Speech Series Collection, vol. 65, file 996, John Diefenbaker, "Partial notes for an address to the Canadian Bar Association," Winnipeg, 1 September 1961, 23–5.

115 JGD Centre, John Diefenbaker Speech Series Collection, vol. 30, file 7795, untitled draft of speech, 7 June 1959, 6.

116 JGD Centre, Diefenbaker Speech Series Collection, box 14, file 5075, untitled speech to the House of Commons, Ottawa, 6 April 1954, 13–14.

117 *Hansard*, 4 August 1960, 7556–7557.

118 JGD Centre, Prime Minister's Office Papers, vol. 52, draft of letter to Mr. Khrushchev, Ottawa, 9 May 1958, 2.

119 John G. Norris, "New 'Lock' to Curb A-Weapon Use," *Washington Post*, 16 June 1962.

120 PCO, Cabinet Conclusions, 25 October 1962, 3 [secret].

121 In the following chapter, I point out that Howard Green sometimes
called attention to the dangers of nuclear proliferation (e.g., in the
Middle East), due in part to the "example" that would be set by
Canada in acquiring nuclear weapons. See chap. 7, 180. Harkness
rejected this argument. Instead, he maintained that because there
were no plans for Canada to exert "unilateral" control over the
nuclear weapons, Canada would not contribute to nuclear proliferation. As he explained to a graduate student who wrote him asking
about this issue: "Under the law, the custody of such nuclear weapons must remain with the United States until they are released in an
emergency by the authority of the President. This, in effect, ensures
that there is no increase in the number of countries having unilateral
control over the use of nuclear weapons." NA, Douglas Harkness
Papers, MG 32, B19, vol. 28, file 42–66, letter from Douglas Harkness
to Thomas Hockin, 20 March 1962, 1. See a similar argument in NA,
MG 32, B19, Douglas Harkness Papers, vol. 28, file 42–66, draft of
letter to Joan Buffey from Douglas Harkness, 13 December 1962, 4.

CHAPTER SEVEN

1 PCO, Cabinet Conclusions, 23 October 1962, 4–5; 24 October 1962, 5
[secret]; and PAC, Douglas Harkness Papers, MG 32, B19, vol. 57,
"Unnumbered series on 'The Nuclear Arms Crisis.'"

2 Patrick Nicholson, *Vision and Indecision*, 159.

3 *Ibid.*, 165; Nash, *Kennedy and Diefenbaker*, 199.

4 PCO, Cabinet Conclusions, 30 October 1962, 10 [top secret].

5 PCO, Cabinet Conclusions, 21 February 1961, 1 [secret].

6 PCO, Cabinet Conclusions, 25 August 1961, item k), 6 [secret].
Diefenbaker also told Cabinet during this 1961 meeting: "The President had said he would go as far as possible to meet the Canadian
position in the matter, and there had been reliable reports in the last
few days that members of the US Senate Foreign Relations Committee would agree to joint control with Canada over nuclear weapons
stockpiled in this country for Canadian use. It would not have been
possible two years ago to obtain US agreement to this principle.
A change in US law might not be required to give effect to an agreement to share with Canada joint control over nuclear weapons
stockpiled in Canada." These comments seem to indicate that some
measure of Canadian joint control, as Diefenbaker conceived it, was
being seriously discussed in the United States in 1961.

7 In another example, Diefenbaker told Cabinet in 1961 that not to
obtain joint control "would be an abandonment of responsibility on

the part of Canada." PCO, Cabinet Conclusions, 25 August 1961, 4 [secret].

8 Basil Robinson interview, 14 September 1992. Thirty years later, when asked during this interview what he thought Diefenbaker had meant exactly by joint control, Robinson threw his hands in the air and shrugged. He said he was not sure that Diefenbaker "fully understood all the jargon."

9 John Diefenbaker, *One Canada, 1962–1967*, vol. 3, 80.

10 NA, Howard Green Papers, MG 32, B13, vol. 12, transcript of an interview of Howard Green by Edwin Eades, 21–22 October 1980, 66.

11 NA, Arnold Heeney Papers, MG 30, E 144, vol. 2, file "Memoir, 1960, chapter 15, diary #2," 20 September 1960 entry.

12 *Ibid.*

13 *Ibid.*, 17 November 1960 entry. Green's tendency to criticize the United States as a whole, not individual Americans, may have led him much later to discount any suggestion that he had distrusted individual Americans during his time as minister of External Affairs. As he recalled in 1980, "We stood on our own feet. We were very friendly with the Americans, got on very well with them actually I did ... They're awfully easy to work with you know." NA, MG 32, B13, Howard Green Collection, vol. 12, transcript of interview of Howard Green by Edwin Eades, 21–22 October 1980, 45.

14 *Ibid.*, 20 September 1960.

15 *Ibid.*

16 NA, Arnold Heeney Papers, MG 30, E 144, vol. 2, file "Memoir, 1960, chapter 15, diary #2," 20 September 1960. Heeney also made the same assertion in his book *The Things that are Caesar's*, 162.

17 *Ibid.*

18 PCO, Cabinet Conclusions, 23 August 1961, 6 [secret].

19 JGD Centre, Diefenbaker Speech Series Collection, vol. 65, file 996, "Partial notes for an address at the Canadian Bar Association Dinner," Winnipeg, 1 September 1961, 12–13.

20 NA, Arnold Heeney Papers, MG 30, E 144, vol. 2, file "Memoir, 1960, chapter 15, diary #2," 30 August 1960. Notably, James Minifie was the author of a book which argued for Canadian neutrality. *Peacemaker or Powdermonkey: Canada's Role in a Revolutionary World.*

21 *Ibid.*, 20 September 1960.

22 The joint control approach was premised on the condition that the nuclear weapons would not be obtained pending a complete breakdown of disarmament negotiations. The missing parts idea was based on the condition that the United States would consent to store the nuclear warheads or parts of the warheads on American soil. In the event that Canada authorized their deployment during an emergency,

the us would undertake to transport the parts to Canada and install them in the Bomarc missiles and Voodoo interceptors.

23 PCO, Cabinet Conclusions, 23 August 1961 [secret].

24 PCO, Cabinet Conclusions, 25 August 1961, 3 [secret].

25 NA, MG 32, B13, Howard Green's Papers, vol. 12, transcript of interview of Howard Green by Edwin Eades, 21–22 October 1980, 79–81.

26 DHist, Raymont Papers, 73/1223, file 768, "Canadian Defence Policy 07/029/63–03/23/64," Douglas Harkness, minister of National Defence, draft of speech to the House of Commons, 13 September 1961, 7.

27 DEA, *Statements and Speeches*, no. 60/11, Howard Green, "Current International Problems: A Canadian View," House of Commons, 10 February 1962, 6–7.

28 Basil Robinson interview, 14 September 1992.

29 NA, MG 32, B13, Howard Green's Papers, vol. 12, transcript of interview of Howard Green by Edwin Eades, 21–22 October 1980, 43.

30 According to DEA, *Statements and Speeches*, no. 59/38, Howard Green, "A Canadian View of NATO" to the NATO Council, 28 October 1959, 2; and DEA *Statements and Speeches*, no. 60/11, Howard Green, "Current International Problems: A Canadian View," House of Commons, 10 February 1962, 8.

31 DEA, *Statements and Speeches*, no. 59/38, Howard Green, "A Canadian View of NATO" to the NATO Council, 28 October 1959, 2.

32 DEA, *Statements and Speeches*, no. 62/17, Howard Green, "NATO's Most Harmonious Meeting," House of Commons, 17 December 1962, 2.

33 DEA, *Statements and Speeches*, no. 60/11, Howard Green, "Current International Problems: A Canadian View," House of Commons, 10 February 1962, 5.

34 NA, Howard Green Papers, MG 32, B13, vol. 12, file 22, "Notes on the Topic of Defence and Disarmament," n.d.

35 These three "streams of thought" are explained in chapter 4, 80–3. In summary, the first stream assumed Canada's military contribution to the Alliance was relatively insignificant and might therefore be reduced. The second stream was primarily concerned that strengthening Canada's military commitments would exacerbate a dangerous situation and increase the likelihood of conflict. The third stream presumed that because of the nuclear balance, Canada's conventional forces to NATO were largely unnecessary. In addition to these three streams of thinking, Critics sometimes recommended that Canada de-emphasize or restructure a particular military commitment to the Alliance without assessing its strategic rationale and implications. For instance, it was sometimes recommended that certain weapons systems be cancelled, downsized, or not acquired because Critics

wanted, above all, to depart from a prescribed course of action or policy direction.

36 According to Dalton Camp in Peter Stursberg, *Diefenbaker: Leadership Lost, 1962–1967*, 19; and Nash, *Kennedy & Diefenbaker*, 189.

37 PCO, Cabinet Conclusions, 25 October 1963, 16 [secret].

38 General C. Foulkes on CBC TV, *Citizen's Forum*, 6 November 1960, transcribed in *News & Views*, no. 92, 22 November 1960, 11.

39 For Diefenbaker's own reference list of his statements referring to joint control, see JGD Centre, Prime Minister's Office, vol. 74, file 10385, "Public Statements by Members of the Government Regarding the Acquisition and Storage of Nuclear Weapons," 24 November 1960.

40 Ignatieff, *The Making of a Peacemonger*, 189.

41 According to Nash, *Kennedy & Diefenbaker*, 152.

42 Ignatieff, *The Making of a Peacemonger*, 189.

43 JGD Centre, Diefenbaker Speech Series Collection, vol. 65, file 996, "Partial Notes for an Address to the Canadian Bar Association," Winnipeg, 1 September 1961, 22.

44 JGD Centre, Diefenbaker Speech Series Collection, vol. 87, file 1122, 28 May 1962, 2.

45 PCO, Cabinet Conclusions, 24 October 1962, 2 [secret].

46 Diefenbaker, *One Canada 1962–1967*, 71.

47 PCO, Cabinet Conclusions, 24 October 1962, 2 [secret].

48 Nash, *Kennedy & Diefenbaker*, 189.

49 PCO, Cabinet Conclusions, 23 October 1962, 4 [secret].

50 PCO Cabinet Conclusions, 24 October 1962, 7 [secret].

51 DEA, *Statements and Speeches*, no. 60/11, Howard Green, "Current International Problems: A Canadian View," House of Commons, 10 February 1962, 6.

52 NA, Arnold Heeney Papers, MG 30, E 144, vol. 2, file "Memoir, 1960, chapter 15, diary #2," 20 September.

53 *Ibid*.

54 For example, see JGD Centre, Diefenbaker Speech Series Collection, vol. 30, file 779, speech to Michigan University, Lansing, USA, 7 June 1959, 6, 18, 20.

55 NA, Arnold Heeney Papers, MG 30, E 144, vol. 2, file "Memoir 1960, chapter 15, diary #2," 20 September.

56 Interview with Basil Robinson, 14 September 1992. For more on Norman Robertson's anti-nuclear convictions, see Basil Robinson, *Diefenbaker's World*, 108; Nash, *Kennedy and Diefenbaker*, 84; and J.L. Granatstein, *A Man of Influence: Norman Robertson and Canadian Statecraft, 1929–1968*.

57 Interview by author with Basil Robinson, 14 September 1992.

302   Notes to pages 173–4

58 *Hansard*, 25 January 1963, 3128.

59 By 1962, Diefenbaker referred to Green as "one of the greatest leaders in the field of disarmament and world peace," and someone who had achieved for Canada "an undisputed place in the field of international affairs and the pursuit of peace for all mankind." JGD Centre, Prime Minister's Papers, vol. 87, file 1122, "International Affairs – Defence Policy," 28 May 1962, 3.

60 According to JGD Centre, Diefenbaker Speech Series Collection, vol. 59, file 967, "Notes for an Address on 'The Nation's Business,'" 21 June 1961, 1. Also according to Arnold Heeney's diary, Diefenbaker was powerfully affected by the shift toward anti-Americanism which he detected in his letters beginning in 1959. NA, Arnold D. Heeney Papers, MG 30, E 144, vol. 2, file "Memoir 1959, chapter 15, diary #1," 29 March.

61 A case in point was his assertion during a Cabinet meeting in February 1961 that the public's appreciation of the need to have nuclear weapons had been weakened by the government's recent emphasis on disarmament negotiations, but that negotiations to acquire the nuclear weapons should continue. PCO, Cabinet Conclusions, 17 February 1961, 2 [secret].

62 Pierre Sevigny, *This Game of Politics*, 256.

63 There is no indication that polls were heavily influential. In 1961, for example, when the issue of nuclear weapons began to attract greater public attention, the Cabinet briefly discussed poll results but concluded that different polls produced diametrically opposite results. PCO, Cabinet Conclusions, February 17, 1961, 2 [secret]. Certainly, if polls had heavily influenced Diefenbaker and Green, they would have supported the acquisition of nuclear warheads in January 1963, since the polls they saw indicated that a strong majority favoured acquiring nuclear weapons for all the nuclear weapons systems. NA, Douglas Harkness Papers, MG 32, B19, vol. 57, "'The Nuclear Arms Question,' Background Correspondence, memoranda, etc.," CTV, *Telepol*, 27 January 1963. Generally speaking, therefore, Diefenbaker relied on letters but not on public opinion polls to detect shifts in public opinion. This is confirmed by Pierre Sevigny's remarks in Peyton Lyon, *Canada in World Affairs: 1961–1963*, 71; and Harkness's comments in Peter Stursberg, *Leadership Lost, 1962–1967*, 25.

64 JGD Centre, Diefenbaker Speech Series Collection, vol. 56, file 950, "Speech on CBC Radio International," 5 May 1961, 2.

65 *Hansard*, 25 January 1963, 3129.

66 For example, see PCO, Cabinet Conclusions, 23 August 1961, 6 [secret].

67 JGD Centre, Diefenbaker Speech Series Collection, vol. 87, file 1122, "International Affairs – Defence Policy," 28 May 1962, 2.

68 Nash, *Kennedy & Diefenbaker*, 296.

69 Lyon, *Canada in World Affairs*, 205. Although Diefenbaker claimed during the election that he had always sought to acquire conventional warheads from the United States for the Bomarc A missiles, there is no denying that the Cabinet, including Diefenbaker, knew in August 1961 that "there were no conventional warheads for the Bomarc B in production." PCO, Cabinet Conclusions, 23 August 1961, 8 [secret].

70 DHist, Raymont Papers, 73/1223, series 1, file 303, draft of a Joint Staff Working Paper, "Nuclear Weapons for Canadian Forces," 11 October 1961.

71 PCO, Cabinet Conclusions, 23 August 1961, 6 [secret].

72 PCO, Cabinet Conclusions, 23 August 1961, 4–5 [secret].

73 Nash, *Kennedy & Diefenbaker*, 212. When Peyton Lyon interviewed Green in 1965, Green made no distinction between the weapons based in Canada, with a strike-radius of less than five hundred miles, and the strike aircraft in Europe, which could deliver nuclear bombs well behind enemy lines. Lyon, *Canada in World Affairs*, 118, footnote 114. Years later, however, Green did distinguish between first-strike and second-strike weapons. He argued that Canada should not have become involved in the strike-reconnaissance role in Europe, although in 1962 he had agreed to it. The problem, he later explained, was due to "confusion" at the beginning and "the defence people." As he explained, "With the CF-104s, Canada got herself into the position where we were the strike force in NATO. We should never have got into that position in the first place but the defence people got us into that." NA, MG 32, B13, Howard Green Collection, vol. 12, transcript of interview of Howard Green by Edwin Eades, 21–22 October 1980, 79–81.

74 The backyard analogy is from Nash, *Kennedy & Diefenbaker*, 212.

75 As Nash writes, Harkness tried several times after the Cuban missile crisis to get Diefenbaker to sign the papers authorizing nuclear weapons for the Canadian NATO forces in Europe, but each time Diefenbaker put him off, saying there was no hurry and that he wanted to sign the deals for all the nuclear weapons systems at the same time. *Ibid.*, 213.

76 PCO, Cabinet Conclusions, October 30, 1962, 10–11.

77 These comments are excerpted from Diefenbaker's statement in the House of Commons and the Prime Minister's officially released statement. See *Hansard*, 20 January 1963, 3129 and Diefenbaker, "Transcript of Prime Minister's Statement," *One Canada, 1962–1967*, vol. 3, 92.

78 DEA, *Statements and Speeches*, no. 60/11, Howard Green, "Current International Problems: A Canadian View," House of Commons, Ottawa, 10 February 1962, 6.

79 George Ignatieff, CIIPS transcripts, 120.

80 PCO, Cabinet Conclusions, 23 August 1961, 8 [secret].

81 JGD Centre, Diefenbaker Speech Series Collection, vol. 65, file 996, "Partial notes for an address at the Canadian Bar Association Dinner," Winnipeg, 1 September 1961, 11; Nash, *Kennedy & Diefenbaker*, 228.

82 Nash, *Kennedy & Diefenbaker*, 81.

83 NA, Arnold Heeney Papers, MG 30, E 144, vol. 2, file "Memoir 1960, chapter 15, diary #2," 20 September.

84 Quoted in Patrick Nicholson, *Vision and Indecision*, 171. For more on Green's fear of nuclear war during the Cuban missile crisis, see Nash, *Kennedy and Diefenbaker*, 203.

85 Nash, *Kennedy & Diefenbaker*, 172.

86 Nicholson, *Vision and Indecision*, 172.

87 As Arnold Heeney wrote Howard Green in 1960: "This policy of 'nuclear deterrent' and 'massive retaliation,' although much maligned in some quarters has, ironically, recently received the highest tribute, that of Soviet emulation. [In January 1960] Premier Khrushchev announced a similar policy for the Soviet Union, based on the striking power of the Soviet ICBM, at the same time declaring the Soviet intention to reduce military forces in the next two years to below levels planned for the United States forces." DEA, file 4901-Y-40, vol. 58, Ambassador Arnold Heeney to the secretary of state for External Affairs, "The Defence Debate: The Relative Strengths of the United States and the Soviet Union," Washington, 14 March 1960, 2 [confidential].

88 JGD Centre, Diefenbaker Speech Series Collection, vol. 87, file 1122, "Untitled draft of speech," 28 May 1962, 1.

89 DEA, *Statements and Speeches*, no. 62/17, Howard Green, "NATO's most harmonious meeting," House of Commons, 17 December 1962, 3.

90 *Ibid.*, 1.

91 PCO, Cabinet Conclusions, 23 August 1961, 6 [secret].

92 Ignatieff, *The Making of a Peacemonger*, 197.

93 At that time, three NATO nations (the United States, the United Kingdom, and France) possessed their own nuclear weapons. Five other NATO countries (Belgium, the Netherlands, Italy, Greece, and Turkey) entered into bilateral agreements with the United States under which they would acquire nuclear weapons systems. As a 1968 DND study for the Special Task Force on Europe added, these warheads were to be retained under US custody until their release was authorized by "joint decision." DHist, DND for STAFEUR, "Canadian Military Interest in Europe," V 2390–1 (STAFEUR), 1 November 1968, 26 [secret].

CHAPTER EIGHT

1 Jervis, *Perception and Misperception in International Politics*, 239.
2 Steinbrunner, *The Cybernetic Theory of Decision*, 134.
3 Jervis, *Perception and Misperception in International Politics*, 239, 256.
4 Nash, *Kennedy and Diefenbaker*, 80, 317. Nash has since carefully quali-
   fied this thesis. He writes: "Combined with his distaste for Kennedy,
   I am also persuaded that Diefenbaker's motivation was political
   rather than philosophical. Green and Norman Robertson had fundamental philosophical problems with the warheads, but I believe with
   Diefenbaker it was essentially a question of how it would play with
   the voters as well as his dislike for Kennedy. The warhead was of
   course the object under discussion, but it was his hatred of Kennedy
   and 'standing up to the Americans' that stimulated his vacillation
   and eventual negativeness. One of the problems in assessing Dief's
   motivations, though, is that he was such a bundle of paranoia."
   Correspondence with the author, 1991.
5 Newman, *Renegade in Power*, 3.
6 NA, Douglas Harkness Papers, MG 32 B19, vol. 57, "Unnumbered
   Series, 'The Nuclear Arms Crisis.'"
7 Robinson, *Diefenbaker's World*, 17, 309.
8 Lyon, *Canada in World Affairs*, 76, 223.
9 As Irving Janis points out, an adequate explanation for phenomena
   (such as "groupthink") must also specify the observable *causes* – that
   is, the antecedent conditions that produce, elicit, or facilitate the
   occurrence of the syndrome. *Groupthink: Psychological Studies of Policy
   Decisions and Fiascoes*, 2nd ed., 176.
10 Ideally, this chapter should be based on in-depth interviews with
   influential decision-makers and their colleagues around the time of
   the decision-making. In most cases, however, interviews were impossible because many of the influential decision-makers have since died
   (e.g., Diefenbaker, Green, Harkness, Foulkes, Pearkes, Smith, Norman
   Robertson, Leo and Marcel Cadieux, Ignatieff, etc.). It was also difficult to arrive at firm conclusions because information documenting
   many of the reasons for these decision-makers' thought processes
   does not exist, is difficult to find, or has not yet been declassified.
   Consequently, although this chapter puts forward various possible
   explanations for the prevalence of these two belief systems, these
   explanations are presented with the caveat that they are informed
   conjecture, not irrefutable fact.
11 For example, John Diefenbaker briefly recounts his military training
   and his impressions of war in Diefenbaker, *One Canada: The Crusading*

Years, 1895–1956, 89; Pierre Sevigny mentions lessons he learned during his military career in *This Game of Politics*; Paul Hellyer describes the impact of the military on his attitudes to defence in *Damn the Torpedoes: My Fight to Unify Canada's Armed Forces*; Lester Pearson describes the impact of World War I on himself in *Mike: The Memoirs of the Right Honourable Lester B. Pearson, 1897–1948* and John English does the same in *Shadow of Heaven: The Life of Lester Pearson, 1897–1948*, vol. 1; Paul Martin records the impact of World War I and II on his thinking in *A Very Public Life*; and Allard, Belzile, Cameron, Campbell, Halstead, and Nixon refer to their wartime experiences in the CIIPS transcripts.

12 CIIPS transcripts, 1987, 542; see also PCO, STAFEUR report, February 1969, chap. 2 "Canada's Stake in Europe," 10–28 [confidential – Canadian eyes only].

13 Interview with Basil Robinson, 14 September 1992.

14 NA, Douglas Harkness Papers, MG 32 B19, vol. 28, file 42–66, letter from Douglas Harkness to Master Peter MacMillan, 26 January 1962, 1.

15 DHist, Raymont Papers, 73/1223, series 1, file 768, "Canadian Defence Policy 07/29/63–03/23/64," Draft of speech by Douglas Harkness, minister of National Defence for the House of Commons, 13 September 1961, 3.

16 *Ibid.*, 5. Whether the air defence of North America should be conceived of as "a single problem" was debated in the military from 1956 onward. Not all military representatives agreed that Canadian commitments to North American defence should be based on the idea that air defence was one problem. See Raymont Papers 73/1223, series 1, "Air Defence Command 79/24 – 'Committees-Canada/US Military Study Group,' August 19, 1953 – June 16, 1958," Memorandum TS-801–200-A166 from P.A. Gilchrist A/C D/Ops, 19 November 1956 [top secret].

17 At that time, Canadian diplomats such as Pearson and Escott Reid were inclined to emphasize the need for stronger non-military ties. But the other allies, particularly the Americans and Dean Acheson, thought of closer ties in terms of military commitments. Whereas the majority of Canadian politicians generally supported the establishment of NATO (including leaders of the CCF), some emphasized strengthening military commitments while others deemphasized the military aspects of the Treaty, in favour of promoting the Altantic community's cultural, economic, and "Judeo-Christian" ties. On the founding of NATO, the importance of Article II to Canadian diplomats, and the relative importance of promoting non-military ties, see Harald von Riekhoff, "The Changing Function of NATO," *International Journal*, 164; and the CIIPS transcripts, 1987, particularly the comments

by John Holmes, 52–53; George Ignatieff, 93; Geoffrey Pearson, 159; and Robert Cameron, 199, 201–203.

18 Lester Pearson to Canada's ambassador to France, Georges-Phileas Vanier, 13 August 1948, quoted in Escott Reid, *Time of Fear and Hope: The Making of the North Atlantic Treaty, 1947–1949*, 27.

19 John Holmes, CIPPS transcripts, 24 and Robert Cameron, 199.

20 JGD Centre, Diefenbaker Speech Series Collection, vol. 65, file 996, "Partial notes for an address to the Canadian Bar Association," Winnipeg, 1 September 1961, 15–19; PCO, Cabinet Conclusions, 25 August 1961, items m) and n), 7 [secret].

21 Ross Campbell, CIIPS transcripts, 1987, 625, 633, 650–51.

22 Confidential source, 17 November 1982.

23 For example, the "flagging" Canadian performance was criticized by representatives from the United States, the United Kingdom, the Federal Republic of Germany, the Netherlands, the NATO Military Committee, SHAPE, and SACLANT at a meeting on 27 October 1980. It was pointed out that, at a time when the need to modernize the Canadian Forces was becoming increasingly urgent, postponement and procrastination seemed to be the dominant characteristics of the Canadian decision-making process. Confidential sources. For the attitude of high-level Canadian representatives to this sort of criticism, see for example, DEA, 27-1-1-USA and DEA, 27-1-1-29.

24 Confidential source, 9 April 1980.

25 DHist, Air Marshall Campbell Speeches, 1960, file 74/426, speech to RCAF Staff College, "Farewell for A/C Orr," 24 June 1960 [declassified].

26 *Ibid.*

27 Douglas Harkness, speech to the Air Industries & Transport Association, 1 November 1961, as reprinted in JGD Centre, vol. 74, file 10385, "Public Statements by Members of the Government regarding the Acquisition and Storage of Nuclear Weapons."

28 George Ignatieff, CIIPS transcripts, 120.

29 The attitudes of English Canadians to fighting for Britain again, and Mackenzie King's political strategy in the final years before World War II, are analysed in Gwynne Dyer and Tina Viljoen, *The Defence of Canada: In the Arms of the Empire*, 332–6. During the interwar years, Prime Minister Mackenzie King seemed wary of entrapment in another European war as well and, consequently, hesitated to make commitments on behalf of Canada. As he explained to the House of Commons on 30 March 1939, "The idea that every 20 years this country should automatically and as a matter of course take part in a war overseas for democracy or self-determination of other small nations, that a country which has all it can do to run itself should feel called upon to save, periodically, a continent that cannot run itself, and to

these ends to risk the lives of its people, risk bankruptcy and political disunion, seems to many a nightmare and sheer madness." *Hansard*, 1939, vol. 3, 2419 and quoted in Escott Reid, *Time of Fear and* Hope, 127. As John Holmes pointed out later in an interview, "There had been long tensions in Canada between those who did not want Canada to be dragged into European wars, and those who either for imperial or internationalist reasons thought we should be more involved in the war." Holmes, CIIPS transcripts, 24.

30 Paul McRae's study, 10.

31 NA, Howard Green Papers, MG 32 B13, vol. 12, transcript of an interview with Howard Green by Edwin Eades, 21–22 October 1980, 66.

32 NA, Arnold Heeney Papers, MG 30 E 144, vol. 2, file "Memoir, 1960, chapter 15, diary #2," 20 September. Heeney also made the same assertion in his book *The Things that are Caesar's*, 162.

33 NA, Arnold Heeney Papers, MG 30 E 144, vol. 2, file "Memoir, 1960, chapter 15, diary #2" 30 August 1960; see also Nash, *Kennedy and Diefenbaker*, 58.

34 Ignatieff, CIIPS transcripts, 104.

35 *Ibid.*, 118.

36 Diefenbaker, *One Canada, 1956–1962*, vol. 2, 51–52.

37 For a detailed account of Diefenbaker's growing suspicions once Kennedy came to power, see Nash, *Kennedy & Diefenbaker*. Nash argues Diefenbaker's perception of the United States shifted because he heartily disliked Kennedy. In fact, Diefenbaker's "anti-American" imagery began to affect his decision-making in 1960, well before Kennedy became president.

38 Ignatieff interview, CIIPS transcripts, 119.

39 Holmes, CIIPS transcripts, 49–50.

40 Confidential high-level source, 5 July 1984 [confidential].

41 According to Sutherland's committee, the argument that Canada should reduce its expenditures on defence in the interest of greater expenditures on foreign aid was also a convenient and unsatisfactory rationalization for "isolationism." Therefore, the committee stated: "If Canada is to play a significant role in foreign aid, as opposed merely to talking about it, this can only be done in close cooperation with our present allies ... Canada cannot play a significant role in relation to Europe other than in close partnership with the United States. She cannot play a significant role in Africa or Asia other than as an ally of the United States and as a member of the North Atlantic community." 74, 76, 109 [secret – Canadian eyes only].

42 On psychological short-cuts such as "historical analogy," "availability," and "standard operating procedures" (SOPs), see Janis, *Crucial Decisions: Leadership in Policymaking and Crisis*, 38.

43 Ad Hoc Committee on Defence Policy, 94 [secret – Canadian eyes only].

44 Confidential source, 10 April 1968 [secret]. This memo also argued that France was able to retain its military and political interests while withdrawing its forces committed to NATO because "France does not need NATO as much as NATO needs France. Canada does not have the same bargaining power at all."

45 On "satisficing," see Herbert Simon, *Models of Man: Social and Rational*, cited in Steinbrunner, *The Cybernetic Theory of Decision*, 62–3. Anecdotal evidence of tendencies in the Departments of External Affairs and National Defence to adopt the first acceptable alternative is presented by Jeff Sallot in "How to Feed the Ministers More than Mush?" *Globe and Mail*, 29 November 1991 and in the account by Charles Nixon of the defence procurement process and its relationship to the strategic overview, CIIPS transcripts, 1987, 585–588.

46 Nixon, CIIPS transcripts, 1987, 571.

47 PCO, STAFEUR report, February 1969, 110.

48 For a discussion of "uncommitted thinking" among high-level policy-makers, see Steinbrunner, *The Cybernetic Theory of Decision*, 128–131.

49 PCO, Cabinet Document 310/69, Ivan Head's study, March 1969, 6–7 [secret – Canadian eyes only].

50 PCO, Cabinet Document 165–558, R.G. Robertson, "Memorandum for the Prime Minister: The Defence Policy Review and the Report of the Special Task Force on Europe," 25 March 1969, 3 [secret].

51 The predominantly legal backgrounds of Ivan Head and Donald Macdonald are remarked on in Richard Gwyn, *The Northern Magus: Pierre Trudeau and Canadians*. For similar commentary, see G. Bruce Doern, "The Policy-Making Philosophy of Prime Minister Trudeau and his Advisers," *Apex of Power: The Prime Minister and Political Leadership in Canada*, ed. Thomas A. Hockin.

52 PCO, Cabinet Conclusions, 19 July 1968, 8–9.

53 Confidential source, December 1968.

54 Trudeau explained in his memoirs that, upon his election in 1968, he decided "to introduce a measure of order and rationality to the whole question of procedure" and to improve the decision-making process of Cabinet. He spent the summer "putting in place a more rational (my obsession!), better organized system of procedure." Pierre Elliott Trudeau, *Memoirs*, 108. Richard Gwyn argues that "rational planning" did not work. The new tools, including flow charts, flip charts, decision trees, and new problem-crunching theologies such as PPBS (Program, Planning and Budgeting Systems) amounted to a new religion but produced, in the end, very little. As Mitchell Sharp admitted later, "I'd have to say that the system didn't produce any better

legislation than Pearson's." Gwyn, *The Northern Magus: Pierre Trudeau and Canadians*, 97–9.

55 There have been many historical recounts of Soviet intransigence and threatening behaviour between 1943 and 1989. Not many scholars, however, have examined the impact of these incidents on the belief systems of high-level Canadian decision-makers. For the most part, historical accounts have focused on relating the historical events and describing the reaction of leaders. But some scholars have engaged in a sustained effort to track down original documents, memos, confidential letters, and diaries so as to recreate the actual thought processes of some important politicians and diplomats vis à vis the threat to NATO from the Soviet Union, communism, or the USSR. Scholars such as Robert Bothwell, James Eayrs, John English, J.L. Granatstein, Norman Hillmer, John Holmes, Kim Richard Nossal, Geoffrey Pearson, Denis Smith, Denis Stairs, Peter Stursberg, and Basil Robinson have contributed a great deal in this regard. For example, on different diplomats' perceptions of the lessons of both world wars; of the tenure of Canada-Soviet relations between 1943–48; the origins of the Cold War; and the lessons of the Gouzenko affair, see Denis Smith, *Diplomacy of Fear: Canada and the Cold War, 1941–1948*; James Eayrs, *In Defence of Canada: Growing Up Allied*; John Holmes, *The Shaping of Peace: Canada and the Search for World Order, 1943–1957*, vols. 1 and 2; Kim Richard Nossal, *The Politics of Canadian Foreign Policy*, 2nd ed., chap. 5. For brief analyses of the impact of different events such as the Czech coups, the Berlin crises, the Korean War, the Suez crisis, and the Cuban missile crisis on some decision-makers see, for example, Geoffrey Pearson, *Seize the Day: Lester B. Pearson and Crisis Diplomacy*; J.L. Granatstein, *Canada, 1957–1967: The Years of Uncertainty and Innovation*; Kim Richard Nossal, "A European Nation?: The Life and Times of Atlanticism in Canada," in *Making a Difference: Canada's Foreign Policy in a Changing World Order*, ed. John English & Norman Hillmer; Peter Stursberg, *Diefenbaker: Leadership Lost: 1962–1967*; and *Lester Pearson and the Dream of Unity*; and the CIIPS transcripts. For John Holmes's recollection of the perception of Soviet behaviour after World War II, see the John Holmes interview in CIIPS transcripts, 1987, 29–30. For Ross Campbell's interpretation of the impact of the 1968 invasion on his conception of the threat from the East bloc, see CIIPS transcripts, 1987, 639–44. And on John Halstead's recollection of the effect that he thought the invasion of Aghanistan had on NATO's out-of-area problem, see CIIPS transcripts 834–6. The official memoirs of high-level officials are also sometimes useful. For example, see Lester Pearson, *Memoirs*, vols. 2 and 3; John Diefenbaker, *One Canada*, vols. 1–3; Paul Martin, *A Very Public Life*, vol. 1; Pierre Elliott Trudeau, *Memoirs*; Ivan L. Head and Pierre Elliott

Trudeau, *The Canadian Way: Shaping Canada's Foreign Policy, 1968–1984*; and Mitchell Sharp, *Which Reminds Me: A Memoir*.

56 Ross Campbell, CIIPS transcripts, 1987, 619.

57 JGD Centre, Diefenbaker Speech Series Collection, vol. 30, file 779, Speech to Michigan University, Lansing, USA, 7 June 1959, 15.

58 On the important contribution of "social corroboration" to strengthening belief systems, see Steinbrunner, *The Cybernetic Theory of Decision*, 121.

59 *Hansard*, 4 March 1988, 13406.

60 On the psychological dynamics of "we" versus "they" imagery, see John Gleisner "The Enemy Within," *New Internationalist*, 1. Defenders also may have projected the threat to be monolithic, inexorable, and external to the Alliance because of other related psychological characteristics. It is not clear why some individuals conceive of the enemy as an external stranger and are more afraid of the "stranger-enemy" than others, but very early experiences and childhood upbringing can play an important role in determining shared enemies. Studies show that the mind of the developing child may create the concept of "enemy" because of early "stranger anxiety." In the long run, the potential for having individualized enemies can find its way into the formation of "shared enemies." See Vamik D. Volkan, MD, *The Need to have Enemies and Allies: From Clinical Practice to International Relationships*, 17–23. On the other hand, Rob Walker points out that the process through which the enemy is identified and constructed is not just a matter of the psychological quirks and misperceptions of decision-makers. It involves a much more complex historical process in which other societies are judged to be similar to, or different from, one's own. It involves "accounts of the other" that are racist; that are religious or ideological negations; and that are embraced in order to legitimize political processes at home. Rob Walker, "Canadian Security Policy and the Language of War and Peace," unpublished paper, University of Victoria, 1988, 82. Sue Mansfield and Mary Bowen Hall point out, however, that the human need to have an adversary, the tendency to project our own hostility and aggressiveness on an enemy, and the warrior-like desire to engage in combat against an equal and worthy opponent are all basic human characteristics that can affect the way in which a threat is perceived. *Some Reasons for War: How Families, Myths & Warfare are Connected*, 57, 101.

61 Confidential source, January, 1969.

62 *Hansard*, 14 June 1983, 26324.

63 Lieutenant-General Charles Belzile, CIIPS transcripts, 1987, 443.

64 In this context, Diefenbaker mentioned "freedom" six times in one short paragraph of another draft for a speech. JGD Centre, Diefenbaker Speech Series Collection, vol. 30, file 779, untitled draft of speech, 20.

For a flavour of his frequent remarks on freedom-loving nations, see also vol. 30, file 779, Speech to Michigan University, Lansing, USA, 7 June 1959, 6, 18.

65 DHist, Raymont Papers, 73/1223, series 1, file 768, "Canadian Defence Policy 07/29/63–03/23/64," Draft of speech by Douglas Harkness for the House of Commons, 13 September 1961, 18.

66 DEA, *Statements and Speeches* 58/19, Sidney Smith, "Canada and NATO" to the Life Insurance Officers Association, Montreal, 27 May 1958, 2.

67 Ad Hoc Committee on Defence Policy, 65 [secret – Canadian eyes only].

68 DEA, *Statements and Speeches*, Paul Martin, secretary of state for External Affairs, "Prospects for Peacekeeping," 17 November 1965, 8; see also similar comments by Marcel Cadieux in DEA, 27-1-1 USA, "Canada-US Defence Relations in 1965," 24 June 1965 [confidential].

69 *Hansard*, 14 June 1983, 26322. The sentiment that the United States could not possibly be conceived of as a threat was oft repeated during the cruise missile testing debate in the House of Commons. As one member of Parliament put it: "The objectives of the United States, one of the superpowers, is peace. The US protects people. The Americans have no ambitions to take over the world. The declared objective of the Soviet Union, of communism, is world domination." Mr. Taylor, MP, *Hansard*, 14 June 1983, 26355.

70 On the tendency to see all adversaries as similar and to believe that whoever caused the last war may cause the next one, see Jervis, *Perception and Misperception in International Politics*, 244, 267. Jervis points out that beliefs about the origins of the Second World War seemed to make the NATO allies more apt to see Russia and China as aggressors to whom few concessions could safely be made.

71 Charles Nixon interview, CIIPS transcripts, 530.

72 Geoff Johnson, "Mis-speak," *Ottawa Citizen*, 18 March 1982.

73 Ad Hoc Committee on Defence Policy, 45 [secret – Canadian eyes only].

74 PCO, STAFEUR study, February 1969, 44 [secret – Canadian eyes only].

75 Confidential memo, 14 May 1971 [confidential].

76 Jervis, *Perception and Misperception in International Politics*, 168, 288–310.

77 PCO, Cabinet Conclusions, 24 October 1962, 2 [secret].

78 Paul McRae's study, 17

79 Comments of Donald Macdonald, Eric Kierans, and the minister of Consumer and Corporate Affairs in PCO, Cabinet Conclusions, 1 November 1968, 3 [secret]. On the other hand, the minister of External Affairs, Mitchell Sharp, agreed that, "the Czechoslovak invasion

had been a sign of weakness, not strength within the Soviet bloc." He argued, however, that, "it was important that there should be a reaffirmation of the principle of collective defence and no weakening of NATO ... If the government did nothing at this stage, other members would likely interpret this to mean that Canada was in the process of withdrawal from NATO since there had not been a more serious threat to the Alliance than the invasion of Czechoslovakia"; 2. In the same discussion, Prime Minister Trudeau proposed that, when considering whether Canada should earmark its CF-5 squadrons as part of its military contribution to NATO, Cabinet ministers should not enter into a discussion of how events in Czechoslovakia should be interpreted in that regard. The prime minister's openness to interpreting incoming evidence differently was also evident in his comments to reporters in July 1968: "Perhaps what is happening in Czechoslovakia could be interpreted to indicate that certain countries, members of the Warsaw Pact would be prepared to pull out of that if other members of NATO were prepared to pull out of NATO. Or you could argue to the contrary that the USSR's new show of strength should be an incentive to us not to pull out of NATO. In other words it is the sort of thing you can argue both ways." DEA, 27-1-1, *verbatim* record of Trudeau's press conference on arrival at Uplands after tour of Arctic, 29 July 1968.

80 During a 1983 press conference, Trudeau mentioned the impact of the downing of the KAL airliner on his own thinking about the threat. He explained that, in part, his peace initiative was undertaken because, "I think there has been a bit of a blitz since the Korean Airline disaster, a hardening of the dialogue, followed by a NATO statement." As he saw it, "until the Korean airline thing happened," world leaders such as Reagan, Thatcher, Mitterrand, and himself had been intent on seeking arms control negotiations, as agreed upon at the Williamsburg summit. The peace initiative, therefore, was part of "the dynamics of what we had wanted to do at Williamsburg" before the downing of the KAL airliner. Library of Parliament, "Transcript of the Prime Minister's Interview with a Group of American Journalists," Washington, 15 December 1983. See also McRae's study, 17.

81 Paul McRae's study, 10.

82 For example, see John Diefenbaker's comments in Cabinet during the Cuban missile crisis that certain military leaders in the United States appeared determined to fight the USSR, PCO, Cabinet Conclusions, 24 October 1962, 2 [secret]; for brief remarks on the way in which McCarthyism seemed to sour Lester Pearson's attitude to the United States, see English, *Shadow of Heaven: The Life of Lester Pearson, 1949–1972*, vol. 2, 88–9; see Trudeau's comments in Cabinet in 1969 (after

the Soviet invasion of Czechoslovakia) that "it should be the primary concern of the Canadian Government to ensure that Canadian soil was not used to assist or abet a first strike by United States military forces." PCO, Cabinet Conclusions, 20 November 1969, 2 [secret]; and see McRae's commentary to Trudeau that President Reagan "constantly belittles the power of his own military, and at the same time, enhances the Soviet threat." As McRae saw it, Reagan dangerously downplayed "America's might," compared to the Soviet Union's military capabilities, and the president's ideas (e.g., about a "window of vulnerability") were "dangerous nonsense." Paul McRae's study, 12.

83 Arthur Menzies, CIIPS transcripts, 1987, 709.

84 For a similar analysis, see Jervis, *Perception and Misperception in International Politics*, 204. For a short description of Canada's civil defence plans in the event of nuclear war, see DND Hist, no. 82/80, CFP 200, Defence planning guidance (U) (Shortened Version), chap. 3, sec. 7, 2 December 1970, 41–2 [secret].

85 *Ibid*, 185.

86 NA, MG 32 B19, Douglas Harkness Papers, vols. 15 and 28, file 42–66, draft of letter from Douglas Harkness to Joan Buffey, 13 December 1962, 4.

87 The idea that leaders have wanted to make the use of nuclear weapons a rational defence strategy because of deep psychological needs is explored by Morris Bradley, "Conflict Dynamics and Conflict Resolution," *The Nuclear Mentality: A Psychosocial Analysis of the Arms Race*, 50.

88 "When a person acknowledges that a bit of evidence contradicts his beliefs and is not satisfied merely to put it to one side, he may engage in bolstering – seeking new information and considerations that support his views ... Bolstering usually refers to the development of new arguments and data, but it can also be applied to the rearranging of attitudes in order to decrease the impact of the discrepant information." Jervis, *Perception and Misperception in International Politics*, 294.

89 On the tendency of decision-makers to be slow to alter their beliefs and to undergo "premature cognitive closure," see Jervis, *Perception and Misperception in International Politics*, 187.

90 Hanna Segal, "Political Thinking: Psychoanalytical Perspectives," *The Nuclear Mentality: A Psychosocial Analysis of the Arms Race*, 45.

91 PCO, Cabinet Conclusions, 15 October 1958, 11.

92 PCO, Cabinet Conclusions, 20 May 1969, 3 [secret].

93 PCO, Cabinet Conclusions, 22 July 1970, 3 [secret].

94 Documented comments indicating that Diefenbaker and Green were inclined to question military opinion are in JGD Centre, vol. 44, file 865, Draft of June 1960 speech, 6; PCO, Cabinet Conclusions, 23, 24,

26 October 1962 and NA, Arnold Heeney Papers, MG 30 E 144, vol. 2, File "Memoir 1960, chapter 15, diary #2." Robinson, Nash and Ignatieff also remark on these tendencies in *Diefenbaker's World*, 20, 22; *Kennedy & Diefenbaker*, 100–101; and the CIIPS transcript, 104, 118. Ivan Head's fundamental criticisms of the STAFEUR report and the Defence Review are found throughout his study, PCO, Cabinet Document 310/69 (165–461), "Canadian Defence Policy: A Study," 28 March 1969 [secret – Canadian eyes only]. Donald Macdonald's detailed criticism of the main points and underlying assumptions of the "Report of the Task Force on Europe" and the "Defence Policy Review" are found in PCO, Cabinet Document 302/69, 27 March 1969 [secret]. Synopses of Eric Kierans's critical attitude to defence priorities and military expenditures are found in the Cabinet Conclusions, and in memoranda succinctly describing the different Cabinet Minister's attitudes to withdrawal. For example, see PCO, Cabinet Conclusions, 1 November 1968, 3 [secret] and PCO, Cabinet Document 165–551, Memorandum describing meeting of the Cabinet Committee on External Policy and Defence, "Defence Policy Review," 11 March 1969 [secret]. A flavour of Kierans' attitude to military doctrine is also found in the transcript of his speech to a fundraising dinner for the Liberal association, Nanaimo, B.C., 25 January 1969. As well, there is considerable documented evidence of Pierre Trudeau's tendency to question established military doctrine in the confidential sources cited in chaps. 4 and 7; PCO, Cabinet Conclusions, 1, 7, 21 November 1968; 22 July 1970; and in the transcript of his speech entitled "The Relation of Defence Policy to Foreign Policy," in DEA, *Statements and Speeches*, No. 69/8, Speech to the Alberta Liberal Association, 12 April 1969. From 1968–71, although other ministers were also inclined to question Canada's traditional military commitments to NATO and to query established military doctrine, they were outside the inner core of defence decision-making; hence their arguments are not dealt with here. For a flavour of the debate in Cabinet, however, see the memoranda describing comments by ministers Otto Lang, Gerard Pelletier, Lewis Richardson, and Paul Hellyer in PCO, Cabinet Document 165–551, Memorandum describing meeting of the Cabinet Committee on External Policy and Defence, "Defence Policy Review," 11 March 1969 [secret] and PCO, Memorandum for the Prime Minister, "Ministers' Views on Defence Policy," 18 March 1969 [secret].

95 PCO, Cabinet Document 310/69, "Canadian Defence Policy: A Study," March 1969, 18 [secret – Canadian eyes only].

96 Paul McRae's study, 3.

97 Interview by author with Basil Robinson, 14 September 1992. Robinson also speculates that Norman Robertson's comparatively early exposure

to the peace movement stemmed from his strong interest and close reading of developments in UK politics. Similarly, J.L. Granatstein points out that Robertson's anti-nuclear sentiments reflected those put forth in an article in the British magazine, *The Spectator*, 1 May 1959. The author, Christopher Hollis, argued that the H-bomb had changed the nature of war and, even if the West was the nominal victor, "there is no chance that the pattern of our national life with which we entered the war will still survive when we emerge from it." Just two days before Howard Green became Minister of External Affairs, a memorandum that Basil Robinson attached to Hollis's article informed Prime Minister Diefenbaker that "Mr. Robertson wishes you to know that his personal views coincide with those of the author of the article." J.L. Granatstein, *A Man of Influence: Norman Robertson and Canadian Statecraft, 1929–1968*, 338–9.

98 In this regard, as Jervis points out, people tend to absorb the values and beliefs that dominate the climate of opinion when they first begin to think seriously about an issue. *Perception and Misperception in International Politics*, 253.

99 Precise information about the possible effects of nuclear weapons on the general population was not widely circulated until the early 1960s. The public was not generally aware until 1963, for example, of the fact that each CF-104 in Europe could carry a one-megaton bomb, equivalent to one million tons of TNT, or fifty times as powerful as the bomb which destroyed Hiroshima. As Dave McIntosh explained in 1963, "The RCAF division in Europe, with eight squadrons of 18 CF-104s each, would thus have the power to destroy 144 cities at one blow." Dave McIntosh, "Canadian CF-104s in Europe can carry 'Million-Ton' Bomb," *Toronto Star*, 16 April 1963.

100 *Hansard*, 25 January 1963, 3128.

101 Library of Parliament, Transcript of the Prime Minister's "Reflections on Peace and Security" to the Conference on Strategies for Peace and Security, University of Guelph, Ontario, 27 October 1983.

102 Library of Parliament, Transcript of the Prime Minister's Interview with a Group of American Journalists, Washington, 15 December 1983. See also J.L. Granatstein and R. Bothwell, *Pirouette: Pierre Trudeau and Canadian Foreign Policy*; Harald von Riekhoff and John Sigler, "The Trudeau Peace Initiative: The Politics of Reversing the Arms Race," in *Canada Among Nations*, 1988, 50–69.

103 According to J. L. Granatstein and R. Bothwell, *Pirouette: Pierre Trudeau and Canadian Foreign Policy*, 363–76. They also point out that Trudeau spoke with Helen Caldicott, an Australian doctor opposed to nuclear weapons, and lunched with Robert McNamara, a former US defence secretary who advocated drastic changes in nuclear policies.

104 General Foulkes on CBC TV, *Citizen's Forum*, 6 November 1960, transcribed in *News and Views*, no. 92, 22 November 1960, 10.

105 PCO, Cabinet Conclusions, 15 October 1958, 10 [secret].

106 PCO, Cabinet Conclusions, 23 August 1961, 6–7 [secret].

107 JGD Centre, Prime Minister's Office Papers, vol. 52, "Extract from Mr. Diefenbaker's Statement to the NATO Heads of Government Meeting, 16 December 1957," 1 [secret].

108 PCO, Cabinet Document 165–551, Memorandum describing meeting of the Cabinet Committee on External Policy and Defence, "Defence Policy Review," 11 March 1969, 2 [secret].

109 DEA, *Statements and Speeches*, no. 69/3, Mitchell Sharp's Speech to Carleton University, 20 February 1969, 4. As in this speech, the term "collective security" was often used interchangeably with the concept of "collective defence." John Holmes analyses the prevailing belief in collective defence, as opposed to collective security, and the difference between these concepts in "Canada and Collective Security," in *Canada: A Middle-Aged Power*.

110 For example, on the lessons of World War II for choosing not to withdraw the CFE, see PCO, Cabinet Document 158/69 (165–163), Report of the Special Task Force on Europe, "Canada and Europe," February 1969, 24 [confidential – Canadian eyes only]. On the implications of the war's lessons for deciding in favour of testing the cruise missile see, for example, Minister Garnet Bloomfield's admonitions to members of the House of Commons, *Hansard*, 14 June 1983, 26359.

111 According to Jervis, "This is most dramatically true of generational effects, where a whole age-band of people is influenced by the events and opinions that are salient when it first becomes politically aware." *Perception and Misperception in International Politics*, 260.

112 For these sorts of interpretations of the lessons from the Korean War, see CIIPS transcripts, John Holmes, 43, 45; Charles Nixon, former deputy minister of National Defence, 528–32; Arthur Menzies, 703; and Denis Stairs, "The Political Culture of Canadian Foreign Policy," *Canadian Journal of Political Science*.

113 Steven Kull, *Minds at War*, 151, 161. "Out-of-area" refers to locations outside the allies' geographical territory (e.g., Vietnam, Yugoslavia). For different interpretations by Canadian decision-makers of the lessons of Indochina (e.g., a "conservative," Paul Martin versus a "liberal-moderate," Lester Pearson), see Douglas Ross, *In the Interests of Peace: Canada and Vietnam, 1954–1973*, 6, 10–14, 268–71.

114 Mitchell Sharp, secretary of state for External Affairs, "NATO from a Canadian Perspective," *Statements and Speeches*, no. 69/4, Canadian Institute of International Affairs Conference, Calgary, 1 March 1969, 3.

115 J. Gilles Lamontagne, *Hansard*, 14 June 1983, 26324.

116 *Ibid.*, 26321. He added: "For it to work, NATO must possess the means to respond to aggression, both conventional and nuclear. The maintenance of a credible deterrent has helped to make western Europe strong and to keep the peace between East and West for over 30 years, despite circumstances that were often very difficult."

117 Jervis, *Perception and Misperception in International Politics*, 346.

118 Alastair Mackie, "Military Pomp and Nuclear Circumstance," *The Nuclear Mentality: A Psychosocial Analysis of the Arms Race*, 111–12. For further analysis of the military mind, as opposed to the diplomat's psychological make-up, see the "ants" versus "bees" analogy in Legault and Fortmann *A Diplomacy of Hope: Canada and Disarmament, 1945–1988*, 7–34.

119 Only Lieutenant-General E.L.M. Burns, Major-General Leonard Johnson, and Admiral Robert Falls openly criticized the principal tenets of Canadian defence policy, including different permutations of nuclear deterrence: E.L.M. Burns, *General Mud*; *Megamurder*; Leonard Johnson, *A General for Peace* and "Canada and NATO: What Price Symbolism," in *Defending Europe: Options for Security*, ed. Derek Paul, 50–63. See also Maurice Archdeacon and Robert Falls, "Decision making in NATO," in *Defending Europe: Options for Security*, 246–60; and the interview of Robert Falls, CIIPS transcripts, 1987.

120 On these tendencies within a policy bureaucracy and SOPs, see Steinbrunner, *The Cybernetic Theory of Decision*, 71–2, 122.

121 Confidential memo, 17 May 1968 [confidential].

122 DEA, file 4901-Y-40, vol. 58, "The Defence Debate I: Adequacy of the Deterrent," Ambassador Heeney, Washington to the secretary of state for External Affairs, 8 March 1960, 3 [secret].

123 NA, Douglas Harkness Papers, MG 32 B19, vols. 15 and 28, file 42–66, Draft of letter from Douglas Harkness to Joan Buffey, 13 December 1962, 4.

124 Morris Bradley, "Conflict Dynamics and Conflict Resolution," in *The Nuclear Mentality: A Psychosocial Analysis of the Arms Race*, 50.

125 Defensive avoidance occurs in many common forms including procrastination, buck passing, wishful thinking, and bolstering. Its functional value lies in the temporary reduction of high conflict, enabling the decision-maker either to continue living up to past commitments in the face of distressing challenges or to make a relatively unambivalent choice of a new course of action rather than remain demoralized and immobilized. For a general explanation of these denial mechanisms, see Irving Janis, *Decision-making: A Psychological Analysis of Conflict, Choice and Commitment*, chap. 4, 5.

126 PCO, Cabinet Conclusions, 25 October 1962, 3 [secret].

127 NA, Douglas Harkness Papers, MG 32 B19, vol. 57, "Unnumbered Series, 'The Nuclear Arms Crisis'."

128 PCO, Cabinet document 165–461, Ivan Head's study, 18 [secret].

129 Pierre Elliott Trudeau, "Text of the Prime Minister's Remarks in the House of Commons on Peace and Security," Ottawa, 9 February 1984, 1. Reprinted in Trudeau, *Lifting the Shadow of War*, 106.

130 Paul McRae's study, 14.

131 PCO, Cabinet Document 310/69, Ivan Head's study, 28 March 1969, 9 [secret – Canadian eyes only].

132 Paul McRae's study, 3. See also Trudeau's comments in "Reflections on Peace and Security," Transcript of the Prime Minister's Remarks to the Conference on Strategies for Peace and Security in the Nuclear Age, University of Guelph, Ontario, 27 October 1983.

133 Interview by author with Basil Robinson, 14 September 1992.

134 NA, Arnold Heeney Papers, MG 30 E 144, vol. 2, file "Memoir, 1960, chapter 15, diary #2," 20 September.

135 Paul McRae's study, 17.

CONCLUSION

1 H.W. Wells, *The Outline of History*, 1100 and cited in Trudeau, *Lifting the Shadow of War*, 128.

Bibliography

PRIMARY SOURCES

Records, Papers, Collections, and Minutes

* indicates certain records are restricted under various programs for academic research
** indicates certain records were accessed under the Access to Information Act (1982)

ARCHIVAL

Department of Foreign Affairs and International Trade, (DFAIT), formerly the Department of External Affairs (DEA)
Classified documents accessed under the programme for academic research. Cited simply as DFAIT document.* **
Declassified documents.

Department of National Defence, Directorate of History, Ottawa (DHist)
General Records
Chairman, Chiefs of Staff and Chief of Defence Staff, The Raymont Collection, Series One and Two (Raymont Papers 73/1223)
Chief of the Defence Staff Minutes
Meetings of the Chiefs of Staff Committee
Meetings of the Defence Council

Rt. Hon. John G. Diefenbaker Centre, Saskatoon, Saskatchewan (JGD Centre)
John G. Diefenbaker Papers*
Diefenbaker Speech Series Collection

National Archives of Canada, Ottawa (NA)
Marcel Cadieux Papers
Chiefs of Staff Records
H.C. Green Papers
D.S. Harkness Papers
A.D.P. Heeney Papers
Paul Hellyer Papers
L.B. Pearson Papers, Leader of the Opposition Series, 1957–63
L.B. Pearson Papers*
G. Pearkes Papers
N.A. Robertson Papers
Basil Robinson Papers

Privy Council Office, Ottawa (PCO)
Cabinet Agendas, 1959–1979
Cabinet Conclusions, 1959–1979* **
Cabinet Documents* **
Privy Council Office Records* **
Cabinet Committee on External Affairs and Defence, Conclusions* **
PCO File Index – NATO – General File

Canadian Institute for International Peace and Security, Ottawa (CIIPS)
Transcripts of interviews conducted by Roger Hill, David Cox, Nancy Gordon,
    et al., unpublished transcripts, 1987, 1–924*
Newspaper clippings

Canadian Institute for International Affairs, Toronto (CIIA)
Newspaper clippings and microfiche

Library of Parliament, Ottawa
Transcripts of Trudeau's speeches (microfiche)

GOVERNMENT DOCUMENTS

Department of Foreign Affairs and International Trade,
formerly the Department of External Affairs (DEA)
Statements and Speeches, 1957–99
Parliament. Report of the Standing Committee on Foreign Affairs and Inter-
    national Trade, *Canada and the Nuclear Challenge: Reducing the Political Value*
    of Nuclear Weapons for the Twenty-First Century, December 1998. Available at
    http://www.parl.gc.ca/InfoComDoc/36/1/FAIT/Studies/Reports/faitrp07-e.htm
Department of Foreign Affairs and International Trade, *Government Response to*
    the Recommendations, 1999. Available at *http://www.dfait-maeci.gc.ca/nucchallenge/*
    ANNEXB-e.htm

Department of National Defence (DND)
Statements and Press Releases, 1957–99
White Paper on National Defence. Ottawa 1964.
Defence in the 1970s: White Paper on Defence. Ottawa 1971.
Challenge and Commitment: A Defence Policy for Canada. Ottawa 1987.
Statement by the Honourable Marcel Masse, September 17, 1991. Ottawa 1991.
Canadian Defence Policy. Ottawa, April 1992.
1994 Defence White Paper. Ottawa, 1994.

House of Commons
Debates of the House of Parliament, *Hansard*
Parliament. Standing Committee on External Affairs and National Defence. *Fifth Report to the House Respecting Defence and External Affairs Policy.* Ottawa, 25 March 1969
Parliament. Standing Committee on External Affairs and National Defence. *Minutes and Proceedings of Evidence*, First Session, 28th Parliament, nos. 19–35.
Parliament. Special Joint Committee of the Senate and the House of Commons on Canada's Defence Policy. *Security in a Changing World.* Ottawa, 1994.
Parliament. Special Joint Committee of the Senate and the House of Commons on Canada's Defence Policy. *Minutes and Proceedings of Evidence.* Ottawa, 1994.
Parliament. Special Joint Committee Reviewing Canadian Foreign Policy. *Canada's Foreign Policy: Principles and Priorities for the Future.* Ottawa, 1994.

Interviews, Briefings, and Correspondence

* indicates off-the-record and confidential

Barrett, John, Disarmament, Arms Control and Cooperation Section, Political Affairs Division, NATO, briefing, Ottawa, March 1990; and interview, NATO HQS, October 1992*
Bentley, Bill, Lt. Col., deputy defence counsellor to the Permanent Representative of Canada to NATO interview, NATO HQS, October, 1992*
Bishop, Jim, Armaments Planning Section, Defence Support Division, NATO, interview, NATO HQS, October 1992*
Bogden, Angela, Canadian Delegation, NATO, interview, NATO HQS, October 1992
Brown, Glen, Canadian Liaison Officer, NATO, interview, October 1992*
Bruce, Dr. Erika, Office of Information and Press, NATO, discussion, NATO HQS, October 1992
Bujold, Lt. Col. Luc, SHAPE, former senior policy-planner, assistant deputy minister (Pol), NDHQ, Ottawa briefing, SHAPE, October 1992
Buteux, Paul, professor of Political Science, Winnipeg, Manitoba, briefing, Toronto, 10 March 1988*

Calder, Ken, assistant deputy minister and former director-general policy planning, Department of National Defence, briefings to the Military and Strategic Studies Conference sponsored by the Department of National Defence, Ottawa, April 1991 and April 1992*

Cameron, Robert, former assistant under-secretary of External Affairs, discussion, January 1993

de Chastelain, John, Chief of the Defence Staff, NDHQ, briefing, DFAIT, Ottawa, 12 June 1991*

Darling, Stan, member of Parliament and member of the Standing Committee on National Defence (SCOND), interview, Ottawa, 10 March 1988

Delvoie, Louis, assistant deputy minister (Pol), NDHQ, Ottawa, briefing to the Military and Strategic Studies Conference sponsored by the Department of National Defence, Ottawa, 18 April 1990 and April 1991*

Delworthy, Thomas, former Canadian ambassador to Federal Republic of Germany, briefing, Toronto, 19 April 1990

Donnelly, Chris, sovietologist-in-residence, NATO, briefing, NATO HQS, 20 June 1990

Duncan, Hedley, chief policy section, Policy Branch, SHAPE, briefing, SHAPE, October 1992

Evraire, Richard J, Lieutenant-General, Canadian ambassador to NATO, briefing, Ottawa, September 1991

Fielding, Lt. Col. Roger, Policy Branch, SHAPE, briefing, SHAPE, October 1992

Fowell, John, director, Defence Relations Division, DEA, interview, Ottawa, 17 August 1990

Furtado, Francis, defence scientist, D-Strat A, NDHQ, briefing, NDHQ, March 1990

George, Vice-Admiral Robert E, Canadian military representative to the Military Committee, briefing, October 1992

Grinius, Marius, premier secretaire, Canadian Delegation, NATO HQS, discussion, NATO HQS, 21 June 1990

Halstead, John, professor of Political Science, Carleton University and former Canadian Ambassador to NATO, briefing, Toronto, 18 April 1990*; discussions, Ottawa, March 1995 and St. John's, Newfoundland, 10 June 1997

Haydon, Admiral (ret.) Peter, Dalhousie University, discussions, Halifax, 23 August 1990 and correspondence, Fall 1990

Hayward, Robert, former news reporter for *Montreal Gazette*, correspondence, October 1990

Henry, Colonel Sean, program evaluation director, NDHQ, Ottawa, interview, NDHQ, 8 November 1990*

Hill, Roger, director of research, Canadian Institute of International Peace and Security, briefing, Ottawa, 9 March 1990

Katsirakis, George, Defence Planning and Policy, NATO, NDHQ, discussion, Halifax, 19 June 1990

Law, David, ad hoc Canadian liaison officer, NATO HQS, briefings, Toronto, 7 February 1990 and NATO HQS, 20 June 1990

Lunn, Simon, deputy secretary general of the North Atlantic Assembly, NATO HQS, briefings, Toronto, March 1989 and NATO HQS, October 1992

Lysyshyn, Ralph, deputy ambassador to the North Atlantic Council, NATO, briefing, NATO HQS, October 1992

Macdonald, Donald S, former president of the Privy Council and Cabinet minister, correspondence, March 1999

McDougall, Robert P, counsellor, NATO HQS, briefing, NATO HQS, June 1990 and interview, Toronto, September 1991

Nash, Knowlton, author and journalist, correspondence, 1991

Pearson, Geoffrey, author, former executive director of the Canadian Institute for International Peace and Security and Canadian ambassador to Moscow, interview, 7 December 1990 and discussions, 1990–99

Pearson, Mike, senior policy adviser to the minister of Foreign Affairs, DFAIT and former member of the National Liberal Caucus Research Bureau, Ottawa, discussions, October 1992, March 1994, July 1997

Pugh, John. D, Disarmament and Arms Control Section, Political Affairs Division, NATO, briefing, NATO HQS, June 1990 and October 1992

Rauf, Tariq, senior research associate, Canadian Centre for Arms Control and Disarmament, Ottawa, discussions, October 1992

Robinson, Basil (ret), former under-secretary of External Affairs, Ottawa, interview, Ottawa, September 1992

Rossignol, Michel, Research Branch, Library of Parliament, Ottawa, discussion, Ottawa, November 1994

Shea, Jamie, Dr., special projects officer, Political Affairs Division, NATO, briefing, NATO HQS, June 1990 and interview, NATO HQS, 12 July 1990*

Simmons, Robert, political advisor to U.S. Delegation, NATO, interview, Toronto, 11 March 1990*

Sippert, Erwin, defence counsellor, Defence Policy and Planning, NATO, interviews, Toronto, October 1992 and 21 June 1990*

Smith, Gordan, ambassador to the European Community, former Canadian ambassador to NATO, briefing, NATO HQS, June 1990 and interview, EC, October 1992*

Sokolsky, Joel, professor, Royal Military College, Kingston, discussions, 11 September 1990, 13 September 1998

Snyder, Denis, deputy director of International Defence Relations Division, DEA, briefing, Ottawa, 8 March 1990

van Boeschoten, Lieutenant-Colonel J.P, deputy, national military representative, NATO, interview, NATO HQS, October 1992*

von Riekhoff, Harald, professor of Political Science, Carleton University, Ottawa, briefing, CIIA, Toronto, 11 March 1988 and discussions, January 1993

Watson, Chuck, Arms Control Branch (Cdn.), SHAPE, briefing, SHAPE headquarters, 21 June 1990

SECONDARY SOURCES

Allison, Graham T., Albert Carnesale and Joseph S. Nye. *Hawks, Doves, and
Owls: An Agenda for Avoiding Nuclear War.* New York: W.W. Norton, 1985.
Archdeacon, Maurice, and Robert Falls. "Decision Making in NATO." In
Defending Europe: Options for Security, edited by Derek Paul. London: Taylor
& Francis Ltd, 1985.
Axworthy, Lloyd and Christine Stewart (on behalf of the Liberal Party of
Canada). "The Liberal Foreign Policy Handbook." Ottawa: May 1993.
Babbie, Earl. *The Practice of Social Research.* 3rd ed. Belmont, California:
Wadsworth Publishing, 1983.
Barnett, Lynn and Ian Lee, eds. *The Nuclear Mentality: A Psychosocial Analysis
of the Arms Race.* London: Pluto Press, 1989.
BBC Two program. "NATO's Inner Kosovo Conflict," 20 August 1999. Online tran-
script at *http://news.bbc.co.uk/hi/english/world/europe/newsid_425000/425468.stm*
Bell, George. "Whither Canada: Long Term Strategic Requirements." In *A
Continuing Commitment: Canada and North Atlantic Security,* edited by Alex
Morrison. Toronto: Canadian Institute of Strategic Studies, 1992.
Bland, Douglas. *The Administration of Defence Policy in Canada, 1947 to 1985.*
Kingston, Ont.: Ronald P. Frye & Company, 1987.
Blight, James G., and David Welch. *On the Brink: Americans and Soviets Reex-
amine the Cuban Missile Crisis.* 2nd ed. New York: Noonday Press, 1990.
Booth, Ken. "New Challenges and Old Mindsets: Ten Rules for Empirical
Realists." In *The Uncertain Course: New Weapons, Strategies and Mindsets,*
edited by Carl Jacobsen, Frank Kerr, George Quester. SIPRI: Oxford Uni-
versity Press, 1987.
Boutros-Ghali, Boutros. *An Agenda for Peace: Preventive Diplomacy, Peacemak-
ing, and Peace-keeping: Report of the Secretary-General Pursuant to the State-
ment Adopted by the Summit Meeting of the Security Council on 31 January
1992.* New York: United Nations, 1992.
Bradley, Morris. "Conflict Dynamics and Conflict Resolution." In *The Nuclear
Mentality: A Psychosocial Analysis of the Arms Race,* edited by Lynn Barnett
and Ian Lee. London: Pluto Press, 1989.
Brebner, John Bartlet. *North Atlantic Triangle: The Interplay of Canada, the United
States and Great Britain.* New Haven: Yale University Press, 1945.
Brewin, Andrew. *Stand on Guard: The Search for a Canadian Defence Policy.*
Toronto: McClelland and Stewart Ltd., 1965.
Bromke, Adam, and Kim Richard Nossal. "Trudeau Rides the 'Third Rail.'"
International Perspectives (May/June 1984):3–6.

Bronfenbrenner, Urie. "The Mirror-Image in Soviet-American Relations: A Social Psychologist's Report." *Journal of Social Issues* 117, no. 3 (1961):45–56.

Burns, E.L.M. *Megamurder.* Toronto: Clarke, Irwin & Company, 1966.

Burns, E.L.M. *General Mud: Memoirs of Two World Wars.* Toronto: Clarke, Irwin & Company Limited, 1970.

Buteux, Paul. *The Politics of Nuclear Consultation in NATO, 1965–1980.* Cambridge: Cambridge University Press, 1983.

Buzan, Barry. *People, States and Fear.* Chapel Hill: University of North Carolina Press, 1983.

Byers, R.B. "Canadian Defence: The Genesis of a Debate," *Current History* 83, no. 493 (May 1984):197–201.

Byers, R.B., et al. *Canada and Western Security: The Search for New Options.* Toronto: University of Toronto Press: Centre for International Studies, 1982.

Campognolo, Iona., et al. *Transformation Moment : A Canadian Vision of Common Security: The Report of the Citizens' Inquiry into Peace and Security.* Waterloo, Ont: Project Ploughshares; Toronto: Canadian Peace Alliance, 1992.

Canada 21 Council. *Canada and Common Security in the Twenty-First Century.* Toronto: Centre for International Studies, 1994.

Canadians Against War on Yugoslavia. "While We Were Sleeping." Available at *http://www.stopwar.net/*

CBC News Online, "Canada on the Attack: Daily Military Updates." Available at *http://www.cbcnews.cbc.ca/news/indepth/canadaattack/updates.html*

CBC News Online. "Canada on the Attack: The Debate." Available at *http://cbcnews.cbc.ca/news/indepth/canadaattack/debate.html*

CBC TV, The National Online. "The Question of Ground Troops," 7 April 1999. Online transcript at *http://tv.cbc.ca/national/pgminfo/kosovo2/eggleton990407.html*

CBC TV, The National Online. "Mission to Moscow," 26 April 1999. Online transcript of Axworthy's comments at *http://tv.cbc.ca/national/pgminfo/kosovo2/axworthy990426.html*

CBC TV, The National Online. "The Dilemmas of War: What Went Wrong for NATO?" 11 June 1999. Online transcript at *http://tv.cbc.ca/national/pgminfo/kosovo3/nato.html*

Clarkson, Stephen. *Canada and the Reagan Challenge.* Toronto: James Lorimer & Company Publishers, 1982.

Clarkson, Stephen. *Trudeau in Our Times.* Toronto: McClelland & Stewart, 1987.

Clearwater, John. *Canadian Nuclear Weapons: The Untold Story of Canada's Cold War Arsenal.* Toronto: Dundurn Press, 1998.

Cohen, Andrew. "Security and NATO." In *Canada Among Nations, 1994: Global Jeopardy,* edited by Maureen Appel Molot, and Harald von Riekhoff. Ottawa: Carleton University Press, 1994.

Cohen, Raymond. *Threat Perception in International Crisis.* Wisconsin: University of Wisconsin Press, 1979.

Common Security Consultants (Howard Peter Langille and Erika Simpson). CFB *Cornwallis: Canada's Peacekeeping Training Centre.* Halifax: Government of Nova Scotia, 1991. A proposal prepared for presentation by the premier of Nova Scotia to the prime minister (August 1991).

Common Security Consultants (Howard Peter Langille and Erika Simpson) and Stratman Consulting Inc. (Brigadier-General Clayton Beattie). CFB *Cornwallis: Canada's Peacekeeping Training Centre – A Blueprint for a Peacekeeping Training Centre of Excellence.* Halifax: Government of Nova Scotia 1992, reprinted in Minutes of Proceedings of the Standing Committee on National Defence and Veterans Affairs, issue no. 45 (1 April 1993).

Common Security Consultants. (Howard Peter Langille and Erika Simpson). *A 1994 Blueprint for a Canadian and Multinational Peacekeeping Training Centre at CFB Cornwallis.* Halifax: Government of Nova Scotia, 1994, reprinted in Minutes of Proceedings of the Special Joint Committee of the Senate and the House of Commons on Canada's Defence Policy, issue no. 21 (14 June 1994).

Cox, David. "The Cruise Testing Agreement." *International Perspectives* (July/August 1983): 3–5.

D'Aquino, Thomas. Address to the Royal Military College on behalf of the Business Council of National Issues. 15 June 1984.

Davis, Jerome D. "To the NATO Review: Constancy and Change in Canadian NATO Policy, 1949–1969." Washington, D.C.: Johns Hopkins University, unpublished PhD dissertation, 1973.

Dewitt, David, and John Kirton. *Canada as a Principal Power.* Toronto: John Wiley & Sons, 1983.

Diefenbaker, John D. *One Canada: The Crusading Years, 1895–1956.* Vol. 1. Toronto: Macmillan, 1975.

Diefenbaker, John D. *One Canada: The Years of Achievement 1956–1962.* Vol. 2. Toronto: Macmillan, 1976.

Diefenbaker, John D. *One Canada: The Tumultuous Years, 1962–1967.* Vol. 3 Scarborough, Ont.: Macmillan-NAL Publishing Limited, 1977.

Dobell, Peter C. *Canada's Search for New Roles.* Toronto: Oxford University Press, 1972.

Doern, B. Bruce. "The Policy-Making Philosophy of Prime Minister Trudeau and his Advisers." In *Apex of Power: The Prime Minister and Political Leadership in Canada,* edited by Thomas A. Hockin. Scarborough, Ontario: Prentice-Hall of Canada Ltd, 1971.

Douglas, W.A.B. "Why Does Canada Have Armed Forces?" *International Journal* 30, no. 3 (spring 1975): 259–83.

Dow, James. *The Arrow.* Toronto: James Lorimer & Co., 1979.

Dyer, Gwynne, and Tina Viljoen. *The Defence of Canada: In the Arms of the Empire.* Toronto: McClelland & Stewart, 1990.

Eayrs, James. "Military Policy and Middle Power: The Canadian Experience." In *Canada's Role as a Military Power*, edited by J. King Gordon. Toronto: Canadian Institute of International Affairs, Contemporary Issues Series, 1965.

Eayrs, James. *In Defence of Canada: Growing Up Allied*. Vol. 4. Toronto: University of Toronto Press, 1980.

Elworthy, Scilla, John Hamwee, and Hugh Miall. "The Assumptions of Nuclear Weapons Decision-Makers." In *The Nuclear Mentality: A Psychosocial Analysis of the Arms Race*, edited by Lynn Barnett and Ian Lee. London: Pluto Press, 1989.

English, John. *Shadow of Heaven: The Life of Lester Pearson, 1897–1948*. Vol. 1. Toronto: Lester & Orpney Dennys, 1989.

English, John. *The Worldly Years: The Life of Lester Pearson, 1949–1972*. Vol. 2. Toronto: Alfred A. Knopf Canada, 1992.

Eustace, Marilyn. *Canada's European Force, 1964–1971: Canada's Commitment to Europe*. National Security Series no. 4/82. Kingston, Ontario: Centre for International Relations, Queen's University, 1982.

Fisher, Dietrich. *Preventing War in the Nuclear Age*. Totowa, N.J.: Rowman & Allanheld, 1984.

Freedman, Lawrence. *The Evolution of Nuclear Strategy*. London: Macmillan Press, 1983.

Gaddis, John Lewis. *Strategies of Containment: A Critical Appraisal of Postwar American National Security Policy*. New York: Oxford University Press, 1982.

Galtung, Johan. *There are Alternatives! Four Roads to Peace and Security*. Chester Springs, P.A.: Dufour Editions, 1984.

Gleisner, John. "The Enemy Within." *New Internationalist* (March 1983): 26.

Gordon, Walter. *Walter Gordon: A Political Memoir*. Toronto: McClelland and Stewart, 1977.

Gordon, Walter. "The Liberal Leadership and Nuclear Weapons." In *Canada and the Nuclear Arms Race*, edited by Ernie Regehr and Simon Rosenblum. Toronto: James Lorimer and Company, 1983.

Granatstein, J.L. *A Man of Influence: Norman Robertson and Canadian Statecraft, 1929–1968*. Ottawa: Deneau, 1981.

Granatstein, J.L. *The Ottawa Men: The Civil Service Mandarins, 1935–1957*. Toronto: Oxford University Press 1982.

Granatstein, J.L. *Canada, 1957–1967: The Years of Uncertainty and Innovation*. Toronto: McClelland & Stewart, 1986.

Granatstein, J.L., ed. *Canadian Foreign Policy Since 1945: Middle Power or Satellite*. 3rd ed. Toronto: Copp Clark Publishing, 1973.

Granatstein, J.L., and Robert Bothwell. *Pirouette*. Toronto: University of Toronto Press, 1990.

Gray, Colin. *Canadian Defence Priorities: A Question of Relevance*. Toronto: Clarke, Irwin & Company, 1972.

Gwyn, Richard. *The Northern Magus: Pierre Trudeau and Canadians*. Edited by Sandra Gwyn. Toronto: McClelland and Stewart, 1980.

Haglund, David, and Olaf Mager, eds. *Homeward Bound? Allied Forces in the New Germany*. Boulder, Colo.: Westview Press, 1992.

Haglund, David, and Joel Sokolsky. *The US-Canada Security Relationship*. Boulder, Colo.: Westview Press, 1989.

Halstead, John. "A Defence Policy for Canada: the White Paper Two Years On." In *Behind the Headlines*, vol. 47, no. 2 (winter 1989–1990).

Hart, Paul. *Groupthink in Government: A Study of Small Groups and Policy Failure*. Ablasserdam: Offsetdrukkeriz Kanters B.V., 1990.

Haydon, Peter. *The Cuban Missile Crisis: Canadian Involvement Reconsidered*. Toronto: Canadian Institute for Strategic Studies, 1993.

Head, Ivan, and Pierre Trudeau. *The Canadian Way: Shaping Canada's Foreign Policy, 1968–1984*. Toronto: M&S, 1995.

Heeney, Arnold. *The Things that Are Caesar's: The Memoirs of a Canadian Public Servant*. Toronto: University of Toronto Press, 1972.

Hellyer, Paul. *Damn the Torpedoes: My Fight to Save the Canadian Forces*. Toronto: McClelland & Stewart Inc, 1990.

Hermann, Margaret G., and Charles F. Hermann. "Who Makes Foreign Policy Decisions and How: An Empirical Inquiry." *International Studies Quarterly* 33 (1989): 361–88.

Hermann, Richard K. "Analyzing Soviet Images of the United States." *Journal of Conflict Resolution* 29, no. 4 (December 1985): 665–98.

Hertzman, Lewis, John Warnock, and Thomas Hockin. *Alliances and Illusions: Canada and the NATO-NORAD Question: Odd Man Out*. Edmonton: M.G. Hurtig Ltd, 1969.

Hill, Roger. *Political Consultation in NATO*. Wellesley Papers 6/1978, Toronto: Canadian Institute of International Affairs, 1978.

Hilliker, John F. "The Politicians and the 'Pearsonalities': The Diefenbaker Government and the Conduct of Canadian External Relations." *Historical Papers*, 1984, reprinted in Granatstein, J.L. ed., *Canadian Foreign Policy: Historical Readings*. Toronto: Copp Clark Pitman Ltd, 1993.

Hockin, Thomas. *Apex of Power: The Prime Minister and Political Leadership in Canada*. Scarborough, Ont.: Prentice Hall of Canada, 1971.

Holmes, John. *Canada: A Middle-Aged Power*. Toronto: McClelland and Stewart, 1976.

Holmes, John. *The Shaping of Peace: Canada and the Search for World Order, 1943–1957*. Vols. 1 and 2. Toronto: University of Toronto Press, 1979.

Holmes, John. "Canada, NATO and Arms Control." Edited by Shannon Selin. Ottawa: Canadian Centre for Arms Control and Disarmament, 1987.

Ignatieff, George. *The Making of a Peacemonger*. Markham, Ontario: Penguin Books, 1987.

Janis, Irving. *Decision Making: A Psychological Analysis of Conflict, Choice, and Commitment*. New York: Collier Macmillan, 1977.

Janis, Irving. *Groupthink: Psychological Studies of Policy Decisions and Fiascoes.* 2nd ed. Boston: Houghton Mifflin Company, 1982.

Janis, Irving. *Crucial Decisions: Leadership in Policy-Making and Crisis.* New York: Collier Macmillan, 1989.

Jervis, Robert. *Perception and Misperception in International Politics.* Princeton: Princeton Press, 1976.

Jervis, Robert. "Cooperation Under the Security Dilemma." *World Politics* 30, no. 2, (January 1978): 167–214.

Jervis, Robert, Richard Ned Lebow, and Janice Gross Stein, eds. *Psychology and Deterrence.* Baltimore: Johns Hopkins University Press, 1985.

Jockel, Joseph T. *Canada and NATO's Northern Flank.* Toronto: Centre for International and Strategic Studies, York University, 1986.

Jockel, Joseph T. *No Boundaries Upstairs: Canada, the US, and the Origins of North American Air Defence, 1945–78.* Vancouver: University of British Columbia, 1987.

Jockel, Joseph T., and Joel J. Sokolsky. "Defence White Paper Lives Again," *International Perspectives* 18, no. 4 (July/August 1989): 5–8.

Johnson, Leonard V. "Canada and NATO: What Price Symbolism?" In *Defending Europe: Options for Security,* edited by Derek Paul. London: Taylor & Francis Ltd, 1985.

Johnson, Leonard V. *A General for Peace.* Toronto: Lorimer, 1987.

Keating, Tom. *Canada and World Order.* Toronto: McClelland and Stewart, 1993.

Keating, Tom, and Larry Pratt. *Canada, NATO and the Bomb: The Western Alliance in Crisis.* Edmonton: Hurtig Publishers, 1988.

Kelman, Herbert C. *International Behaviour: A Social Psychological Analysis.* New York: Holt, Rinehart and Winston, 1965.

Kennedy, Robert F. *Thirteen Days: A Memoir of the Cuban Missile Crisis.* New York: Norton, 1968.

Kull, Steven. *Minds at War: Nuclear Reality and the Inner Conflicts of Defense Policy-makers.* New York: Basic Books, 1988.

LaMarsh, Judy. *Memoirs of a Bird in a Gilded Cage.* Toronto: McClelland and Stewart Pocketbook, 1970.

Langille, Howard Peter. *Changing the Guard: Canada's Defence in a World in Transition.* Toronto: University of Toronto Press, 1990.

Langille, Howard Peter, and Erika Simpson. "Peaceful Conversion: A Training Centre for Peacekeepers." *Ploughshares Monitor* (December 1991).

Larson, Deborah Welch. *Origins of Containment: A Psychological Explanation.* Princeton: Princeton University Press, 1985.

Larson, Deborah Welch. "Problems of Content Analysis in Foreign-Policy Research: Notes from the Study of the Origins of Cold War Belief Systems." *International Studies Quarterly* 32, no. 2 (June 1988): 241–55.

Legault, Albert. *Deterrence and the American Alliance.* Toronto: Canadian Institute of International Affairs, 1966.

Legault, Albert, and Michel Fortmann. *A Diplomacy of Hope: Canada and Disarmament, 1945–1988*. Kingston: McGill-Queen's University Press, 1992.

Lentner, Howard. "Foreign Policy Decision-making: The Case of Canada and Nuclear Weapons." *World Politics* 29, no. 1 (October 1976): 29–66.

Lijphart, Arend. "Comparative Politics and the Comparative Method." *American Political Science Review* 65 (September 1971): 682–93.

Little, Richard, and Steve Smith. *Belief Systems and International Relations*. New York: Oxford University Press, 1988.

Lloyd, Trevor. *Canada in World Affairs 1957–1959*. Toronto: Oxford University Press, 1968.

Lyon, Peyton. "Independent Control of Nuclear Weapons?" *Canadian Commentator* (September 1962): 7–8

Lyon, Peyton. *Canada in World Affairs*. Toronto: Oxford University Press, 1968.

Lyon, Peyton. *NATO as a Diplomatic Instrument*. Toronto: The Atlantic Council of Canada, 1970.

Mackie, Alastair. "Military Pomp and Nuclear Circumstance." In *The Nuclear Mentality: A Psychosocial Analysis of the Arms Race*, edited by Lynn Barnett, et al. London: Pluto Press 1989.

Macmillan, Margaret, and David Sorenson, eds. *Canada and NATO: Uneasy Past, Uncertain Future*. Waterloo: University of Waterloo Press, 1990.

Mandelbaum, Michael. *The Nuclear Revolution: International Politics Before and After Hiroshima*. Cambridge, UK: Cambridge University Press, 1981.

Mansfield, Susan, and Mary Bowen Hall. *Some Reasons for War: How Families, Myths and Warfare Are Connected*. New York: Thomas Y. Crowell, 1988.

Martin, Lawrence. *The Presidents and the Prime Ministers*. Toronto: Doubleday, 1982.

Martin, Paul. *A Very Public Life*. Vols. 1–3. Ottawa: Deneau, 1983.

McCaffrey, Diana, and Katherine Starr, eds. "Consequences of Kosovo – Views from Western Europe and Canada." United States Information Agency, Office of Research and Media Reaction, 9 July 1999. Available at *http://www.usia.gov/admin/005/wwwh9709.html*

McDougall, Barbara, et al. *Canada and NATO: The Forgotten Ally?* Washington: Institute for Foreign Policy Analysis, Brassey's, 1992.

McIntosh, David. *Ottawa Unbuttoned*. Toronto: Stoddart, 1987.

McKinsey, Lauren, and Kim Richard Nossal. *America's Alliances and Canadian-American Relations*. Toronto: Summerhill Press, 1988.

McLin, Jon B. *Canada's Changing Defense Policy, 1957–1963: The Problems of a Middle Power in Alliance*. Baltimore: Johns Hopkin Press, 1967.

Middlemiss, D.W., and J. L. Sokolsky. *Canadian Defence: Decisions and Determinants*. Toronto, Harcourt Brace Jovanovic Canada Inc, 1989.

Minifie, James M. *Peacemaker or Powder-Monkey: Canada's Role in a Revolutionary World*. Toronto: McClelland and Stewart, 1964.

Morgan, Patrick. *Theories and Approaches to International Politics*. 2nd ed. Palo Alto, California: Page-Ficklin Publications, 1975.

Morgenthau, Hans. *Politics Among Nations.* 6th ed. New York: Alfred A. Knopf, 1985.

Morrison, Alex, ed. *A Continuing Commitment: Canada and North Atlantic Security.* Toronto: Canadian Institute of Strategic Studies, 1992.

Morton, Desmond. "Defence Policy for a Nice Country." *Peace and Security* 5, no. 2 (summer 1990): 2–3.

Munton, Don. "Going Fission: Tales and Truths about Canada's Nuclear Weapons." *International Journal* 51, no. 3 (summer 1996): 506–28.

Naidu, M.V. "Canada, NATO and the Cruise missile." *Peace Research* 15, no. 2 (June 1983):1–12.

Nash, Knowlton. *Kennedy and Diefenbaker: Fear and Loathing Across the Canadian Border.* Toronto: McClelland and Stewart, Inc, 1990.

Newman, Peter. C. *Renegade in Power.* Toronto: McClelland and Stewart, 1963.

Nicholson, Patrick. *Vision and Indecision.* Don Mills, Ont.: Longmans Canada Limited, 1968.

Nossal, Kim Richard. "A European Nation? The Life and Times of Atlanticism in Canada." In *Making a Difference? Canada's Foreign Policy in a Changing World Order,* edited by John English and Norman Hillmer. Toronto: University of Toronto, 1977.

Nossal, Kim Richard. *The Politics of Canadian Foreign Policy.* 2nd ed. Scarborough, Ont.: Prentice-Hall Canada Inc, 1989.

Osgood, Charles E. "Suggestions for Winning the Real War with Communism." *Journal of Conflict Resolution* 3 (December 1959): 295–325.

Pearson, Geoffrey. "Trudeau Peace Initiative Reflections." *International Perspectives* (March/April 1985): 3–6.

Pearson, Geoffrey. *Seize the Day: Lester B. Pearson and Crisis Diplomacy.* Ottawa: Carlton University Press, 1993.

Pearson, Lester B. *Diplomacy in a Nuclear Age.* Toronto: S. J. Reginald Saunders, 1959.

Pearson, Lester B. *Words and Occasions.* Toronto: University of Toronto Press, 1967.

Pearson, Lester B. *Mike: The Memoirs of the Right Honourable Lester B. Pearson.* Edited by John A. Munro and Alex I. Inglis. Vol. 1, 1897–1948, vol. 2, 1948–1957, vol. 3, 1957–1968. Toronto: University of Toronto Press, c1972–c1975.

Peden, Murray. *Fall of an Arrow.* Stittsville: Canada's Wings, 1978.

Pratt, Cranford. "Dominant Class Theory and Canadian Foreign Policy." *International Journal* 39, no. 1 (winter 1983–1984): 99–135.

Preston, Richard A. "Two Centuries in the Shadow of the Behemoth: The Effect on the Canadian Psyche." *International Journal* 31, no. 4 (autumn 1976): 423–33.

Pross, Paul A. *Group Politics and Public Policy.* Toronto: Oxford University Press, 1981

Reay, Gordon. "The Canadian Army and Atlantic Security." In *A Continuing Commitment: Canada and North Atlantic Security,* edited by Alex Morrison. Toronto: Canadian Institute of Strategic Studies, 1992.

Regehr, Ernie, and Simon Rosenblum, eds., *Canada and the Nuclear Arms Race.* Toronto: James Lorimer and Company Publishers, 1983.

Reid, Escott. *Time of Fear and Hope: The Making of the North Atlantic Treaty, 1947–1949.* Toronto: McClelland and Stewart, 1977.

Rempel, Roy. "Canada's Troop Deployments in Germany: Twilight of a Forty-Year Presence." In *Homeward Bound: Allied Forces in the New Germany,* edited by David Haglund and Olaf Mager Boulder. Colorado: Westview Press, 1992.

Rempel, Roy. *Counterweights: The Failure of Canada's German and European Policy, 1955–1995.* Montreal & Kingston: McGill-Queen's University Press, 1996.

Richter, James G. "Perpetuating the Cold War: Domestic Sources of International Behaviour." *Political Science Quarterly* 107, no. 2 (1992): 271–302.

Rigby, Ken, et al. "Factors Predisposing Individuals to Support Nuclear Disarmament: An International Perspective." *Journal of Peace Research* 27, no. 3 (1990): 321–30.

Ritchie, Charles. *Storm Signals.* Toronto: Macmillan, 1983.

Robinson, Basil. *Diefenbaker's World: A Populist in Foreign Affairs.* Toronto: University of Toronto Press, 1989.

Roche, Senator Douglas (chairman, Middle Powers Initiative). "Analysis of NATO Action on Nuclear Weapons," 28 April, 1999. Available at *http://sen.parl.gc.ca/droche/*

Rose, Christopher. "Canada: Government Policy Towards NATO." In *Semi-Alignment and Western Security,* edited by Nils Orvik. Kent: Croom Helm Ltd, 1986.

Rosenblum, Simon. *Misguided Missiles: Canada, the Cruise and Star Wars.* Toronto: James Lorimer and Company Publishers, 1985.

Ross, Douglas. *In the Interests of Peace: Canada and Vietnam, 1954–1973.* Toronto: University of Toronto Press, 1984.

Rossignol, Michel. "Peacekeeping Training Centres," Ottawa: Library of Parliament, Political and Social Affairs Division, 26 October 1992.

Sapardanis, Christopher. "'The World Is Entitled to Ask Questions': The Trudeau Peace Initiative Reconsidered." *International Journal* 41, no. 1 (winter 1985–1986): 129–58.

Segal, Hanna. "Political Thinking: Psychoanalytical Perspectives." In *The Nuclear Mentality: A Psychosocial Analysis of the Arms Race.* London: Pluto Press, 1989.

Sevigny, Pierre. *This Game of Politics.* Toronto: McClelland and Steward Limited, 1965.

Sharp, Jane. "Arms Control and Alliance Commitments." *Political Science Quarterly* 100, no. 4 (winter 1985–1986): 239–58.

Sharp, Jane. "After Reykjavik: Arms Control and the Allies." *International Affairs* 63, no. 2 (spring 1987): 649–68.

Sharp, Mitchell. *Which Reminds Me: A Memoir.* Toronto: University of Toronto Press, 1993.

Simon, Herbert. *Models of Man: Social and Rational*. New York: John Wiley and Sons, Inc, 1957.

Simpson, Erika. "Redefining Security." In *The McNaughton Papers*. vol. 1. Toronto: Canadian Institute for Strategic Studies, 1991.

Simpson, Erika. "Canada's Defence Costs will Jump with NATO Expansion." *Peace Research* 30, no. 1 (February 1998): 1–10.

Simpson, Erika. "New Ways of Thinking about Nuclear Weapons and Canada's Defence Policy." In *Diefenbaker's Legacy*, edited by D.C. Story and R. Bruce Shepard. Regina: Canadian Plains Research Centre, 1998.

Simpson, Erika. "The Looming Costs of NATO Expansion in the 21st Century," *International Journal* 54, no. 2 (spring 1999): 324–39.

Simpson, Erika. "The Principles of Liberal Internationalism According to Lester Pearson." *Journal of Canadian Studies* 34, no. 1 (spring 1999): 64–77.

Simpson, Erika. "Canada and the UN Security Council: New Strategies to Advance International and National Security." *Peace Research* 31, no. 2 (June 1999): 79–99.

Simpson, Erika. "Canada's NATO Commitment: Current Controversies, Past Debates, and Future Issues." In *Behind the Headlines* 57, no. 2, winter 1999–2000.

Simpson, Erika. "Games, Strategies, and Human Security." In *Human Security*, edited by M.V. Naidu. Winnipeg: Canadian Peace Research and Education Association and the Canadian Centre for Foreign Policy Development, forthcoming 2000.

Singer, J. David. "The Level-of-Analysis Problem." In *The International System*, edited by Klaus Knorr and Sydney Verba. Princeton: Princeton University Press, 1961.

Smith, Denis. *Diplomacy of Fear: Canada and the Cold War 1941–1948*. Toronto: University of Toronto Press, 1988.

Smith, Denis. *Rogue Tory: The Life and Legend of John G. Diefenbaker*. Toronto: MacFarlane Walter & Ross, 1995.

Snyder, Glen. "'Prisoner's Dilemma' and 'Chicken' Models in International Relations." *International Studies Quarterly* 15, no. 1 (March 1971): 66–103.

Snyder, Glen H. "The Security Dilemma in Alliance Politics." *World Politics* 36, no. 4 (July 1984): 461–95.

Snyder, Glen, and Paul Diesing. *Conflict Among Nations*. Princeton: Princeton University Press, 1977.

Snyder, Richard, H.B. Bruick, and Burt Sapin. *Foreign Policy Decision-Making*. New York: Free Press of Glencoe, 1962.

Sokolsky, Joel J. "Trends in United States Strategy and the 1987 White Paper on Defence" *International Journal* 42, no. 4 (Autumn 1987): 675–706.

Sokolsky, Joel J. "A Seat at the Table: Canada and its Alliances." In *Canada's Defence: Perspectives on Policy in the Twentieth Century*, edited by B.C. Hunt, and R.G. Haycock. Toronto: Copp Clark Pitman Ltd, 1993.

Sokolsky, Joel J., and Jockel, Joseph. *Canada and Collective Security: Odd Man Out*. New York: Praeger, 1986.

Somerville, David. *Trudeau Revealed by His Actions and Words*. Richmond Hill, Ontario: BMG Publishers, 1978.

Stairs, Denis. "The Political Culture of Canadian Foreign Policy." *Canadian Journal of Political Science* 15, no. 4 (December 1982): 667–90.

Stein, Janice Gross. "The Misperception of Threat: Building Politics into Psychology." *Political Psychology* 9, no. 2 (1988): 245–71.

Steinbrunner, John. *The Cybernetic Theory of Decision*. Princeton: Princeton University Press, 1974.

Stewart, Walter. *Shrug: Trudeau in Power*. Toronto: New Press, 1971.

Stoessinger, John G. *Crusaders & Pragmatists: Movers of American Foreign Policy*. New York: W.W. Norton & Company, 1979.

Story, D.C., and R. Bruce Shepard, eds. *Diefenbaker's Legacy*. Regina: Canadian Plains Research Centre, 1998.

Stursberg, Peter. *Diefenbaker: Leadership Gained, 1956–1962*. Toronto: University of Toronto Press, 1975.

Stursberg, Peter. *Diefenbaker: Leadership Lost, 1962–1967*. Toronto: University of Toronto Press, 1976.

Stursberg, Peter. *Lester Pearson and the Dream of Unity*. Toronto: Doubleday, 1978.

Stursberg, Peter. *Lester Pearson and the American Dilemma*. Toronto: Doubleday, 1980.

Sutherland, R. J. "Canada's Long Term Strategic Situation." *International Journal* 17, no. 3 (summer 1962): 199–223.

Swift, Jamie. *Odd Man Out: The Life and Times of Eric Kierans*. Toronto: Douglas & McIntyre, 1988.

Thériault, Gérald, et al. "What Is to Be Done?: Canada's Military Security in the 1990s." *Peace and Security* 5, no. 2 (summer 1990): 2–6.

Thordarson, Bruce. *Trudeau and Foreign Policy*. Toronto: Oxford University Press, 1972.

Trudeau, Pierre Elliott. *Lifting the Shadow of War*. Edited by David C. Crenna. Edmonton, Alberta: Hurtig Publishers, 1987.

Trudeau, Pierre Elliott. *Memoirs*. Toronto: McClelland & Stewart Ltd, 1994.

Trudeau, Pierre Elliott, and Head, Ivan. *The Canadian Way*. Toronto: McClelland & Stewart Inc, 1995.

Tucker, Michael. "Canada and Arms Control: Perspectives and Trends." *International Journal* 36 no. 3 (summer 1981): 635–56.

Volkan, Vamik D. *The Need to Have Enemies and Allies: From Clinical Practice to International Relationships*. New York: Jason Aronson Inc, 1988.

von Riekhoff, Harald. "The Changing Function of NATO." *International Journal* 21 no. 2 (spring 1966): 157–72.

von Riekhoff, Harald. *NATO: Issues and Prospects*. Toronto: Canadian Institute of International Affairs, 1967.

von Riekhoff, Harald. "NATO: To Stay or Not to Stay." In *An Independent Foreign Policy for Canada?*, edited by Stephen Clarkson. Toronto: McClelland and Stewart Limited, 1968.

von Riekhoff, Harald. "The Impact of Prime Minister Trudeau on Foreign Policy." *International Journal* 33, no. 2 (spring 1978): 267–86.

von Riekhoff, Harald, and John Sigler. "The Trudeau Peace Initiative: The Politics of Reversing the Arms Race." In *Canada Among Nations 1988*, edited by Brian Tomlin and Maureen Appel Molot. Ottawa: Carleton University Press, 1988.

Walker, R.B.J. "Canadian Security Policy and the Language of War and Peace." Unpublished paper, University of Victoria (September, 1988).

Warnock, John. "Canada and North American Defence." In *Alliances and Illusions: Canada and the NATO-NORAD Question: Odd Man Out*, edited by Lewis Hertzman, John Warnock, and Thomas Hockin. Edmonton: M.G. Hurtig Ltd, 1969.

Warnock, John. *Partner to Behemoth: The Military Policy of a Satellite Canada.* Toronto: New Press, 1970.

Washington Summit communiqué. "An Alliance for the 21st Century." *NATO Press Release*, 24 April 1999. Available at: *http://www.nato.int/docu/pr/1999/p99-064e.htm*

Wells, H.G. *The Outline of History.* New York: Macmillan Company, 1923.

Wertsch, James V. "Modes of Discourse in the Nuclear Arms Debate." *Current Research on Peace and Violence* 2–3 (1987): 102–11.

Wheeler, Nicholas, and Ken Booth. "Beyond the Security Dilemma." In *The Uncertain Course: New Strategies, Weapons and Mindsets*, edited by Carl Jacobsen, Frank Kerr, and George Quester. SIPRI: Oxford Press, 1987.

Whitaker, Reg. "Prisoner of the American Dream: Canada, the Gulf and the Future World Order." In *International Relations in the Post-Cold War Era*, edited by Mark Charlton and Elizabeth Riddell-Dixon. Toronto: Nelson, Canada, 1993.

Wood, Bernard. "The Gulf Crisis and the Future World Order." In *International Relations in the Post-Cold War Era*, edited by Mark Charlton and Elizabeth Riddell-Dixon. Toronto: Nelson, Canada, 1993.

Yee, Albert S. "The Causal Effect of Ideas on Policies." *International Organization* 50, no. 1 (winter 1996): 69–108.

Index